INTRODUCTION TO
STOCK EXCHANGE INVESTMENT

Second Edition

Janette Rutterford

MACMILLAN

First published 1983 by
THE MACMILLAN PRESS LTD
Houndmills, Basingstoke, Hampshire RG21 2XS
and London
Companies and representatives
throughout the world

ISBN 0–333–59387–1 hardcover
ISBN 0–333–59388–X paperback

A catalogue record for this book is available
from the British Library.

First edition reprinted (with corrections) six times
Second edition 1993
Reprinted 1994

Printed in Great Britain by
Mackays of Chatham PLC
Chatham, Kent

INTRODUCTION TO
STOCK EXCHANGE INVESTMENT

WITHDRAWN

To my father and mother, without whom
I would never have finished this book

Contents

Preface

Aim of the book

The desire to write this book arose from the lack of a good textbook suitable for my third-year undergraduate course on Stock Exchange investment. The books available fell into two main categories. The first category consisted of US texts which described the US stock markets and were thus of only indirect interest to UK-based students. The second category was aimed at the UK market but the books were either simple, factual texts which described rather than attempted to value securities, or 'how to make a million' books which were strong on recommendations but weak on theory.

This book therefore aims not only to provide an introduction to the world of investment, describing how the Stock Exchange works, the types of security quoted on it and the main types of investor, but also to explain the *principles* underlying Stock Exchange investment. The book concentrates on the two main characteristics of any security, risk and return and, using these characteristics, shows how securities such as equities, gilts and options and overseas investments can be compared and valued. The book also explains how to approach the design of an investment portfolio and discusses alternative investment strategies, both those advocated in theory and those used in practice in the stock market.

Structure of the book

The book is divided into four main parts, together with an introductory chapter which explains the role of the Stock Exchange and how it works. Part I begins with Chapter 2, which shows how any quoted security can be evaluated according to its risk and return and how risk and return can be measured. Chapters 3–5 show how these measures can be derived for the different types of security quoted on the Stock Exchange – fixed interest securities and shares. Chapters 6 and 7 show how derivatives of securities, namely futures and options, can be used to alter the risk and return of investments according to the requirements of the investor.

Part II concentrates not on how to value and compare individual securities but on how to *combine* securities into portfolios. Portfolio theory and the capital asset pricing model, described in Chapters 8 and 9, show how substantial diversification can lead to portfolios with better risk and return characteristics than portfolios consisting of only a few securities. Chapter 10 contrasts an investment strategy based on these models, where the emphasis is on diversification and on the expectation of a 'fair return' for the risk level of the portfolio, with the more common investment strategy where only a few securities are held in the expectation that these securities will produce 'abnormal' returns for the risk involved.

Part III is devoted to two somewhat peripheral subjects which are nevertheless of increasing importance to UK investors. The first subject, covered in Chapter 11, is that of international investment, which has traditionally been of greater importance to UK investors than, say, to their US counterparts, and which has become of even greater significance with the relaxation of exchange controls. The second subject, discussed in Chapter 12 is that of the investing institutions, which is again perhaps of greater significance in the UK stock market than in other major stock markets. The impact of the investing institutions on the UK Stock Exchange has been major, both as a result of their dominance as security-holders and their importance as traders in securities.

Part IV comprises Chapter 13, the concluding chapter, and considers the general objectives of the investor and the factors which should be taken into account when determining those objectives. The chapter also describes the alternative investment strategies available to the investor. By the time Chapter 13 has been reached, the reader should be clear as to which type of policy he or she prefers. The chapter concludes by describing performance measures which investors can use to evaluate their own or other investors' investment performance.

The text reflects the major changes which have taken place in the UK stock market, in particular the methods of trading securities, the greater emphasis on futures and options, and the increasing amount of international investment.

Readership

The book thus attempts to put a theoretical framework, based on the quantifying of risk and return, on the subject of Stock Exchange investment. This should be of interest both to students of Stock Exchange investment and to individuals who come into contact with Stock Exchange investment, such as bankers, accountants, analysts, actuaries and, of course, investors. Because the book is not confined to a student readership, the aim has been to keep the maths to a minimum, concentrating on explaining concepts by the use of examples rather than equations. Most of the calculations shown in this book can be carried out on a simple, hand-held calculator. The exceptions are valuing options and finding optimal portfolios; these require small computer programs which can be run on a personal computer.

One point which I must make. Throughout the book I have referred to the investor as 'he'. I obviously expect a female as well as male readership, especially since the author is female, but I felt that to change constantly from 'he' to 'she' throughout the book would disturb the readers' concentration more than would be gained by striking a blow for equality of the sexes.

Acknowledgements

The author and publishers are grateful to the *Financial Times*, the International Stock Exchange, HMSO, BZW, the *Wall Street Journal*, the Midland Bank, LIFFE, UBS Phillips & Drew, Goldman Sachs, James Capel, the Bank of England and the London Business School for permission to reproduce extracts from their publications. These extracts are crucial to the book, since one of its aims was to show how published financial data, in particular that provided in the *Financial Times*, can be used in investment decision-making. Thanks are also due to Datastream, the *Financial Analysts' Journal* and the *Journal of Finance* for figures in Chapters 8, 10, 11 and 13, and to Van Nostrand Reinhold for Appendix data.

Finally, I would like to thank all those who helped me to start *and* to finish this book. In particular, my thanks go to my father who was the only person who had the courage to comment on the whole book and on the new material for the second edition. My thanks also go to colleagues from the LSE who commented on the first edition. For the second edition, my especial thanks to Patrick Thomas who prepared a first draft of the entirely new chapter, Chapter 6, on futures. My editor, Stephen Rutt, has had the courage to believe that I would eventually produce a second edition and the willpower to continue to encourage me to produce it, ten years on.

May 1993   JANETTE RUTTERFORD

Glossary of terms used

ACT	Advance corporation tax
AM	Arithmetic mean
APT	Automated pit trading
β	Beta risk of a security (derived from the capital asset pricing model, CAPM)
$\beta_i^2 S_m^2$	Market risk of a security
C	Value of call option
CBOT	Chicago Board of Trade
CME	Chicago Mercantile Exchange
$CORR_{AB}$	Correlation coefficient of returns of securities *A* and *B*
COV_{AB}	Covariance of returns of securities *A* and *B*
CULS	Convertible unsecured loan stock
CT	Corporation tax
D	Duration (measure of volatility of gilt to changes in interest rates)
DTB	Deutsche Terminen Bourse
D_i	Dividend or income to be paid on a security in period *i*
dps	Dividend per share
e	Exponential function
E(infl)	Expected annual rate of inflation
$\epsilon_{j,t+1}$	Excess return on security *j* in period $t + 1$
eps	Earnings per share
E(R)	Expected return on a security
$E(R_m)$	Expected return on the market (all risky, marketable assets)
$E(R_m) - R_F$	Market premium for taking on risk
$E(R_p)$	Expected return on a portfolio
$e^{-R_{Ft}}$	The present value of £1 invested risk-free for a period *t* where the interest payments are continuously compounded
E(U(W))	Expected utility of wealth

$_if_j$	Forward interest rate for loans from year i to year j
ϕ_t	Information on a security known in period t
g	Constant growth rate of dividends
GM	Geometric mean
HPR	Holding period return
IDB	Inter dealer broker
ITC	Investment trust company
k_i	Proportion of earnings paid out as dividends for security i
LIFFE	London International Financial Futures Exchange
n	General term for the number of years, securities, etc.
LTOM	London Traded Options Market
NASDAQ	National Association of Securities Dealers Automated Quotations system
$N(d_i)$	The value of the cumulative normal probability distribution (with a mean of 0 and an area under the curve of 1) evaluated at d_i
NMS	Normal market size
P	Value of put option
P_0	Current market price or value of a security (sometimes abbreviated to P)
P_1	Value of a security at the end of period 1
PE	Price–earnings ratio
p_i	Probability of state i occurring
PSBR	Public sector borrowing requirement
PTM	Panel on Takeovers and Mergers
$PV(X)$	Present value of future cash flow X
R or r	Holding period return or annual return on a security
$R_\$$	Return expressed in dollar terms
R_F	Return on a risk-free security
r_i	Spot rate in year i, i.e. the annual rate of interest required for lending for n years starting now
$R_{j,t+1}$	Return on security j in period $t+1$
ROI	Return on investment
$R_\pounds$	Return expressed in sterling terms
RPI	Retail Price Index
S or S_1	Current share price used for option valuation
S_A	Standard deviation of returns of security A (sometimes the subscript is omitted)

SEAQ	Stock Exchange Automated Quotation system
SOFFEX	Swiss Options and Financial Futures Exchange
S_p	Standard deviation of returns of portfolio
$S^2(e_i)$	Specific or diversifiable risk of security i
Σ	Summation sign
t	Time period
TOPIC	Teletext Output of Price Information on Computer
TWROR	Time-weighted rate of return
USM	Unlisted securities market
$U(W)$	Utility of wealth
V_A	Variance of returns of security A (square of standard deviation)
V_p	Variance of returns of portfolio
X	Exercise price of option
x	General term used for an unknown variable
X_0	Spot exchange rate
X_1	Spot exchange rate at the end of period 1
X_f	Forward exchange rate

The stock exchange

Introduction

This book is about investment in securities quoted on the UK Stock Exchange. This is not as limiting as it appears. As can be seen from Example 1.1, the total market value of all securities listed on the UK Stock Exchange on 30 June 1992 was £2,101 b. There are over 7,300 different securities to choose from and turnover in these securities averaged £1,425 m. for each day of trading in 1991.

Such opportunities for Stock Exchange investment do not exist in many countries. The London Stock Exchange is the third largest in the world in terms of value after New York and Tokyo. In early 1992, it was the second largest in terms of turnover after New York, overtaking the rather depressed Tokyo market. This can be explained by two major factors. Firstly, the Stock Exchange developed much earlier than in other countries in response to a demand for risk capital during the industrial expansion of the

1

Example 1.1   Market values of all Stock Exchange listed securities
(30 June 1992)

	Number of securities	Market value (£b.)
UK public sector		
0–7 years	36	60.1
7–15 years	30	44.6
Over 15 years	22	25.2
Index-linked	13	18.2
	101	148.1
Irish public sector		
0–7 years	27	7.8
7–15 years	16	3.9
Over 15 years	8	1.3
	51	13.0
Corporation and county stocks		
Great Britain and Northern Ireland	71	0.2
Public board, etc.	29	0.1
Public sector: overseas	166	4.4
Eurobonds		
UK and Irish companies	741	52.6
Overseas companies	1,545	93.8
	2,286	146.4
Company securities		
UK and Irish		
Loan capital	763	14.8
Preference capital	1,054	13.5
Ordinary and deferred	1,953	554.5
	3,770	582.8
Overseas		
Loan capital	22	0.1
Preference capital	97	0.9
Ordinary and deferred	752	1,204.5
	871	1,205.5
TOTAL	7,345	2,100.5

Source: Stock Exchange Quarterly (April–June 1992).

late nineteenth and early twentieth centuries. It has retained a relatively greater importance as a source of finance than stock exchanges in countries with greater economic activity than the UK. Secondly, the Stock Exchange has become a dominant force in the trading of shares which are *not* listed and hence do not appear in Example 1.1. Nearly three-quarters of these trades relate to Continental European shares and as much as half of the trades in the major French shares, for example, are done through London. This creates an additional boost to turnover; for example, daily turnover in overseas equities in London averaged £1,120 m. in 1991, equivalent to 80% of the turnover in UK listed securities for that year. This type of trading explains why the Stock Exchange's official name was the International Stock Exchange although they have reverted to the less confusing 'London Stock Exchange'.

Financial investment

Whether investing directly, by holding Stock Exchange securities, or indirectly, by saving through a pension fund or insurance company, the individual investor is providing funds for investment in the company sector, be it manufacturing or services.

For example, an entrepreneur setting up a business making Wellington boots will have to provide the money needed to pay for machinery, equipment and other start-up costs. He will invest this money at the outset in the hope that he will earn more money in the future, thereby making an overall gain on the venture. This type of investment is known as 'physical' investment because the entrepreneur is directly involved in the physical activity of making Wellington boots. The stock market investor, on the other hand, makes a 'financial' investment. He has no direct interest in the size or colour of the Wellington boots nor of the number produced; he is only concerned with the amount of money he has invested in, say, the equity or shares[1] of the company making boots and how much money he will receive in the future. This type of investment is 'pure' in the sense that the investor has no interest in his investment other than the future income it will generate.

By restricting ourselves to pure financial investments, we also exclude investments in works of art. These can be acquired in the expectation of financial gain but are usually purchased for display and appreciation of their beauty. During the 1980s the British Rail pension fund used paintings and sculptures as financial investments in the hope that they would provide a good return for the beneficiaries of the pension fund. The problem with such investments is that other investors may be buying them for consumption, in the form of enjoyment of their beauty, or for status as well as for investment purposes, and this makes it difficult to value them as pure

---

[1] A share is a specific type of security, sometimes known as equity to reflect *ownership* of the company. 'Security' is a general term for any type of financial investment traded on the Stock Exchange.

investments. Attitudes towards the beauty of an ICI share certificate will not change as rapidly as attitudes towards a Picasso. Also, works of art may not store as well as money. An entry in a Swiss bank ledger will not deteriorate in the way a fine carpet may do in a damp cellar![2]

Quoted investments

Financial investments are therefore easier to value than more subjective types of investment. They always consist of the exchange of a known amount of money in return for the expectation of future receipts of money. The distinguishing feature of those financial investments which are quoted on the Stock Exchange is that, at least in theory, these securities can be bought and sold at any time. In other words, another investor can always be found who is willing to acquire the security and hence the entitlement to the future payments due on that investment. Of course, the price he is prepared to pay may not be the one the seller expected to receive. This can be due either to changes in expectations concerning the amount of money the investment will pay in the future (for example, a company is doing badly and likely to cut its dividend) or to more general market factors such as a change in interest rates. Uncertainty about the future characterises all financial investments and this inherent risk will be discussed in detail in Chapter 2.

The concentration of this book on securities which are quoted on the Stock Exchange means that we exclude such financial investments as bank deposit accounts and National Savings certificates. In these cases, money is invested for a certain period from a day to several years, which is sometimes specified and sometimes flexible. However, the transaction is entirely between the borrower and provider of funds. No third party can buy the entitlement to the proceeds of your National Savings certificates from you and the value of your investment in National Savings is not quoted daily in the *Financial Times*. The concentration on the Stock Exchange also excludes investments in commodities such as gold and cocoa (although the securities of mining or commodity trading companies do come within the scope of this book).

Quoted or marketable securities are those which have a *market price*. The investor can consult his newspaper or telephone his stockbroker to find out the current quoted price. However, a stock market quotation is

---

[2] Similarly, gambling and other forms of speculation are excluded from our definition of 'pure' investment. The thrill of gambling will be included in the price in the form of a lower return than that on an equally risky financial investment. This is not to say that the topic of this book, Stock Exchange investment, is not enjoyable!

not to be confused with a *listing*. Although most quoted securities are listed, which means that the issuers of the securities have to comply with rules laid down by the Stock Exchange, some are unlisted, for example the shares quoted by the Independent Company Exchange Limited, run by the investment bankers Granville & Co. Limited,[3] and yet can be bought and sold at a market price.

Comparing investments

Although securities represent funds provided to finance a wide range of investment, from North Sea oil exploration to the takeover of an advertising agency, they are all basically about receiving future cash flows in return for an initial investment. So, how do we compare quoted securities?

Market price and return

Each security has a market price and an expected pattern of future cash flows. Market prices can be compared easily enough. If one security costs £20 and another £100, the effects of purchasing either the £100 security or five of the £20 securities can be considered. Another way of comparing two securities which have different prices is to examine not the absolute cash flows they yield but the returns relative to their cost. For example, suppose the £100 security pays £5 per year in perpetuity and the £20 security £1.10 per year in perpetuity. From this we can deduce that their annual returns are respectively 5% and 5½% of the initial cost.

Irregular future cash flows are more difficult to compare since both the amounts *and* timing of these future payments will differ between investments. For example, suppose Mr Hope can buy either security *A* or security *B* for £100. Security *A* will pay £5 per year for two years and at the end of that time the £100 will be returned to the investor. Security *B* will make one payment of £110.25 in two years' time. Example 1.2 illustrates the cash flows of the two investment possibilities. By convention it is assumed that year 0 represents the point in time when the investment is made; the cash flows at time 0 are negative because they represent

---

[3] Companies dealt in on the over the counter (OTC) market (run by Granville & Co. Limited and other dealers in securities) are usually either too small or too new to have the track record required for a full listing.

Example 1.2   Comparing securities with different cash flows (£)

	Year		
Security	0	1	2
A	−100	+5	+105
B	−100	−	+110.25

purchase payments by the investor. It is also common practice to assume that all cash flows occur at the end of each year, to simplify calculations. This implies a gap of twelve months between each payment related to securities *A* and *B*.

Suppose both securities are issued by the same company and all future payments are certain to be made. Mr Hope must compare two securities which have the same price (£100), the same life of two years and no risk (since all the payments are certain).

Mr Hope will first consider the *return* on securities *A* and *B* – how profitable they are relative to his investment cost of £100. Consider security *A*. Mr Hope gets 5% interest each year and his money back. This must represent an annual return of 5%. Now consider security *B* and compare it with an investment of £100 at 5%. At the end of one year such an investment would be worth.

$$£100 (1 + 0.05) = £105$$

If Mr Hope then reinvested the original sum plus the accrued interest for a further year at 5%, it would be worth

$$£105 (1 + 0.05) = £110.25$$

So, an investment of £100 for two years earning 5% interest (with no withdrawals) would be worth £110.25. Since Mr Hope is due to receive £110.25 in two years' time on security *B*, he must be getting an annual return of 5% on his investment of £100 in *B*.

Timing of cash flows

Thus, both security *A* and security *B* yield 5% annual return. Mr Hope cannot distinguish between them by choosing the security which offers the highest return as he would like to do. He must compare the different timings of cash flows by considering his *consumption preference*, that is, when he would prefer to receive the cash payments, bearing in mind how much he wishes to spend or consume at each point in time. For example, Mr Hope may need a regular income and so prefer *A*, or have no need of money for the next two years and so choose *B*.

In practice, Mr Hope will hold several different securities with a variety of cash flow patterns and so, even if he needs a regular income, he will be able to buy security *B* since his other investments will provide the income he needs before year 2. He can also either sell security *B* via the stock market whenever he decides he needs some money or borrow from the bank on the strength of owning security *B*. Thus, the requirement for a particular pattern of cash flows to match consumption preferences does not limit Mr Hope in his choice of investments. In fact, in a market where Mr Hope is able to borrow and lend freely at the same rate of interest, he can alter the cash flows from any security to match his consumption preferences exactly.

Uncertainty of cash flows

The pattern of future cash flows attached to each security will usually differ not only in amount and timing but also in the uncertainty attached to them. A British government security, for example 2½% Consols, quoted at £15 (for £100 nominal)[4] will promise to pay the owner £2.50 per annum in perpetuity and the investor can be certain of receiving that income for as long as he holds the security (since the government will always pay the interest on its debt even if it has to borrow money to do so). On the other hand, an investor holding shares in a company may *expect* to receive regular dividend payments but there is no certainty attached to either the amount of the future dividends or even to the payment of any dividend at all. The company concerned may in a bad year cut the dividend, as many large companies did in 1992, or even go into liquidation and cease dividend payments altogether.

Suppose Mr Faith is comparing the purchase of £15 worth of 2½% Consols with £15 of shares in Colimited, whose shares cost £1 each and are expected to pay a dividend of 20p per share in the next year. Mr Faith has to compare two different income streams, one of which is fixed indefinitely and one of which is unknown after the first year. Example 1.3 emphasises Mr Faith's problem.

---

[4] £100 nominal means that the holder will receive interest on £100 (e.g. 2½% Consols will pay £2.50 for each £100 nominal held, whatever the market price) and eventual repayment on maturity of £100 if the stock is dated.

Example 1.3   Comparison of two securities of different risk (cash flows, £)

	Year					
Security	*0*	*1*	*2*	. . .	*n*	. . .
2½% Consols	−15	+2.5	+2.5	. . .	+2.5	. . .
Colimited shares	−15	+3.0	?	. . .	?	. . .

He will have to estimate what income he expects Colimited shares to generate from year 2 onwards and how certain he is of his estimates. He will then have to decide whether he is prepared to take on the risk of receiving more or less income than he expects or whether he prefers the more certain return of the government bond. Chapter 2 discusses in more detail the different types of risk inherent in financial investment and the relationship between the risk and return of securities.

Role of the stock market

The financial securities we have been considering are all traded on the UK Stock Exchange. This body provides the market for stocks and shares in the UK. Centred on London, the Stock Exchange provides the inter-mediary mechanism whereby buyers and sellers of securities are brought together.

The Stock Exchange offers the advantages of any regulated market. Investors know where to go, they do not have to worry about finding the other party to the transaction they wish to make and they are to some extent protected from negligence or fraud by the rules the Securities and Futures Authority requires Stock Exchange members to follow and by its arbitration procedure.

However, the stock market also performs two unique functions within the economy.

Transfer of risk

Firstly, physical investment is a risky business. Uncertainty clouds future demand for a manufacturer's products and other factors which will affect the future profits of the venture. Suppose Mr Wheeler wishes to set up a factory making tandems. If he is prepared to take on the risk[5] of the business himself, he can provide the necessary finance from his own resources, so that whatever profits or losses he makes belong to him alone. Mr Wheeler may decide, though, to share or transfer some of the risk of making and selling tandems by issuing securities to investors. He could issue fixed interest securities called stocks where he would promise to pay a fixed amount of interest on the money loaned to him by the investors. In this case, investors would not take on as much risk as Mr Wheeler. They would receive the same payment on their investment every year whereas Mr Wheeler would collect the fluctuating balance of profits. They would, however, bear the risk of the venture failing, in which case they could lose some or all of their initial investment.

Mr Wheeler might decide to transfer more risk to investors by issuing shares in his company, Twosome Tandems plc. Instead of receiving fixed interest payments, these shareholders would take payment in the form of dividends, high in good years, low or non-existent in bad years. They would also rank last in the queue of creditors should the company fail.

Whichever securities Mr Wheeler decides to issue, investors will take on the risk of Twosome Tandems via the medium of the Stock Exchange, which will arrange the issue of securities for Mr Wheeler's company. In this way, the Stock Exchange in its role of *primary* market (for the issue of *new* shares) enables the risk of physical investment to be transferred to financial investors.

New issues for UK public companies were already £245 m. in the post-war boom year of 1920 and were only at the same level in real terms by 1981 when new issues totalled £2,600 m.[6] However, by 1991, new issues raised £21.7b. for UK public companies, five times the 1920 amount in real terms.

Two major factors have stimulated the growth since the nineteenth century of new issues of securities for companies via the Stock Exchange. Firstly, the creation of the limited liability company in 1855 meant that any losses incurred by a shareholder were limited to the capital he had invested in the company. Previously, liabilities incurred by the owners of a business (and still today by members of partnerships) were not limited to their investment in the failed concern but could extend to the whole of their personal wealth. The risk of loss for shareholders in Twosome Tandems, a limited liability company, is therefore restricted to the amounts they invest in Twosome whereas their possible gains are unbounded.

---

[5] Risk can be viewed as quantifiable uncertainty, that is where more than one outcome is likely but where the likelihood of each possible outcome can be assessed. See Chapter 2 for a discussion of risk.

[6] See the *Midland Bank Review* (Spring issues), and the *Stock Exchange Quarterly*.

Secondly, the new businesses spawned by the Industrial Revolution – railways, steel, mass manufacture – were capital-intensive and required more investment than the entrepreneurs running them or wealthy individuals could provide. Banks were unwilling to furnish more than a proportion of the funds needed since they required relatively safe investments for their depositors. The issue of shares via the Stock Exchange offered a means of allowing a large number of small investors to supply the risk capital required by these industries. It also implied, with suppliers of investment capital being able to choose between alternative ventures, an efficient allocation of resources. Investors would use the stock market to allocate their funds to the companies which provided the best return, given the risk involved, and which would bring the most financial benefit to the economy.[7]

Transfer of waiting

The Stock Exchange, as well as providing a primary market for new securities, also acts as a *secondary* market, where securities can be traded throughout their lives. This can be for an indefinite period, as in the case of shares. For example, Marks and Spencer shares have been traded on the stock market since 1927 and are expected to be traded as long as Marks and Spencer continues in existence. An investor buying a Marks and Spencer share now would not expect to see his investment repaid by the company. He could, however, realise his investment at any time by selling his shares via the Stock Exchange to another investor. Similarly, investors in fixed interest stocks which usually have a finite life of between 10 and 25 years, can trade in these stocks at any time. Whoever holds a particular stock at maturity will be entitled to the repayment of the original amount lent to the issuer of the stock but this does not have to be, and most likely will not be, the person who originally invested in the stock ten or twenty years before.

This marketability of stocks and shares strongly affects the willingness of investors to hold long-term securities (by which we usually mean securities with an original life of at least ten years).

Each investor will have different consumption preferences and these may not match the maturity of the securities the investor holds, or the investor's consumption preferences may change over time. Suppose Mrs Field in-

---

[7] The efficient allocation of resources depends on there being a perfect capital market, discussed in more detail in Chapters 9 and 10. One factor which could prevent efficient allocation of resources is imperfect knowledge. Stock Exchange and accounting rules governing the quality of information in share prospectuses left much to be desired in the first decades of this century. See, for example, the case of the Royal Mail (1931), described in Hastings (1977).

vested £10,000 five years ago in a fixed interest stock which had a ten-year life and envisaged holding that stock until maturity. She suddenly decides that she wishes to buy a larger house and needs the money invested in the stock now. In the meantime, Mr Wake has inherited a lump sum on the death of his mother and wishes to invest it. Through the medium of the Stock Exchange, Mr Wake could purchase all or some of Mrs Field's stock. Both Mrs Field and Mr Wake are willing to hold a long-term security because they know they can sell at any time if they so wish. Even though Mrs Field expected to hold the stock to maturity, she would have been unwilling to buy it if she had known that she would be unable to realise it before the ten years were up.

The nature of most physical investment is such that it can take many years before the business has generated enough cash for the original investors to be able to withdraw their funds. As a result, securities based on physical investment are naturally long term. The primary market for new issues of these securities would not be successful were it not for the existence of the secondary market, which transforms these long-term securities into short-term ones by offering permanent marketability. If these stocks and shares could not be traded throughout their life, investors would require a 'liquidity premium', in the form of a higher return, for holding an asset which could not be sold before the end of its life.[8] The existence of a stock market prevents investors from having to wait before realising their investments and, by removing the need for a liquidity premium, reduces the cost of issuing long-term securities.

Buying and selling securities

There are essentially two ways of running a stock market – either with a 'single' capacity or a 'dual' capacity role for brokers. Prior to Big Bang in 1986,[9] the Stock Exchange operated a single capacity system. Stockbrokers acted in the single capacity of agent for the buyer or seller of shares whom they represented. Market makers were called 'jobbers' and their sole function was to make a market in the shares for which they were responsible. Brokers were forced to buy and sell shares through jobbers and not allowed to take positions in shares in return for being able to charge a minimum level of commission to their clients. Jobbers were forced to quote

---

[8] For example, building societies offer extra interest for deposits which cannot be withdrawn on demand.

[9] 'Big Bang' is the term used for the deregulation of the Stock Exchange which occurred after pressure from the Office of Fair Trading which had spent ten years investigating restrictive Stock Exchange practices.

prices on shares to the brokers on demand, in return for knowing that all trades would go through jobbers. Prices quoted by jobbers were supposed to be competitive since stockbrokers had a choice of jobbers for each share listed on the Stock Exchange. Trading took place on the floor of the Stock Exchange in the City of London.

After Big Bang, the Stock Exchange introduced dual capacity. Under this system, brokers can choose to act only as agents, in which case they are known as 'agency brokers' or can choose to also act as a market maker, in which case they are known as 'broker dealers'. If acting as a market maker, the broker has the right to take a position in shares, for example, buying 10,000 ICI shares with a view to selling them to a client for a 'turn' between the price at which he buys the shares – the 'bid' price – and the price at which he sells them – the 'ask' price – making the difference of a few pence per share profit. If acting as a market maker, the broker has to commit himself to quoting bid and ask prices on shares continuously during trading hours. The prices the market maker quotes are input into a computer system run by the Stock Exchange known as SEAQ and displayed on a computer screen, known as a TOPIC screen,[10] and investors or other market makers buy or sell shares based on these prices by telephone. Each share will have a number of market makers quoting a bid–ask spread and the maximum number of shares for which this quote is 'good', that is, the maximum number the market maker is prepared to buy or sell at the quoted prices. Because computers and telephones are the means of communication, the trading floor of the Stock Exchange is no longer in use.

The post-Big Bang system is based on the US system called NASDAQ (the National Association of Securities Dealers Automated Quotations system) which operates on computer screens throughout the United States, predominantly for over the counter shares. The largest stock market in the United States, the New York Stock Exchange, is still based on a trading floor although some trades are computerised and it does allow strictly regulated dual capacity for brokers. The UK Stock Exchange chose NASDAQ as a model rather than the New York Stock Exchange since they perceived NASDAQ, with its computer-based system, to be more up-to-date. Other stock markets around the world operate various types of single capacity or dual capacity system, with some dual capacity systems being floor-based and others computer-based. Some of the newer markets, especially the newly developed futures markets,[11] use computers without the aid of telephones. Buyers or sellers advertise the number of securities they wish to buy or sell and the price they are prepared to accept on the screen and

---

[10] SEAQ stands for Stock Exchange Automated Quotations and TOPIC for Teletext Output of Price Information by Computer.

[11] Such as SOFFEX in Switzerland and the DTB in Germany. See Chapter 6 on Futures for more explanation of how futures markets work.

other market participants can 'take' the trade by keying into the computer. This type of computer system is known as 'order driven' since the investors or traders put their orders directly onto the screen. The UK Stock Exchange SEAQ and TOPIC system is known as 'price driven' since the screens show the prices at which the market makers are *prepared* to buy or sell up to a certain number of shares.

The aim of a stock market is to act as both a primary and a secondary market in securities. In order to be successful in its primary role, it has to ensure a liquid secondary market. In order to ensure liquidity, the market must be seen to be fair to all investors. The aim of the old 'single' capacity system was to ensure that the broker would have no conflict of interest and that prices would be competitive through having a number of jobbers prepared to trade. This system worked well in terms of fairness but failed on competitive pricing as there were no longer enough firms of jobbers by the mid-1980s to compete with each other.

By allowing brokers to act as market makers and by allowing firms of market makers to be limited liability companies rather than the unlimited liability partnerships required pre-Big Bang, the Stock Exchange successfully increased the number of competing market makers. The larger brokers were keen to become market makers because they resented giving the market maker the bid–ask spread profit when they had both a buyer and a seller already matched. However, the rights of the investor to a fair price had to be protected. It would be all too easy for the broker to take an unfairly large bid–ask spread if the investor had no idea of what the 'fair' price should be. In order to protect the investor from unfair pricing, the Stock Exchange requires market makers receiving orders from the broking side of the business to at least match the best price quoted on the TOPIC screen. If the investor wishes to deal in a larger number of shares than the market makers have indicated they are willing to buy or sell at the quoted prices, the broker is given more discretion since he is only then required to deal at the 'best' price he thinks he can get.

Essentially, investors get fair prices for their share purchases and sales if a stock market is 'transparent' in disclosing actual prices at which they can trade. Institutional investors can do this by having TOPIC screens in their offices and by talking directly to market makers. Small investors can receive share prices via various television news services or can subscribe to TOPIC via their televisions for a monthly charge. This gives access to prices at which market makers are prepared to trade and to the prices at which the last few trades have been carried out.[12] However, there are certain trades which do not have to be disclosed via SEAQ within the five minutes usually required by the Stock Exchange. These are large

---

[12] These are shown at the top of the TOPIC screen.

trades[13] which do not have to be disclosed for 90 minutes after the trade has been done to allow the market maker time to offset his position with counterbalancing purchases or sales. This clearly biases the recent trade information given on TOPIC. Also, the prices at which the small investor trades are usually 'at the touch', that is the best bid or best ask price on the screen. Institutional investors, trading larger numbers of shares, are able to negotiate prices 'inside the touch', that is at more advantageous prices than are quoted on the screen, in more than 60% of their transactions.[14]

Description of a transaction

Let us now examine exactly how a transaction is processed through the UK Stock Exchange. Mr Wake wishes to buy some shares with the proceeds of his legacy. He will do this via his stockbroker who may also be a market maker. Suppose that the broker is a small agency broker, who is not a market maker, although Mr Wake might also approach his High Street bank, which probably is a broker/dealer, making markets in shares through its merchant banking subsidiary. All Mr Wake has to do is to notify the broker which shares he wishes to buy, usually by telephone. Suppose he decides to buy 5,000 BP shares. The broker will then look on his TOPIC screen and tell him the lowest quoted price for BP; there should be several, possibly up to 10, competing quotes for the shares of a major UK company such as BP.

Suppose there are only three market makers with quotes:

Market maker A:	207p–210p	Up to 1,000 shares
Market maker B:	209p–213p	Up to 10,000 shares
Market maker C:	207p–211p	Up to 10,000 shares

This means that market maker A, for example, is willing to buy BP shares at 207p and sell them at 210p and that the prices shown are good for transactions of up to and including 1,000 shares either way.[15]

---

[13] These are defined to be three times the 'normal market size' (NMS) of a share which is the normal market size traded for a particular share and can vary from 500 for a small company share to 100,000 for a share such as ICI.

[14] See the *Stock Exchange Quarterly* (January–March 1992) pp. 25–31.

[15] In practice, codes are used to indicate the volumes at which the market makers are prepared to honour the prices quoted.

Clearly, the best price for a purchaser such as Mr Wake is 210p. However, he wishes to buy 5,000 shares which is above the limit shown by market maker *A*. The broker would then probably telephone market maker *A* to see if the price was good for 5,000 shares or take the price of 211p offered by market maker *C*. If 100,000 shares were required by Mr Wake, he would expect to be able to pay, say, 209p by negotiation with a market maker. If Mr Wake only wished to buy 500 shares, the broker dealer could use the SEAQ Automatic Execution facility and trade automatically at the best price for Mr Wake (210p) by computer and without having to make a telephone call.

Currently, dealings in shares are not cash settled but are 'on account' and settled on 'account day'. The year is divided into account periods, normally of two weeks in duration, with account day the Monday following the last Friday of the two week period. Some account periods are for three weeks, usually around holiday periods. This means that Mr Wake could carry out several transactions in BP shares during the account and would only have to settle the *net* amount plus transaction costs on account day.

The broker will then send Mr Wake a *contract note* detailing the transaction done, that is, the number of shares bought, the price to be paid, the transaction costs to be paid, the total cost, and the settlement date by which money is to be received by the broker. The settlement of shares listed on the UK Stock Exchange is done via a system called Talisman which uses a central Stock Exchange nominee account called SEPON into which all share purchases and sales are transferred.[16] Shares listed on the UK Stock Exchange are *registered* shares; that is, the company (or an agent on behalf of the company) keeps a share register of all shareholders of that company. So, when shares are bought or sold, the transactions have to be registered via a Talisman sold transfer form. In practice, in this example, ownership of BP shares would be passed into the SEPON account from a seller before being transferred into the name of Mr Wake. He in turn would forward cash and ultimately receive a share certificate to acknowledge his ownership of the shares and the adding of his name to the BP share register.

However, this settlement system is archaic in that it requires much paperwork in the form of transfer documents (which can be numerous if, for example, a large sale has to be divided into many small purchases), registration of new share certificates, and the issuance of share certificates. A new system was due to be instituted, called Taurus,[17] which would do away with the need for share certificates, thus 'dematerialising' the system, in other words, removing the need for paper proof of ownership by switching

---

[16] TALISMAN stands for Transfer Accounting Lodgement of Investors, Stock Management for Principals and SEPON for Stock Exchange Pool Nominees.

[17] This stands for Transfer and Automated Registration of Uncertified Stock.

to computerised 'book entry' transfer. Such a system is already used for holders of units in unit trusts. Taurus would also have led to the replacement of the account system with a five-day settlement system. However, the introduction of Taurus was delayed for years in part due to a reluctance to implement it on the part of Stock Exchange members (some with subsidiaries running share registers) who benefit from the current systems. The Bank of England has now taken responsibility for introducing a more modern settlement system.

Transaction costs

Transaction costs on securities dealing consist of the broker's commission, a 'PTM' levy of 10p on bargains to purchase or sell shares worth more than £5,000 towards the costs of the costs of the Panel of Takeover and Mergers (PTM), and transfer stamp duty. Transfer stamp duty is a tax on the *purchase* of shares (not the sale) and is payable at the rate of 0.5% on the value of shares. Although it raises substantial revenues for the government, transfer stamp duty is due to be abolished on the introduction of Taurus, since the stock transfer forms on which the transfer stamp duty is payable will no longer be issued.

Before Big Bang, a minimum commission system was in operation. Different rates were charged on different bands, the effect of which was a charge of 1.65% on small transactions, with a minimum of, say, £10, and a charge of around 0.53% on a transaction worth £300,000. After Big Bang, brokerage commissions became negotiable although rates have settled and there is not an enormous difference between brokers. However, small investors will probably use a broker specialising in small trades and offering competitive rates for such transactions whereas the institutional investor will negotiate competitive rates direct with several broker/dealers using the large volume of transactions that they will conduct with the broker/dealer to negotiate very fine commissions.

Most of the High Street banks offer a fixed charge stockbroking service aimed at the small investor. Typical charges are around 1.5% for small trades of up to £7,000 with a minimum charge of around £25 or £30. Again a band system will operate with, say, the next £8,000 chargeable at 1% and thereafter at 0.75%–0.5%, depending on the broker. Although rates with banks are unlikely to be negotiable, an individual investor with frequent transactions can negotiate special rates with brokers in return for the promise of regular business. Without special concessions, the normal small investor would therefore pay 2.5% brokerage commission on a £1,000 share purchase or sale (based on a minimum charge of £25) and a brokerage commission of 1.35% on a £10,000 share transaction. Example 1.4

Example 1.4   Transaction costs on £10,000 share transaction

		£
Cost of purchase		
Shares		10,000.00
Brokerage commission		
1.5% of first £7,000	105.00	
1.0% on next £3,000	30.00	
		135.00
Transfer stamp duty at 0.5%		50.00
PTM levy		0.10
TOTAL COST		10,185.10
Cost of sale		
Shares		10,000.00
Brokerage commission		
1.5% of first £7,000	105.00	
1.0% on next £3,000	30.00	
		135.00
PTM levy		0.10
TOTAL COST		10,135.10

details the typical transaction costs on a £10,000 share purchase or sale. Notice that brokerage commission does not attract VAT.

Of course, the contract note will only state the costs which are added to the price paid for the shares. But an important element of the cost is the difference between the bid and ask price. For example, if Mr Wake paid 210p for his BP shares, he could sell them back at only 209p if the three hypothetical market makers maintained the prices quoted earlier. This 1p difference is small when expressed as a percentage of the share price. However, the typical bid–ask spread for liquid shares is around 1–2% whereas less liquid shares will have a wider bid–ask spread of up to 5% or more of the share price. This means that the share price will have to move up by over 5%, plus transaction costs for the small investor of around 2% to buy and 1.5% to sell, a total of over 8.5%, before the investor can recoup his cost on an illiquid share.

Appendix 1 (p. 415) gives fuller details of the costs of buying and selling shares, gilts, futures and options.

Institutional investors, typically buying or selling 50,000–100,000 shares at a time, worth around £100,000–£500,000, can negotiate commission rates as low as 0.2% (with no banding). A further option available to the institutional fund manager is to agree a 'soft commission' deal with the broker. Here, the broker provides research services, not necessarily his own, in return for an agreed amount of transaction business from the fund manager.[18] These services are not normally the research produced by the broker, but are on-line analysis services such as Datastream and Bloomberg,[19] which use 'real time' prices to analyse share price and bond price performance and to help the fund manager make investment decisions.

From this brief description of commission rates, it can be seen that the impact of Big Bang has been negligible on the small investor in terms of the commission rates he pays whereas the institutional investor has dramatically reduced *his* commission rates. However, the impact on brokers has been an overall reduced revenue from commissions, since the majority of transactions are carried out by institutional investors. Some brokers attempted to encourage small investor business in the first few years after Big Bang, but their cost base in the City of London was too high for the substantial administrative costs associated with processing large numbers of small transactions. As a result, broker/dealers are now more dependent on market making in shares as a source of profit (although we noted how their spreads are smaller for institutional investors who deal, as we saw earlier, 'inside the touch') and are cost conscious about equity research. It is now much more difficult for small investors to obtain research from broking houses. Before Big Bang, high minimum commissions from institutional investors subsidised the service offered to small investors. Today, this is no longer so, with the large investors having access to computer analytic services and written broker research not available to the small investor. However, we shall see in Chapters 9 and 10 whether or not this research can help investors to improve their performance.

Fixed interest securities

We now turn to fixed interest securities, and gilts in particular, to see how dealings in gilts differ from dealings in shares.

Firstly, the market making system is almost identical in that a number of market makers (not necessarily the same as the market makers in equities) agree to provide continuous two way prices in all gilts during trading hours. As for equities, computer screens are used to display prices and transactions are agreed over the telephone. However, there is one major difference between the two types of security trading. For equities, the prices

---

[18] Although there is some controversy over this system since some argue that the institutional investor is tempted to churn his portfolio in order to generate the purchase and sale volumes necessary to pay for the research services he is given.

[19] These are described in more detail in Appendix 3 (p. 422).

given on the screen *must* be honoured for the number of shares indicated. For gilts, the prices shown are indicative only and each gilt market maker displays his prices on a separate screen available only to the broker or institutional investor. The market maker cannot, as he can for equities, see the gilt prices displayed by competing market makers.

However, market makers have access to computer screens provided by 'inter-dealer brokers' (IDBs) which show 'order driven' prices input by themselves and other market makers. The inter-dealer broker is there to ensure anonymity between market makers. This IDB system, as it is known, is designed to allow market makers to offset positions they have taken on from, say, an investor. For example, suppose an institutional investor sells £1 m. of a particular gilt to the market maker. The market maker can then contact the inter-dealer broker saying that he is willing to sell £1 m. of that gilt at a slightly higher price than he paid for it. This will then appear on the screen and a market maker who has just *sold* £1 m. of that gilt to a customer can ring the inter-dealer broker to accept the offer and buy the gilts. The inter-dealer broker charges a *tiny* commission of 1/128th of 1% to the market maker who accepts the screen offer for the service provided. So, with the IDB system (which also operates for equity market makers), gilt market makers are not as isolated as first appears.

Brokerage commission on gilts is lower than for equities because the average transaction size is larger. Institutional investors will typically deal in millions of pounds' worth of gilts whereas a usual institutional share transaction would be worth of the order of several hundred thousand pounds. Indeed, for large trades in round millions of pounds, gilt market makers charge no commission at all, hoping to make all their profit from the bid–ask spread. For smaller transactions, at the individual investor level, commissions are typically 1% on the first £7,000, falling to 0.125% thereafter. Again, a minimum commission charge of around £25 will be charged. Transfer stamp duty is not payable on gilt purchases or sales, since the government is naturally keen to encourage a liquid secondary market in order to be able to sell new gilts on the primary market. Thus, the purchase and sale costs for gilts is the same and an example of a purchase is shown in Example 1.5.

Investors wishing to make small purchases of gilts can do so, at the sacrifice of a little flexibility, via the National Savings Stock Register using forms obtainable in any Post Office. A stockbroker will execute a gilt transaction within minutes of a telephone call and can confirm the price of the gilt to the investor during the same call whereas the National Stock Savings Register can take a day to execute an order, during which time the gilt price will have changed – in either direction. However, the transaction costs are low, around 0.4% of the value of the gilts bought or sold, which is competitive with the broker's charges shown in Example 1.5 for transactions worth less than £25,000.

Notice that gilt transactions are cash settled, that is the cheque is

Example 1.5   Transaction costs of buying gilts

		£
Cost of purchase		
£10,000 in value[20] of Treasury 8¾% 2017		10,000.00
Brokerage commission		
1.0% of first £7,000	70.00	
0.125% on next £3,000	3.75	
		73.50
TOTAL COST		10,073.50

required immediately for settlement the day following the purchase. This is also the case for options, whose transaction costs are given in Appendix 1 and which are described in detail in Chapter 7. Transactions on futures contracts (described in Chapter 6) require an initial deposit known as a margin to be paid on the *same* day as each transaction; brokers will therefore require the investor to deposit cash with them in advance before they will accept orders for any transactions in futures.

The changing face of the stock market

Types of security

Over the past few years, Stock Exchange investment has become more interesting, since investors have been given a wider range of types of investment to choose from. Firstly, as well as the main stock market whose securities are given in Example 1.1, there is also the Unlisted Securities Market for companies which do not satisfy the criteria required for the main stock market. This market was opened in 1980 and now has 333 different ordinary shares listed with a total market capitalisation of £5b. in June 1992, compared with £529b. for the UK shares listed on the main stock market. As will be described in more detail in Chapter 5 on equities, the USM, as it is known, was devised to allow small, relatively new

---

[20] As we shall see in Chapter 3, gilts are quoted as a percentage of their nominal value, for example £98 per £100 nominal. However, the buyer of gilts will also pay what is known as 'accrued interest', representing the interest rate payable on the gilts.

companies to gain access to the capital markets. Investors now have the opportunity to buy shares in these companies, safe in the knowledge that they are regulated (although less onerously than for companies listed on the main market) by the Stock Exchange.

Another development has been an increase in the number of futures and options contracts based on Stock Exchange securities which can be traded. Chapters 6 and 7, on futures and options respectively, show how investors can use futures and options to alter the risk profile of their investments, either reducing risk by 'hedging' with futures or options or increasing risk by using the leverage inherent in futures and options instead of buying or selling the underlying securities.

We have also already mentioned the large volume of non-UK listed shares bought and sold by London-based brokers and market makers. The volume of these transactions is almost as great as for domestic securities. The tradition of international investment, discussed in more detail in Chapter 11, is peculiar to the Stock Exchange's history and investors based in the UK therefore have access to international investment opportunities, backed up by research, which are without parallel elsewhere in the world.

Type of investor

As well as the types of security traded on the Stock Exchange having changed over time, the major types of investor have also altered, with the main change being the decline of individual investors and the rise of institutional investors. Individuals, especially the younger generations, now invest *indirectly* in the stock market through the institutional investors. Their savings are channelled into pension funds and insurance companies and, to a lesser extent, into unit trusts and investment trusts. Individual investors, who held nearly two-thirds of the market value of UK ordinary shares in 1957, now hold only one-fifth. On the other hand, the investing institutions (comprising pension funds, insurance companies, unit trusts and investment trusts), who held only 19% in value of UK company ordinary shares in 1957, now hold 60% in value. They also hold over 50% in value of British government securities and over two-thirds in value of UK company fixed interest securities. The implications of this trend, which is continuing apace, and the roles of these investing institutions are considered in Chapter 12. The formulation of investment objectives, investment policy and the measurement of investment performance for both individual and institutional investors are described in the final chapter, Chapter 13.

Summary

This chapter has described what is meant by financial investment in a quoted security which can be bought and sold through the Stock Exchange and which promises the holder a series of future payments, the amount, timing and certainty of which vary according to the type of security.

The vital role of the stock market as a centre of trading in securities and, more importantly, as a means of transferring risk and the postponement of consumption was discussed. The primary market allows companies to spread the risk of physical investment among shareholders and between holders of different securities. The secondary market in effect converts long-term securities into short-term ones by allowing them to be bought and sold throughout their life. No investor need postpone consumption by having to wait for the maturity of his investment.

The Stock Exchange dealing systems were then described, in particular the roles of the broker and of the market member. The technicalities of buying securities were explained and the typical transaction costs of buying and selling shares and fixed interest securities outlined. The chapter concluded with a brief look at the major changes which have taken place in the stock market in recent years, especially the changes in the types of security traded and the change from direct investment in the stock market by individual investors to indirect investment via the investing institutions.

Problems

1. Mary Contrary has just joined a pension fund as a securities clerk. She has asked her departmental manager to describe how the buying and selling of securities are carried out on the London Stock Exchange – she has vaguely heard of such terms as 'market making' and 'settlement day'. She also asks what are the transaction costs of buying government bonds and shares.

   Assume you are the departmental manager and provide Mary with the information she requires.

2. You are a private investor wishing to buy 1,000 ICI shares and instruct your stockbroker accordingly. Explain the process which will take place between you, the broker and the market maker of the 500 shares and show how much the transaction will cost the investor in total. What would be the transaction costs associated with the purchase of the same amount of long-term, fixed interest government stock? When would the payment for the ICI shares or the government stock have to be made?

3. Describe the main changes in type of security and type of investor which have taken place on the UK Stock Exchange over the past few decades. Why do you think these changes have occurred?

4. (i) What is the difference between quoted and unquoted securities and between physical and financial investment?

(ii) What is meant when the Stock Exchange is described as a primary and secondary market for securities?

(iii) Describe the main functions of a stock market within the economy.

(iv) Explain the roles of agencies, brokers and market makers in the UK stock market. What changes have taken place in recent years?

PART I

EVALUATION OF SECURITIES

Risk and return

Introduction

This chapter discusses the two most important attributes of stock market securities – risk and return. When considering any security, the investor is always concerned with the *return* expected on the investment and the *risk* of the investment, that is, how likely it is that the return expected will be achieved. In a certain world, the return would always be exactly as expected and there would be no risk. The investor would merely have to compare the returns available on different investments and choose those which offered the highest returns.

Unfortunately, the existence of uncertainty means that returns on investments are not always as expected. The hoped-for dividends on the shares in the speculative Australian mining company may never materialise or the company whose junk bond you hold may go into liquidation. All securities are subject to risk. Different types of securities will have different kinds of risk attached to them (for example, UK government securities do not suffer the risk of default but are vulnerable to changes in interest rates). However, the effect of all these different kinds of risk is the same – the *actual* returns achieved will be different from those *expected* by the investor. The riskier the security the more likely it is that the hoped-for return will not be achieved or the greater the likely shortfall from the expected return.

So, the investor needs to be able to quantify both the uncertain return and the level of that uncertainty for each security before he can make investment decisions. Depending on his attitude towards risk and return, he will then be able to choose the securities which offer him the combination of risk and return which best suits him.

The chapter starts by introducing the standard measure of return, known as the *holding period return*, which is all the investor would need to be able to make investment decisions under certainty. We then go on to consider investment decisions made under uncertainty and different types of risk to which securities are subject, namely, uncertainty of income, default risk, interest rate risk and inflation risk.

Given uncertainty, it is not possible to determine the future holding period return on any security, since a range of returns is likely. The concept of a probability distribution of returns is then introduced. This enables the investor to quantify both the return he *expects* to get and the risk of not achieving that return. The investor can then decide, according to the level of return he wishes to achieve and the amount of risk he is willing to bear, which securities he prefers. If he is averse to taking on risk, he will prefer the securities which offer the least risk for any given return or the most return for any given level of risk. We will assume that the average investor on the Stock Exchange is what is known as 'risk averse'.

The concept of *utility*, which combines the attitudes of each investor to both risk and return into one measure, is then discussed. Utility also takes into account the wealth of the investor and so each security must be analysed to see how its returns will affect the investor's wealth. Utility enables the investor, if he knows his utility function (which he can estimate by evaluating his attitude to certain risk–return alternatives) to calculate the expected utility of each investment opportunity. All he then has to do is to choose the one which offers him the highest expected utility.

The chapter concludes with a section on two ways of reducing risk without reducing expected return. These are 'pooling' and 'hedging' and the Stock Exchange investor can apply these methods of reducing risk by diversifying his securities portfolio (discussed in detail in Chapter 8) and by making use of the various futures markets referred to in the text.

Holding period return

Any investor, when deciding on which securities he wishes to hold in his portfolio, has to be able to compare them directly. Each security is characterised by a market price, the cost of the security, and a pattern of cash flows. Suppose share A cost 486p and, at the end of six months, paid a dividend of 20p before it was sold for 500p. How can it be compared with share B, bought at 30p, held for one year and then sold for 35p with no dividend payment? Obviously the different costs of the shares must be taken into account, as well as the different time periods involved.

Calculating the percentage holding period return for each security avoids the problem of comparing different size investments. This return is simply the gain during the period held (money received less cost) divided by the cost. So,

$$R = \frac{D_1 + P_1 - P_0}{P_0} \tag{2.1}$$

where P_0 is the cost, P_1 the value of the investment at the end of the holding period and D_1 any interest or dividend payments made during the period. Using equation (2.1), the holding period returns of shares A and B can be calculated and compared as in Example 2.1.

The holding period returns of A and B are not yet directly comparable since B was invested for twice as long as A. When A was sold, the proceeds could have been reinvested for another six months but we do not know what return would have been available to the investor at that time. An alternative solution would be to calculate the equivalent six-monthly return on B. This is done in Example 2.2 by equating the return on money invested for two six-month periods, at a return r_B per period, to money invested for an equivalent one-year period at return R_B, the one-year holding period return.

Example 2.1 Holding period returns of A and B

Share	Holding period return	Holding period (months)
A	$R_A = \dfrac{(20 + 500) - 486}{486}$	
	$= 0.070$	
	$R_A = 7.0\%$	6
B	$R_B = \dfrac{(0 + 35) - 30}{30}$	
	$= 0.167$	
	$R_B = 16.7\%$	12

Example 2.2   Six-month holding period return

Suppose £100 is invested for 6 months at 5%

At the end of 6 months, it will be worth

£100 (1 + 0.05) = £105

If reinvested for another 6 months at 5% it will be worth

£105 (1 + 0.05) = £110.25

or

£100 (1 + 0.05)^2

If we define r_B to be the six-monthly return equivalent to an annual holding period return on B of R_B, we can write

$(1 + r_B)^2 = 1 + R_B$

We know R_B = 16.7% or 0.167, giving

$(1 + r_B)^2 = 1.167$

Solving,

$r_B = 0.080$

$r_B = 8.0\%$

We can now compare A, which offered a return of 7% over six months, with B which offered a higher return over the same period of 8%.

Most investors would no doubt choose the investment which offered the highest return over any particular period. If we look at Example 2.3 to see which investments have typically yielded the highest returns in the past, we note that ordinary shares have, on average, out-performed long-term gilts on annual return over the past seventy years.

Example 2.3   Returns and risk of different types of security

1919–90	Annual average return (%)	Range of returns (%)
Long-term gilts	2.6	−14 to +40
Ordinary shares	8.2	−24 to +54

Source: Frank Russell International and BZW Gilt Survey 1991.

With this evidence before him, the investor would surely always buy shares. And yet, many investors choose gilts or hold at least some gilts in their investment portfolio. The reason why people invest in gilts can be seen from the third column in Example 2.3, which shows the *variation* in annual return achieved on shares and gilts. Although gilts have offered a lower return on average, they have also offered less chance of a large negative return or loss. This means that the investor cannot just look at return alone when making investment decisions, he must also consider *risk*.

Types of risk

There are several different types of risk which can lead to variability in return on a security. Some securities, such as gilts, will have few risks attached to them, whereas company shares will be subject to many possible reasons for fluctuations in return. One of the risks to which ordinary shares are subject is *uncertainty of income*.

Uncertainty of income

The risk of uncertainty of income is a risk to which all ordinary share-holders are subject. This can be seen by looking at the holding period return on an ordinary share, which can be written as

$$R = \frac{D_1 + P_1 - P_0}{P_0}$$

where D_1 is the dividend expected to be paid during the holding period, P_0 the share purchase price and P_1 the price at the end of the period. When we considered shares A and B, we knew the values of D_1, P_0 and P_1 because in that case we were looking at *past* returns achieved on the investments. Unfortunately, an investor is always making investment decisions concerning the future. All he knows is P_0, the current market price of the share. He has no idea what the share price will be when he sells it, nor what dividend payments he will receive. In contrast with its fixed interest securities, such as debentures or loan stocks, a company does *not* contract to pay its ordinary shareholders any fixed or even any minimum level of dividend.

Ordinary shareholders own the assets of the company after all other claims on it have been satisfied but the company is under no obligation to pay out these shareholders' funds as dividends. Probably only part of the total profit attributable to ordinary shareholders in any one year will be paid out as dividends, the remainder being retained within the company. If a company is doing well, the ordinary shareholder will expect both to receive a dividend D_1 and for the share price P_1 to exceed P_0, reflecting the retention of earnings by the company.[1]

However, if the company does badly, it does not have to make any payments to ordinary shareholders as it does to its debt-holders. The profitability of any company is subject to certain risks. For example, an economic recession could lead to a reduction in sales, or a political decision could mean higher tax payments. Technical change could render the company's products obsolescent or, on a simpler level, an event such as a fire could wipe out some of the assets of the company. These factors render the profits of the company uncertain and, since ordinary shareholders are entitled only to the balance of income and capital after all other security-holders have been paid, ordinary shares are the most risky of all securities. On the other hand, ordinary shareholders stand to gain more than fixed interest security-holders, whose return is more limited.

Corporate fixed interest debt-holders suffer, as we have mentioned above, less uncertainty of income since they are promised specific interest payments by the company. However, they are subject to another type of risk, the risk of *default*.

Default risk

If a company does badly, it may be unable to pay the interest on a fixed interest security or to repay the principal on maturity. Only government bonds, fixed interest securities issued or guaranteed by a government, such as UK gilts, are not subject to default risk; governments are the only borrowers which can always avoid default in the last resort by printing more money – provided the debt is in their own currency.

All types of fixed interest corporate debt are subject to default risk, from debenture stocks secured on the assets of the company to unsecured loan stocks and junk bonds,[2] but each will be subject to a different *level* of risk of losing on their investment. On default, debenture holders can appoint a receiver whose job it is to realise the security they hold and, if it is worth at

---

[1] Some fast-growing companies have a policy of paying no dividends at all over a period of years. In these cases the holding period return is purely the capital gain or loss, $P_1 - P_0$.

[2] Debenture stocks, unsecured loan stocks, and other corporate bonds are described at the end of Chapter 4, pp. 113–19.

least the sum they are owed,[3] will suffer no loss. Unsecured loan stock holders have no security and rank behind the secured creditors of the company.

Corporate fixed interest securities do not represent a major part of the Stock Exchange in this country (less than 1% of 1990 turnover and 1% of 1990 market value),[4] but in the US they are an important form of investment. Each major US company will have several corporate bonds, each with carefully defined rights to the assets of the company in the event of default. For example, a 'subordinated' debenture means that it comes lower down in the queue than an 'unsubordinated' debenture, and will only be entitled to payment, in the event of default, after the unsubordinated debenture holders have been fully repaid.[5] Example 2.4 shows an extract from the *Wall Street Journal* giving market information on just a few US corporate bonds. Opinions on the credit-worthiness and hence the default risk of these bonds, from AAA for, say, a highly rated bond to C or D for bonds which are probably already in default, are provided by Moody's and by Standard & Poors. Junk bonds, referred to earlier, are simply lower grade bonds, in other words poorly rated by the credit-rating agencies and hence more subject to default risk.

Ordinary shareholders do not suffer default risk since they are not entitled to any particular level of income or to any prespecified repayment which might run the risk of not being paid. Preference shareholders[6] lie somewhere between fixed interest debt-holders and ordinary shareholders; although they are entitled to fixed interest payments, if these are not made the company is not legally in default, since preference shareholders are part-owners and not creditors of the company.

Other risks

It is easy to see why securities issued by companies, even if they promise a fixed income, have an element of risk. In an uncertain and competitive world some companies may well fail and, given that companies have limited liability, investors in these companies will, in the last resort, only have recourse to the assets remaining within the company which may not be sufficient to repay their investments in full. It is less easy, though, to understand why fixed interest securities issued by the British government offer uncertain returns.

---

[3] Net of the costs of using the receiver to realise the security.

[4] However, UK corporate bonds are issued in increasing numbers in the eurosterling market.

[5] Notice that, in the UK, debentures are secured and, in the US, are unsecured fixed interest securities.

[6] Preference shares are described on pp. 120–1.

Example 2.4 Dow Jones Bond averages

Quotations as of 4 p.m. Eastern Time
Thursday, November 29, 1990

Volume $38,390,000

SALES SINCE JANUARY 1
(000omitted)

1990	1989	1988
$10,037,021	$7,992,268	$6,902,773

	Domestic Thu.	Domestic Wed.	All Issues Thu.	All Issues Wed.
Issues traded	564	586	566	589
Advances	218	233	219	236
Declines	213	209	213	209
Unchanged	133	144	134	144
New highs	8	13	8	13
New lows	12	12	12	12

Dow Jones Bond Averages

–1989– High	–1989– Low	–1990– High	–1990– Low		–1990– Close	–1990– Chg.	–1990– %Yld	–1989– Close	–1989– Chg.
94.15	87.35	93.04	88.44	20 Bonds	90.39	-0.02	9.66	93.51	-0.07
95.26	86.95	94.48	89.23	10 Utilities	92.55	-0.08	9.54	94.86	-0.19
93.26	87.60	91.60	86.43	10 Industrials	88.24	+0.05	9.79	92.16	+0.05

Bonds	Cur Yld	Vol	Close	Net Chg.
GMA 8½91	8.5	27	99 21/32	...
GMA 8⅞96	8.9	61	99½	...
GMA 8¼16	9.8	17	84	...
GMA 8⅛92	8.2	5	99½	- ½
GMA 8s93J	8.1	25	98⅝	+ ¼
GMA 8s93O	8.2	50	98⅛	- ⅞
GMA 8s94	8.3	115	96¾	+ ⅛
GTE 9⅜99	9.3	2	100½	...
GTCal 8⅞96	9.0	5	99⅛	...
Genrad 7¼11	cv	28	34	- 1
GaGlf 15s00	16.0	248	93½	...
GaPw 8⅞00	9.3	25	95⅛	+ ⅛
GaPw 8⅛01	9.0	21	90⅛	...
GaPw 7⅝01	8.9	11	86⅛	- ⅝
GaPw 7½02J	8.8	5	84¾	- ½
GaPw 7½02D	8.8	4	85½	- ½
GaPw 11⅝00	11.3	12	103	+ ½
GaPw 11¾05	11.5	32	102	+ ⅛
GaPw 9¾08	9.8	27	99¼	+ ¼
GaPw 10½09	10.4	10	101	+ ⅜
GaPw 11s09	10.8	20	101½	+ ⅛
GaPw 10s16J	10.1	84	98⅞	- ⅛
GaPw 10s16A	10.1	17	98¾	+ ¾
GdNgF 13¼95	35.3	384	37½	...
Gdrch 8¼94	8.6	10	95½	+ ⅛
GreyF zr94	...	40	61½	+ ⅜
GrowGp 12½94	14.7	40	84¾	- ¼
Gulfrd 6s12	cv	70	54	...
HalwdGp 13½09	...	1	72⅛	- ⅛
HarDav 7¼15	cv	8	73½	+ 3¼
Hartfd 8½96	12.7	8	67	- ⅞
Hawn 7⅝02	9.1	1	84¼	+ ⅝
Hawn 8.35s03	9.1	2	92	+ 3
Hltsou 7¾14	cv	4	125	...
Holnam 9¼00	11.4	1	81⅛	+ 4⅛
HmeDep 6s97	cv	15	96	+ ½
HomFSD 6½11	cv	13	37	- ¼
Hmcrp 14⅞99	45.1	53	33	...
HudFd 8s06	cv	19	60	- 3
HudFd 14s08	cv	1	90¾	- ¼
Huffy 7¼14	cv	48	87	+ 1
IBM Cr 9⅝92	9.4	18	102½	...
ICN 12⅞98	25.9	8	49¾	+ ⅝
ICI 9.05s95	9.1	10	100	+ ¾
IllBel 7⅝06	8.8	16	87⅛	+ ½
IllPw 10s98	9.9	11	100¾	- ¼
IllPw 9⅞16	9.9	20	99¾	+ 1
IndBel 8⅛11	8.9	5	91	+ 1⅞
InldStl 8¾95	9.2	17	95	...
InspRs 8½12	cv	1	59½	+ 2
IBM 9⅜04	9.3	48	100⅞	- ¼
IBM 7⅞04	cv	117	100½	...
IBM 10¼95	9.8	188	104¾	- ¼
IBM 9s98	8.8	10	102¼	...
InMin zr05	...	5	30	+ ¾
IPap 8.85s95	8.9	25	100	...
IntRec 9s10	cv	175	71⅝	+ 2⅛
Intnr 11s95	10.8	25	102⅛	- 2⅞
ckpt 8¾14	cv	3	64½	...
amswy 8s05	cv	26	40	- 1

Bonds	Cur Yld	Vol	Close	Net Chg.
LoewCp zr04	...	15	38	- ¼
viLomF 10¾93f	...	114	14	+ ¼
LglsLt 10⅞99	10.8	135	100⅝	+ ⅛
LglsLt 11½14	11.5	95	99⅞	+ ⅛
Loral 7¼10	cv	5	96	+ 2
Lorilld 6⅞93	7.2	34	94⅞	+ ⅛
viLykes 7½94f	...	10	5½	- ⅛
viLykes 11s00f	...	10	5⅝	- ⅜
MACOM 9¼06	cv	8	68½	...
MGMUA 13s96	29.4	27	44¼	+ ½
MfrH 8⅛04	10.9	2	74⅞	- ⅛
MfrH 8⅛07	11.1	52	73¼	- ½
Manvl zr03	...	60	37¼	- ¼
MarO 8½00	9.4	25	90	+ 1
MarO 8.5s06	9.8	25	87	- ¼
MarO 9½94	9.6	102	99	...
Masco 5¼12	8.6	76	61	- ½
Mattel 14¾00	14.1	59	104½	- 1⅜
McCro 7½94	31.3	33	24	- 1
McDe 10s03	11.0	20	90⅞	+ ⅜
McDInv 8s11	cv	11	62	+ 5
McDnl zr94	...	6	77⅝	+ ⅛
Mead 6¾12	cv	16	76	- 1
Melln 8.6s09	10.4	11	83	- 1½
Melln 7¼99	7.8	10	93½	...
MLCPS 15¾06	14.4	4	109	- ½
MerLy zr06	...	25	30	+ ⅛
MesaCap 13½99	16.1	45	83⅞	...
MichB 7¾11	9.1	18	85¼	- ¼
MichB 9.6s08	9.5	25	101	- 1½
MichB 9⅛18	9.4	40	97½	- 1
MidlBk 11.35s93	12.8	446	89	+ ⅜
MKT 5½33f	...	1	24	...
MPac 4¼05	7.2	1	59¼	...
MPac 4¾20f	...	5	51½	...
MPac 4¾30f	...	1	48	+ ¼
MPac 5s45f	...	4	50	...
Mobil 8½01	8.7	25	97¼	- ¼
Mobil 8⅝94	8.5	55	101½	...
Mobil 8¾91	8.7	10	100½	- ½
MohD 5½94	cv	4	19½	- ½
Motrla zr09	...	28	32	+ ¼
MtSTl 9⅝15	9.6	3	100	+ ¼
MtSTl 7⅞16	9.4	1	84	- 1⅞
MtSTl 8s17	9.4	70	85	- ¾
MtSTl 8⅝18	9.4	5	91¾	+ ¼
NCNB 11⅛97	10.9	137	102¼	+ ⅛
NCNB 8½96	9.0	10	94	...
NConv 9s08	cv	5	40	+ ½
NtEdu 6½11	cv	20	39½	+ 2
viNtGyp zr04	...	1852	2¾	...
NMed 12¾99A	12.5	2	102¼	- ¼
NMed 12⅛99B	12.0	1	101	- 1
NMEd 12s00	11.9	1	101¼	...
NMed 12½00	12.4	1	100½	- 1½
NMed zr04	...	20	44	...
NRUt A9¾09	9.8	5	99⅞	+ ⅞
Navstr 8⅝95	9.8	5	88⅛	...
Navstr 9s04	11.3	5	79⅝	- 1⅜
NavFin 8⅝91	8.8	14	98½	...

Bonds	Cur Yld	Vol	Close	Net Chg.
PacTT 9¾19	9.8	239	99⅞	- ⅜
Paine 9⅜96	10.5	10	89½	...
PAA dc13½03	51.4	144	26¼	...
PAA 15s04	55.6	268	27	+ ⅛
PAA 9s10	cv	55	19¾	- ¼
Paten 8¼12	cv	13	22	+ ½
PennC 11s97	10.7	5	102⅜	+ 1⅜
Penny 8⅞95	8.9	50	99⅞	+ ⅝
PepBoy 6s11	cv	1	79¾	- ¼
Pepsic 7⅝98	8.2	10	93¼	+ 1⅛
PeryDr 8½10	cv	25	58	- ⅜
Petrie 8s10	cv	94	86½	+ ½
Pfizer 8½99	8.6	4	98¾	+ 1⅜
PhilEl 9s95	9.0	10	99½	+ ¾
PhilEl 8½04	9.5	106	89¼	...
PhilEl 11⅝00	11.1	15	105	...
PhilEl 9⅝02	9.8	3	98¼	...
PhilEl 9⅛08	9.9	5	92⅜	- ⅛
PhilEl 11¾14	10.8	25	108⅜	+ 1⅞
PhilEl 11s11	10.9	21	100⅞	- 1
PhilEl 10¼16	10.3	14	100	- ½
PhilEl 11s16	10.6	30	104	+ ⅞
PhilEl 12⅛16	11.2	7	108⅛	- ⅛
PhilM 9⅛03	9.2	41	99½	+ ⅞
PhillP 7⅝01	9.1	10	84	...
PhillP 13⅞97	12.0	134	108¾	+ ⅛
PhilP 14¾00	13.7	237	109¾	+ ⅛
PogoP 8s05	cv	10	69	+ ¾
PopeTl 6s12	cv	10	64½	+ ½
PotEl 9½s05	9.5	15	100½	- ½
PotEl 9¼16	9.5	10	97½	...
PotEl 9¾19	9.8	40	99¾	- ¼
viPrmM 6⅝11f	cv	95	5	- ½
viPrmM 7s13f	cv	2	5½	- ¼
Primca 7¾01	9.2	1	84	+ 2¾
ProcG 8¼05	8.7	2	94¾	...
PSInd 8⅞08	9.6	10	92⅝	+ ⅛
viPSNH 15¾88f	m...	10	102¾	...
viPSNH 14⅜91f	...	70	106	+ 2
viPSNH 15s03f	...	10	108	+ 1½
viPSNH 17½04f	...	127	99	+ 1
viPSNH 13¾96f	...	141	143½	- 1⅜
PSEG 9s95	9.0	9	100½	+ ½
PSEG 8.45s06	9.3	20	90⅞	+ ⅜
PSEG 9⅜08	9.5	30	98½	- ½
PSEG 8¾94	8.7	50	100½	...
QuaStC 9s95	9.1	50	99	+ ¼
RJR Nb zr01	...	2415	47⅝	+ ¼
RJR Nb 13⅛01	13.7	100	96	+ ⅜
RJR Nb 13½01	14.1	683	95½	+ 1⅛
RJR Nb 15s01	19.7	689	76¼	+ ⅜
RJR Nb 17s07	21.6	4018	78¾	+ ⅛
RJR Nb 17⅜09	17.6	518	98⅝	- ⅜
RJR 7⅜01	10.8	1	68	- ¼
RalsP 9½16	9.9	20	95⅝	- ⅜
RalsP 9s96	9.0	15	100⅛	...
RalsP 9⅜16	9.8	35	95½	+ 1½
RapA72 7s94	35.0	11	20	...
RapA69 7s94	38.9	12	18	...
RapA 10¾03	69.4	9	15½	+ ½
RapA 12s99	55.8	5	21½	- ½
RelGp 11s96	17.8	18	61⅝	+ ⅜
viRepStl 12⅛03f	...	100	5¾	- ¾
Revl 10⅞10	19.6	230	55½	- 3¼
Revln 11¾95	16.0	257	73½	...
ReyTb 7⅞94	8.8	24	89	...
Rohr 7s12	cv	2	64½	...
Rowan 13¾96	13.3	45	103	...
StLSaF 4s97	5.2	4	76¼	...
StLSaF 5s06f	...	4	62¾	+ ¼
Seafst 9¼01	10.1	33	92	- 1½
Seagrm zr06	...	12	38	+ 1
Sears 13¼92	12.4	30	106⅞	...
Sears 12s94	11.1	40	107⅝	+ ⅞
Sears 9½99	9.7	140	97¾	- ⅝
SvceCp 6½11	cv	18	98	- ½
ShrLehm 10¾96	11.0	18	98⅛	...
ShellO 8s07	8.8	25	91¼	+ 1¼
SoestB 6½99	cv	53	53¾	+ ¼
SoNG 11⅜94	11.2	30	101¼	- ⅛
SNET 8⅛08	9.1	40	89½	+ 1
SNET 9⅝10	9.5	25	101⅝	- ⅛
SPac 2¾96r	4.0	5	69	+ 1
StdOil 7.6s99	8.0	4	95⅜	...
StdOil 8½00	8.9	11	95½	+ ⅝
StrlSft 8s01	cv	21	59⅞	...
StoneCn 13⅝95	16.8	226	80⅞	+ ⅜
StoneCn 11½99	15.9	18	72½	+ ½

JCP 9¾06	9.9	6	98½	− 1⅜
viJonsLI 6¾94f	...	6	5	− ½
viJoneL 9⅞95f	...	25	57⅛	− ⅜
K mart 8⅜17	10.0	25	84	− ¼
KerrGl 13s96	18.3	30	71	− 4½
KerrMc 7¼12	cv	15	105	+ 1
KogerP 9¼03	cv	30	52	− 1½
Kraft 6⅞96	7.7	50	89¾	− ½
viLTV 5s88mf	...	119	6¼	− ⅛
viLTV 9¼97f	...	3	13	+ ¼
viLTV 11s07f	...	186	5¾	+ ⅛
viLTV 95t f	...	78	6⅝	− ⅞
viLTV 14s04f	...	50	13½	...
viLTV 11½97f	...	15	6½	+ ½
viLTV 8¾98f	...	5	5¾	+ 1½
LaQuin 10s02	cv	5	86	− 1¼
NavFin 7½94	9.0	5	83	...
NJBTI 7¼11	8.8	10	82¾	− ¼
NJBTI 7¾13	8.9	30	87⅜	+ 1⅝
NJBTI 8¾18	9.1	2	96½	...
NYEG 8⅝07	9.6	5	90	+ 1⅞
NblAfl 7¼12	cv	15	103	...
NoPac 3s47	4.0	7	75	+ 1
NoPac 3s47str	9.8	7	30½	...
NwnBl 7⅞11	9.2	10	85¼	− ¼
NwnBl 10s14	9.7	14	103⅜	− ⅛
NwnBl 8⅝12	9.3	1	92½	+ 1
NwnBl 8⅛17	9.3	4	87	− 1¼
NwnBl 9½16	9.6	12	99⅜	− ⅛
Oakwd 6½12	cv	15	60	+ 2½
OccP dc9.65s94	10.3	202	93¾	− ⅛
OcciP dc8.95s94	9.8	45	91	+ ⅝
OcciP 9.64s92	9.7	10	99⅝	− ¼
OccP 10½93x	10.5	85	99¾	− ⅛
OcciP 10⅞96	11.1	84	97⅞	+ ⅛
OcciP 11¾11	12.3	90	95⅜	− 1⅛
OccP 10½93y	10.4	1	101	...
OcciP 11⅛19	12.0	10	92½	+ 1½
OcciP 9⅝99	10.9	671	88⅝	+ ⅛
OcciP 10⅛09	11.8	20	86	+ 1
OcciP 10⅛01	11.2	20	90⅝	− ⅜
Ogden 5s93	cv	4	127	− 1½
OhBIT 7½11	9.0	15	82⅞	− ⅝
OhBIT 7⅞13	9.0	25	87⅞	+ ⅞
OhEd 8⅜07	9.4	25	89	...
OhEd 9½08	9.8	15	97¼	− ⅞
Orion 11s98	18.8	10	58½	+ ¾
Orion dc10s94	19.3	16	51⅞	+ ⅞
Oryx 7½14	cv	5	123	− ½
PPG 9s95	8.9	56	100⅝	+ ⅝
PGE 4¼95r	5.2	7	81½	...
PGE 8⅞s02	9.1	39	97	+ ⅜
PGE 8s2003	9.0	12	89¼	− ¾
PGE 9⅛s06	9.4	112	97	...
PGE 9⅝s06	9.7	35	99⅝	− ⅝
PGE 9⅜11	9.6	135	97¾	− ⅜
PcLumb 12s96	15.3	44	78½	− ⅜
PcLumb 12.20s96B	15.9	17	76½	− ⅜
PNwT 8¾08	9.3	2	94	+ 1½
PNwT 9s12	9.4	1	95⅜	...
PacTT 8.65s05	9.1	10	95⅜	+ ¾
PacTT 8¾06	9.1	13	96¼	+ ½
PacTT 7.8s07	8.9	36	87¼	− ½
PacTT 7⅝09	8.9	7	85⅜	+ ½
PacTT 9½11	9.5	70	99¾	+ ⅛
PacTT 8⅞15	9.5	63	93¼	...
PacTT 9⅝14	9.7	40	99½	...
PacTT 9s18	9.5	8	94¼	+ ⅛
PacTT 9⅝18	9.7	165	99⅜	− ¼
PacTT 9⅞16	9.8	6	101¼	− ⅛
Sunsh 9½94	12.2	7	78	...
Sunsh 9½95	...	1	79	...
TJX 7¼10	cv	9	68½	− 1½
Teledy 7s99	8.4	15	83¾	+ 1⅞
Teledy 10s04A	10.6	8	94⅜	− ⅝
Teledy 10s04C	10.6	11	94¼	...
TencCr 9¾94	9.7	100	100½	+ ⅝
Tenco 9⅜93	9.4	12	100	...
TencoCr 9s95	9.1	5	98½	− 1⅜
TennGas dc6s11	9.8	50	61⅜	+ ⅛
TennGas 11⅛13	10.8	5	103	...
TennGas 9¼96	9.4	10	98¾	...
TV 7.35s97C	7.9	15	93	+ ⅝
TV 7.35s98A	8.0	15	92	+ ¾
TV 7.35s98B	8.0	50	92	+ ¼
TV 7¾98Cr	8.3	5	93⅛	...
Texco 13⅝94	13.2	5	103½	− ¼
Texco 5¾97	6.9	5	83½	...
Texco 8⅞05	9.3	65	95⅛	− ½
Texco 8½06	9.3	5	91½	− ¾
TxInd 9s08	cv	35	58½	− 1½
Texfi 11¼91	cv	6	96½	+ ½
Textrn 11¾95	11.6	10	101	...
Textrn 11s95	10.8	10	101⅝	− ⅝
Thermo 5¾12	cv	26	101¼	− ¾
Tidwtr 7s10	cv	1	79	− ½
viTodSh 14s96f	...	100	104	...
TolEd 9s00	9.7	10	93	− ½
TolEd 7½02	9.3	5	80⅞	...
TolEd 8s03	9.2	10	87	− ⅜
Toyota 8¾91	8.8	10	99½	− ¾
Trvlr 8.7s95	9.2	72	94½	+ ⅝
Trvlr 7⅝97	9.0	15	85	+ ¾
Trvlr 8.32s15	cv	57	75½	+ 1
TrinLs 6¾12	cv	27	70	+ 1½
TucEP 7.55s02	10.4	27	72¾	+ 7
TucEP 10½05	12.4	102	85	+ 2
TCFox 13¼00	15.0	15	88⅝	− 1⅞
UNC 7½06	cv	40	53½	+ ¼
USG na16s08	...	381	10⅝	+ ⅛
USLICO 8s11	cv	5	78⅛	+ 2⅛
USX 4⅝96	5.6	3	83⅛	...
USX 5¾01	cv	14	68¾	+ ¼
USX 9s92	9.0	291	100	...
USX 7s17	cv	45	91¼	− 1
UBk 7.35s01	9.5	10	77	+ 1¾
UCarb 5.3s97	6.7	2	78⅞	+ 2⅞
UCarb 8½05	9.7	20	87½	+ ⅞
UCarb 7½12	cv	59	71	− ¼
UCarb 9¾94	9.8	101	99¾	...
UnEl 8⅞06	9.3	8	95	− ⅝
Unisys 8.2s96	19.5	10	42	+ ¾
Unisys 13⅞92	24.6	99	56½	+ ⅛
Unisys 10¾95	27.5	1000	39⅛	− ⅛

Source: *Wall Street Journal* (November 30, 1990).

The British government first borrowed from the City of London in the sixteenth century although the secondary market in government securities only became fully developed in the nineteenth century when London was the financial centre of the world. These securities came to be known as gilts because there was absolutely no risk of default. There was never any doubt that the government would pay the interest or repay on maturity, since the government could create the money when needed. In fact, in the nineteenth century, a group of people called the 'three percenters' lived on unearned income from investment in gilt-edged stocks which provided an annual return on capital of around 3%. With a £5,000 investment in gilts, the annual income of £150 was sufficient to maintain a family in middle-class ease.

However, inflation and rapidly changing interest rates have dealt a blow to the stability of gilt prices. For example, 3% Treasury are currently quoted at around £35 for £100 nominal.

Yield on gilts

Before we can fully analyse the risks inherent in investing in gilts, we must understand more about the *return*, or yield as it is known, of gilts.

Let us again consider 2½% Consols,[7] one of the undated gilts. The term 'undated' means that the government promises to pay £2.50 per annum (for every £100 held) indefinitely. The quoted price of 2½% Consols always refers to £100 nominal of the stock. However, each year the £2.50 received by the investor will appear less valuable to him. £2.50 received now is worth more than £2.50 received next year because it can be invested to yield more than £2.50 in one year's time. Suppose the current one-year interest rate is 10%. £2.50 could be invested to become £2.50 × (1.10) or £2.75 in twelve months' time and so £2.50 received in one year's time is only worth £2.50/(1.1) or £2.27 today. This £2.27 is known as the *present value* of £2.50. The present value of receiving £x in the future is always less than £x because of the opportunity cost of not being able to invest the money in the interim. In other words, the investor has forgone the opportunity of investing £x for one year.

The investor can now calculate the present value of receiving a string of future £2.50s if he knows the prevailing interest rate, R, on equivalent investments.[8]

The present value of £100 nominal of 2½% Consols is P_0, and P_0 can be written as

$$P_0 = \frac{D}{(1 + R)} + \frac{D}{(1 + R)^2} + \ldots \frac{D}{(1 + R)^n} + \ldots \tag{2.2}$$

where D represents the yearly interest payment of £2.50. Of course, the present value, P_0, of the gilt must be its market price if the market is efficient.[9] So, knowing P_0, the investor can determine R, called the discount rate because it is used to discount future cash flows, and which represents the actual rate of return he will get on his gilt-edged investment.[10]

---

[7] Gilts, such as 2½% Consols, 3% Treasury, etc. are described in detail in Chapter 3. 2½% Consols is just one of the UK government securities issued to the public to finance government borrowing. Holders of 2½% Consols are entitled to receive interest of £2.50 every year until such time as the government chooses to redeem them. Other gilts may have a specified date on which they will be redeemed. For simplicity, it is assumed that interest on 2½% Consols is paid annually.

[8] In fact, there will be a string of different interest rates, $R_1, R_2, R_3 \ldots$ for each future time period which will not necessarily all be the same. See Chapter 4 for a description of this yield curve.

[9] See Chapter 10 for the meaning of an 'efficient' stock market.

[10] Assuming the gilt is held indefinitely.

Example 2.5 Value of a fixed interest security

The holding period return is

$$R = \frac{D_1 + P_1 - P_0}{P_0} \tag{2.1}$$

Multiplying by P_0

$$RP_0 = D_1 + P_1 - P_0$$

$$P_0 (1 + R)) = D_1 + P_1$$

$$P_0 = \frac{D_1}{(1 + R)} + \frac{P_1}{(1 + R)}$$

where P_1 is the price of the security at the end of the holding period, say one year. Now suppose the security is held for two years. We can write

$$P_0 = \frac{D_1}{(1 + R)} + \frac{D_2}{(1 + R)^2} + \frac{P_2}{(1 + R)^2}$$

where D_2 is the income received in year 2 and P_2 the price of the security at the end of the two years. If the security is held for n years we can write

$$P_0 = \frac{D_1}{(1 + R)} + \frac{D_2}{(1 + R)^2} + \cdots \frac{D_n}{(1 + R)^n} + \frac{P_n}{(1 + R)^n}$$

In the special case of an undated gilt, such as 2½% Consols, this becomes

$$P_0 = \frac{D}{1 + R} + \frac{D}{(1 + R)^2} + \cdots + \frac{D}{(1 + R)^n} + \cdots \tag{2.2}$$

where D is the fixed annual interest payment received indefinitely.

Equation (2.2), for an undated gilt which will pay interest in perpetuity, can be simplified.

$$P = \frac{D}{(1 + R)} + \frac{D}{(1 + R)^2} + \cdots + \frac{D}{(1 + R)^n} + \cdots \tag{2.3}$$

If we multiply through by $(1 + R)$

$$(1 + R)P = D + \frac{D}{(1 + R)} + \cdots = \frac{D}{(1 + R)^{n-1}} + \frac{D}{(1 + R)^n} + \cdots \tag{2.4}$$

and subtract (2.3) from (2.4), most of the terms on the right-hand side cancel out because we have the same infinite series.

We are left with

$$(1 + R)P - P = D$$

$$P = \frac{D}{R} \tag{2.5}$$

Equation (2.2) is exactly equivalent to equation (2.1) (p. 29) for the holding period return:

$$R = \frac{D_1 + P_1 - P_0}{P_0} \tag{2.1}$$

This can be seen in Example 2.5 where equation (2.1) is first rearranged to be an expression for the initial price P_0 and then the holding period is extended by one year at a time until the investment is assumed to be held indefinitely.

Equation (2.5) states that the price of an undated fixed interest stock is equal to its coupon (the nominal interest rate) divided by the required yield. The lower the coupon, relative to the required yield, the lower the price. If we substitute, say, a current market price of £20 for 2½% Consols we can find its required yield.

$$£20 = \frac{£2.50}{R}$$

$$R = 12.5\%$$

Currently, investors require an annual return of 12½% on this undated gilt-edged stock. Because the coupon is so far below this, the price of £100 nominal is very low at £20. When Consols were issued, the required yield would have been around 2½–3% and the market price approximately equal to the nominal price of £100. Interest rates are now much higher and so the present value, or market price, of a stream of £2.50 interest payments is worth substantially less than its value 100 years or more ago.

This introduction to the yield on gilts now allows us to analyse the two main types of risk affecting all fixed interest securities including gilts, interest rate risk and inflation risk.

(i) INTEREST RATE RISK

Let us consider the case of an investor who purchases £100 nominal of 2½% Consols when the prevailing yield on the gilt is 10%. His purchase price, P_0, will be

$$P_0 = \frac{£2.50}{0.10} = £25$$

(A) Suppose, after one year, interest rates and hence required yields on gilts increase. The required yield on 2½% Consols rises to 15%. The market price of his gilt will be

$$P_1 = \frac{£2.50}{0.15} = £16.70$$

(B) Alternatively, suppose in that time the required yield on 2½% Consols falls to 5%. The market price in this case will be

$$P_1 = \frac{£2.50}{0.05} = £50$$

If the investor then sells the gilt, his return, if scenario (A) takes place, will be

$$\text{Return } R_A = \frac{D_1 + P_1 - P_0}{P_0} = \frac{2.50 + 16.70 - 25}{25}$$

$$R_A = -23\%$$

If scenario (B) takes place, his return will be

$$\text{Return } R_B = \frac{D_1 + P_1 - P_0}{P_0}$$

$$= \frac{2.50 + 50 - 25}{25}$$

$$R_B = 110\%$$

A change in interest rates has had a dramatic impact on the investor's return on his supposedly risk-free gilt. Only when interest rates, and hence prices of gilts, are stable can a gilt be truly considered risk-free.

So, an investor in an undated stock runs the risk that, when he wishes to dispose of the stock, interest rates will have risen and the value of his gilt fallen. How does interest rate risk operate on gilts which are not undated and have a finite life with explicit redemption dates?

Suppose the investor knows that he has a need for funds at a specified date in the future. For example, he has to repay a £10,000 loan in exactly five years' time. If he puts his money into gilts with longer than five years to run or, indeed, undated stocks, he runs the risk that interest rates will rise during the five years he will hold the stock and that, when he comes to sell the gilts to pay off his loan, their value will be less than the £10,000 he needs. On the other hand, if he invests in short-term gilts, with less than five years to run, he runs the opposite risk of a possible fall in interest rates. If the gilts mature before he needs the £10,000, he will have to reinvest them. This leaves the investor open to the risk that interest rates will fall before the gilts are repaid, so that he will only be able to reinvest the proceeds at a lower yield than if he had chosen gilts with the full five-year life. This example illustrates the fact that, unless an investor matches the maturity of his gilt-edged investments exactly with the maturity of his liabilities, in this case chooses gilts with a five-year life, he will expose himself to risks due to changes in interest rates. In fact, even if the investor matches maturities, the gilt will pay interest before maturity which he may not wish to spend. The interest may therefore have to be reinvested, perhaps at a lower rate than that yielded by the gilt.

Pension funds and insurance companies have commitments at specified dates in the future which they can quantify more or less exactly, for example maturing insurance policies and pension payments. These institutions can thus choose gilts which match their commitments and to a great extent avoid interest rate risk. Other investors are unlikely to be able to specify exactly *when* they will need money in the future and are probably unable to state the future value of these commitments. Life assurance payments or pensions may be expressed in nominal[11] terms which can be matched by the maturity of nominal amounts of gilts. In contrast, an investor wishing to buy a house in five years' time which costs £140,000 today does not know how much money he will then need to be able to afford an equivalent house. The *real* value of the house may remain constant, but inflation will increase the nominal cost of the house. For example, £200,000 may be needed in five years to be able to buy what £140,000 would buy today.

(ii) INFLATION RISK

This brings us to the second type of risk attached to gilts, and in fact all other fixed interest securities. Suppose Mr Stone, wishing to buy a house

---

[11] A future liability of £100 in nominal or money terms means that £100 will actually have to be paid out in the future. A future liability of £100 in *real* terms means that an unknown amount; £x, will have to be paid out, where £x then has the same purchasing power as £100 today.

which currently costs £140,000, invests a sufficient amount in gilts maturing in five years' time to repay him £140,000. He will probably find that this will not be enough to buy the house of his dreams. Even if he *expects* inflation to be such that he will need £200,000 in five years' time and he invests in gilts which will repay £200,000, Mr Stone still runs the risk that inflation will not be as he anticipated and he will need more (or less) than £200,000 to buy that house.

Let us look at a simple numerical example which brings out the impact of inflation.

Suppose Mrs Silver buys a gilt for £95 which only has one year to maturity, at which time she will receive the principal of £100 plus an interest payment of £5.

Mrs Silver's return on that gilt held for one year will be

$$R = \frac{D_1 + P_1 - P_0}{P_0}$$

$$R = \frac{(5 + 100) - 95}{95}$$

$$R = 10.5\%$$

Now suppose she expects inflation to be 5% during the next year so that £105 in one year's time will have the same purchasing power as £100 now. Mrs Silver can calculate her expected real return by expressing all cash flows in current purchasing power terms.

$$\text{Expected real return } R_{Real} = \frac{100 - 95}{95} \times 100$$

$$R_{Real} = 5.3\%$$

There is no risk as yet in this investment decision. If the market as a whole requires a real rate of return of 5.3% on a one-year gilt, Fisher[12] has postulated that nominal interest rates (actual market interest rates) will fully reflect expected inflation. Thus, if inflation is expected to be 5%, the nominal interest rate can be calculated as follows:

---

[12] See Fisher (1930).

$$(1 + \text{nominal}) = (1 + \text{real}) (1 + \text{expected inflation rate})^{13} \quad (2.6)$$

$$= (1.053) (1.05)$$

$$= 1.106$$

Nominal interest rate = **10.6%**

The market prices the gilt at £95 to take into account the expected 5% inflation. If no inflation were expected, the market price would be higher at £99.72.

$$P_0 = \frac{D_1 + P_1}{1 + R}$$

$$= \frac{105}{1.053}$$

$$= \textbf{£99.72}$$

According to Fisher's theory, nominal interest rates rise to take account fully of expected inflation and this pushes down the prices of gilts. We now have an explanation of why gilt prices have fallen so dramatically over the past thirty years. The current purchasing power of £100 is one-tenth of what it was in 1960.

So far, inflation risk is not a problem to Mrs Silver, provided she is aware of expected inflation and provided expected inflation is included in nominal interest rates, as Fisher suggests. She will be able to compare investments and make investment decisions with equanimity. However, there are two factors which can make inflation risk a real risk.

Firstly, interest rates may not exactly adjust to expected inflation as Fisher predicts. However, it is difficult to test Fisher's theory since, although tests can be carried out to see whether interest rates have taken account of *actual* inflation, it is more difficult to determine whether interest rates have taken account of *expected* inflation, because of the difficulty of

---

[13] This formula is often approximated to

Nominal IR = real IR + expected inflation rate

In this example, we would get

Nominal IR = 5.3% + 5%

= **10.3%**

measuring expected inflation. (If interest rates do adjust in this way, one would expect investors to require the same *real* rate of interest on, say, gilts, over time, with the nominal, required return actually varying from this constant because of expected inflation.)

Secondly, even if expected inflation is fully catered for in market prices, *un*expected inflation can affect the real returns of investors and prevent Mr Stone from realising enough in real terms to buy his house.

Suppose Mrs Silver buys the gilt described above for £95 and that inflation during that year turns out to be 10%. The purchasing power of £105 received at the end of that year will only be £105/(1.1) or £95.45. So Mrs Silver's *actual* real return will be

$$R_{actual} = \frac{95.45 - 95}{95}$$

$$R_{actual} = 0.5\%$$

Inflation risk, in the sense that the actual real returns achieved on investments could be less than the expected real returns, is a risk for all types of fixed interest securities. So, Mrs Silver cannot avoid inflation risk by investing in particular fixed interest securities. However, if next year's inflation can be estimated more accurately than inflation in several years' time (and if nominal interest rates do fully take account of expected inflation), then Mrs Silver will suffer less inflation risk if she invests in short-term rather than long-term or undated securities-simply because current estimates of inflation are less likely to be wrong in the short rather than the long term. In that sense, Mrs Silver will suffer less inflation risk, the shorter-term the gilt she buys.[14]

However, although inflation risk is present to a greater or lesser extent when investing in any fixed interest security, it need not be attached to ordinary share investment. The dividends paid on shares are *not* fixed. If inflation is high, the company should be able to achieve high nominal profits and to pay out high nominal dividends.[15] In fact, if the company has issued a substantial number of fixed interest securities, the value of the ordinary shares may increase by more than inflation to balance the loss incurred by the fixed interest security-holders whose investments are worth less because of unexpected inflation.

---

[14] The impact of different amounts of inflation risk on different maturity gilts is discussed further in Chapter 4.

[15] Although see a discussion of the possible impact of inflation on equity prices in Chapter 13.

Measurement of risk and return

The previous section discussed the different types of risk attached to investment in securities – uncertainty of income, default risk, interest rate risk and inflation risk. As well as being subject to various types of risk, different securities suffer these risks to greater or lesser extents. However, whatever the risk, it is always reflected in the variability of returns achieved on any security and derives from the fact that we live in an uncertain world.

When looking into the future, we can predict different possible states of the world, for example the company whose loan stock we are considering buying may or may not default; the actual inflation rate, which we expected to be 5%, may turn out to be 10 or 8 or 3%. If only one possible state could occur, we would live in a certain world with certain returns on investment and zero risk.

Having identified the different types of risk which exist and realising that they are the result of the possibility of different states of the world occurring in the future, how can we quantify the risk and likely return of any investment?

We use probabilities to attach numbers to the likelihood of each possible state of the world occurring. For example, suppose we look at what happened to £100 invested in company X shares at the beginning of each year for the past fifty years. What were the end-of-year values of the investment in each of those fifty years? Suppose we find that the end-of-year value was £104 in ten of those years, £106 in fifteen of those years and so on as in Example 2.6.

What can we say about the end-of-year value of £100 invested now in company X? If the factors underlying company X's share performance are fundamentally unchanged, we can convert these long-run frequencies of past returns into probabilities concerning the future. We can say that there is a probability of 10 in 50 or a 0.2 chance that the value will be £104 giving a 4% return and so on, as in Example 2.7.

These probabilities (p_i) add up to 1 because we have taken into account all eventualities and no more than one of these could occur. (The states of the world considered are, in other words, exhaustive and mutually exclusive.) All we have done here is apply the way we think about, say, cards to investments in shares. Since there are four aces in a pack we deduce that there is a probability of 4 in 52 or 1 in 13 that an ace will be picked at random from the full pack. What we mean by this is that if we pick cards at random often enough from the full pack we will expect 1 out of every 13 picked to be an ace. We are using *long-run average frequencies* to estimate the likelihood of future events.

Probabilities derived from inspecting past frequencies are known as 'objective' probabilities. They have been calculated by looking at actual past events. With investments in securities, objective probabilities can be

Example 2.6   *Frequency distribution of the value of one-year investments of £100 in company X in each of the last fifty years*

End-of-year value £	Frequency with which value occurred
104	10
106	15
108	15
110	10
	50

calculated by looking at the frequency distribution of returns the security has achieved in the past. If a particular share has provided variable returns in the past and if it has not fundamentally changed its business, it is likely to be equally volatile in the future. Frequency distributions will therefore provide a good picture of what may happen in the future. Alternatively, data on past performance may not be available or factors affecting the security's return may have altered. In this case, 'subjective' probabilities based on the best estimates of the investor or his advisers will have to be used to provide the probability distribution of future returns.

Expected return

Armed with our probability distribution, we still need to measure risk and return to be able to compare investments. We have an idea of the different returns which are likely, but is there one figure which will give us the best

Example 2.7   *Probability distribution of end-of-year values of £100 invested now in company X*

End-of-year value £	Holding period return on investment (%)	Probability P_i
104	4	0.2
106	6	0.3
108	8	0.3
110	10	0.2
		1.0

estimate of the return we will actually achieve? The most likely outcome, known as the *mode* (the one with the highest probability), is either 6% or 8% in this example – both have a probability of 0.3. This measure of return is inconvenient if there is, as in this case, more than one mode in the probability distribution. The *median*, defined to be that return where there is a 50% chance that the actual return will be less than or more than this figure must, in our example, lie somewhere between 6 and 8%. The median, as with the mode, does not take into account all the possible returns in the distribution.

The third possible estimate of the future return is the *mean* or expected return. This is the average of all the possible returns weighted by their probabilities. It is equivalent to the *average* return one would expect to get if one kept on investing each year in company X. The expected return gives a single figure which takes into account all possible returns, and which is useful statistically as we shall see later. For these reasons, and because it is intuitively easy to understand, the expected return is the measure normally used for estimating future, uncertain returns.

$$\text{Expected return} = p_1R_1 + p_2R_2 + p_3R_3 + \ldots + p_nR_n$$

where each $R_i(i = 1, \ldots, n)$ is a possible return and p_i the probability that this return will occur

In this case, the expected return $E(R)$ is

$$E(R) = p_1R_1 + p_2R_2 + p_3R_3 + p_4R_4$$

$$E(R) = (0.2 \times 4) + (0.3 \times 6) + (0.3 \times 8) + (0.2 \times 10)$$

$$= 7\%$$

More generally we can write $E(R)$ as

$$E(R) = \sum_{i=1}^{i=n} p_iR_i \tag{2.7}$$

where Σ is a summation sign indicating that we should add together as many p_iR_i terms as there are.

At the beginning of the chapter, we compared securities by looking at their actual returns. Because we were looking at historic returns, we knew the P_0, P_1 and D_1 for each security and hence its return, R. When comparing future investments to be made in an uncertain world, the values of P_1 and even D_1 may not be known in advance. Estimates of the possible returns which could be achieved and the probabilities of these returns must be made and, from these estimates, the *expected* return can be calculated.

Securities can therefore be compared by looking not at their actual but at their expected returns.

Definition of risk

However, we know that in a risky world, we would not necessarily always buy the security which offered the highest expected return because each security will have a different level of risk attached to it. For example, suppose an investor is comparing the two investment opportunities, each costing £100, described in Example 2.8.

In this example, both *A* and *B* offer the same expected return. The investor cannot choose between them on the basis of expected return alone. He needs to consider the risks of *A* and *B*, firstly to see whether they are worth purchasing at all and secondly to see which of *A* and *B* he prefers.

Intuitively we can see that security *B* is riskier than *A* but how do we measure that risk? Is it the risk relative to the initial investment of £100 or relative to the expected value of £120? If security *B* becomes worth £60, the investor will actually lose £40 in cash but he will lose £60 relative to the *expected* value of *B*. The £60 will be the more relevant figure, since not only will the investor have lost £40, if *B* turns out to be worth £60, but he

Example 2.8   Comparison of risk and return of securities A and B

	End-of-year value £	Return (%)	Probability
Security A	110	+10	0.3
	120	+20	0.4
	130	+30	0.3
			1.0

Expected return of A: $0.3 \times 10 + 0.4 \times 20 + 0.3 \times 30 \quad = 20\%$

Security B	60	−40	0.3
	120	+20	0.4
	180	+80	0.3
			1.0

Expected return of B: $0.3 \times -40 + 0.4 \times 20 + 0.3 \times 80 \quad = 20\%$

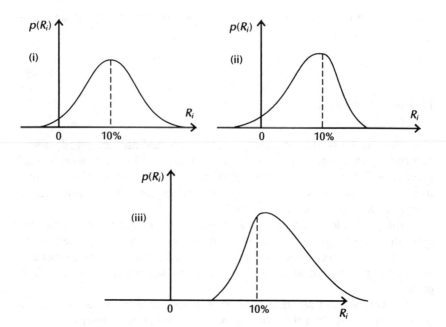

Figure 2.1   Normal and skewed probability distributions

will also have lost the opportunity of investing his £100 in something else of equivalent risk which could have yielded him £20. His concern will therefore be with how different the return could be from £120.

Another problem in deciding on how to measure risk is whether the investor is concerned only with downside risk (risk that the return will be *less* than he expects) or the risk that the return will be more *or* less than he expects. Consider the probability distributions in Figure 2.1. They all have the same expected return of 10%.

Figure 2.1(i) shows a normal distribution. This is the well-known probability distribution which occurs when a number of random and separate possibilities are envisaged. It is symmetric, which means that the distribution below the expected value is the mirror image of the distribution above the expected value. Thus, in this case of a normal probability distribution, any measure of downside risk (the risk that the return will be *less* than expected) will give the same result as a measure of total dispersion about the expected value (the risk that the return will be less *or* more than expected).

On the other hand, if the distributions are skewed (not symmetrical), as in Figures 2.1(ii) and 2.1(iii), measures of downside risk and total dispersion do not give the same result. In Figure 2.1(ii), the downside risk is greater than the risk of doing better than expected, whereas in Figure 2.1(iii) the opposite is the case. A measure of total dispersion would not be able to distinguish between Figures 2.1(ii) and 2.1(iii).

However, a measure of total dispersion, the *standard deviation*, is the most common measure of risk used in the theory of investment. There are three major reasons for this. Firstly, if security return distributions are normal, as in Figure 2.1(i), the expected return and standard deviation are the only two measures needed to describe fully the probability distribution of any security. It is also true, in this case, that the standard deviation is equivalent to a measure of downside risk. Secondly, most frequency distributions of past security returns do appear to conform more to normal than to skewed distributions. Even if they are not exactly normal, it is a statistical fact that the returns of a portfolio made up of a collection of such securities will be normal and most people do hold portfolios of securities. Thirdly, the standard deviation is a particularly easy measure to handle, as we shall see below.

The remainder of this book will assume that the standard deviation adequately quantifies the total risk of investing in a security – the uncertainty surrounding the actual returns which will be achieved. The greater the uncertainty, the greater the standard deviation and vice versa. If there is no uncertainty, that is, the return is known for certain, the dispersion, and hence the standard deviation, will be zero. However, we cannot be sure that investors do regard the standard deviation as an adequate measure. They may prefer another measure of risk altogether (such as the maximum possible cash loss from an investment, which does not require knowledge of the full probability distribution of returns) or they may require more than one measure of risk, perhaps needing a measure for skewness as well as dispersion. Nevertheless, the above-mentioned attractions of the standard deviation have led to its supremacy as a measure of risk, and until more is known about how investors do quantify risk, the standard deviation is an adequate and simple measure.

Measurement of risk

The formula for the standard deviation of a probability distribution is rather complicated to look at but simple to understand. The square of the standard deviation, known as the *variance*, is usually calculated first. The variance is the sum of the *squares* of the dispersions around the expected return, $E(R)$, weighted by their probabilities (as for the expected return). Squares are used because if actual dispersions were added they would cancel each other out and sum to zero. So we can calculate the variance, V, as

$$V = \sum_{i=1}^{i=n} ((E(R) - R_i)^2 \, p_i(R_i)) \qquad (2.8)$$

The standard deviation S is then the square root of V. In Example 2.9 we

Example 2.9   Calculation of variance

End-of-year return R_i	Dispersion $E(R) - R_i$	Square of dispersion $(E(R) - R_i)^2$	Probability p_i	$(E(R) - R_i)^2 p_i$
4	3	9	0.2	1.8
6	1	1	0.3	0.3
8	−1	1	0.3	0.3
10	−3	9	0.2	1.8
$E(R) = 7\%$	0	20	1.0	$V = 4.2$

$V = 4.2$
$S = \sqrt{V}$
$S = \sqrt{4.2} = 2.1\%$

The standard deviation, S, is 2.1%

---

use the investment in shares of company X, described in Example 2.7, as an example.

As an exercise, check that the standard deviations of securities A and B, described in Example 2.8, are 8% and 46% respectively. The standard deviation is always expressed in the same units as the expected return and is intuitively easier to use than the variance, especially with a normal distribution. With a normal distribution, we can say that there is approximately a 2 in 3 (more accurately, 68.3%) chance that the return will actually be within + or − 1 standard deviation of the expected value. For example, if the expected return on a security is 10% and its standard deviation (on a normal distribution) is 2%, there is a 2 in 3 chance that the return will actually be between 8 and 12%. Similarly, there is only 1 chance in 100 that the return will lie outside the range 5–15%. These generalisations cannot be applied to securities A and B of Example 2.8 since their probability distributions are only very simple approximations to a normal distribution.

Knowing only the expected returns of A and B did not allow the investor to make any investment decisions under uncertainty. Knowing both their expected returns and their risks now enables the investor to do two things:
  (i) decide whether A and B offer sufficient reward in the form of expected return for their risks;
  (ii) assuming both A and B are attractive investments, decide which of A and B to choose.

The theories discussed in this book assume the investor is averse to taking on risk – in other words, he requires more expected return before he will take on more risk. Since A has a lower standard deviation, for the same expected return, the investor will prefer A.

Expected utility

Although all investors are presumed risk averse, each investor will make different *trade-off decisions* between risk and expected return. This trade-off will be affected by such factors as unwillingness to bear risk which will be reflected in how much additional expected return the investor requires for taking on an additional unit of risk. Similarly, another factor will be how much the investment could affect the investor's total wealth. A potential loss of £1,000 would probably worry a millionaire less than someone with earnings of £100 per week.

The concept of utility allows the investor to combine his attitudes to risk and return at different levels of wealth into one measure – *utility of wealth*. Utility in this case can be thought of as the satisfaction the individual gets from different amounts of wealth. The different probable outcomes of any investment will lead to different probable levels of wealth. If an investor knows how much utility he will get from each level of wealth, he can calculate his *expected* utility from each investment – just as he can determine the expected return of any investment. He will then choose any investment which increases his expected utility and, in particular, those which increase it most.[16] Each investor will have a different utility function which will lead to his preferring different investments.

As an example, let us consider Mr Black who is evaluating the investments described in Example 2.10.

Example 2.10   Comparison of securities I and J with different expected returns and different risks

Security	Cost of invest-ment £	End-of-year value £	Return R_i (%)	Proba-bility P_i	Expected return $E(R)$	Standard deviation S (%)
I	100	105	5	0.5	10	5
		115	15	0.5		
J	100	102	2	0.5	12	10
		122	22	0.5		

---

[16] In order for an investor to wish to maximise expected utility, we assume he is rational, i.e. prefers more wealth to less wealth, etc. See Alexander (1986), chs II and III, for a more detailed discussion of utility functions. We need to calculate *expected* utility because we are dealing with uncertain returns.

Unlike the case in Example 2.8, the investments do not offer the same expected return nor do they have the same standard deviation. The choice is no longer as simple – it depends on whether Mr Black requires more or less than the additional 2% expected return offered by *B* in exchange for an additional 5% standard deviation. With a simple expected return/standard deviation analysis, Mr Black can choose only if he lays down rules such as 'no more than 7% standard deviation' (in which case he prefers *A*) or 'at least 12% return' (in which case he prefers *B*). However, knowledge of his utility function allows him to choose the one which maximises his expected utility. Suppose Mr Black has the following utility of wealth function where *W* is his wealth:

$$U(W) = 0.1W - 0.000025W^2 \tag{2.9}$$

Equation (2.9) is a quadratic equation in W.[17] This means that, when plotted on a graph (as in Figure 2.2 on p. 54), Mr Black's utility function is a curve with a decreasing slope, the larger W. We shall see later that this type of curve implies that Mr Black is risk averse. In other words, he requires a higher expected return, the higher the risk of the investment.

In this example, we are concerned with whether Mr Black, given his particular utility function, prefers *I* or *J*. To ascertain this, we must know his current actual wealth – suppose it is £500. We now calculate the expected utility he would derive from each investment. We do this in the same way as we calculated expected return in equation (2.7). Thus, expected utility is simply the sum of the utilities attached to the possible wealth after investment, weighted by their probabilities. Expected utility of wealth, written *EU(W)*, is:

$$EU(W) = \sum_{i=1}^{i=n} p_i\, U(W_i) \tag{2.10}$$

The expected utilities of wealth after investing in *I* or *J* are shown in

---

[17] A quadratic equation of the type $Y = f(x)$ is one which has a squared term in x

$$Y = a + bx + cx^2$$

where a, b and c are constants. The equation of a straight line does not have a squared term in x:

$$Y = a + bx$$

Utility functions for risk averse investors do not have to be quadratic, for example, we can have $U = a + bW + cW^2 + dW^3$ (cubic), etc. See Alexander (1986) for further details. However, if a probability distribution of returns is *not* normal, the investor's utility function has to be quadratic for expected return and standard deviation to be the only characteristics which concern him (that is, he is unconcerned about skewness).

Example 2.11   Mr Black's expected utility of wealth from investments I and J

(1) End-of-year value of security £	(2) Proba- bility of outcome, p_i	(3) End-of-year wealth, W_i (net of cost of investment) £	(4) Utility of wealth $U(W_i) =$ $0.1W_i - 0.000025W_i^2$ (U)	(5) = (2) × (4) $p_iU(W_i)$ (U)
Initial wealth £500, cost of investment £100				
I 105	0.5	505	44.12	22.06
115	0.5	515	44.87	22.44
				$EU(W_I) = 44.50$ U
J 102	0.5	502	43.90	21.95
122	0.5	522	45.39	22.69
				$EU(W_J) = 44.64$ U

Example 2.11. Mr Black's *current* utility of wealth is $U(W)$ where $W = £500$:

$$U(W) = 0.1(500) - 0.000025(500)^2$$

$$= 50 - 6.25$$

$$U(W) = 43.75 \text{ U}$$

The actual values we calculate for utility do not matter. What counts is the relative ranking of utilities.[18]

In both cases, expected utilities are greater than Mr Black's existing utility and both investments are worthwhile. However, investment *J* offers the highest expected utility to Mr Black and would be preferred by him.

So, expected utility enables Mr Black to make investment decisions under uncertainty using one simple measure rather than separately evaluating the expected return of each investment, its risk and its effect on his wealth.

If we plot Mr Black's utility function on a graph, we get a curve as in Figure 2.2. This is the curve of a risk averse investor. Mr Black is averse to risk in the sense that he requires additional expected return for taking on additional risk. We saw that this was true when we looked at the expected utilities he derived for securities *I* and *J*. He preferred *J* because, in his view, the additional 2% it offered in expected return more than compensated for the additional 5% in standard deviation.

---

[18] Units of utility are usually termed 'utiles' (U). They can be of any size, like temperature. What counts is whether *A* is hotter than *B*, not the absolute heat values of *A* or *B*.

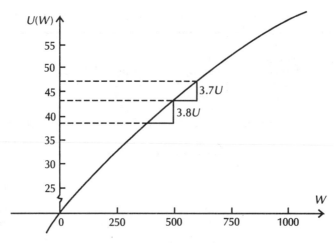

Figure 2.2   Mr Black's utility function

Another way of showing that this is the graph of a risk averse investor is to consider Mr Black's attitude to a 'fair gamble', that is, a gamble with an expected value of zero. For example, suppose Mr Black were offered a 50% chance of winning £50 and a 50% chance of losing £50. If his current wealth is £500, we can see from the graph that he loses more utility (−3.8 U) if his wealth is reduced to £450 than if he gains from increasing his wealth to £550 (+3.7 U). A risk averse investor, like Mr Black, will always refuse a fair gamble.

Most gambles in real life, such as on horse races or the football pools, have a negative expected value because of the government tax on gambling and the profits of the companies organising the betting. The question then arises as to how we can assume investors have risk averse utility functions when the incidence of gambling is so high. Various solutions to this paradox have been proposed, for example that the shape of the utility function changes according to the level of wealth and incorporates both a risk averse and risk preferring section,[19] as in Figure 2.3.

Alternatively, gamblers might ascribe better odds (probabilities) to the possible outcomes of the gamble than actually hold because they believe they are 'lucky'.

The underlying topic of this chapter has been: how do investors compare different securities? We have suggested that they should determine the probability distribution of returns for each security, although only the expected return and standard deviation need in practice be calculated.

Each individual then has to decide whether the expected return offered on each security is sufficient to reward him for its risk, assuming he is risk averse, and then has to compare the risk-return trade-offs offered by those

---

[19] A risk preferrer is an individual who will always *accept* 'fair gambles'.

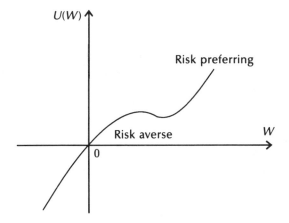

Figure 2.3   Graph of cubic utility function

securities. Knowledge of his utility of wealth function enables the investor to choose between securities, taking into account in a single measure his attitudes to risk and return at each level of his wealth. In this way, he can easily choose between securities, such as between *I* and *J* in Example 2.10. In practice, however, investors do not know what their utility function is, and certainly not its mathematical expression. What risk averse investors *can* do is to choose the security or portfolio which offers the highest expected return for a given risk *or* the lowest risk for a particular desired return. We shall return, in Chapter 8, to the topic of investors' choice between portfolios of varying returns and risks to achieve this 'optimal' portfolio.

Reduction of risk

Since we assume throughout this book that investors are risk averse, it would be interesting to finish this chapter by investigating whether there are any simple mechanisms whereby risk can be reduced, without sacrificing return. If there are, any sensible investor will follow them.

There are, in fact, two principal ways in which risk can be reduced. The first, pooling, is the reason for the existence of such bodies as insurance companies and investment trusts, and the second, hedging, requires the participation of speculators in the market.

In Chapter 1 we considered the role of a stock market as a means of *transferring* risk from entrepreneurs to investors and between investors. Pooling and hedging offer means whereby the overall level of risk can not only be transferred but actually *reduced*.

Pooling

Consider the risk of your house being totally destroyed. Each house owner bears this risk which can be well quantified by probabilities using past frequencies of houses being destroyed.[20] Although this risk is small, the house may well represent the most valuable asset in the investor's portfolio and he may therefore wish to insure against an occurrence which has a high expected cost to him. In other words he will pay a fixed premium to an insurance company in return for the insurance company guaranteeing to pay him should his house be damaged or destroyed. If many house owners pool their risks in this way, the insurance company will actually bear less risk than if each house owner had separately borne the risk. This is because the risk of each house being destroyed is *independent* of the risk of another house being destroyed (events which might affect all houses such as nuclear war are specifically excluded in insurance policies) and, when these independent risks are considered, the standard deviation of the pooled risk is less than the sum of the individual risks.

Why this is so will be shown when we discuss portfolio theory in Chapter 8. We will merely state the result here. If each house is insured for the same amount and the risk of each house being destroyed is equal and has standard deviation S_H, then the risk borne by the company insuring n such houses is S where

$$S = \frac{S_H}{\sqrt{n}}$$

For example, if the company insures 10,000 houses, its standard deviation or risk will be 1/100th of the risk of the individual house owner. The overall risk of these n houses being destroyed has been reduced by pooling. An important proviso must be attached to this statement. The overall risk will be reduced by the presence of the insurance company only if the probability of the event occurring is not increased as a result of the insurance being taken out. If people, knowing that they are insured, are more careless, the overall risk borne by the insurance company may not be less than the sum of the individual risks. This is called the 'moral hazard' problem.

Of course, insurance has nothing to do with the stock market. Insurance policies are arranged via Lloyds, a completely separate market, or with insurance companies (who may then use Lloyds). Also, the returns on securities are not independent; they are affected by common economic factors. Nevertheless, it will be seen, again in Chapter 8, that the combina-

---

[20] The underlying factors affecting events such as houses being destroyed or the expected life span of individuals (for life assurance) do not change so rapidly over time that they cannot easily be adjusted.

tion by an investor of securities into a portfolio will always be worthwhile in the sense that his overall risk will be reduced to less than the weighted average of the risks of the component securities. This method of reducing the risk of investing in securities is called diversification, and forms the basis of portfolio theory.

Hedging

As with pooling, the possibility of reducing risk by hedging applies only to a specific kind of risk. This is one where two parties are subject to exactly opposite risks, say one person bears the risk of event A happening and the other of event A not happening. If these two people can get together and agree on a transaction before the outcome of A is known, they will both have hedged their risk. For example, a producer of cocoa wishes to know how much cocoa to grow next year. He will be influenced by the price of cocoa prevailing next year which he would like to know now. Similarly, a manufacturer of chocolates wishes to plan his production of sweets and would like to be assured of future supplies at fixed prices. If the producer and manufacturer get together to agree today on a price for cocoa to be delivered next year, they will both have hedged their risks. The producer's uncertainty of the future price he can get for his cocoa and hence how much he should grow has been resolved. The manufacturer's uncertainty concerning future prices and supplies of raw materials is removed. Both parties have hedged the risk of a change in the price of cocoa – on the manufacturer's side the risk of cocoa prices going *up* and on the producer's side the risk of cocoa prices going *down*. They have used what is known as the *forward* market for their transaction. Forward markets exist in major commodities such as sugar, cocoa, metals and in foreign exchange. They are markets in which future transactions are agreed now but not paid for or delivered until a specified date in the future. These markets provide hedges in exactly the same way as we described in the cocoa market. For example, in the foreign exchange forward market, UK buyers of US goods bear the risk of the cost of the dollars they need for their purchase going up in sterling terms, whereas British sellers of goods priced in dollars bear the risk of the value of dollars falling in sterling terms. Forward transactions in dollars will enable them both to hedge their risks.

These forward markets (or futures markets as the more regulated ones are known[21]) have evolved in response to the need for certain risks, such as

---

[21] Futures markets are more regulated in the sense that there is a physical market place. Also, all transactions are recorded, prices are published, transactions are standardised and there is an intermediary clearing house which requires security (in the form of deposits of money) from parties to all transactions to prevent default.

fluctuations in commodity prices or exchange rates, to be hedged. Such markets require the existence of speculators since there may not be an even balance of opposite risks to be hedged. More traders may wish to hedge against the price of cocoa rising in value than against its falling and so speculators will have to step in to take the risk of the cocoa price falling. In fact, if speculators accurately forecast which way prices are going to move, they will improve the market in cocoa, for they will buy when prices are low, hold stocks and sell when prices are high. In this way, they will remove excess quantities of cocoa from a depressed market and provide needed cocoa in a buoyant market. However, inexpert speculators will have the opposite and damaging effect. The existence of speculators willing to take on risk means that not only can risk be reduced by hedging but also transferred to investors willing to accept risk as on the Stock Exchange.

We may ask ourselves: of what use is hedging to the stock market investor? Commodities and foreign exchange markets operate separately from stock markets and do not involve transactions in quoted securities. There are two main reasons why the stock market investors should be interested in hedging.

Firstly, the investor now has the opportunity to undertake hedging transactions in quoted securities. As far as shares are concerned, he can use futures contracts on stock market indices and options on both stock market indices and individual shares. Futures and options are described in Chapters 6 and 7. In addition, the interest rate risk inherent in bond investment can be hedged through the use of bond futures and options in all the major markets. Even inflation risk can to some extent[22] be hedged, in the UK at least, through the use of index-linked gilts described in more detail in Chapters 3 and 4.

The second reason why the stock market investor should be interested in hedging is because the foreign exchange markets, both spot[23] and forward, must be understood before international investment can be undertaken. Most overseas investments require the purchase of foreign currency and so involve two considerations, that of the risk and return of the investment itself *and* that of the risk of holding the foreign currency in which they are denominated. The subject of international investment and the hedging of currency risk is discussed in Chapter 11.

---

[22] We shall see in Chapter 3 that the coupon and redemption payments of an index-linked gilt are, in fact, only fully hedged against the retail prices index (RPI) for a period which is not exactly the same as the holding period.

[23] A spot transaction is one where a commodity is paid for and delivered on the spot (now) rather than at some future date.

Summary

This chapter has described the two major characteristics of any investment, its expected return and risk. The different types of risk underlying various types of investment were discussed, from supposedly risk-free bonds to company shares. The major types of risk described were uncertainty of income, default risk, interest rate risk and inflation risk.

The chapter then considered how uncertain return and risk could be measured so that different investments could be compared. Probability distributions, either derived objectively from observation of past returns or subjectively by estimating future possible returns, were used to quantify expected return. The standard deviation of the probability distribution of returns is a suitable measure of risk provided the distribution is normal or investors ignore skewness.

The investor's attitude to the risk and expected return of investment can be neatly described in his utility function. Each investor may have a different attitude to risk and return and hence a different utility function. Such a utility function is expressed in terms of the investor's wealth and not the rates of return of the investment. Obviously different returns will imply different changes in the investor's wealth. In the special case where the investor only compares the expected returns and standard deviations of investments, his utility function can be shown to be quadratic and such an investor will be risk averse.

This book assumes that, when considering Stock Exchange investments, investors can be viewed as risk averse. If this is the case they will be interested in any means whereby risk can be reduced, and the last section of the chapter considered two possible methods of reducing risk, pooling and hedging.

Problems

1. Mr Woolly is choosing between two possible investment opportunities:
   (a) A gilt-edged stock which will mature in exactly one year and on that date the nominal amount (£100) and a 3% interest payment will be made. The price of £100 nominal of this stock is £98 today.
   (b) 100 shares costing 98p each in a company specialising in software for personal computers. The return on the shares is uncertain but the investor has read a report on the company which estimates the one-year return to be as follows, subject to how the economy behaves and how the company's products are received by the market:

	Economic	
	Growth	Recession
Well received	30% $p = 0.2$	15% $p = 0.3$
Poorly received	10% $p = 0.3$	−10% $p = 0.2$

New products

where p = probability

(i) Using expected values and standard deviations, calculate the expected return and risk of the two investments.
(ii) Bearing in mind that inflation is expected to be 5% in the next twelve months, which investment would you advise Mr Woolly to make?
(iii) What other factors would you take into consideration?

2. Mr Gray has derived his utility function (by comparing his preference for various gambles and certain outcomes) as

$$U(W) = 1 - \frac{10,000}{W}$$

He is now considering investing his entire wealth of £10,000 (he has no earned income) in fixed interest securities for a period of one year. His stockbroker recommends one of the following gilts, both priced at £90:

Gilt	Coupon (annual)	Possible price in one year's time	Probability
A	10	90	0.3
		95	0.4
		100	0.3
			1.0
B	7	80	0.3
		100	0.4
		120	0.3
			1.0

Their interest payments (to be paid in twelve months' time) are certain, but their end-of-year prices are uncertain due to interest rate risk. Mr Gray wishes to invest all £10,000 in either gilt A or gilt B.
(i) Calculate the expected return and risk of each gilt. Does this knowledge help Mr Gray to decide? Why/why not?
(ii) Which gilt will Mr Gray choose?

3. Mrs de Salvera is fifty-five and self-employed. She wishes, on retirement, to use her investments to buy a house in the country and believes that house prices will remain constant in real terms. She is unwilling to buy shares and intends to invest her savings for the next five years in fixed interest securities.
   (i) Which types of risk will Mrs de Salvera incur if she buys fixed interest securities?
   (ii) How can she choose particular fixed interest securities to minimise those risks?

4. To what kinds of risk are the different types of financial investments subject? Explain how such risks can be reduced in the various financial markets without sacrificing return.

Gilt-edged securities

Introduction

Chapters 3 and 4 are devoted to a type of security often ignored in investment text books – fixed interest securities.[1] Such a lack of emphasis on this type of investment can partly be explained by the preference for the more glamorous company share sector and partly by the poor performance of fixed interest securities in this century. (For example, £100 spent on 2½% Consols at the beginning of 1919 would have been quoted at £25$\frac{11}{16}$% on the first day of 1992 and worth in real terms only 1½% of its 1919 value.)

This view of fixed interest securities is changing. Interest rates now fluctuate both up and down, allowing the value of fixed interest securities to rise as well as fall. Also, the sheer size of the fixed interest securities market, in particular gilts,[2] has brought these securities back into prominence.

The National Debt of the British government has dramatically increased during the twentieth century, fuelled by two World Wars, the nationalisation of the major public utilities and growing budget deficits. The early

---

[1] That is, securities which entitle the holders to a fixed rate of interest throughout the life of the loan. Note that in the UK, fixed interest securities are often called 'stocks', whereas in the US this term refers to the ordinary shares of companies.

[2] See Chapter 2, p. 35 for an explanation of why UK government fixed interest securities are called 'gilt-edged' or 'gilts'.

1990s saw an increase in the size of the National Debt, and by March 1992 the UK's National Debt was £213b. of which the majority, over £133b., was financed by gilt-edged securities. The British government's aim has been to lengthen the maturity of its debt and this has led to the UK Stock Exchange offering one of the best markets in the world for long-term government fixed interest securities.

Turnover in gilts of £1,113b. was *three* times as great as for UK equities in 1991. Corporate fixed interest securities, such as debentures, loan stocks and preference shares, are relatively less important than gilts, with UK listed fixed interest securities a very small element of the UK Stock Exchange, with total turnover of only £65b.

However, there has been an increase in new issues of corporate fixed interest securities via the eurobond market, which we will discuss in more detail in Chapter 4. Given the dominance of gilts in terms of turnover and market value over other fixed interest securities in the stock market, this chapter, although relevant to *all* fixed interest securities, will concentrate predominantly on gilts.

Example 3.1 shows who holds these government securities. It can be seen that all the major financial institutions hold substantial portfolios of gilts of differing maturities. The attractions of holding gilts to these investors are various. For example, insurance companies have long-term commitments. If they buy gilts with the same maturities as these commitments they can be certain of being able to meet their liabilities in nominal terms. Also, banks and building societies keep a certain proportion of their investments in what are known as liquid assets[3] (easily realisable short-

Example 3.1 Holders of gilt-edged securities (31 March 1992)

	Gilts held (%)		
	0–5 years	*5–15 years*	*over 15 years*
Official holders	11	10	6
Banks	3	3	4
Building societies	6	–	–
Insurance companies	13	41	38
Pension funds	8	21	41
Overseas holders	22	17	5
Individuals	14	6	4
Other	23	2	–
	100	100	100
TOTAL (£b.)	**40.4**	**61.2**	**31.5**

Source: *Bank of England Quarterly Bulletin*, November 1992.

---

[3] Liquid assets include treasury bills (ninety-one-day securities), certificates of deposit (securities relating to large bank deposits), short-term gilts and deposits with the Bank of England.

term investments of minimal risk) in order to be able to pay depositors wishing to withdraw funds from their accounts. Short-term gilts are considered to be suitable liquid assets.

Another reason why both institutions *and* individual investors include gilt-edged securities in their portfolios will become clear on reading Chapters 8 and 9. Since gilts are less risky than company shares, both portfolio theory and the capital asset pricing model (discussed in those chapters) show that any investor wishing to hold a portfolio which is less risky than one consisting entirely of company shares should include some gilt-edged securities in his portfolio.[4]

However, these reasons why investors hold gilts do not explain the higher turnover of gilts relative to company shares experienced on the Stock Exchange. For example, eight times the market value of all gilt-edged securities was turned over during 1991 including inter-market maker business compared with only 60% of the value of all UK company shares. How can we explain this high turnover in gilts?

The price, and hence the returns, of gilts are affected above all by present and future interest rates, although different gilts are affected to different extents by changes in these rates. In recent years, interest rates and expectations concerning future interest rates have changed frequently. This has provided scope to any investor who feels he or she can accurately predict interest rate changes either by switching between gilts or by switching between gilts and other securities such as shares. The high turnover in gilts is partly due to the transactions of such investors. Even the financial institutions which have long-term commitments actively deal in part of their gilt portfolios. Unless gilts are held to match a specific nominal liability, they can no longer be considered investments which can be bought and then ignored – as we saw with the 2½% Consols acquired in 1919. Investors who wish to do this may be better advised to put their money on deposit with a bank or building society where interest rates will not be fixed but will vary according to prevailing market rates. The volatility of interest rates, and hence the prices of gilts, implies that investors must carefully choose when to buy and when to sell gilts to maximise their returns.

Most investment advice to the small investor concentrates on share investment, for two reasons. Firstly, share investment has been the traditional first love of the small investor and, secondly, the gilt-edged market is dominated to a much greater extent than the share market by large institutions dealing in large amounts (see Example 3.1). The average size of a gilt-edged bargain in 1990 was £1.5m., and institutions expect to deal in amount of £5–10m. Also, the type of analysis needed to understand gilt

---

[4] An investor could also reduce risk by investing in company fixed interest securities (which have default risk) or non-quoted investments such as National Savings accounts. However, gilts represent the least risky *quoted* investments available.

price movements is different from that required for shares and the small investor unversed in these techniques is at a considerable disadvantage.

However, the principles underlying these techniques are relatively straightforward and, as we shall see, the traditional valuation methods used by investors in the market, such as redemption yields, are now being superseded by more sophisticated and accurate analyses of interest rates. Any investor who understands both techniques need have no fears of investing in fixed interest securities.

This chapter will first describe the gilts available and how they can be distinguished from one another, in terms of coupon, maturity and accrued interest. The method of issue of gilts is then outlined for conventional as well as index-linked gilts. The chapter concludes with a section on how to calculate returns on investments in gilts, describing the two most common measures, the interest yield and the redemption yield. Chapter 4 continues the discussion on gilts with a more sophisticated approach to determining returns and to measuring the impact of interest rate changes on gilt prices.

Description of gilts

The description 'gilt-edged' is sometimes applied to fixed interest securities issued by borrowers other than the British government such as UK corporations and local authorities, Commonwealth governments and quasi-official UK bodies. Technically, only those securities issued or guaranteed by the British government, known as British funds, should be considered as free of default risk and therefore 'gilt-edged' in that sense. Other bodies may, in exceptional circumstances, default.[5]

We will concentrate on the securities known as British funds, whose prices are quoted daily in the *Financial Times*. Example 3.2 gives an extract from the *Financial Times* where details of 83 different British funds (or gilts) are given.

Most gilts are registered securities, which means that the name of each holder is noted in a register. A few gilts, such as 3½%[6] War Loan, can be issued in bearer form. Bearer securities are not registered anywhere, the only proof of ownership being the physical possession of the relevant certificate. Some investors consider that the disadvantage of bearer securities, their risk of being lost or stolen, is outweighed by their anonymity. However, it is not common for gilts to be issued in bearer form nowadays.

---

[5] For example, the fixed interest debt of the Mersey Docks and Harbour Board had its quote suspended from 1970 to 1974 with only reduced interest payments being made during that period.

[6] The *Financial Times* notation is 3½ pc.

Investors wishing to acquire bearer fixed interest securities can acquire eurobonds, discussed in Chapters 4 and 10.

The gilts in Example 3.2 have different names, the three most common being Exchequer, Treasury and Funding, all of which simply denote the British government as borrower. Only one gilt issued to fund the national-isation of a utility can now be easily identified: Exchequer 3% Gas 1990–1995; the remainder were not specifically named after the industry concerned. A few longstanding gilts with different names remain, for example, 2½% Consols, which consolidated several different gilts into one, and 3½% War Loan, issued in 1932 to replace a First World War issue.

Clearly, this handful of different names is not sufficient to be able to distinguish one gilt from another. Two other distinguishing features are usually included in the full name of each gilt: its coupon and its maturity date.

Coupon

For example, Treasury 10% 2001 will pay the holder £10 per annum for every £100 of the gilt held until 2001. The amount of the gilt held, the 'nominal' value of the investment, is the amount to be repaid (in 2001, in this case). As interest rates change, the value of the gilt, and hence its market price, will vary and may be very different from the nominal amount.

Although gilts can be bought in any amount, they are usually quoted in amounts of £100 nominal. In the case of Treasury 10% 2001, the price for £100 nominal quoted in Example 3.2 is £100⅜ – the gilt-edged market has not yet converted to decimals![7] For an outlay of £100.38,[8] an investor will be entitled to receive £10 each year until the government repays the nominal amount of £100 in 2001.

The interest rate on the nominal amount, in this case 10%, is known as the 'coupon' of the gilt. This refers to the coupon which is attached to bearer securities and which has to be physically surrendered to the bor-rower when interest is due to show entitlement to receive that interest. Since gilts are mostly registered securities, this term is a misnomer. Interest

---

[7] In fact, this pricing system is due to the pre-decimal pounds, shillings and pence; there were 240 old pence to the pound. The irony is that the most important government bond market in the world, the US Treasury bond market, prices in 32nds, having adopted the UK pricing system a long time ago.

[8] In practice, the total outlay will include accrued interest, see p. 70.

Example 3.2   Details of British funds as given in the Financial Times

BRITISH FUNDS

"Shorts" (Lives up to Five Years)

BRITISH FUNDS - Cont.

Over Fifteen Years

Undated

BRITISH FUNDS - Cont.

Index - Linked

OTHER FIXED INTEREST

Source: Financial Times (1 April 1992).

on gilts is automatically paid to the registered holders. Such interest payments are usually made in two equal six-monthly instalments on two prespecified dates. (Only 2½% Consols pay interest quarterly.) With Treasury 10% 2001, £5 (net of personal income tax at the basic rate) will be paid on 26 February and 26 August each year until 26 February 2001 when the last interest payment and the £100 repayment will be made.[9]

As can be seen from Example 3.2, the coupons currently payable on gilts vary from 2½ to 15½%. The very low coupon gilts were issued when prevailing interest rates were low, for example 2½% Consols in 1905, whereas the 14 and 15% coupons were issued in the high-interest 1970s. However, some low-coupon gilts are still issued today because they are preferred by certain types of investor for tax reasons. The taxation of income from gilts affects different investors in different ways, as will be seen below.

The return actually achieved on a gilt, as with any security, is made up of income received during the period held and a capital gain or loss. So the holding period return, R, can be written

$$R = \frac{D + (P_1 - P_0)}{P_0}$$

where D represents, for a gilt, the interest payments received, and $P_1 - P_0$ the capital gain or loss either on disposal or on redemption of the gilt. Now, the interest payments on gilts, D, are taxable at the personal or corporate tax rate of the investor depending on who the investor is. The capital gain, $P_1 - P_0$ (if this is positive), suffers capital gains tax or is not taxed at all if the gilt is held for twelve months or more before disposal or redemption. High rate taxpayers will generally prefer to receive their return in the form of capital gain rather than interest payments whereas low rate or non-taxpayers will be less concerned as to how they receive their return. So, high rate taxpayers will tend to go for low coupon gilts which have a high capital gain potential; see, for example, in the five to fifteen years section in Example 3.2, Funding 3½% 1999–2004 whose market price of £60⁹⁄₃₂ is less than two-thirds of its nominal value on redemption. Higher coupon gilts, for example in the same section Conversion 9½% 2004 priced at £97²³⁄₃₂, have a higher income and price and so a smaller potential capital gain. In fact, if the coupon of a gilt exceeds prevailing interest rates, the price will be greater than £100, giving the holder income and a capital *loss* on redemption. For instance, Treasury 11½% 2001–4 is priced in Example 3.2 at £107¹³⁄₁₆, £7.81 more than will be received on maturity.

---

[9] For details of coupon payment dates, see Monday issues of the *Financial Times*, when they replace the high/low figures in Example 3.2. However, be careful. The *Financial Times* does *not* tell you which of the two coupon dates is the maturity date.

Most interest payments on gilts have standard rate personal tax deducted from them before being paid out. If the taxpayer pays tax at a different rate, he either claims tax back or pays the balance to the Inland Revenue. Interest can be paid gross (before deduction of tax) to *overseas* investors on certain gilts (those marked ‡‡ in the *Financial Times*) and to UK resident[10] investors who have bought their gilts via the Post Office and are thus registered on the National Savings Stock Register. This latter facility is helpful to small investors who do not pay tax and do not want the bother of claiming it back.

Maturity

The other distinguishing feature of gilts is their maturity – the date at which the nominal amount borrowed by the government will be repaid. In fact, gilts are listed by maturity and divided up into groups by maturity in Example 3.2.[11] Gilts which will be redeemed at the latest within five years are known as 'shorts'; 'mediums' are those which are redeemable within five to fifteen years and 'longs' those which will be repaid at a date more than fifteen years away from now. Treasury bills, which are the short-term marketable government debt, are not traded on the Stock Exchange but sold via the discount houses to the institutions.[12]

Of course, 'longs' will eventually become 'mediums' and then 'shorts' before being redeemed. Only the fourth category of gilts, 'undated' gilts, will probably never be redeemed and so never change category. This group of six gilts consists of those stocks which the government has no obligation to repay by a specific date. The government may have stated that it would not repay *before* a certain date, for example, 3½% War Loan 1952 or after, but no final redemption date has been specified. The government would only redeem these undated stocks if it could replace the debt more cheaply – issue gilts with a lower coupon on the same nominal value. So, the undated stocks will only be repaid if interest rates fall below, say, 4 or 3%. It may seem incredible now that this should ever be the case, but in 1948, 3½% War Loan was viewed as a 'short' because it was considered likely that it would be redeemed in 1952.

---

[10] Investors who are liable to UK tax.

[11] Except for a section, discussed below, devoted to index-linked gilts.

[12] A bill is a promise to pay the bearer a fixed sum of money on maturity (usually no more than one year away). Treasury bills are bills of ninety-one days' maturity issued by the UK government. A discount house is a financial institution which discounts bills – both commercial and Treasury – that is, pays the issuer a sum less than the face value, this discount being equivalent to a rate of interest in return for providing funds.

Some gilts have a spread of maturity dates, for example, Funding 3½% 1999–2004. In this case the government can repay on any 14 July between 1999 and 2004. How can investors estimate the maturity of a gilt on which the government has the option of when to repay? As with the undated stocks, the government will only repay if it can replace with a lower coupon stock. So unless interest rates fall below 3½%, the government will not replace Funding 3½% 1999–2004 until the last possible moment in 2004. If the coupon of a gilt is above or at the same level as prevailing interest rates, redemption may be before the last possible date (since the government may choose to refinance at a lower coupon) and is therefore more difficult to estimate.

Another factor which could alter the effective maturity of any fixed interest security would be the existence of a *sinking fund*. This means that a sum of money is set aside by the issuer to buy back securities each year, either by repurchasing through the market or by repaying certain securities selected at random (by drawings) at a predetermined price. If a stock has a sinking fund, its *expected* life will be less than the period to maturity. However, only one small gilt issue, 3½% Conversion 1961 or After has a sinking fund although sinking funds are more popular with company fixed interest securities in the eurobond market. The advantage of a sinking fund to an issuer or borrower is that it does not have to refund the whole amount at maturity with another issue when interest rates may be high. The advantage of a sinking fund to an investor is that it reduces the life of the bond (if the bonds are bought back early) and hence reduces default risk.

Accrued interest

All gilt prices are quoted 'clean', that is, net of accrued interest. However, when a gilt is paid for, accrued interest is added to the clean price to obtain the 'gross' or 'dirty' price owed. This method of quoting gilt prices is now common to all the bond markets and is to help traders and investors judge the impact of interest rate changes on bond or gilt prices.[13] For example, suppose an investor bought a 10% coupon gilt 89 days after the last coupon was paid for a clean price of £102.00. The dirty price would be

Clean price	£102.00
plus Accrued interest = 89/365 × £10	£2.44
Dirty price	**£104.44**

---

[13] In markets other than the UK, 'dirty' prices are sometimes called 'gross' prices and 'clean' prices 'net' prices.

Suppose, one month later, the price is £103.00. The investor is clear that this price is due to a general interest rate fall and *not* to the fact that the gilt will have accrued, say, another 30 days of coupon. When he sells the gilt he will receive:

Clean price	£103.00
plus Accrued interest = 119/365 × £10	£3.26
Dirty price	**£106.26**

He will have effectively made a capital gain of £1.00 and received income of £3.26–£2.44 or £0.82, ignoring transaction costs.[14]

Sometimes accrued interest has to be *deducted* from the price. This will occur when a short is purchased 'ex div'. Some gilts in Example 3.2 have 'xd' after their price, standing for 'ex dividend'. If a gilt is purchased 'ex div', the purchaser will not be entitled to the imminent interest payment whereas if he purchases the gilt 'cum div' he will be buying the gilt plus the entitlement to that interest payment. Gilts are usually quoted 'ex div' five weeks and two days before the interest payment. So, with a gilt purchased 'ex div', say, fifteen days before the interest payment, the price would be adjusted to take account of the two weeks' interest foregone. For example, again with a 10% gilt quoted at £102.00, the price paid would be

Clean price	£102.00xd
minus Interest foregone 14/365 × £10	£(0.38)
Dirty price	**£101.62**

Special ex div

Normally, a security is quoted 'cum div' one day and 'ex div' the next so that holders registered on the last day before the security goes 'ex div' receive the dividend or interest payment. However, gilts other than shorts and War Loan 3½% can be traded both 'cum div' *and* 'special ex div' at the same time for the three weeks prior to going officially 'ex div'. This enables market makers to balance their books.

---

[14] For details of transaction costs, see Chapter 1, p. 16.

Example 3.3   Effects of tax on buying gilts 'cum' or 'ex' dividend

Funding 3½% 1999–2004	Net cost to pension fund (0% tax rate) £	Net cost to individual on, say, 40% tax rate £
Ex div price	60	60
Cum div price	61.50	61.50
Less interest	(1.75)	(1.05)
Net cost cum div	59.75	60.45
Prefers to buy:	**Cum div**	**Ex div**

Investors with different tax rates can therefore choose whether they wish to buy or sell a gilt 'cum' or 'ex' dividend without having to wait until the gilt goes officially 'ex div'. Suppose a high marginal rate taxpayer wishes to buy a gilt during these three weeks. If he buys a gilt full of accrued interest ('cum div'), he will have to pay tax, say at 40%, on the interest payment. If he buys the gilt 'special ex div', the price will be lower to reflect the loss of the interest payment (remember, gilts other than shorts have accrued interest included in the price). The price will not in fact fall by as much as the whole gross interest amount, but by, say, 75–90% of it, depending on the relative demand and supply from high and low rate taxpayers.

For example, suppose Funding 3½% 1999–2004 is quoted at £61.50 'cum div' and £60 'special ex div', a difference of £1.50. If the high rate taxpayer buys 'cum div', he will pay £61.50, be entitled to £1.75 interest, £1.05 after tax on a 40% tax rate. His net cost will be £60.45 compared with £60 if he buys 'special ex div'. On the other hand, a pension fund will prefer to buy 'cum div' since it pays no income tax. By paying £61.50 it will be entitled to receive the full £1.75 interest (after reclaiming tax) to give a net cost of £59.75. Example 3.3 outlines the situation.

The difference in amount between the fall in the gilt price due to the interest payment and the interest payment itself will depend on prevailing tax rates and the tax positions of buyers and sellers of the gilt.[15]

---

[15] These changes in price around interest payment dates could lead to tax being always avoided on interest payments. Taxpayers could sell 'cum div' to non-taxpayers and repurchase 'ex div'. However, the Inland Revenue has stamped on these practices, known as 'bond-washing', by treating any such profits as income, rather than capital gain.

Methods of issue

The traditional method of issuing gilts has been via the 'tap' method. Gilts which have recently been issued this way can be identified by a • against their name in the list of British Funds in the *Financial Times*. The Bank of England is responsible for the long term financing of the Public Sector Borrowing Requirement and will be aware of the approximate amount of money to be raised in each financial year via the issuance of gilts. The gilts which are to be issued are decided by the Bank and will depend on various factors: whether the liquidity of a particular gilt needs to be improved with the issue of a new 'tranche'; whether a particular maturity or coupon of gilt is in short supply and can therefore be sold at a relatively high price; or whether the average maturity of government debt needs to be lengthened or shortened.

Once the characteristics of the gilt to be issued have been decided by the Bank of England, the Bank announces the issue and requests applications to tender[16] on a specific day, normally a few days after the announcement. To protect itself from unexpected falls in the market between the announcement date and the tender date, the Bank will usually set a minimum price at or just below the current market level. (By not having to issue gilts at their nominal value of £100, the government can issue gilts whose coupons are different from prevailing interest rates and yields.) If the market improves before the closing date, the tender offers received by the Bank of England will be higher than the minimum price. If the market does not improve or even falls, any unsubscribed stock goes to official government departments for sale via the Bank at a later date 'on tap'. The tap will be turned on every time the market reaches the minimum price level, until the entire amount of the issue has been sold into the market.

This method of issue gives the Bank of England the maximum amount of flexibility. It can choose exactly when to issue any gilt and can choose the coupon, maturity and amount to be issued. On the other hand, market makers in gilts and investors are vulnerable to sudden unexpected announcements of a large gilt issue; this can depress the prices of existing gilts in expectation of the increased supply.

In the last few years, the Bank of England has switched a large proportion of its issues to an auction system, which is the method used in most major government bond markets, in particular the US Treasury Bond market. The major difference between an auction and a tap issue is that there is no minimum price. However, the Bank of England still reserves the right to refuse bids which they believe are too low.

---

[16] A tender offer for securities is one where all would-be purchasers state the price at which they are willing to buy the securities. The issuer will then allot the securities to bidders ranked by bid price until the issue is exhausted.

Despite the shift towards the US-style auction system, there are still subtle differences between government bond auctions in the UK and the US. In the UK, the gilt market is given only a few days' notice of the issue and of the type of gilt which is to be issued. Also, because the Bank can choose the coupon of the gilt as well as its maturity, the auction price is not necessarily close to the par or nominal value of £100. In the US, the US Treasury, which in the 1980s had a massive Public Sector Borrowing Requirement (PSBR) to fund and therefore had to conciliate investors as much as possible, the maturity of the bonds to be issued, the amounts to be issued and the dates on which they will be issued are known well in advance. The offer price is always the nominal value of $100; what bidders bid is the coupon they would like on the bond – known as the par yield. The lower the coupon bid, the more likely the bid is to be accepted. And, most importantly, the US Treasury is obliged to sell the entire amount of the issue, regardless of whether or not it deems the bids to be too low.

Index-linked gilts

Any increase in uncertainty about future inflation and interest rates makes the holding of fixed interest long-term securities relatively less attractive than under more stable conditions. Over the years, the government has introduced variations on the traditional type of gilt to attract lenders into continuing to fund the ever-growing National Debt. It has experimented with short gilts convertible into long-dated gilts and with gilts with a variable coupon. However, the only innovative type of gilt currently in issue is the index-linked gilt which offers a fixed *real*[17] interest rate rather than a fluctuating *nominal* rate. It can thus protect investors against both inflation and interest rate risk for a longer period. Insurance companies and pension funds are by far the most important purchasers of long-dated gilts and they have future liabilities such as pension payments which are mostly based on earnings in the few years prior to retirement and so will increase in line with inflation. These institutions find index-linked gilts attractive because such gilts enable them to match their liabilities with an income from investment which similarly keeps up with inflation.[18]

---

[17] A real rate of interest is one where the nominal or money interest rate (IR) (the one usually quoted for securities) has been adjusted for the effects of inflation. So,

$$(1 + \text{nominal IR}) = (1 + \text{inflation rate})(1 + \text{real IR})$$
$$\text{e.g. } (1 + 10\%) = (1 + 7.8\%)(1 + x\%)$$

where $x\%$ is the *real* interest rate, which must in this instance be 2%.

[18] See Chapter 12 for a discussion of how the objectives of these institutions affect the securities they hold.

The demand for index-linked stock grew throughout the inflationary 1970s, culminating in a recommendation for the encouragement of such issues in the Wilson Committee Report of 1980.[19] The government finally responded in 1981 by issuing a gilt offering a 2% *real* interest rate and maturing in 1996.[20] This issue was designed to help the pension funds meet their real liabilities and was, in fact, initially restricted to institutions engaged in pension fund business. However, the 1982 budget allowed all investors to acquire index-linked gilts and several more such issues were made. As can be seen in Example 3.2, by April 1992 there were eleven index-linked gilts in issue worth in nominal terms around £13b and 10% of all gilts in issue.

What exactly does the term "index-linked' mean, and how does this link reduce inflation risk? Index-linked stocks have their interest payments and redemption payments linked to the retail prices index (RPI), an index made up of the prices of various goods and services assumed to represent the typical expenditure of the average consumer. Thus, the RPI will include the cost of petrol, mortgage repayments, bread, tea and so on in proportions representative of actual consumption. This index is the most widely quoted measure of inflation in the UK and is, for example, an index against which earnings are measured. If earnings (and pensions) do keep up with inflation, gilts whose payments are linked to the RPI will indeed allow pension funds to meet their liabilities. If, on the other hand, an individual investor has liabilities which are not the same as those included in the RPI, he will not be able completely to hedge inflation risk by investing in index-linked stocks. In fact, the gilts' interest and redemption payments are based on the RPI eight months before each payment. So, an interest payment in November will be based on the RPI in March. This lagging allows the actual amount of the interest (or redemption payment) to be known several months in advance of the payment and certainly before the gilt goes ex div. However, it also means that index-linked gilts do not provide a perfect hedge against inflation throughout their lives. This will become evident when we discuss how to calculate returns on index-linked gilts at the end of the next section.

Of course, government bonds do not have to be linked only to the RPI. The French government, with its 7% fifteen-year government bond issued in 1973, chose to index it instead to the price of gold – the French have traditionally viewed gold as the most secure investment. The disadvantage of this is that a government has even less control over the price of gold than it does over the RPI. Between 1976 and 1988 the price of gold fluctuated

---

[19] See the Wilson Report (1980) ch. 17.

[20] Before this, several index-linked government National Savings Certificate issues offering a real return of around zero had already been made. Such issues can only be bought via the Post Office and are *not* marketable securities.

between \$104 and \$667 an ounce. The 1981 interest payment alone was worth over 60% of the original amount issued and the final redemption value was 831% of the face value. However, the man responsible for this bond, Giscard d'Estaing, subsequently went on to become President of France!

Returns on investments in gilts

We now investigate the various methods used to calculate the return on gilt-edged securities which are, in fact, applicable to all fixed interest securities. We consider first of all the straightforward gilts which are not index-linked.

We have defined the holding period return of a security as

$$R = \frac{D + P_1 - P_0}{P_0}$$

where D represents any dividend or interest payments made during the period, P_0 the cost and P_1 the selling price of the security. In the case of a gilt, D is known with certainty (in money terms) and so the risk of holding the gilt comes from two sources. Firstly, from the change in its price, $P_1 - P_0$, during the holding period which, for a gilt with no default risk, will be due to changes in market interest rates and hence required yields on gilts – interest rate risk. Secondly, there is the risk that the values of P_1 and D when received will be less in *real* terms than expected – inflation risk.

Holding period return is useful for comparative purposes since it can be applied to all securities. It can also be used to calculate the deviation of the *actual* return from the *expected* return. Unfortunately, in order to calculate R, P_1 must be known. This is a simple matter if we are calculating the *historic* return achieved on disposal of a security. It is not so easy when trying to calculate the return we *expect* to get from the security. P_1 must be estimated and, to obtain a reasonable estimate, we need an understanding of how gilt prices are affected by interest rate changes as well as a forecast of how and why interest rates themselves will change. We leave a discussion of these topics until Chapter 4. For the moment, we concentrate on two measures of return commonly used for gilts and fixed interest securities, both of which get round the problem of having to estimate P_1.

Interest yield

If we go back to Example 3.2, we can see that the *Financial Times* provides two different types of yield (return) for each gilt, interest yield and redemption yield. Interest yield, the simpler measure of the two, avoids the problem of having to estimate P_1 to calculate the capital gain or loss on the gilt by simply ignoring it. It concentrates only on the first part of the holding period return – the return from income (or interest in this case), D/P_0, where P_0 is the current market price.

For example, in Example 3.2, Treasury 10% 2001 has an interest yield (sometimes called the coupon, running, income or flat yield) of 9.96% This is calculated as follows

$$\text{Interest yield} = \frac{D}{P_0} \times 100$$

In this case, the current market price, P_0, is £100⅜ or £100.38, which gives

$$\text{Interest yield} = \frac{£10}{£100.38} \times 100$$

$$= \mathbf{9.96\%}$$

Similarly, the interest yield on Funding 6% 1993 is

$$\text{Interest yield} = \frac{£6}{£95.44} \times 100$$

$$= \mathbf{6.29\%}$$

The investor can also adjust the interest yield to reflect his particular tax position. So, if he pays tax at 40% on the income from Treasury 5½% 2008–12, his net interest yield will be

$$\text{Net interest yield} = \frac{£5.50}{£63.72} \times (1 - 0.4) \times 100$$

$$= \mathbf{5.18\%}$$

In financial terms, interest yields are calculated on the 'clean' original price of each gilt. Strictly speaking, they should be calculated as coupon divided by dirty price (that is, clean price *plus* accrued interest) since this is what the investor pays out. The return in the form of income should be determined by a percentage of the total outlay on the gilt.

For example, Treasury 10% 2001 pays interest on 26 February and 26 August each year. The gilt prices shown in Example 3.2 were published on 1 April 1992 and refer to closing prices for 31 March 1992. Settlement for Treasury 10% 2001 bought on 31 March 1992 would be on 1 April 1992 (one day after purchase), 34 days after the last interest payment on 26 February 1992 (a leap year). So, 34 days' accrued interest or £0.93 would have to be added to the 'clean' price quoted of £100.38 to give a dirty price of £101.31. Thus the 'true' interest yield will be:

$$\text{True interest yield} = \frac{£10}{£101.31} \times 100 = \mathbf{9.87\%}$$

Of what use is the interest yield? It does not reflect the *total* return from holding a gilt since it ignores any capital gain or loss. What it does give is a simple indication to the investor of his return in terms of income by comparing the interest he receives with the actual price he paid for the gilt rather than its nominal value. For example, with Treasury 5½% 2008–12, although the coupon shows a return of 5½% on the nominal value of £100, interest rates are higher than when this gilt was issued; the price of the gilt has fallen by one-third to give an income before tax of over 8.5% on the investment. In other words, if an investor bought Treasury 5% 2008–12 on 24 October 1991 and held it until redemption he would be certain of receiving an annual gross income of over 8.5% on his original investment.

As well as being relevant for determining income from gilts, the other major use of the interest yield is when determining what is known as the 'cost of carry'. This is particularly useful for traders and shorter-term investors. For example, suppose a trader wants to buy a gilt in the expectation that the price will rise over the next few days. He will have to fund this purchase with short-term borrowing. However, he will receive accrued interest (in the form of an interest yield) from the gilt. Therefore his cost of carry will be:

Cost of carry = Borrowing cost − Interest yield

For example, suppose his borrowing cost is 12% and he wishes to buy the Treasury 10% 2001. The cost of carry will be:

Cost of carry = 12% − 9.87%

$$= \mathbf{2.13\%}$$

Notice that the interest yield is a function of the coupon of the gilt and that the higher the interest yield, the lower the cost of carry (it can even be negative). The lower the cost of carry, the less the trader has to worry about large price rises to make a profit.

However, the interest yield ignores the possible impact of capital gain or loss on the overall return of a gilt. Most individual investors are unlikely to hold Treasury 5½% 2008–12 until maturity (probably in 2012), a period of almost thirty years, and so must come to terms with the possibility of a gain or a loss on disposal. It also ignores the time value of money, since it assumes that the interest paid in any year up to 2012 is as valuable to the investor as this year's interest payment. The redemption yield or 'yield to maturity', as it is called in the US, is the second measure of return used in relation to gilts and overcomes the disadvantages of the interest yield as a measure of return.

Redemption yield

In Chapter 2 we saw that the price P of an undated gilt could be written as

$$P_0 = \frac{D}{(1 + r)} + \frac{D}{(1 + r)^2} + \frac{D}{(1 + r)^3} + \ldots \tag{3.1}$$

where D was the annual interest payment and r the opportunity cost of the funds used to buy the gilt. For example, if the investor did not receive the first interest payment D for twelve months, he could not invest D in an equivalent risk-free investment paying r interest to give him $D(1 + r)$ at the end of the twelve months. So D received in one year's time would be worth only $D/(1 + r)$ to the investor now, and so on.

For a gilt with a maturity date, the price can be written as

$$P_0 = \frac{D}{(1 + r)} + \frac{D}{(1 + r)^2} + \ldots \frac{D}{(1 + r)^n} + \frac{100}{(1 + r)^n} \tag{3.2}$$

where £100 is due to be repaid at the end of n years. The price P_0 is simply the present value of a future income stream made up of regular interest payments D, and a redemption payment of £100 on maturity.

In other contexts, r may have been encountered as the 'internal' rate of return. In the case of gilts, r is known as the redemption yield (or yield to maturity), that is, the rate of return achieved on a gilt if it is purchased at the quoted price P_0 and held to maturity. The redemption yield is an improvement on the interest yield since it takes into account the time value of money. For example, the shorter the term of the gilt the more valuable the final redemption payment in present value terms. The redemption yield also avoids the problem of having to estimate the selling price P_1 by assuming that the gilt is not sold but held to maturity. In other words, P_1 is always equal to £100.[21] Again, this assumption will only be realistic for the investor who intends to hold each gilt purchased to maturity.

The calculation of the redemption yield is actually somewhat more complex than appears from equation (3.2) because the 'dirty' price has to be used and interest payments are in fact made six-monthly not yearly as was assumed in equation (3.2). Also, the first interest payment may not be in exactly six months' time. However, redemption yields can be calculated very quickly, despite these complexities, by using bond tables, a calculator or a computer. There follows a simple example to show how redemption yields are determined.

Take Exchequer 12¼% 1999. Suppose that a purchase was made on 31 March 1992 at the price of £110¼ quoted in Table 3.2. Redemption will be on 26 March 1999 and interest payments will be on 26 March and 26 September each year. Since the gilt was purchased just after a coupon payment, the first interest payment of £6.125 will be almost exactly six months from purchase on 26 September 1992. Because interest is paid at six-monthly intervals, we calculate the *six-months* redemption yield, r. The number of periods, n, is fourteen. We can therefore write

$$110\tfrac{1}{4} = \frac{6.125}{1 + r} + \frac{6.125}{(1 + r)^2} + \ldots + \frac{6.125}{(1 + r)^{14}} + \frac{100}{(1 + r)^{14}} \qquad (3.3)$$

We have to calculate r by iteration, that is, by trying different values of r to see which will fit equation (3.3): $r = 5\%$ is tried first, using either a calculator or annuity and present value tables, to calculate the present value of a stream of payments discounted at 5%. These tables are provided in Appendix 2 on pp. 418–21. Present value tables will give the present value of a sum received in n periods' time, discounted at $r\%$ per period. Annuity tables will show the present value of an amount received *each period* for n periods with a discount rate of $r\%$ per period.

In the above case, we are due to receive £6.125 per period for fourteen periods discounted at 5%. From the annuity tables on p. 420, we find that the value of £1 received every period for fourteen periods discounted at 5% is £9.90. Since we will receive £6.125 per period, we must multiply by 6.125 to give a present value of the interest stream of £60.64. It remains for us to calculate the present value of £100 received in fourteen periods' time. The present value table on p. 418 shows that £1 received in fourteen periods' time discounted at 5% is worth £0.5051 today. So the present value of that £100 is £50.51. Adding together the present value of the

---

[21] Unless we are discussing index-linked gilts. See below.

interest payments and the present value of the redemption payment gives a price for the gilt of £110.15.[22]

If we deduct the 6 days of accrued interest since the first coupon date of 26 March, we obtain a clean price of £109.95, very near to the quoted clean price of £110¼. This implies that the semi-annual redemption yield estimate of 5% was a good estimate. Iteration with estimates of the semi-annual redemption yield just above 5% would eventually lead to the present value (net of accrued interest) being exactly £110¼ and an exact value for the semi-annual redemption yield. We would find, by using a fairly arduous method, that the six-months redemption yield was 5.08%. However, with the prevalence of calculators and computers to estimate accurate redemption yields we will leave the approximate method here.

In order to be able to compare fixed interest securities with different frequencies of interest payment, it is usual to quote the *annual* redemption yield, R. To calculate R, we know that £1 invested at R% for twelve months will yield the same amount as £1 invested compound for two periods at r%. So, for the example above,

$$£1(1 + R) = £1(1.0508)^2$$

giving

$R = 10.42$%

The redemption yield given in Example 3.2 for Exchequer 12¼% 1991 is slightly lower than our estimate, at 10.15%. This is because the annual redemption yields in the *Financial Times* are obtained simply by multiplying the semi-annual redemption yield, r, by two. If we use this simplified method to find the annual redemption yield, we get 5.08% × 2 = 10.14%, the same (allowing for rounding error) as the *Financial Times* figure. The compounded redemption yield of 10.42% is higher because it allows for reinvestment of the six-monthly interest payments. However, in bond markets where coupons are paid semi-annually, the redemption yield quoted is twice the semi-annual rate and *not* the compounded figure which gives a more accurate return estimate. This can cause complications when semi-annual bonds such as gilts are compared with annual coupon bonds such as eurobonds.

Notice how the redemption yield for Exchequer 12¼% 1999 (10.15%) is less than the interest yield (11.11%). This is because, with the market price at £110¼, there will be a capital loss on redemption of £10.25, not taken

---

[22] Note that if the price of a gilt is close to £100, choosing a semi-annual redemption yield equal to the semi-annual coupon will always give a price of exactly £100.

into account in the interest yield. When the market price is less than £100, involving an eventual capital *gain* on redemption, the redemption yield will be *greater* than the interest yield.

Return on index-linked gilts

So far, we have seen how to calculate the interest yield and the redemption yield for gilts whose interest and redemption payments are fixed in nominal terms. The problem we now consider is how to estimate measures of return for index-linked gilts, whose interest and redemption payments are fixed in *real* terms and *not* fixed in nominal terms.

(i) REAL INTEREST YIELD

One solution would appear to be to calculate the interest yield in real terms since all the future cash flows are certain in real terms. Unfortunately, there are two factors which complicate the calculations.

Firstly, index-linked gilts listed in Example 3.2 under the heading 'Index-Linked' are quoted 'clean' in the same way as conventional gilts. In order to determine the 'dirty' price, the accrued interest must be determined. This is a simple matter for ordinary gilts, since the next coupon payment (and hence the proportion of it included in the price) is always known. In the case of index-linked gilts, if these were truly inflation-proof, the nominal amount of each coupon to be paid would never be known in advance. This is because the rate of inflation right up to the date of the coupon payment would be used to determine how much the coupon would actually be. In fact, since the retail prices index (the index used as a measure of inflation) is usually published with a lag of around one month, it would be impossible to match exactly the RPI and the coupon payments. So, in order to be able to calculate the clean price of an index-linked gilt up to six months before a coupon payment,[23] and allowing for the lag of around one month in the publication of the RPI, the government has linked each coupon or redemption payment of an index-linked gilt to the change in the RPI from the base date (which is *eight* months before the gilt was issued) to *eight* months before the payment is made.

For instance, if we look at Treasury 2½% Index-linked (I.L) 2001 as at 1

---

[23] The Bank of England announces the amount of each coupon payment no later than one business day before the previous coupon payment date.

April 1992 (the date of Example 3.2), the next coupon payment will be made on 24 September 1992 and will be based on the RPI level eight months earlier, that is, of January 1992, which is already published. Since the Treasury 2½% I.L. 2001 was issued in August 1982, the base date for the index-linking of its coupon and redemption payments must be eight months before, December 1981, when the RPI stood at 78.3.[24] By January 1992, the RPI had risen to 135.6. Thus, by April 1992 it was known that the September 1992 coupon payment would be

$$£1.25 \times \frac{135.6}{78.3} = £2.1654$$

where £1 was the semi-annual coupon in 'real' terms.

Since the future coupon was then certain in nominal terms, the dirty price could be calculated. Because the previous coupon payment had been on 24 March, by 1 April 8 days of accrued interest had been included in the price.

Clean price	=	£144.313
plus Accrued interest = $\frac{8}{365/2} \times 2.1654$[25]	=	(£0.095)
Dirty price	=	**£144.408**

Unfortunately, although the lag of eight months between the RPI used and each actual coupon payment allows investors to know what the next coupon payment will be in nominal terms, it does mean that index-linked gilts are not fully hedged against inflation risk.

For example, we can see that the 24 September 1992 coupon payment is hedged against the inflation which occurred between December 1981 (eight months before the gilt was issued) and January 1992 (eight months before the actual payment of the coupon). For the investor to be fully hedged against inflation risk, the September 1992 payment should be linked to the rate of inflation between the day when the gilt was issued and 24 September 1992. We consider this problem in more detail when we try to calculate a 'real' redemption yield in the next section.

---

[24] The base date RPI has been adjusted by a factor of 3.945 to allow for rebasing to 100 in January 1987. In our calculations the more accurate figure has been used for determining accrued interest. The RPI is published in the monthly government publication, *Employment Gazette*, and recent RPI figures are also available at Post Offices.

[25] We divide by 365/2 instead of 365 because we are using a semi-annual interest payment.

Returning to the calculation of the real interest yield, we need to be able to express both the coupon and the clean price of the gilt in real terms, as of the same base date. We could then write

$$\text{Real interest yield} = \frac{\text{Real coupon}}{\text{Real price}}$$

Since there is a lag of eight months between the date of the RPI used to protect the payments against changes in prices and the actual dates of these payments, we are not sure of the true real value of the next coupon payment and so we are forced to express both the coupon and the price in 'real' terms with a lag of eight months.

We know that the annual coupon for Treasury 2½% I.L. 2001 is £2.50 in real terms (with a lag of eight months) and so we determine the price in real terms using the same base date of December 1981 and applying the same lag of eight months. So, we deflate the price by

$$\frac{RPI_{August\ 1991}}{RPI_{December\ 1981}} = \frac{134.1}{78.3} = 1.7126$$

The 'real' dirty price is thus $\dfrac{£144.408}{1.7126} = £84.32$

The 'real' interest yield is therefore

$$\frac{\text{'Real' coupon}}{\text{'Real' price}} = \frac{2.50}{84.32}$$

$$= 2.96\%$$

Despite having attained a result which approximates a 'real' interest yield, we now find that it is not of much use. As with nominal interest yields, it ignores both the time value of money and any capital gain or loss on redemption. In addition, it lacks the main attraction of the nominal interest yield, namely the speed and ease with which it can be calculated, and it is not a true 'real' yield. Finally, it is not of much use to the investor since it gives little idea of the level of income to be received from the gilt.[26] Because of these disadvantages, the *Financial Times* does not publish an interest yield for index-linked gilts, preferring to concentrate on the more complete redemption yield with two alternative inflation rate assumptions.

---

[26] A nominal interest yield might give a better indication of this but is relevant only to the next coupon payment.

(ii) REAL REDEMPTION YIELD

If all the cash flows relating to a particular index-linked gilt were fully index-linked, it would be a simple matter to express all the cash flows in real terms and to calculate a real redemption yield. For example, if all the interest and redemption payments were guaranteed to maintain their value in real terms relative to base date B, we could write

$$P_{0,B} = \frac{D}{(1 + r)} + \frac{D}{(1 + r)^2} + \ldots + \frac{D}{(1 + r)^n} + \frac{100}{(1 + r)^n} \tag{3.4}$$

where $P_{0,B}$ is the market price of the index-linked gilt expressed in purchasing power terms as at date B, and r is the *real* redemption yield. Unfortunately, as we saw above, the future cash flows of an index-linked gilt are not guaranteed in real terms right up to the date of payment but up to a date eight months earlier. This lag of eight months means that the investor (who holds the gilt to maturity) is protected against the increase in the RPI between eight months before the gilt was issued and eight months before final redemption.

The lag in inflation-proofing is emphasised in Figure 3.1 where I_1 is the inflation the investor is protected against and I_2 the actual inflation he experiences over the life of the gilt. Whether he is fully protected for the holding period t_0 to t_n will depend on whether $I_1 = I_2$, or more particularly, $i_1 = i_2$, where i_1 is the inflation during the eight months before the gilt is issued and i_2 the inflation which occurs during the last eight months of the life of the gilt. If the historic inflation rate, i_1, is greater than the future inflation rate, i_2, the investor will be overprotected from inflation and if i_1 is less than i_2, he will be underprotected.

Figure 3.1 Inflation-proofing of index-linked gilts

The problem, therefore, with determining a real redemption yield is that the period during which the cash flows are guaranteed in real terms is not the same as the period during which the cash flows occur. For example, when discounting a coupon payment to be made in six months' time in nominal terms the calculation would look like this:

$$\frac{D\,(1\,+\,\mathit{infl}_1)}{(1\,+\,r)\,(1\,+\,\mathit{infl}_2)}$$

where D was the latest coupon paid in nominal terms, infl_1 was the rate of inflation from eight months ago to two months ago, infl_2 the rate of inflation expected over the next six months and r the real redemption yield. Because infl_1 is not necessarily the same as infl_2, they cannot be cancelled out to give one of the terms in equation (3.4).

Since we cannot calculate a simple real redemption yield, we are forced to make an assumption about inflation – what I_2 will be. There are two principal methods of doing this. One is to take the most recent level of inflation and to extrapolate this into the future. Basically, this is equivalent to taking i_2 as a forecast for I_1 (and hence i_1) and thereby assuming $i_1 = i_2$. By doing this, one is implicitly assuming that the investor will be more or less fully protected against inflation if he holds the index-linked gilt to maturity.

The second method, preferred by gilt analysts, is to make a 'sensible' estimate of future inflation. This is extremely difficult especially when looking at a time horizon of up to thirty years. However, it must be remembered that one of the assumptions of the redemption yield is that the required rate of return is constant over the life of the gilt, whatever the maturity of the gilt. It is no more unrealistic to assume a constant inflation rate for the same period.

The real redemption yields provided by the *Financial Times* are calculated using the second method, with two estimates of inflation, 5% and 10%, as in Example 3.2. These can be altered as expectations concerning future inflation rates change. Example 3.4 shows how the real redemption yield can be calculated approximately for Treasury 2½% I.L. 2001, using the price given in Example 3.2 (adjusted for accrued interest) and assuming a future annual inflation rate of 5%.

Example 3.4   Calculation of real redemption yield for index-linked gilt

Clean price	£144.313 (31 March 1992)
Dirty price	£144.408
Next coupon payment	£2.1654 on 24 September 1992 (index-linked from base date to January 1992 – see page 83)
Other payments	(to be based on 30 March coupon and inflated by the relevant factor $(1\,+\,i)^n$ where i is the forecast semi-annual inflation rate)

Example 3.4 continued

Principal repayment

$$£100 \times \frac{135.6}{78.3} (1 + i)^n = £173.232 (1 + i)^n$$

(where 135.6/78.3 is the index linking to September 1992 and $(1 + i)^n$ the index-linking thereafter)

Let R be the semi-annual *nominal* redemption yield

Let r be the semi-annual *real* redemption yield

We can write

$$P_0 = \sum_{i=1}^{i=n} \frac{D_i}{(1 + R)^i} + \frac{V}{(1 + R)^n}$$

where P_0 is today's price, D_i the interest payments in nominal terms, and V the amount paid on redemption, also in nominal terms. Substituting in known values, such as $D_1 = £2.1654$ and $P_0 = £144.408$, we get

$$144.408 = \frac{2.1654}{(1 + R)} + \frac{2.1654 (1 + i)}{(1 + R)^2} + \cdots + \frac{2.1654 (1 + i)^{18}}{(1 + R)^{19}}$$

$$+ \frac{173.232 (1 + i)^{18}}{(1 + R)^{19}} \tag{3.5}$$

Taking out a factor $1/(1 + i)$ in the right-hand side of equation (3.5),

$$144.408 = \frac{1}{(1 + i)} \left\{ \frac{2.1654 (1 + i)}{(1 + R)} + \frac{2.16. 4 (1 + i)^2}{(1 + R)^2} + \cdots + \frac{2.1654 (1 + i)^{19}}{(1 + R)^{19}} \right.$$

$$\left. + \frac{173.23. (1 + i)^{19}}{(1 + R)^{19}} \right\} \tag{3.6}$$

If we substitute for R in equation (3.6) by using the relationship between the required real and the required nominal rate of return postulated by Fisher

$$(1 + R) = (1 + r) (1 + i) \tag{3.7}$$

we get

$$144.408 = \frac{2.1654}{(1 + i)} \left\{ \frac{(1 + i)}{(1 + r) (1 + i)} + \frac{(1 + i)^2}{(1 + r)^2 (1 + i)^2} + \cdots + \frac{(1 + i)^{19}}{(1 + r)^{19} (1 + i)^{19}} \right.$$

$$\left. + \frac{80.000 (1 + i)^{19}}{(1 + r)^{19} (1 + i)^{19}} \right\}$$

$$= \frac{2.1654}{(1 + i)} \left\{ \frac{1}{(1 + r)} + \frac{1}{(1 + r)^2} + \cdots + \frac{1}{(1 + r)^{19}} + \frac{80.000}{(1 + r)^{19}} \right\}$$

Multiplying both sides by $(1 + i)/(2.1654)$

$$\frac{144.408 (1 + i)}{2.1654} = \frac{1}{(1 + r)} + \frac{1}{(1 + r)^2} + \ldots + \frac{1}{(1 + r)^{19}} + \frac{80.000}{(1 + r)^{19}}$$

Since we have taken the forecast of 5% annual inflation rate, approximately equivalent to 2.5% for the six-months rate,[27] we can substitute for i.

The left-hand side of the equation becomes

$$\frac{(1.025) \, 144.408}{2.1654} = 68.356$$

We therefore have

$$68.356 = \frac{1}{(1 + r)} + \frac{1}{(1 + r)^2} + \ldots + \frac{1}{(1 + r)^{19}} + \frac{80.000}{(1 + r)^{19}} \qquad (3.8)$$

Equation (3.8) looks like the equation for the nominal redemption yield, as given in equation (3.2), except that, since we are looking for a real yield, we will expect a much lower r. Using the same method as for the nominal redemption yield and ignoring the fact that we do not have *exactly* six months to the next coupon, we get a real redemption yield of just under $r = 2.20\%$. For the annual figure, we double 2.20% to get an annual real redemption yield of 4.4%. This is just below the figure given in Example 3.2.

How can we use the real redemption yield for index-linked gilts? We can either make an investment decision based on real yields or we can work out the nominal redemption yield implied by the real redemption yield, since we have assumed an inflation rate in our calculations.

Looking at the real yield of 4.42% promised each year until 2001, we can compare this with, say, an average of 1%–2% annual real return on Treasury bills over the last fifty years. Alternatively, we can gross up the real redemption yield to get a nominal figure as follows:

$$(1.0442) \, (1.05) = (1.0964)$$

giving a nominal yield of 9.64%. We can then compare this with the nominal yields on comparable conventional gilts and decide which is the best buy, depending on our inflation forecast.

For example, Treasury 10% 2001 has a gross redemption yield of 9.91% from Example 3.2, which is higher than that on the index-linked gilt with

---

[27] It is usual in the City simply to divide by two to get six-monthly interest or inflation rates from annual figures.

the same maturity date and so looks a better buy if inflation is forecast to be 5% per annum or less on average up until 2001.

Another way of making the comparison, is to calculate the implied breakeven inflation rate on a comparable conventional gilt. So, the breakeven inflation rate is i

$$i = (1 + R)/(1 + r) - 1$$

where R is the nominal redemption yield and r is the real redemption yield. In this case, for Treasury 10% 2001, the breakeven inflation rate is

$$(1.0991)/(1.0442) - 1 = 0.053 \text{ or } 5.3\%$$

Thus, if inflation is 5.3% or less each year over the life of the gilts, the Treasury 10% 2001 is the best buy. If inflation is 5.3% per annum or higher, the index-linked gilt will yield higher average nominal returns. However, the two gilts are not strictly comparable in net yield terms. The coupons on the index-linked gilt are lower than on Treasury 10% 2001, and so may be more attractive to the higher rate taxpayer.

Summary

This chapter has looked at gilts, the most important type of fixed interest security quoted on the UK Stock Exchange. Gilts vary according to their coupon and maturity but all gilts have their interest and redemption payments guaranteed by the UK government. They are thus not subject to default risk.

Most gilts have interest and redemption payments fixed in nominal terms and are therefore subject to both interest rate risk and inflation risk. However, to encourage investors to continue to lend long-term to the government during periods of uncertainty over future inflation rates, new types of gilts were developed, called index-linked gilts, quoted in a separate section under British funds in the *Financial Times*.

The remaining section of the chapter was devoted to a description of how the two main types of return for gilts given in the *Financial Times*, interest yield and redemption yield, are calculated both for nominal and for index-linked gilts. The interest yield and, more importantly, the redemption yield are the two most common measures of return used for gilts. They are relatively easy to calculate and to understand. However, it remains to be seen whether these estimates of return on gilts help the investor to compare different gilts or to decide when to buy and sell gilts. A more detailed discussion on these questions is left to the next chapter.

Problems

1. The following gilt-edged securities were quoted in the *Financial Times* as follows on 24 March 1992.

Stock	Price £	Interest yield (%)	Redemption yield (%)
Exchequer 12¼% 1992	100¹¹⁄₁₆	12.17	10.57
Treasury 3% 1992	98¹³⁄₁₆	3.04	8.20

(i) Explain how the interest and redemption yields have been calculated and why you think Exchequer 12¼% is quoted at a price which is greater than its nominal value.

(ii) Suggest types of investor who might be interested in buying Exchequer 12¼% 1992, explaining why they would prefer it to the Treasury 3% 1992.

2. The *Financial Times* of Monday 30 March 1992 gives you the following information on Treasury 9% 1992–96, which is due to mature on 15 March in any year 1992–1996 at the government's discretion.

Interest due	Price	Last xd date
15 Sep. 15 Mar.	97³⁄₁₆	7 Feb.

(i) How much accrued interest should be added to the clean price to determine the full price to be paid?

(ii) Using the dirty price, calculate the interest yield on the gilt. Is it higher or lower than the gilt's coupon? In which year do you think the gilt will be redeemed?

(iii) Estimate the redemption yield for the gilt.

3. (i) Calculate the gross redemption yield on an Exchequer 8¼% gilt assuming the interest and capital repayment will both occur in exactly twelve months' time from today. The price is £97⅞.

(ii) Another gilt which will be redeemed at exactly the same time is Exchequer 3%, which is currently priced at £94½. Which gilt would you buy if you expect to hold it to redemption and
(a) you are a charity paying no income or capital gains tax,
(b) you are an individual with a marginal tax rate on investment income of 59% but not liable for capital gains tax on gilt investments.

(iii) At what marginal income tax rate would an investor be indifferent between the two gilts?

(iv) Is it possible that you could receive a greater yield/lesser yield than you have calculated above if you sell the gilt before redemption? Why? Would the tax situation change?

4. Suppose it is March 1992. The quoted price of Treasury 2% index-linked 2006 is £140 and the next semi-annual interest payment is due on 19 July. The base date for index-linking of the gilt is November 1980 when the retail prices index was 69.4. The monthly retail price indices for January–November 1991 were:

Jan.	130.2
Feb.	130.9
Mar.	131.4
Apr.	133.1
May	133.5
Jun.	134.1
Jul.	133.8
Aug.	134.1
Sep.	134.6
Oct.	135.1
Nov.	135.6

(i) What will the July 1992 coupon payment be in nominal terms?
(ii) Calculate the 'real' interest yield on the gilt.
(iii) Suppose the *Financial Times* told you that the 'real' redemption yields on this gilt, assuming 5 and 10% p.a. inflation, were 4.5% and 4.3% respectively. How would you go about comparing this gilt with, say, Treasury 8% 2002–6 which, on the same day, had a quoted redemption yield of 9.7%?
(iv) What factors would lead an investor to invest in the index-linked gilt, rather than an ordinary gilt of the same maturity?

5. How has the issue of index-linked gilts by the UK government:
   (i) Affected the cost of funding to the government?
   (ii) Affected the investment opportunities available to potential investors in gilts?

CHAPTER 4

Investing in fixed interest securities

Introduction

In Chapter 3, we looked at how gilts differ from one another, through their coupons and maturities, and examined how measures of return on gilts, notably the interest yield and the redemption yield, can be calculated. In this chapter, we concentrate on how to choose between fixed interest securities, in particular gilts, from the point of view of investment.

We saw in Chapter 2 that all fixed interest securities are subject to interest rate risk and inflation risk (as well as default risk for non-UK government securities). However, given its particular coupon and maturity, each fixed interest security will respond in a different way to changes in interest rates and unexpected inflation. So, in order to be able to choose between fixed interest securities, we need an understanding of how each one will be affected by such changes.

What we shall in fact find is that fixed interest security prices reflect what the market as a whole expects interest and inflation rates to be in the future. However, redemption yields do not give us this information. Forward interest rates, which are implicit in gilt prices, do. Armed with this knowledge of expected future interest rates, the investor can then follow one of two types of investment strategy. In the first instance, he can accept the market projections of future interest rates implicit in gilt prices. He can then attempt to minimise interest rate risk by matching the maturities of the gilts with the maturities of his liabilities or minimise inflation risk by either investing short term or by buying index-linked gilts. On the other hand, he can compare his own projections of future interest and inflation rates with those of the market and choose those gilts which will do best if his forecast proves a more accurate picture of the future than that of the market. If, for example, he believes that interest rates will fall over the next year by more than is predicted by the market and is reflected in gilt prices, he will invest in those gilts which are the most volatile to changes in interest rates and which will therefore experience the biggest price rises if his forecast is correct. We shall see that this volatility can be assessed by a measure called 'duration'.

Thus, the investor has a choice. He can either accept market forecasts of future inflation and interest rates and minimise the risk that actual rates will be different from those forecast by reducing his exposure to interest rate risk or inflation risk, or he can choose his level of exposure according to how he himself forecasts the future.

The structure of Chapter 4 is as follows. We first of all examine the measures used to describe gilts in Chapter 3 to see how they can help in investment decision-making. We find that the only measure of any potential use is the redemption yield. However, the redemption yield does not help us to obtain market forecasts of future interest rates and, because of this, we turn to spot and forward interest rates for this information. We can then determine the term structure of interest rates, both now and in the future, which allows us to estimate the volatility of different gilts to expected changes in interest rates and thus to choose in which gilts to invest. The remaining section of the chapter is devoted to corporate fixed interest securities such as Eurobonds which can be valued in a similar way to gilts but which are also subject to default risk.

Comparing gilts

In this section we look at the gilt measures discussed in Chapter 3 to see how they can help us compare gilts. For example, given the information on gilts provided in *Financial Times*, as shown in Example 3.2 on p. 67, the investor can compare the price, coupon, maturity, interest yield and redemption yield of every gilt.

Knowledge of the price alone will not help the investor since, on a cursory inspection, the longer-dated the gilt, the cheaper it looks. This is simply due to the fact that, the nearer the gilt is to maturity, the closer the price is to £100. No matter what happens to interest rates or inflation, the value of any gilt on its redemption date must be £100 and this value acts like a magnet to which the price of the gilt is drawn over its life. Only undated stocks, which have no prospect of redemption as long as prevailing interest rates are higher than their coupons, and index-linked gilts, whose redemption values are not fixed at £100, do not have this inexorable tendency.

The coupon of the gilt informs the investor whether he will receive a substantial amount of his return by way of income or capital gain. For example, in Example 3.2, Exchequer 3% Gas 1990–95 is priced at £88⅞ and Treasury 12% 1995 at £104³/₃₂. Exchequer 3% will yield little in the way of interest over its life, the majority of its return being in the form of capital gain (£100–£88⅞). On the other hand, Treasury 12% 1995 will yield all of its return via interest income with, in fact, a prospective capital loss. The investor, from knowledge of his tax position, may be able to express a preference for high or low coupon stocks. Knowledge of the coupon and the price combine to give the interest yield and with this some understanding of the level of return the income from the gilt will generate. In the above example, the interest yield from Exchequer 3% 1990–95 would only be 3.38% compared with 11.53% from Treasury 12% 1995.

However, the interest yield, as mentioned earlier, ignores the capital gain or loss element of return and the shorter the term of the gilt or the lower the coupon, the more misleading this will be as a measure. This can be clearly seen from Example 4.1.

For example, the difference between the interest yield and the redemption yield (the latter allows for the capital received on redemption) is over 3% for the short, Exchequer 3%, and less than 0.1% for the long, Conversion 9½% 2004. For long-term or high coupon gilts, therefore, the interest yield can be used as an estimate of the overall return to redemption whereas for short-term or low coupon gilts it gives only a partial measure of return. However, for undated stocks such as Consols 4%, the interest yield

Example 4.1   Comparison of interest yields and redemption yields

	Price £	Interest yield (%)	Redemption yield (%)	Difference (%)
Exchequer Gas 3% 1990–95	88⅞	3.38	6.89	+3.51
Treasury 12% 1995	104³/₃₂	11.53	10.29	−1.24
Funding 3½% 1999–04	60⁹/₃₂	5.81	8.86	+3.05
Conversion 9½% 2004	97²³/₃₂	9.72	9.80	+0.08
Consols 4% undated	40⅜	9.91	–	–

Source: Example 3.2.

is the only measure of return available, since undated gilts have no expected redemption date.

Maturity is a useful comparative measure for gilts since investors can choose gilts according to their pattern of consumption preferences or their future liabilities. As was discussed in Chapter 2, one way of avoiding interest rate risk is to match exactly the maturities of assets and liabilities.[1] If a gilt with a longer maturity than the liability is chosen, the investor runs the risk that interest rates will have risen and the price fallen when the gilt has to be sold to meet the liability. If a gilt with too short a maturity is chosen, the investor runs the risk that interest rates will have fallen and the money received on redemption will have to be reinvested for the remaining term at a lower interest rate than the investor could have obtained on a gilt with the same maturity as the liability.

However, the investor may be unable or unwilling to match the maturity of his investments to that of his liabilities. Or he may wish to compare two gilts with the same maturity. In order to choose between gilts in these circumstances, he must be able to compare the interest rate risk and the return on each of the gilts he is considering and, to do this, he must turn to his only remaining measure, the redemption yield.

Comparison of redemption yields

Suppose the Greenfields pension fund knows in 1992 that it has a liability to meet in two years' time but, since it pays no tax, it is indifferent between a high coupon or low coupon gilt of the same maturity, for example between Treasury 8½% 1994 and Treasury 14½% 1994.

From a comparison of redemption yields, it would appear that Treasury 14½% 1994 offers the greater return since it has the higher redemption yield of 10.4% compared with the redemption yield of 10.2% on Treasury 8½% 1994. Redemption yield is a measure of holding period return to redemption, and so, if Greenfields intends to hold the gilt until 1994, it would appear obvious that it should choose Treasury 14½% 1994. A glance at Example 3.2 in Chapter 3 shows that all gilts have different yields to redemption and if redemption yields were the only measure of choice, this state could surely not persist since the gilts would have to provide the same redemption yield or their prices would fall until they did so. If Treasury 8½% 1994 were judged on redemption yield alone, no one would

---

[1] In fact interest rate risk cannot be completely avoided since interest payments during the life of the gilt may not exactly match consumption needs and so have to be reinvested, perhaps at less advantageous rates. Only if an investor were to purchase a zero coupon fixed interest security (one which pays no interest during its life) could he avoid interest rate risk altogether.

Example 4.2   Comparison of redemption yields of gilts with the same maturity

	Dirty price £	Redemption yield (approx.) (%)	1992	1993	1994
Treasury 8½% 1994	99.89	10.2	£99.89 = $\dfrac{8.50}{1.102} + \dfrac{108.50}{(1.102)^2}$		
Treasury 14½% 1994	109.40	10.4	£109.40 = $\dfrac{14.50}{1.104} + \dfrac{114.50}{(1.104)^2}$		

buy it and its price would fall until it too offered a redemption yield of 10.4%.

So, why cannot the redemption yield be used as a measure of comparison between two gilts of the same maturity? Example 4.2 highlights some of the problems of the redemption yield. Firstly, look at the cash flows in 1992/3. The £8.50 income from Treasury 8½% 1994 is discounted at 10.2% whereas the £14.50 income from an investment of equal risk, Treasury 14½% 1994, is discounted at 10.4%. We know that the discount rate which should be used is the rate of interest Greenfields could get by investing in another investment of equivalent risk. The redemption yield does not tell us what that rate of interest is. It is simply the single discount rate which, given the price, coupon and maturity of a gilt, discounts the future cash flows back to the price – the missing number in an equation. Also, if we look at Treasury 8½% 1994 we can see that the discount rate for cash flows in 1992/3 is the same as that for 1993/4 and yet we do not expect interest rates to remain constant throughout the life of any gilt. This is the assumption underlying the use of a redemption yield, even if the gilt has a life of twenty years. So, the redemption yield does not help Greenfields in its understanding of the pricing of equivalent maturity gilts.

Now, consider Mr Gamble. He wishes to take on some interest rate risk since he believes that interest rates will fall within the next twelve months. He would like to know which gilt it would be best to choose to take advantage of this expected fall in interest rates and to maximise his gain from it. In other words, Mr Gamble wishes to estimate the sensitivity of each gilt to interest rate risk.

Does an analysis of redemption yields help Mr Gamble identify the sensitivity of different gilts to interest rate risk? One way of doing this would be to examine the effect of a given change in redemption yield on the prices of gilts with different maturities and coupons (the two major distinguishing factors). Example 4.3 quantifies the effect of a 2% rise or fall in redemption yields from the assumed prevailing yield of 10%. Example

Example 4.3 Effects of changes in redemption yield on prices of gilts with different maturities and coupons

(a) *Different maturity gilts (assume 10% coupon)*

		Years to maturity			
	1	*5*	*10*	*20*	*Undated*
Redemption yield 8%	£102	£108	£113	£120	£125
10%	£100	£100	£100	£100	£100
12%	£98	£93	£89	£85	£83
Price range	£4	£15	£24	£35	£42
Price range as percentage of original price	4%	15%	24%	35%	42%

(b) *Different coupon gilts (assume ten-year maturity)*

	Coupon		
	5%	*10%*	*15%*
Redemption yield 8%	£80	£113	£147
10%	£69	£100	£131
12%	£60	£89	£117
Price range	£20	£24	£30
Price range as percentage of original price	29%	24%	19%

4.3(a) looks at the impact on the prices of gilts with a 10% coupon and different maturities. Example 4.3(b) looks at gilts with a ten-year life but different coupons. In both cases interest is assumed to be paid once a year at the year end.

From Example 4.3(a), Mr Gamble can see that the longer the maturity of the gilt, the more sensitive it is to changes in redemption yield. So, if he believes that redemption yields will fall, he would probably choose long-dated or undated gilts. Similarly, although the effect is less marked, Mr Gamble can see from Example 4.3(b) that the lower the coupon the more sensitive the gilt will be to changes in redemption yield. This is because investors in low coupon gilts purchased substantially below par receive proportionately more return from repayment on redemption and this effectively makes such stocks into longer-term gilts than high coupon gilts of the same maturity. Mr Gamble will therefore maximise his gain, in the event of a fall in redemption yields, by investing in low coupon long-dated gilts.

Duration

We have seen above how both the coupon and the maturity of a particular gilt affect its sensitivity to changes in interest rates. What we would like is a single measure for each gilt which would quantify this sensitivity. This is provided by what is known as the 'duration' or 'average life' of the gilt. Duration is defined to be

D = Weighted average of length of time before each payment ×
    the relative present value of each payment

By 'relative present value', we mean the present value of each payment divided by the price of the gilt. We do this to make sure that the relative present values of the payments add up to 1 overall. Since the present values of the payments on the gilt add up to the price of the gilt, the present values divided by the price must add up to 1.

For example, consider a two-year zero coupon bond, priced at £82.64 to yield 10%. The duration of this bond must be 2, since 100% of the cash flows are in year 2.

$$D = 0 \times 1 + \frac{100/(1.1)^2 \times 2}{82.64}$$

$$= 2$$

More generally, we can write, for a two-year bond, with annual cash flows,

$$D = (PV_1/\text{Price}) \times 1 + (PV_2/\text{Price}) \times 2 \tag{4.1}$$

where PV_1 is the present value of the coupon due one year from now discounted by the redemption yield and PV_2 the discounted present value of the coupon plus principal payment two years from now.

If we now look at an 8% two-year bond priced at £96.53 to yield 10%, the duration is

$$D = \frac{8/(1.1)}{96.53} \times 1 + \frac{108/(1.1)^2}{96.53} \times 2$$

$$= 1.92$$

or less than 2 years. If we think of duration as the average life of the bond, the concept becomes easier to understand. Think of any gilt as a series of one-payment loans to the UK government. If we for simplicity assume annual coupons, a two-year gilt can be thought of as a one-year zero coupon bond and a larger two-year zero coupon bond. The *average* life of this gilt will depend on the relative importance of the cash flows in years 1 and 2. Since only 8/(1.1)/96.53 or 7.5% of the present value of the cash flows of the 8% coupon two-year bond occur in year 1, 92.5% occur in year 2, causing the average life to be close to but not quite 2. If we calculate the duration of a 15% coupon two-year bond, this will be lower than the duration or average life of the 8% coupon bond since a greater proportion of the cash flows will occur in year 1. For example, if the yield on such a bond is also 10%, giving a price of £108.68, the percentage of the present value of the cash flows occuring in year 1 will be 15/(1.1)/108.68 or 12.5%. In fact, you can check that the duration of this bond is 1.87.

No matter what the coupon or the maturity, every gilt's duration can be determined using the formula given in equation (4.1) but extended for the relevant number of years. The greater the duration of a gilt, the more sensitive it is to changes in interest rates. For any particular maturity, the lower the coupon of the gilt, the more volatile it is, with a zero coupon bond being the most volatile of all. Similarly, the longer the maturity of a bond, the more volatile it is, with perpetual bonds the most volatile of all. Interestingly, the average life of a gilt is never more than 12 years, even if it has a maturity of 30 years or is a perpetual. This is because the coupon payments in the early years of the lives of such gilts dominate the distant cash flows in present value terms and so the latters' weighting is insignificant in comparison. However, a 20-year zero coupon gilt, if it could be acquired, *would* have a duration of twenty years.

Of what use is duration to the bond investor? There are two main uses. Firstly, using duration, the investor can quantify the interest rate risk of any bond portfolio in a single number and is therefore able to work out how to hedge that amount of interest rate risk, either through bond futures or by matching the durations of the assets and liabilities of the fund. Secondly the investor using duration, or a version of it known as modified duration, can work out exactly how much a particular bond price will move for a given change in interest rates.

Hedging

One of the advantages of duration as a risk measure is that the duration of a portfolio of bonds is simply the weighted average of the durations of the individual bonds. For example, suppose Ms Vortex has two gilts in her portfolio priced at £96 and £120 respectively. She has £1,000 nominal of each gilt, and their durations are 3 and 10 respectively. The market values of the two gilts are therefore (96/100) × (£1,000) = £960 and (120/100) × (£1,000) = £1,200 and the duration of the portfolio

$$= \frac{3 \times 960 + 10 \times 1,200}{960 + 1,200}$$

$$= \quad 6.9 \text{ years}$$

As we shall see in Chapter 6 on Futures, we can use this number to decide how many futures contracts to sell in order to neutralise any exposure to interest rate risk. If the duration of the futures contracts sold is also 6.9, if interest rates go up, any loss on the portfolio would be exactly matched by the gain on the repurchase of the futures contracts sold.[2]

Alternatively, pension funds and life insurance companies can insure themselves against interest rate risk on their future liabilities by buying a portfolio of bonds with the same duration or average life as their portfolio of liabilities. For example, suppose that an insurance company works out the duration of its liabilities to be 10 years. It could make sure that these liabilities could be met (if they are expressed in nominal terms) by buying a portfolio of bonds with a duration of 10 years: a single zero coupon bond with a maturity of 10 years would do the trick. However, a portfolio of coupon bearing bonds such as gilts with longer maturities than 10 years but with an average duration of 10 years would also fit the bill. Why would this be so?

One can think of the interest rate risk of the coupon-bearing gilts in terms of a see-saw. If interest rates were to fall over the 10-year period, the reinvestment rates achieved on the coupons would be less than 10% and would drag down the overall return. However, because the gilts would have maturities in excess of 10 years, when they came to be sold at the end of the 10-year period, they would have experienced a price rise because required yields had fallen. If the average duration of the assets is fixed to be equal to the average duration of the liabilities, the reinvestment loss on the portfolio of coupon gilts will be exactly offset by the price gain made on their disposal. Similarly, if interest rates were to rise during the 10-year period, the reinvestment gain would be exactly offset by a capital loss on disposal.

Even if liability matching is not an issue, the duration of a portfolio can be used as a means of guaranteeing returns to investors. We have seen that, if a 10-year time horizon for the investor were appropriate, buying 10-year gilts would not guarantee the investor the redemption yield on the portfolio because the reinvestment risk would not be offset by any price gain or loss on disposal: 10-year maturity bonds would always be worth exactly £100 on maturity. It is the case, however, that if a portfolio of bonds with a 10-year *duration* were acquired, the yield to maturity on the

---

[2] The gilts in the portfolio would go down in price if interest rates fell whereas a profit would be made on the bond futures position taken out since the futures contracts could be bought back for less than the price at which they were sold.

portfolio could be locked in. The simplest possible portfolio with a duration of 10 is a 10-year zero coupon bond; clearly, there is no reinvestment
risk in this case and the redemption yield is locked in. Similarly, with
coupon bonds, if the duration of the portfolio is 10 years, the redemption
yield can also be guaranteed. This has enabled insurance companies to
offer investment products where a return is guaranteed over a number of
years, protecting investors from downside risk.

Thus, the duration of a portfolio of bonds is more important than their
average maturity when it comes to considering their exposure to the
interest rate risk first mentioned in Chapter 2.

Estimating price changes

Duration can also be used to estimate the change in price of a particular gilt
and this is useful, both for hedging and taking risk.

Duration, as well as being thought of as the average life of a bond, can
also be defined as its elasticity with respect to a percentage change in
interest rates. Formally, it is

$$D = \frac{-\,\%\ \text{change in price}}{\%\ \text{change in } (1+R)} \tag{4.2}$$

where R is the redemption yield on the bond.[3] Notice that there is a minus
sign since if R rises, the bond price falls, and vice versa.

Rearranging equation (4.2), we can write

$$\%\ \text{change in price} = -\,D \times \%\ \text{change in } (1+R)$$

or $\qquad dP/P = -\,D \times d\,(1+R)/(1+R)$

where dP is the absolute change in price P and $d\,(1+R)$ the absolute
change in $(1+R)$. Since $d(1+R)$ is the same as dR, and taking P over to
the right-hand side, we obtain

$$dP = -\,D \times P \times dR/(1+R) \tag{4.3}$$

---

[3] For those readers curious to know how this formula is derived and how D can also be
equivalent to a bond's average life, I refer you to Copeland and Watson, 1988, Ch. 13.
Appendix 2. As a first pointer, D is obtained by differentiating the price of a bond with
respect to $(1+R)$ in equation (3.2) on p. 79, which sets the price of a bond equal to the sum of
the present values of the cash flows discounted by $(1+R)$.

With equation (4.3), we can estimate the price change dP for a yield change dR. For example, suppose a bond is priced at par on a yield of 10% and has a duration of 10. If interest rates rise 1%, equation (4.3) becomes

$$dP = -10 \times 100 \times 0.01/(1.1)$$

$$= -9.09$$

In other words, the bond price would fall 9.09 to 90.90 or almost 10% for a 1% interest rate rise. For a 10 basis point (0.1%) rise, the price would fall by 0.909 to £99.09, or a fall of almost 1%.

For a bond priced at £90, yielding 8% with a duration of 3, the equivalent price fall for a rise in interest rates of 1% would be

$$dP = -3 \times 90 \times 0.01/(1.08)$$

$$= -2.5$$

causing the price to fall to £87.50.

In practice, to simplify equation (4.3), some investors prefer to use modified duration instead of duration in the formula. If we define modified duration to be $MD = D/(1 + R)$, equation (4.3) becomes

$$dP = - MD \times P \times dR \qquad (4.4)$$

So for example, if a bond has a duration of 5.5 and a redemption yield of 10%, the modified duration will be 5. If the bond price is £100, equation (4.4) shows how the price change will simply be the modified duration (in this case 5) times the yield change. In this case, a 10 basis point fall in yields will lead to a 50 basis point or 0.5% price rise for the bond.

Equations (4.3) and (4.4) are crucial to investors wishing to switch between bonds of different interest risks and hence durations. Suppose Miss Vortex is given the information in Example 4.4 and told that Gilt A is cheap and Gilt B is dear.[4] If she already holds Gilt B, a simple way to enhance returns on her portfolio would be to sell Gilt B and to buy Gilt A.

Let us suppose that Ms Vortex has no particular view on interest rates and wishes to maintain the interest rate risk exposure of her portfolio at current levels. She can do this by doing a *duration-weighted switch*. Suppose that she has £1,000 nominal of gilt B in her portfolio which she sells.

---

[4] By 'cheap', we mean that the yield on the gilt looks high compared to similar coupon and maturity gilts. By 'dear', we mean that the yield on the gilt looks relatively low by comparison with similar gilts.

Example 4.4 Bond switch with neutral interest rate risk

Gilt	Coupon (%)	Maturity (Years)	Price (£)	Yield (%)	Modified Duration
A	8%	10	100.00	8	6.80
B	12%	4	106.44	10	3.16

How much of gilt A should she buy? All she has to do is calculate the ratio of dPs for the pair of bonds, using equation (4.4) and assuming the same yield shift of, say, 1%, since this will mean that the absolute price change of her portfolio would be the same, *ceteris paribus*, whether she held gilt A or gilt B:

$$dP_A = -6.80 \times 100.00 \times 0.01 \tag{4.5}$$

$$dP_B = -3.16 \times 106.44 \times 0.01 \tag{4.6}$$

Since gilt A is riskier than gilt B in interest rate risk terms (it has a higher duration), Ms Vortex will wish to hold less of gilt A than she did of gilt B. If we divide equation (4.6) by equation (4.5), we get

$$\frac{-3.16 \times 106.44}{-6.80 \times 100.00}$$

$$= \mathbf{0.49}$$

So, Ms Vortex should sell £1,000 nominal of gilt B and buy £490 nominal of gilt A. If the gilts move back into line and become fairly priced, she should make money by carrying out the switch – regardless of what happens to interest rates.

Yield curve

Ms Vortex can now, given an estimated change in redemption yield, calculate the effect of this change on different gilts and make purchase, sale or switching decisions. This is all very well, but what does a change in redemption yield signify and how can Ms Vortex estimate how required redemption yields will change over any given period?

At any point in time, redemption yields of gilts of differing maturities

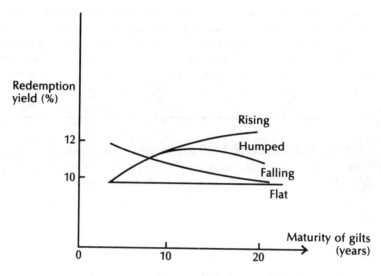

Figure 4.1   Possible redemption yield curves

follow a pattern (with exceptions in the case of low coupon gilts.[5] For example, in April 1992, the date of the gilt prices shown in Example 3.2, redemption yields fell slightly with maturity, reaching a peak 10.62% for the 1992 maturity highest coupon gilt, and then declining slightly thereafter to around 9.5% for the longer dated gilts. This trend in redemption yields can be plotted on what is known as a yield curve which may be rising, humped, falling or flat. These four types of yield curve are drawn in Figure 4.1.

The yield curve is affected by present and expected future interest rates. For example, if short-term interest rates are low and considered likely to rise in the near future, the redemption yield on shorts will be lower than that on five- or ten-year gilts, giving a rising yield curve. On the other hand, if inflation and hence interest rates were expected to decline in the longer term, long-term gilts would have lower redemption yields than medium-term gilts, giving a falling yield curve.

If Ms Vortex could draw today's yield curve and her estimate of this curve in twelve month's time, she would be able to apply her knowledge of sensitivity to redemption yield changes to make investment decisions.

---

[5] Low coupon gilts are out of line in the yield curve for two reasons. Firstly, most of their value lies in the capital repayment at the end of their life and so they act as longer-term stocks than high coupon gilts of the same maturity (they have higher duration). Secondly, tax effects may distort their redemption yields. If there is more demand for low coupon stocks than there is supply, because investors want return in the form of capital gain rather than income, this will push up the prices of low coupon gilts relative to other gilts and lower their redemption yields.

However, a redemption yield is a complex average of interest rates prevailing throughout the life of the gilt.[6] Each redemption yield is a different mixture of these interest rates. It would be far easier for Ms Vortex to concern herself with the relevant underlying interest rates and estimate sensitivities using these, rather than using misleading and complicated redemption yields. Interest rates are also economically significant figures. They are determined by the demand and supply for money and these in turn are determined by the number of productive investment opportunities, the consumption preferences of investors and the expected inflation rates. If inflation is expected to rise by 5% next year, Ms Vortex will be able to estimate the impact on interest rates but not necessarily on redemption yields.

Term structure of interest rates

Since redemption yields do not enable us to get an accurate picture of prevailing interest rates for different maturities of gilt (known as the 'term structure of interest rates'), we go back to the discounted cash flow valuation model for gilts and examine the underlying interest rates which determine their prices.

Spot rates

We know that we must be able to write

$$P = \frac{D}{(1 + r_1)} + \frac{D}{(1 + r_1)^2} + \ldots \frac{D + 100}{(1 + r_n)^n} \tag{4.7}$$

where D is the annual interest payment,[7] r_1 the rate of interest required on one-year investments such as gilts, r_2 the *annual* rate of interest required

---

[6] With a fixed interest security which paid no interest (zero coupon) and had an n-year life, the redemption yield would be the geometric mean of all the n underlying interest rates, or spot rates as they are called. So, in the case of a zero coupon gilt, we could write r as

$$r = \sqrt[n]{(1 + r_1)(1 + r_2) \ldots (1 + r_n)} - 1$$

For gilts with non-zero coupons, the relationship between a redemption yield and underlying interest rates is more complex.

[7] For simplicity, we assume annual rather than six-monthly cash flows.

for money invested now for two years, and so on; r_1 will not necessarily be equal to r_2 nor r_2 to r_3 (as was assumed in the case of the redemption yield) since interest rates will be expected to change over time. These interest rates, the r_i, are called *spot interest rates* because they are rates for investments made now or 'on the spot'. In other words, the investor contracts to lend money now for n years in return for which he receives an annual rate of interest of r_n throughout the n years of the loan.

Since the purchase of a gilt always involves a loan to the UK government, the investor will be guaranteed the interest and principal payments whichever gilt he invests in. Thus, he will require the same interest rate for lending for n years to the UK government for any gilt. This means that, at any point in time, the same set of spot rates can be used to value any gilt. So, different gilts will have cash flows paid in the same years discounted at the same rates. If we go back to Example 4.2 on p. 96, we can now write

$$\text{Treasury } 8\tfrac{1}{2}\% \ 199? \quad 99.89 = \frac{8.50}{(1 + r_1)} + \frac{108.50}{(1 + r_2)^2}$$

$$\text{Treasury } 14\tfrac{1}{2}\% \ 1994 \quad 109.40 = \frac{14.50}{(1 + r_1)} + \frac{114.50}{(1 + r_2)^2}$$

This implies that money invested in either gilt for one year will provide the same interest rate, r_1, whether invested in Treasury $8\tfrac{1}{2}\%$ 1994 or Treasury $14\tfrac{1}{2}\%$ 1994. Similarly, money invested for one year at r_1 will not necessarily provide the same annual interest rate as money invested for two years at r_2, because interest rates vary over time.

Our objective is to be able to draw a spot rate curve now and an expected spot rate curve in twelve months' time (or for whichever holding period is preferred) in order to be able to study changes in gilt prices and calculate expected holding period returns and investment strategies for Ms Vortex. To draw the present curve, the spot rates, r_i, have to be determined.

There are essentially three ways of determining spot rates: iteration; regression; and from zero coupon bonds. Although all three methods are different, the principle is the same in that the spot rates are determined from bond prices. The spot rates are the market consensus rates for lending to the UK government, in the case of gilts, for one year, two years, and so on. The spot rates are not plucked out of thin air; in exactly the same way as redemption yields, they depend on bond market prices for their determination.

Example 4.5 shows how the iteration method can be used. A selection of bonds is needed, one for each maturity of the term structure. In Example 4.5 we start with a one-year annual coupon bond. For this bond, the one-year spot rate is simply the same as the redemption yield and so the

Example 4.5   Estimation of existing spot rates

Gilt	Coupon (%)	Maturity (years)	Price £
A	8.5	1	98.625
B	10	2	98.375

We assume all payments are at the year end and at exactly one-year intervals. From gilt A, we know that

$$P_0 = \frac{D_1 + 100}{1 + r_1}$$

or

$$98.625 = \frac{108.5}{(1 + r_1)}$$

which gives

$$r_1 = 10\%$$

From gilt B, we can write

$$P_0 = \frac{D_1}{(1 + r_1)} + \frac{D_2 + 100}{(1 + r_2)^2}$$

$$98.375 = \frac{10}{(1 + r_1)} + \frac{100}{(1 + r_2)^2}$$

We have already found r_1 to be 10%, so

$$98.375 = \frac{10}{1.10} + \frac{110}{(1 + r_2)^2}$$

Solving, we get

$$r_2 = 11\%$$

one-year spot rate can be readily calculated. For the two-year bond, we write down the price in terms of the one-year cash flow discounted by the one-year spot rate (which we now know) and the two-year cash flow discounted by the two-year spot rate (which we do not yet know). Since we know the price of the bond and the one-year spot rate, we solve for the two-year spot rate. In practice, this process would have to be carried out right through the maturity spectrum and it would be difficult to find bonds with exactly the right maturities.

For this reason, spot rates are normally determined by *regression*. The population of gilt prices, coupons, and maturities is put into the computer and the set of spot rates which best fits the data is estimated by regression analysis. In practice, there will be parts of the yield curve with a large number of bonds, and other parts of the yield curve where there are only a few bonds, and so the estimates will not be perfect. However, the method is good enough to derive for most bond markets a sensible set of spot rates.

One immediate use for such a regression model is to reprice all the bonds in the model with the spot rates estimated from the model. Since the spot rates are the 'best estimates', repricing the bonds will give some bonds which look expensive relative to their market price and others which look cheap. This could simply be a problem with the accuracy of the regression technique but if the 'cheapness' or 'dearness' varies over time, this technique could throw up switch ideas such as that carried out by Ms Vortex earlier.

The third method is only possible if there is a set of zero coupon bonds, one for every maturity in the yield curve. If there is, the redemption yields on the zero coupon bonds are the spot rates. For example, the ten-year spot rate is the redemption yield on a ten-year zero coupon bond, and so on. Where would such a set of zero coupon bonds come from? In the US, banks take coupon bonds and 'strip' them into a set of single-payment bonds, one for each coupon payment on the original bond. Each of these stripped bonds is effectively a zero coupon bond and so their yields can be used to estimate spot rates. This third method is clearly the simplest and most attractive; however, two caveats must be mentioned. Firstly, not many markets have such stripped government bonds and the gilt market is one market without them – although corporate zero coupon bonds have been much more popular in the 1990s, leading to a greater awareness of spot rates. Secondly, the spot rates derived from stripped US Treasury bonds may be different from those derived from coupon bonds using regression techniques because different supply and demand factors influence the two types of Treasury bond, affecting their relative prices and hence the spot rates derived from these two sets of prices.[8]

Forward rates

The next step is to try to determine the future spot rates, that is, a future term structure of interest rates. This will enable Ms Vortex to see how

---

[8] For example, in the section on duration earlier in the chapter, we saw how insurance companies might particularly value twenty-year zero coupon bonds, since they have a higher duration than is available with coupon bonds.

interest rates are expected to change in the future. She can then decide which gilts to buy, given the market's and her own expectations. In fact, we can use the existing spot rate curve to give an indication of future spot rates as follows.

Suppose Ms Vortex is considering the purchase of one of the gilts described in Example 4.5. If she buys A, she will get a one-year return of 10%. If she buys B, she will get an equivalent annual return of 11% for two years. But, if the going rate for lending money for one year is 10%, by buying B Ms Vortex is in effect agreeing to lend for one year at 10% and then for another year at a rate which gives an overall return of 11% per annum for two years. If we call this unknown rate for lending for one year from the end of year 1 to the end of year 2, $_1f_2$, we can write

$$(1 + r_1)(1 + {}_1f_2) = (1 + r_2)^2$$

$$(1.10)(1 + {}_1f_2) = (1.11)^2$$

$$_1f_2 = 12\%$$

$_1f_2$ is the *current* market rate for agreeing *now* to lend money for one year starting in twelve months' time. $_1f_2$ is called the forward rate for lending in year 2. It is implicit, since once r_1 and r_2 are known $_1f_2$ is fixed. Once we know all the spot rates r_i, we can isolate the implicit forward rates $_0f_1$, $_1f_2$, $_2f_3$, and so on ($_0f_1$ is obviously the same as r_1).

For example, to calculate $_2f_3$, we know that the following must hold:

$$(1 + r_1)(1 + {}_1f_2)(1 + {}_2f_3) = (1 + r_3)^3$$

where r_1 (or $_0f_1$), $_1f_2$, $_2f_3$ are the three implicit one-year forward interest rates for years 1, 2 and 3 which combine to give an equivalent annual interest rate of r_3 for three years. So, if we know that r_3 is 12.5% and $_1f_2$ is 12%, we can write:

$$(1.10)(1.12)(1 + {}_2f_3) = (1.125)^3 \tag{4.8}$$

giving

$$_2f_3 = 18.5\%$$

An alternative way of finding $_2f_3$ would be to say

$$(1 + r_2)^2 (1 + {}_2f_3) = (1 + r_3)^3 \tag{4.9}$$

$$(1.11)^2 (1 + {}_2f_3) = (1.125)^3$$

Since the investor is lending for three years at r_3, this must be equivalent to lending for two years at r_2 and for one year in year 3 at $_2f_3$. Equations (4.8) and (4.9) are exactly the same given that $(1 + r_2)^2 = (1 + r_1) (1 + _1f_2)$.

Of what use are these forward rates in estimating the future spot rates which will prevail, say, in one year's time? This depends on two factors: the efficiency of the market for gilts and the element of bias which may be included in forward rates as estimators of future spot rates.

If the market is active with many investors, low transaction costs and expectations on future interest rates are widely disseminated, these expectations will be incorporated into gilt prices and forward rates. Thus, such an efficient market will have forward rates which predict, as accurately as is possible at the time, future spot rates. In previous chapters, we have seen that transaction costs on gilts are very low (with no stamp duties and no brokers' commissions for institutional investors) and turnover in gilts is high. Also, because interest rates form such a major element of government policy, any expectations or comments concerning future interest rates are widely publicised. We would therefore expect forward rates to be good predictors of future spot rates and such empirical evidence as there is, both for UK and US government fixed-term stock, on the whole supports this view.[9]

The implications of having efficient securities markets are very important and the whole of Chapter 10 is devoted to the concept of efficient markets. We simply point out here that an efficient gilts market leads to the conclusion that forward rates are the best estimates available for future spot rates. Although future spot rates will doubtless turn out not to be exactly as predicted by forward rates, it will not pay Ms Vortex to spend time and money on her own market forecasts. Since all that is publicly known about future interest rates is already incorporated into forward rates, it is unlikely that Ms Vortex's own views will add anything to the accuracy of the forward rates' forecasts. Despite this, much trading in gilts is based on the investors' own views of future interest rate movements which are different from those reflected in forward rates and gilt prices.

The second factor to be taken into account when using forward rates as estimates of future spot rates is whether they include any bias in their estimates. There are various hypotheses concerning this which are concerned with whether there is a bias or not and, if so, what is the cause of this bias. The four major hypotheses are outlined in Example 4.6.

The simplest hypothesis in Example 4.6 is the *expectations hypothesis*. This says that forward interest rates are unbiased predictors of future interest rates. So, for example, the forward rate, $_1f_2$, of 12% derived from Example 4.5 is the market's exact estimate of next year's r_1.

---

[9] For a summary of the research in this area, see Nelson (1980) and Fama (1984).

Example 4.6   Hypotheses concerning relationship between forward rates and expected spot rates

Hypothesis	Argument	Effect
(1) *Expectations*	Every forward rate is the best market estimate of the relevant future spot rate.	Forward rates can be used as estimates of expected spot rates.
(2) *Liquidity premium*	Lenders prefer to lend short. Borrowers prefer to borrow long. So investors require a liquidity premium to compensate for the interest rate risk of holding longer-term securities than they wish to. The premium increases with maturity of investment.	Forward rates are overestimates of future spot rates since they include a premium for agreeing to lend long.
(3) *Inflation premium*	Risk is due mainly to inflation risk, that is, uncertainty about future *actual* inflation since only *expected* inflation is incorporated into interest rates. The shorter the term of lending, the better the lender can estimate inflation. So lenders prefer to lend for short periods and forward rates include an inflation premium to compensate lenders for uncertainty about future inflation.	Forward rates are overestimates of future spot rates since they include a premium for inflation risk.
(4) *Market segmentation*	In order to reduce interest rate risk, both borrowers and lenders match their assets and liabilities. For example, banks will prefer short-term gilts and pension funds long-term gilts.	The premium or discount in the forward rate for a particular maturity will depend on the demand and supply for that maturity.

A major implication of the expectations hypothesis is that, if it holds, the investor need not worry about the maturity of the gilts he buys. For example, if Ms Vortex wishes to make a two-year investment in gilts, she can either buy a gilt maturing in two years' time, say, gilt *B* in Example 4.5, or a one-year gilt, say, gilt *A*, followed by a further one-year gilt (or, indeed, a three-year gilt which she will sell at the end of two years). The *expected* two-year holding period return from all these investment strategies is the same. If Ms Vortex buys gilt *B*, she will get an annual return of 11% for the two years. If she buys gilt *A*, she will get a return of 10% in the first year. Since $_1f_2$ is 12%, Ms Vortex expects to get a return of 12% on a one-year gilt if she buys it in one year's time (since 12% is the expected future one-year spot rate). Thus, expected return from either strategy is 11% per annum.

The problem with this argument is that the risk inherent in each of the maturity strategies is not the same, even if the *expected* return is. If Ms Vortex wishes to invest for a period of two years, she will ensure a *certain* nominal return by buying *B*. If she buys *A* and then has to reinvest at the end of one year, she runs the risk that next year's r_1 will not be the 12% currently predicted and thus her return is not certain.

The liquidity premium hypothesis is based on the view that investors usually want to lend for a short time and borrowers (in the case of gilts, this is the UK government) wish to borrow long. So, for example, Ms Vortex would have to be paid a premium to invest in, say, a ten-year gilt when she only wishes to invest for two years.

The inflation premium hypothesis is based on the idea that the risk of concern to the investor is not interest rate risk but *inflation risk*. If inflation can only be forecast accurately a short time ahead, investors (such as Mrs Silver in Chapter 2) will prefer to lend short term, as under the liquidity preference argument. So, again, forward rates will include a premium to persuade investors to lend long. Finally, the market segmentation hypothesis presumes that the demand and supply for each maturity of gilt will be different, with the premium being positive or negative according to whether borrowers outnumber lenders or vice versa for that maturity.

In the UK, a typical yield curve since the early 1980s is humped. This provides some support for the market segmentation hypothesis. Short-dated gilts are in demand as investments or reserves by building societies and banks. Long-dated gilts are in demand for the long-term investment needs of pension funds and of life insurance companies managing pension and life policy business. There is less demand for the 7–10-year maturity gilts and that can cause the 'hump' in this maturity band.[10]

---

[10] This hump is also visible in the US Treasury bond yield curve.

Other fixed-interest securities

The discussion of holding period returns of gilts and the importance of the term structure of interest rates applies to all fixed interest securities. In this section, therefore, we content ourselves with highlighting the major differences between gilts and other fixed interest securities.

'Other' fixed interest securities can be divided into five main groups: other 'public' fixed interest securities which include those issued by local authorities and sterling bonds issued by foreign governments; and four groups of 'private' fixed interest securities – debentures and loans, eurobonds, preference shares, and convertibles, three of which we shall discuss here. Convertibles, which entitle the holder to convert from a fixed interest security or from preference shares into ordinary shares, will be discussed in Chapter 6.

Example 4.7 shows the relative importance of these types of fixed interest security compared to gilts, both in terms of market value and turnover.

Example 4.7   Market value and turnover of fixed interest securities

	Market value (£b.)	Turnover (£b.)
Public		
UK gilts	123.2	973.2
Irish government	12.1	33.1
Overseas governments	4.2	7.1
Local authorities	0.3	0.1
UK and Irish companies		
Debentures and loans	10.2	5.7
Eurobonds	53.0	n/a
Preference shares	2.2	3.4
Convertibles	13.6	6.7
Ordinary shares	522.2	318.2

Source: Stock Exchange Quarterly (July–September 1991).

Other public fixed interest securities

Irish government securities are traded on the Dublin Stock Exchange and can be treated in the same way as gilts by Irish investors. Since they are denominated in punts, they include an element of exchange risk (to be discussed in greater depth in Chapter 11) for UK investors. Commonwealth governments traditionally issued long-term debt securities in sterling but, as can be seen from looking at Example 3.2 under the heading 'Other Fixed Interest', this type of security has been replaced by a handful of issues by other governments.[11]

Local authority stocks are considered almost as default-free as government bonds, and examples of these can also be seen in Example 3.2.

Private fixed interest securities

Since these are issued by companies rather than by government bodies, the risk of non-payment of interest attached to these types of securities is greater than for government securities. Because of their additional risk, the returns available on company fixed interest securities are higher than those on gilts. This can be seen in Example 4.8 which gives the redemption yields on a variety of gilts and debentures and loans on 11 March 1993. For example, on that date, 5 year Debentures and Loans yielded 8.49% on average compared with an average redemption yield on medium coupon 5 year gilts of 6.78%, a premium for risk of 1.71%. The premium was slightly smaller, at 1.09%, for 15 year Debentures and Loans. Preference shares coming behind debentures and loans in the liquidation queue, would command a higher premium yield over gilts.

Example 4.7 clearly shows how company fixed interest securities are now dominated by ordinary shares, both in terms of market value and turnover. This has not always been the case. In the nineteenth century, companies could only borrow very short term from the banks. Any long-term debt had to come from investors via the stock market, in the form of debentures, loans, convertibles and preference shares. Recently, however, the banks have become more willing to lend for longer periods and companies have raised the majority of their debt finance from this source. This is highlighted by the new issue statistics shown in Example 4.9 where, from the 1980s, equity issues dominated debt issues on the UK stock exchange.

This decline in importance of company fixed interest securities relative to equity securities on the UK stock exchange can be attributed to several

---

[11] For example, United Mexican States 16½% 2008.

Example 4.8   Financial Times–Actuaries fixed interest indices

FT-ACTUARIES FIXED INTEREST INDICES

PRICE INDICES	Thu Mar 11	Day's change %	Wed Mar 10	Accrued Interest	xd adj. 1993 to date	AVERAGE GROSS REDEMPTION YIELDS		Thu Mar 11	Wed Mar 10	Year ago (approx.)
British Government						**British Government**				
1 Up to 5 years (24)...	129.87	+0.03	129.83	2.08	1.98	1 Low	5 years..........	6.51	6.51	9.10
2 5-15 years (22)..	150.40	-0.26	150.79	1.84	3.03	2 Coupons	15 years..........	7.65	7.56	9.43
3 Over 15 years (8)...	158.47	-0.78	159.72	0.65	3.10	3 (0%-7¾%)	20 years..........	7.93	7.84	9.43
4 Irredeemables (6)..	181.73	-0.33	182.33	2.58	1.48	4 Medium	5 years..........	6.78	6.77	9.77
5 All stocks (60)...	146.09	-0.25	146.46	1.77	2.66	5 Coupons	15 years..........	8.14	8.06	9.54
Index-Linked						6 (8%-10¾%)	20 years..........	8.32	8.23	9.49
						7 High	5 years..........	6.95	6.94	10.00
6 Up to 5 years (2)..	183.90	-0.03	183.95	0.23	1.51	8 Coupons	15 years..........	8.36	8.29	9.66
7 Over 5 years (12)..	172.94	-0.02	172.97	0.62	1.14	9 (11%-)	20 years..........	8.45	8.38	9.58
8 All stocks (14)...	173.26	-0.02	173.29	0.57	1.19	10 Irredeemables(Flat Yield)		8.38	8.34	9.62
						Index-Linked				
9 Debs & Loans (67)..	129.44	-0.65	130.29	2.14	2.24	11 Inflation rate 5%	Up to 5yrs..	2.02	2.00	3.63
						12 Inflation rate 5%	Over 5 yrs..	3.44	3.44	4.44
						13 Inflation rate 10%	Up to 5 yrs..	1.20	1.18	2.99
						14 Inflation rate 10%	Over 5 yrs..	3.27	3.26	4.26
						15 Debs &	5 years....	8.49	8.43	11.02
						16 Loans	15 years....	9.23	9.14	10.78
						17	25 years....	9.46	9.38	10.62

Source: Financial Times (12 March 1993).

factors. Firstly, the relative attractions of each type of fixed interest security have been affected by their respective tax treatments. For example, in 1965 the introduction of corporation tax rendered preference shares relatively unattractive to issue for UK companies in comparison with debentures and loan stocks.[12]

Secondly, the high interest rates and inflation uncertainty of the 1970s made companies unwilling to incur long-term high fixed interest debt commitments and so they increased their dependence on bank loans for debt finance. As the new issue market in company debt dried up, so did the secondary market for these securities, making them relatively unattractive to hold compared to gilts.

However, one new source of debt finance has emerged to replace the traditional debenture and loan stock issues of old. This is the *eurobond market* which is an offshore market, not regulated by the Stock Exchange or the Bank of England, but where UK companies can issue sterling or foreign currency bonds to UK or foreign investors. From the issuer's point of view, the company can choose from a wider variety of types of debt to issue than is available in the UK market, and the investor base for the securities is larger making a successful issue more likely. In addition, since there is little regulation of this market, the documentation required for an issue is less than for a traditional debenture or loan issue. The eurobond

---

[12] Although, some UK companies have recently found preference shares attractive to issue to US rather than UK investors – again driven by tax factors.

Example 4.9   Company security new issue statistics

Year	Debentures and loans (excluding convertibles) £m	Preference shares £m	Ordinary shares £m	Total £m
1950	72	11	46	129
1960	122	10	346	478
1970	212	17	52	281
1980	45	62	1,098	1,205
1990	814	364	12,035	13,213

Source: *Midland Bank Review* (February issues) and *Stock Exchange Quarterly* (July–September 1991). Note that 1980 and 1990 figures include new issues for Irish companies.

market, which includes bonds issued by all types and nationalities of borrower, has become very liquid, making it attractive to investors as well as to issuers.

(i) DEBENTURES AND LOANS

This consists of debentures and loan stocks. Debentures are secured forms of fixed interest debt. Should the borrower default, the debenture-holders can appoint a receiver to sell those assets of the company which represent their security and to reimburse them with the proceeds, whether or not the company is still operating. This security is either a 'fixed' charge on a particular asset such as property or a 'floating' charge. A floating charge gives the debenture-holders more powers and means that investors are secured on all the assets of the company. The managers can buy and sell these assets until the company defaults, at which time the floating charge 'crystallises' and the debenture-holders can sell as many assets as they need to get the money they are owed. Debenture-holders are usually protected by a trust deed which specifies exactly their rights in the event of default and also places restrictions on the company, for example limits on other debt it can issue.

Unsecured loan stock is less protected against default risk in that it has no security. In the event of default, it is only ranked with all the other unsecured creditors, for example suppliers to the company.

So, in addition to inflation and interest rate risk, to which gilts are subject, investors in company debentures and loan stocks are concerned with whether the income of the company will be sufficient to enable it to fund the interest and capital repayments on the securities – that is, with default risk. They are similarly interested in the company's ability to repay its debts in the event of its being wound up[13] before the due repayment date.

Interest paid on both these types of debt capital is deducted from the company's pre-tax profits and so the cost to the company of the interest payments is net of the associated corporation tax liability. From the investor's point of view, the returns and yields on these securities are calculated exactly as for gilts, and income from these investments is taxed at the investor's personal tax rate.

(ii) EUROBONDS

The market for eurobonds developed in the wake of the eurocurrency market which is briefly described in an Appendix to Chapter 11, p. 347. Eurobonds are fixed interest securities issued in several countries at once by a syndicate of banks. Eurobonds are similar in type of security to gilts and debentures and loan stock, since they are issued by governments and companies, except for their international character and their freedom from national regulation.

Eurobonds are issued in bearer form with interest paid annually. They were orginally bought by individual investors who held them to maturity. (The archetypal eurobond investor was said to be a Belgian dentist seeking to avoid payment of tax!) As the market has grown, so institutional investors have acquired eurobonds and a liquid secondary market, run by banks in the main financial centres and not by a single stock exchange, has evolved. Prices of eurobonds are given in the *Financial Times* and Example 4.10 gives an extract showing some *Financial Times* quotations. Because of the market's freedom from government regulation and its access to an international investor base with a wide variety of tax and income requirements, eurobonds have developed in many different forms in response to demand. For example, Example 4.10 shows a variety of currencies of bonds, and some floating rate (rather than fixed rate) and convertible bonds. The sterling eurobonds are hidden under the heading 'Other Straights'[14] and examples include British Land 12 ½% 2016 and Abbey National Treasury 13 ⅜% 1995.

When buying eurobonds rather than gilts, various differences between the two must be borne in mind. Firstly, although technically listed on the Stock Exchange in London, eurobond prices are actually quoted by market makers in eurobonds who may or may not be market makers in UK equities. The larger ones will sell both. Also, the smallest nominal amount which can be bought is normally £1,000, much larger than an equivalent

---

[13] This occurs when the company goes into voluntary or compulsory liquidation.

[14] A 'straight' bond is one which is a conventional fixed interest rate bond with few or no frills. These types of bond are also known as 'plain vanilla'.

Example 4.10 FT/ISMA international bond service

FT/ISMA INTERNATIONAL BOND SERVICE

Listed are the latest international bonds for which there is an adequate secondary market.

Closing prices on April 1

U.S. DOLLAR STRAIGHTS	Issued	Bid	Offer	Chg. day	Yield
ABN 9 1/8 94	200	104¼	105⅝	+¼	6.82
ALBERTA PROVINCE 9 3/8 95	600	107⅛	107½	+⅛	7.02
AUSTRIA 8 1/2 00	400	104	104⅜	+⅛	7.79
BANK OF TOKYO 8 3/8 96	100	102⅞	103½	+¼	7.52
BELGIUM 9 5/8 98	250	108⅞	109⅜	+¼	7.77
BFCE 7 3/4 97	150	101⅜	102	+⅛	7.40
BNP 8 5/8 94	300	105⅛	105½		6.18
BRITISH GAS 8 3/8 99	350	102¾	103¼		7.86
CANADA 9 96	1000	106¾	107⅛	+⅛	6.96
CARCO 9 1/4 96	650	103⅛	104		8.34
CCCE 9 1/4 95	300	106⅞	107¼	+⅛	6.57
COUNCIL EUROPE 8 96	100	102⅜	103	+⅛	7.32
CREDIT FONCIER 9 1/2 99	300	109	109⅜	+⅛	7.76
DENMARK 8 1/4 94	150	104⅛	104½	+⅛	6.30
DENMARK 9 1/4 95	1571	106⅝	107		6.71
ECSC 8 1/4 96	193	103½	104⅛	+⅛	7.32
EEC 8 1/4 96	100	103½	104⅛	+⅛	7.24
EIB 7 3/4 96	250	102⅜	102⅞	+⅛	7.07
EIB 9 1/4 97	1000	107⅝	107⅞	+⅛	7.52
ELEC DE FRANCE 9 98	200	106⅛	106⅝		7.68
EURO CRED CARD TST 9 94	325	103¾	104⅝	+⅛	7.29
EUROFIMA 9 1/4 96	100	106⅜	107⅛	+⅛	7.33
EXPORT DEV CORP 9 1/2 98	150	108⅝	109	+⅛	7.70
FINLAND 7 7/8 97	200	100¾	101½	+⅛	7.67
FINNISH EXPORT 9 3/8 95	200	106¾	107¼	+⅛	7.14
FORD CAPITAL 9 3/4 97	250	105⅜	105⅞	+¼	8.41
GEN ELEC CAPITAL 9 3/8 96	300	106¾	107¼	+⅛	7.43
GMAC 9 1/8 96	200	103½	104⅛		8.05
GUINNESS FINANCE 8 94	200	103⅛	103⅝	+⅛	6.46
IBM INTL FIN 7 3/4 94	200	102⅞	103⅜	+⅛	6.21
IND BK JAPAN FIN 7 7/8 97	200	100⅞	101½	+⅛	7.66
INTER AMER DEV 7 5/8 96	200	101⅝	102⅛	+⅛	7.17
ITALY 8 1/2 94	1500	105½	105¾	+⅛	6.10
JAPAN DEV BK 8 94	150	103¾	104⅛	+⅛	6.06
KANSAI ELEC PWR 10 96	350	108⅞	109⅜	+⅛	7.36
LTCB FIN 8 97	200	100⅛	100¾		7.96
NEW ZEALAND 9 94	850	105⅜	105¾	+⅛	6.49
NIPPON CRED BK 10 3/8 95	150	107⅞	108⅞	+⅛	7.54
NIPPON TEL & TEL 9 3/8 95	200	107	107½	+⅛	6.65
ONTARIO 8 1/2 01	600	101½	102		8.25
ONTARIO HYDRO 11 5/8 94	200	109	109¾	+⅛	6.31
OSTER KONTROLLBANK 8 1/2 01	200	103¾	104⅛	+⅛	7.90
PETRO-CANADA 7 1/4 96	200	100	100⅝	+⅛	7.24
QUEBEC HYDRO 9 3/4 98	150	107⅞	108⅝		8.12
QUEBEC PROV 9 98	200	104½	105	+⅛	8.03
SAINSBURY 9 1/8 96	150	104⅞	105½	+⅛	7.78
SAS 10 99	200	105⅛	106⅛	+⅛	8.97
SBAB 9 1/2 95	500	106¾	107⅛	+⅛	7.03
SNCF 9 1/2 98	150	108⅝	109	+⅛	7.71
STATE BK NSW 8 1/2 96	200	102½	103¼	+⅛	7.77
SWEDISH EXPORT 8 3/8 96	700	103⅞	104¼	+⅛	7.23
TOKYO ELEC POWER 8 3/4 96	300	104⅞	105⅜	+⅛	7.39
TOKYO METROPOLIS 8 1/4 96	200	103⅜	103⅞	+⅛	7.34
WORLD BANK 8 3/8 99	1500	104⅞	105	+⅛	7.65
WORLD BANK 8 3/4 97	1500	106¾	107	+⅛	7.22
XEROX CORPN 8 3/8 96	100	101⅛	102⅛	+⅛	8.04

DEUTSCHE MARK STRAIGHTS	Issued	Bid	Offer	Chg. day	Yield
ABN AMRO 8 1/2 96	500	100⅝	100⅞		8.31
AUSTRIA 6 3/4 99	750	93⅝	94⅛	−¼	7.97
BNP 8 1/4 01	200	100½	101	−⅛	8.16
DEUTSCHE FINANCE 7 1/2 95	1000	97¾	97¾	+⅛	8.41
EIB 5 3/4 98	400	89¾	89¾	+⅛	7.97
EIB 6 1/4 99	600	91⅜	91⅞		7.93
EUROFIMA 8 3/4 96	400	102⅛	102⅝		8.14
FIRST INTERSTATE 5 3/4 96	100	86¾	86¾	+½	9.82
FORD MOTOR CREDIT 9 1/4 94	300	99¾	100		9.32
IND BK JAPAN FIN 5 5/8 96	200	90¾	90¾	+¼	8.40
INTER AMER DEV 9 00	300	105	105½	+¼	8.16
IRELAND 6 1/2 99	300	91⅝	92⅛	+¼	8.13
LUFTHANSA INT FIN 5 7/8 98	500	89½	89½	+¼	8.14
NAT BK HUNGARY 10 3/4 98	500	99⅞	100⅛	−⅛	10.75
SWEDEN 6 1/8 98	300	91⅛	91⅛		8.06
TURKEY 10 3/4 96	500	104⅜	104⅞		9.49
WORLD BANK 0 15	2000	20¼	20⅞	+⅛	6.96
WORLD BANK 5 3/4 96	300	92¼	92⅞	−¼	8.12
WORLD BANK 8 3/4 00	1250	104¼	104¾	−⅛	8.01

SWISS FRANC STRAIGHTS	Issued	Bid	Offer	Chg. day	Yield
ASIAN DEV BANK 6 10	100	88½	89½	−¼	7.13
AUSTRIA 4 5/8 98	100	88½	89	−¾	7.09
CHUBU ELEC POWER 6 3/4 01	300	99	99¼		6.90
COUNCIL EUROPE 4 3/4 98	250	89¼	89¾		7.04
EEC 5 1/2 00	100	91	91½	+½	6.91
EIB 6 1/2 98	800	99⅝	99¾	+⅛	6.57
ELEC DE FRANCE 7 1/4 06	100	101½		+½	7.07
FINLAND 5 3/8 95	150	94¾		−¼	7.07
GENERAL MOTORS 7 1/2 95	100	98	99		8.28
JAPAN DEV BK 5 1/2 94	100	96¼	97	−¼	7.73
KOBE 6 3/8 01	240	98½	98¾	+¼	6.59
NEW ZEALAND 4 7/8 99	200	88	88½		7.15
QUEBEC HYDRO 5 08	100	77	78½	−1	7.52
WORLD BANK 5 03	150	85	85½	+½	6.95
WORLD BANK 7 01	600	102¼	102⅜		6.66

YEN STRAIGHTS	Issued	Bid	Offer	Chg. day	Yield
AUSTRIA 4 3/4 94	30000	99¼	99½		5.19
CREDIT FONCIER 5 1/4 94	20000	99⅜	99⅞		5.49
DENMARK 7 95	40000	104¼	104⅝	−⅛	5.33
EIB 4 5/8 94	40000	99⅜	99¾	−⅛	4.94
ELEC DE FRANCE 5 5/8 96	20000	100	100⅝	−¼	5.62
FINLAND 6 3/4 96	50000	103¼	103½	−⅛	5.81
INTER AMER DEV 7 1/4 00	30000	109⅛	109⅜	−¼	5.81
KANSAI ELEC PWR 4 5/8 94	60000	98½	98⅞	−⅛	5.40
NIPPON TEL & TEL 5 7/8 96	50000	101⅜	101¾	−¼	5.51
NORWAY 5 1/8 95	50000	99½	99¾	−⅛	5.31
SNCF 6 3/4 00	30000	106⅝	106⅞	−¼	5.69
SWEDEN 5 5/8 95	20000	100⅜	100⅞	−⅛	5.49
WORLD BANK 6 3/4 00	50000	107⅛	107⅜	−⅜	5.61

OTHER STRAIGHTS	Issued	Bid	Offer	Chg. day	Yield
BAYERISCHE VEREINS INT 7 94 LFr	600	94	95		10.01
COPENHAGEN TEL 8 5/8 96 LFr	600	98¼	99¼		9.17
WORLD BANK 8 96 LFr	1000	96¾	97¾		8.99
ENERGIE BEHEER 8 3/4 98 Fl	500	101¾	102¼		8.38
UNILEVER 9 00 Fl	500	104	104½		8.30
ALBERTA PROVINCE 10 5/8 96 C$	500	103¾	104⅛		9.41
BELL CANADA 10 5/8 99 C$	150	103⅞	104½		9.84
BRITISH COLUMBIA 10 96 C$	500	101⅞	102¼		9.42
EIB 10 1/8 98 C$	130	103⅛	104⅛		9.41
ELEC DE FRANCE 9 3/4 99 C$	275	101¼	101¾		9.49
FORD CREDIT CANADA 10 94 C$	100	100	100⅜	+⅛	9.95
GEN ELEC CAPITAL 10 96 C$	300	102⅜	102⅞	+⅛	9.27
KFW INT FIN 10 01 C$	400	102⅛	102⅝	+⅛	9.63
NIPPON TEL & TEL 10 1/4 94 C$	200	102¾	103¼		9.70
ONTARIO HYDRO 10 7/8 99 C$	500	104¼	104⅝	−⅛	10.00
OSTER KONTROLLBANK 10 1/4 99 C$	150	103⅜	103⅞		9.57
QUEBEC PROV 10 1/2 98 C$	200	102⅜	102⅞		9.97
BELGIUM 9 1/8 96 Ecu	1250	100⅞	101		8.85
CREDIT LYONNAIS 9 96 Ecu	125	98¾	99⅞	−⅛	9.37
DENMARK 7 5/8 96 Ecu	250	93¾	94½		9.55
EEC 7 5/8 94 Ecu	200	96⅞	97⅜		9.48
EIB 10 97 Ecu	1125	105½	105¾	−⅛	8.56
FERRO DEL STAT 10 1/8 98 Ecu	500	104⅜	104⅝		9.10
ITALY 10 3/4 00 Ecu	1000	109⅞	110		8.97
UNITED KINGDOM 9 1/8 01 Ecu	2750	102⅜	102½	−⅛	8.72
BP AMERICA 12 1/4 96 A$	100	106¾	107¼	+⅛	10.07
COMM BK AUSTRALIA 13 3/4 99 A$	100	115¼	115⅝		10.65
EKSPORTFINANS 12 3/8 95 A$	75	108¼	108¾	+⅛	9.23
EUROFIMA 14 5/8 94 A$	75	110	110½		9.16
MCDONALDS CANADA 15 95 A$	100	112⅞	113⅜		10.10
NAT AUSTRALIA BANK 14 3/4 94 A$	150	109¼	109¾		9.11
STATE BK NSW 14 1/4 99 A$	100	116⅛	116½	−⅛	10.95
UNILEVER AUSTRALIA 12 98 A$	150	107½	107⅞	+⅛	10.27
VOLKSWAGEN INTL 15 94 A$	100	110	110½	+⅛	9.41
ABBEY NATL TREAS 13 3/8 95 £	100	105¼	105¾	−½	11.14
ALLIANCE & LEICS 11 3/8 97 £	100	100	100⅜	−½	11.36
BRITISH GAS 12 3/4 95 £	300	104⅛	104½	−½	10.96
BRITISH LAND 12 1/2 16 £	150	101½	102	−2⅜	12.68
DEUTSCHE BK FIN 11 94 £	225	100⅛	100½	−¼	10.86
EIB 10 97 £	636.5	98⅜	98¾	−⅝	10.43
FINLAND 10 1/8 97 £	100	98⅛	98½	−½	10.62
ITALY 10 1/2 14 £	400	99½	99⅝	−¾	10.55
LAND SECS 9 1/2 07 £	200	84¾	85⅛	−⅞	11.69
NORWAY 10 1/2 94 £	200	99⅜	99¾	−¼	10.85
ONTARIO 11 1/8 01 £	100	102	102½	−¾	10.75
SEVERN TRENT 11 1/2 99 £	150	100⅞	101¼	−⅝	11.29
SKANDINAVISKA ENSK 13 1/8 95 £	100	104	104½	−½	11.41
TOKYO ELEC POWER 11 01 £	150	102¼	102½	−½	10.59
WORLD BANK 11 1/4 95 £	100	101⅛	101⅝	−½	10.78
ABBEY NATIONAL 0 96 NZ$	100	66½	67½		9.47
BNP 12 96 NZ$	50	109⅜	110⅜		9.12
CEPME 10 95 FFr	2000	101⅞	102¼		9.27
ELF-AQUITAINE 9 99 FFr	600	99⅜	99⅞		9.10
EURATOM 7 5/8 98 FFr	500	93⅜	93¾	+⅝	9.05

FLOATING RATE NOTES	Issued	Bid	Offer	C.cpn
ALLIANCE & LEICS 0.08 94 £	300	99.48	99.63	10.7675
BANCO ROMA 0.03 01	200	92.93	94.11	4.4050
BELGIUM 1/16 97 DM	500	99.96	100.06	9.6875
BFCE −0.02 96	350	100.16	100.26	4.9175
BNP 05	300	97.65	98.50	5.5625
BRITANNIA 1/10 96 £	150	99.04	99.24	10.7875
CCCE 06 ECU	200	99.91	100.02	9.8594
CITIZENS FED 0.15 96	100	99.47	99.85	5.0000
CREDIT FONCIER −1/16 98	200	100.09	100.19	5.3438
DENMARK −1/8 96	1000	99.75	99.86	4.1875
DRESDNER FINANCE 1/32 98 DM	1000	99.94	100.04	9.5938
ELEC DE FRANCE 1/8 99	400	101.16	101.84	5.2500
FERRO DEL STAT 94	200	101.03	101.35	4.4375
HALIFAX 1/10 94 £	200	99.92	100.02	10.5375
IRELAND 98	300	99.67	99.77	4.4600
ITALY 00	500	100.96	101.24	4.5000
LEEDS PERMANENT 1/8 96 £	200	99.36	99.53	10.9375
LLOYDS BANK 1/10 PERP S.3	600	79.08	81.00	4.5375
MITSUI FIN ASIA 1/8 96	100	99.95	100.05	5.2500
NAT WEST FIN 3/16 05	400	93.00	93.96	5.5000
NEW ZEALAND 1/8 96	250	100.23	100.33	4.8130
RENFE 98	500	99.99	100.10	5.0000
SOCIETE GENERALE 96	300	99.71	99.81	4.5625
STATE BK VICTORIA 0.05 99	125	98.70	98.95	4.3625
UNITED KINGDOM −1/8 96	4000	99.99	100.02	4.0625
YORKSHIRE BS 1/10 94 £	165	99.57	99.67	10.5375

CONVERTIBLE BONDS	Issued	Conv. price	Bid	Offer	Prem.
BURTON GROUP 4 3/4 01 £	110	2.38	130	131¾	
CHUBB CAPITAL 6 98	250	86	[illegible]	102¼	+31.93
EASTMAN KODAK 6 3/8 01	300	50.67	[illegible]	100⅝	+24.26
GOLD KALGOORLIE 7 1/2 00	65	1.0554	[illegible]	84	+41.42
HANSON 9 1/2 06 £	500	2.5875	[illegible]	100¼	+19.62
HAWLEY 6 02 PREF	400	19.1	[illegible]	101	
HILLSDOWN 4 1/2 02 £	150	3.97	117½	118½	
LAND SECS 6 3/4 02 £	84	6.72	[illegible]	77¾	+31.91
LASMO 7 3/4 05 £	90	5.64	[illegible]	75½	
MITSUI BANK 2 5/8 03	200	2332.6	[illegible]	60½	+25.32
MOUNT ISA FIN 6 1/2 97	100	2.283	96	97	+8.98
OGDEN 6 02	85	39.077	81½	82½	+42.34
SEGA ENTERPRISES 3 1/2 96	200	13018	100	101	+36.20
SMITH & NEPHEW 4 02 £	90	1.775	121¼	122⅜	+44.44
SUMITOMO BANK 3 1/8 04	300	3606.9	60⅝	61⅝	+35.67
TEXAS INSTRUMENTS 2 3/4 02	300	82⅞	89⅜	90⅜	
THORN EMI 5 3/4 04 £	103	7.16	120¼	121¼	+16.82

* No information available - previous day's price
‡ Only one market maker supplied a price

STRAIGHT BONDS: The yield is the yield to redemption of the bid-price; the amount issued is in millions of currency units. Chg. day = Change on day.
FLOATING RATE NOTES: Denominated in dollars unless otherwise indicated. Coupon shown is minimum. Spread = Margin above six-month offered rate (‡three-month §above mean rate) for US dollars. C.cpn = The current coupon.
CONVERTIBLE BONDS: Denominated in dollars unless otherwise indicated. Cnv. price = Nominal amount of bond per share expressed in currency of share at conversion rate fixed at issue. Prem = Percentage premium of the current effective price of acquiring shares via the bond over the most recent price of the shares.

Data supplied by International Securities Market Association.

Source: *Financial Times* (2 April 1992).

gilt and with much less liquidity. This is why small investors who wish to buy one or more eurobonds should intend to hold them to maturity.

Secondly, the way in which the accrued interest is calculated for euro-bonds differs from the accrued interest method for gilts. The eurobond method is known as the '30/360' method, because traders in eurobonds assume 30 days in each month and hence 360 days in each year. Also, accrued interest can be more important in sterling terms since coupons are only paid annually, on provision of the coupon which has been detached from the bond certificate. For example, if a 10% coupon sterling eurobond pays interest on 16th August each year and the settlement date for the purchase of the bond is 2 April, the accrued interest would be calculated as follows:

Number of days accrued

April 2–30	=	28
May	=	30
June	=	30
July	=	30
August	=	16
Total	=	**134**[15]

Accrued interest

$$\frac{134}{360} \times 10 = £3.72 \text{[16]}$$

Thirdly, care must be taken when comparing the redemption yield on a eurobond with the redemption yield on a gilt. Since gilts pay coupons semi-annually, we showed in Chapter 3 (p. 81) how the yield is calculated on semi-annual cash flows and then multiplied by two to give an annual figure. Thus, if both a gilt and a eurobond have 10% redemption yields, the gilt's true yield would be understated relative to that of the eurobond, because no account would have been taken of the compounding potential of the semi-annual coupon. In order to make accurate comparisons, the eurobond yield must be reduced to a semi-annual equivalent or the gilt yield compounded up. In this case, we could compound the true semi-annual yield of 5% on the gilt as follows:

$$(1 + .05)^2 - 1 = 0.1025$$
$$= 10.25\%$$

yielding an extra 25 basis points compared to the eurobond.

---

[15] This compares with 136 under the UK gilt system of actual days.

[16] This compares with £3.73 for the equivalent coupon gilt.

(iii) PREFERENCE SHARES

These are not strictly speaking fixed interest securities since preference shares are equity and not debt securities and so pay dividends rather than interest. However, because of the fixed nature of most preference shares' dividends, they are valued in the same way as fixed interest securities and are for that reason included in this chapter rather than Chapter 5 on Ordinary Shares.

Preference shares form part of the share capital of the company and so holders can be viewed as part-owners of the company. In return for accepting a fixed rather than a variable amount of dividend, preference shareholders rank before ordinary shareholders who are entitled to whatever is left after all creditors, debt-holders and preference shareholders have been paid. Preference shareholders suffer less uncertainty of income than ordinary shareholders since they know how much income they expect to get. However, the company does not *have* to pay the preference dividend as it does with debt interest. It is in the interests of the ordinary shareholder for the company to pay the preference dividend since no ordinary share dividends can be paid until it has. (With 'cumulative' preference shares, all previous years' unpaid preference share dividends have to be made up before any ordinary dividends can be paid.) Also, preference shares usually rank before ordinary shares, but after debt capital, on a winding up of the company.

It can be seen that preference shares occupy a middle position between debt capital and ordinary shares. Preference shareholders are not strictly subject to default risk, as are other fixed interest securities, since they are part-owners of the company and not creditors who can put the company into liquidation. However, they do run the risk of not receiving a fixed-dividend payment or being fully repaid on winding up. Their risk is greater than the debt-holders' default risk but less than the ordinary shareholders' uncertainty of income.

Another difference between preference shares and debt capital is their tax position. Since the introduction of corporation tax in 1965, preference and ordinary share dividends have been paid out of after-corporation-tax profits. This is in contrast to interest on debt capital which is paid out of the company's pre-tax profits and hence is allowable against the company's tax bill. This tax disadvantage has contributed to the decline of the preference share as a source of funds for companies. The main reason for the continued presence of preference shares on the stock market is the fact that the majority, although perhaps issued in the 1930s or before, are irredeemable.

When looked at from the investor's viewpoint, care must be taken when preference shares are compared with other fixed interest securities all of which are quoted gross (before) income tax. The net preference dividend can be grossed up as in the following example. If a company has 4.9% preference shares in issue quoted at £75 per £100 nominal, the net interest yield on the preference shares will be:

$$\textit{Net interest yield} \quad = \frac{4.9}{75} \times 100$$

$$= \mathbf{6.5\%}$$

Assuming a 25% personal tax rate, the gross interest yield will be:

$$\textit{Gross interest yield} \quad = \frac{4.9}{75} \times \frac{100}{75} \times 100$$

$$= \mathbf{8.7\%}$$

Preference shares do have one advantage to *corporate* investors. In their case, the dividends count as 'franked' income, meaning income which can be offset against the holders' corporation tax bill. This is why well over 75% of all preference shares are held by corporate investors.

A similar tax advantage applies to US corporate investors, and this has encouraged them to buy recent issues by UK companies of floating rate preference shares. Another recent trend has been the issue of convertible preference shares, in other words, preference shares convertible at the option of the holder into ordinary shares. These can be valued using option techniques and are therefore discussed in more detail at the end of Chapter 7 on Options.

Summary

This chapter has discussed how to make investment decisions concerning fixed interest securities, a subject often neglected in investment texts. The chapter has concentrated on gilts, by far the most important type of fixed interest security traded on the UK Stock Exchange, since the valuation of other types of fixed interest security is based on the method used for gilts.

The measures used in Chapter 3 to describe gilts were examined to see how they could help investors to choose between gilts. One of the main requirements was a tool to be able to quantify the interest rate risk of each gilt. This was found to depend on the coupon and on the maturity of the gilt, and a single number, known as 'duration' or 'average life' was derived to measure this interest rate risk accurately. Armed with the duration of each gilt, investors can calculate how many gilts or futures contracts to buy or sell in order to hedge their interest rate risk.

The chapter then described how, given the prices of different maturity and coupon gilts, the underlying term structure of interest rates could be derived. It was seen that the spot and forward rates implicit in the term structure could be used to derive market estimates of future interest rates more accurately than was possible with redemption yields. Given this knowledge, investment decisions could then be made according to investor beliefs (relative to market estimates) of future interest rates.

The chapter concluded with a brief outline of the major differences between gilts and other types of fixed interest security. These included debenture and loan stocks, eurobonds, and preference shares.

Problems

1. Mr Long is considering, in January 1993, investing in low coupon 'shorts' for a period of one year. He has narrowed his selection down to

Gilt	Price £	Redemption yield (%)
Treasury 3% 1988–98	76⅞%	8.0
Treasury 3% 1995	89½%	7.0

   (i) If Mr Long believes that yields in general are going to fall by 1%, which gilt would he choose and why?
   (ii) Calculate the 'duration' for each of the above gilts. Assume an annual coupon. Does the duration measure help Mr Long's choice?
   (iii) Is Mr Long right in looking simply at redemption yields? Explain the problems in using redemption yields.

2. From prevailing gilt prices in January 1993, current spot interest rates have been calculated:

Year	Spot rate (%)
1993	11.50
1994	11.20
1995	11.00
1996	10.80
1997	10.50
1998 onwards	10.00

  (i) What shape is the current yield curve? Is this inconsistent with the inflation or liquidity premium hypothesis?
 (ii) What are the forward rates for 1993 onwards?
(iii) Calculate, using the spot rates, the current market prices of the following gilts:
  (a) 5% Treasury 1995
  (b) 15% Exchequer 1995
  (c) 5% Treasury 1997
  assuming annual interest payments and redemption payments occur at the year end.
 (iv) The redemption yields of gilts (a), (b) and (c) are 11, 11.2 and 10.6% respectively. Why is the redemption yield of gilt (b) higher than the redemption yields (a) and (c)?
  (v) If all redemption yields were to fall by 2%, which of the three gilts would experience the greatest *percentage* price change? What factors could cause such a fall in redemption yields?
 (vi) Suppose Miss Tery wishes to repay a loan of £10,000 in 1995, which gilt should she buy to minimise the risk that she will not be able to meet the loan?

3. The following information is from the *Financial Times* of 24 March 1992, which for the purpose of this question should be assumed to be today's date.

	Clean price £	Interest yield (%)	Redemption yield (%)
Treasury 8¼% 1993	98⅜	8.39	10.17
Exchequer 12½% 1994	104²³⁄₃₂	11.94	10.25
Exchequer Gas 3% 1990–95	88½	3.39	7.25
Treasury 12¾% 1995	107¹⁷⁄₃₂	11.82	10.12

  (i) Explain the meaning of the terms 'interest yield' and 'redemption yield' and discuss the shortcomings of their use for investment decision-making.
 (ii) Explain the meaning of the term 'spot' interest rates and 'forward' interest rates. Estimate, from the above table, approximate spot and forward interest rates for the next three years. What do they tell us about the market's current expectations concerning future interest rates? Assume, for simplicity, that interest on these gilts is paid annually in arrears and that the gilts are all redeemable on 24 March in their respective years.
(iii) Suppose you believe that, in one year's time, one- and two-year spot interest rates will be 2% per annum less than predicted by current forward interest rates. Which of the above gilts would you buy? How much would you stand to make, per £100 nominal, if you buy today and sell, ex dividend, in one year's time?

4. The following fixed interest securities are listed in ascending order of *gross* redemption yields.

	Gross redemption yield (%)
3% PRO Redeemable Debentures 2005	8
Treasury 13½% 2005	10
XZY 10½% Unsecured Loan Stock 2005	11
JLK 6% Redeemable Preference Shares 2005	14

(i) If all the corporate securities had been issued by the same company, in which order would you have expected them to be listed, and why?

(ii) Suggest possible reasons why the securities are in the order listed in the above table.

(iii) Outline the main differences between unsecured loan stock and preference shares. Why are preference shares usually irredeemable?

(iv) Describe the main advantages of gilt-edged securities as fixed interest investments over similar corporate securities.

Ordinary shares

Introduction

We examine in this chapter the valuation of ordinary shares. Ordinary shares, or equities as they are also known, are by far the most important type of security issued by UK and Irish companies. On 31 March 1992, there were 797 loan capital securities and 1,068 preference shares of UK companies quoted on the Stock Exchange (including the Unlisted Securities Market) compared to 2,313 ordinary shares,[1] and yet the ordinary shares represented 95% of the market value of all these UK corporate quoted securities. The ordinary shares were worth £543b., over four times more than the market value of UK gilt-edged stock of £133b. Despite this, ordinary shares represented 26% of the total market value of the UK Stock Exchange on that date. This percentage figure is misleading, since 58% of

---

[1] Including deferred ordinary shares, i.e. shares with one or more rights of the ordinary shareholders for example the right to dividends, deferred until some specified time in the future. Strictly, the rights attached to a share are determined by the terms of the issue and the company's constitution, rather than by its name, which can sometimes mislead. The rights of a listed share can be found by referring to the *Stock Exchange Official Year Book* (see n. 3 below).

the Stock Exchange's total market value consisted of the securities of overseas companies, that is, shares which are quoted primarily on overseas stock exchanges. If these shares are excluded, UK and Irish company ordinary shares represented 72% of the market value of the Stock Exchange with gilts contributing a further 18%. The bulk of the remainder is eurobonds, referred to in Chapter 4.

Turnover in equities during 1991 was £318b., including intra-market maker business, compared with £1,113b. for gilts. Thus, although ordinary shares have a greater market value than gilts, they have a lower turnover. As explained in Chapter 3, the high turnover in gilts is due to the volatility of interest rates and the large average size of each transaction, £1,500,000 compared to £44,000 for ordinary shares. The small average size of bargains in equities reflects the greater involvement of the small investor in ordinary shares as opposed to fixed interest securities.

In fact, this involvement is one of long standing. As industries grew, in the late nineteenth and early twentieth centuries, companies began to raise much-needed capital by issuing securities to the public. Initially, fixed interest securities were the most common form of security issued. Then, as the need for capital increased even further, company owners became unable to raise additional debt on acceptable terms and turned to issuing shares (both preference and ordinary), thereby encouraging investors to participate more fully in the risk and return of their companies. Ordinary shares, in particular, offered the prospect of unlimited returns with the proviso of coming last in the queue after debt-holders, creditors and preference shareholders in the event of a liquidation. Small investors, eager for high returns, were willing to accept this greater risk of ordinary shares because their liability on fully paid-up shares was limited to the amount they invested.[2] If a company went into liquidation with liabilities exceeding assets, shareholders, unlike partners in a partnership, would not have to provide additional funds with which to repay all the creditors.

As the stock market developed, both UK and overseas companies came to the UK investor for funds. A glance at a *Stock Exchange Official Year Book*[3] of sixty years ago reveals that UK and overseas corporate securities of many more different types were in issue than are quoted today. Securities such as redeemable preference shares, convertible debentures and deferred ordinary shares abounded, with a company possibly having well over a dozen different types of security in issue, offering a wide variety of different levels of risk and return. Corporate securities are now much reduced in number and type, with fixed-coupon securities being mostly in

---

[2] Shareholders who held partly paid shares (now no longer allowed by the Stock Exchange for listed shares) were liable for the unpaid element of their shares in the event of a liquidation.

[3] An annual publication by the Stock Exchange, giving details of all securities listed on the Stock Exchange.

the form of straight debentures, unsecured loan stocks and preference shares. The decline in number of these securities can be attributed to such factors as the nationalisation of the utilities (590 companies were merged when the gas companies were nationalised in 1948 compared with *one* new company when privatised in 1986), takeovers and mergers, the decline in popularity of certain fixed interest securities discussed in Chapter 3, and the lower issue costs associated with larger issues of a single type of security. Convertible unsecured loan stock, a fixed interest security convertible into ordinary shares, is still relatively popular but pure equity is by far the most important type of corporate finance raised through the stock market. In 1991, new equity issues on the UK Stock Exchange totalled £18b., representing 84% of all corporate new issues of securities.[4]

Although the small investor still takes a reasonably active part in the market for ordinary shares, his role has diminished in the past few decades *despite* the efforts made by the Conservative governments of the 1980s to encourage individual shareholdings through successive privatisations and the creation of tax-exempt Personal Equity Plans or PEPs. Example 5.1 shows who held listed UK company ordinary shares in 1957, 1969, 1981 and 1989. The proportion, in market value terms, of ordinary shares held directly by the private investor has declined inexorably, from nearly 66% in 1957 to 21% in 1989.

Example 5.1   Beneficial ownership of listed UK equities 1957–89

Category of beneficial shareholder	% of total shareholdings at market value			
	1957	*1969*	*1981*	*1989*
Personal sector	65.8	47.4	28.3	21.3
Investing institutions				
Pension funds	3.4	9.0	26.7	30.4
Insurance companies	8.8	12.2	20.5	18.4
Unit trusts	0.5	2.9	3.6	5.9
Other financial companies	7.7	10.4	6.8	3.2
	20.4	34.5	57.6	57.9
Overseas holders	4.4	6.6	3.6	12.4
Other	9.4	11.5	10.5	8.4
Total	100.0	100.0	100.0	100.0

Source: Wilson (1980) and *Stock Exchange Quarterly* (April–June 1991).

---

[4] Excluding eurobonds. Sterling eurobonds accounted for a further £8.8b. in 1991, but much of this was issued by UK financial institutions.

The private investor has not completely abandoned the stock market. He has changed his method of investment from direct holdings to indirect holdings via insurance companies, pension funds, unit and investment trusts. The primary reasons for this are the tax advantages of, say, investment coupled with life assurance, the often compulsory saving in the form of pension contributions, and the benefits of risk reduction through diversification[5] offered by such funds as unit trusts. As a result, the overall level of direct investment by the private investor has fallen. Investors have been partly discouraged by sudden falls in share prices, such as occurred in 1987 and again in 1989, and have concentrated their savings in housing, life assurance, and pensions.

As can be seen from Example 5.1, institutions have consequently become increasingly important investors on the Stock Exchange over the past twenty-five years, with pension funds, insurance companies, unit trusts and other financial companies (including investment trusts) increasing their percentage holding of UK equities from 20% in 1957 to 34% in 1969 and 58% in 1989. This change has been due to the massive increase in funds they have experienced as the private investor switched from direct to indirect investment. In fact, the effects of this change in type of investor have been substantial, and the whole of Chapter 12 is devoted to institutional investors and their impact on the stock market.

As a result, although the 'players' may have changed, the overall level of interest in the stock market, and in particular in ordinary shares, has been maintained, and this interest will no doubt continue as long as money can still be made and lost from this kind of investment. Investment in equities is to many people the most fascinating form of Stock Exchange investment.

More recent interest in investment in overseas securities (in particular in overseas equities), following on from the relaxation of exchange controls in 1979, to some extent has distracted the attention of UK investors from UK securities. The additional factors which need to be taken into consideration for investment in shares denominated in foreign currencies, for example the risk of changes in exchange rates, are discussed in Chapter 11, but the basic methods of valuing shares are the same, whatever the currency.

This chapter concentrates on the valuation of ordinary shares. The first section details their fundamental characteristics and is followed by a description of the major ways in which ordinary shares are issued to the public. The chapter then goes on to consider the advantages and disadvantages of the most commonly used measures of share performance as well as the more complex problem of how the expected holding period return on a share can be estimated. The chapter concludes with a description of the major share valuation models used in practice.

---

[5] Diversification, a form of reduction through pooling, was mentioned in Chapter 2, p. 56, and is discussed in detail in Chapter 8.

Description of ordinary shares

Ordinary shares are issued by limited liability companies as risk capital. As with fixed interest securities they have a nominal value (required by law), and this can be very different from the market value or price of the share. For example, a 25p nominal share can be quoted at, say, 437p. The actual nominal value of a share may reflect the original amount of money raised by issuing shares (since no share may be issued at a price below its nominal value) but, more likely, has more to do with the tradition in the UK of keeping nominal (or par) values below £1. Ordinary shares are usually described simply by the name of the company which issued them and by the nominal value, as can be seen in the extract from the *Financial Times* given in Example 5.2. Note that the nominal value is given there only if it differs from the most common value of 25p.

Most (but not all) the ordinary and deferred ordinary share prices are given in the *Financial Times*, which lists the share prices of those companies whose shares are traded on the Stock Exchange and who are willing to pay £1,200 fee to the *Financial Times*. The shares are divided into forty-one sectors, for example Brewers & Distillers; Food Retailing; Hotels & Leisure: and Media.[6]

Example 5.2 shows details of the shares listed under the heading of 'Media'. Notice how the shares having the symbol ■ are those deemed to be the most actively traded stocks and those marked with a ✾ are those listed on the USM.

Some companies have the letter A after their name – in Example 5.2 the Daily Mail and Grampian TV. This is because these types of companies have two classes of ordinary share capital, perhaps denominated 'O' and 'A', with the 'O' shares having preferential voting rights over the 'A' shares. This type of capital structure was originally used by family-controlled companies as a means of raising new equity funds without sacrificing control. A small number of ordinary shares with voting rights controlled the company whilst the majority of shareholders held non-voting ordinary shares, identical in all respects save for the right to vote in General Meetings. For example, Marks and Spencer had this dual share structure until 1966 when the 'A' ordinary shares were enfranchised. The Stock Exchange now encourages companies to have only one class of voting share. The exceptions are primarily in the media sector, say with television stations, communications companies, and newspapers (as in the case of Grampian TV, Reuters, and the Daily Mail, where it is considered

---

[6] For a full breakdown, see the back pages of the *Financial Times*. These share groupings are based on those of the FT-Actuaries share indices discussed later in the chapter. They also include three categories for non-UK shares – Americans, Canadians and South Africans – which are represented in the FT-Actuaries World indices.

Example 5.2   Ordinary share prices

MEDIA

	Notes	Price	+ or -	1991/92 high	low	Mkt Cap£m	Yld Gr's	P/E
Abbott Mead	†♦	393		393	175	57.8	2.6	16.8
■Acsis	‡	1³⁄₄		9	1¹⁄₄	4.83	‡	—
Addison	G	14¹⁄₂#		15¹⁄₂	10	9.59	1.4	♦
Adscene	†	95		104	23	14.1	2.8	18.2
■Aegis		114	+1	244	100	141.2	7.0	♦
9³⁄₄ pc Cv Pf		58		94	55	41.8	16.8	—
Allied Radio		18¹⁄₂		27	18	7.77	—	—
8pc Cv 2001		£84¹⁄₂		£107¹⁄₂	£84¹⁄₂	4.91	9.5	—
■Anglia TV		243	+1	246	140	107.1	5.1	11.1
■Avesco		14		31	14	7.87	14.3	10.8
✲BBB Design		10		25	10	0.82	—	—
Birkdale		46	−1	78	29	7.49	—	—
Black (A & C)		340		510	340	5.19	5.1	26.0
■Blenheim		445		463	190	408.8	2.3	20.2
✲Border TV	†	77		87	24	7.79	3.6	10.7
Bristol Eve		291		326	210	47.6	5.3	24.9
✲CIA	†	155		164	83	18.0	2.8	12.0
■Capital Radio		200	−3	231	134	134.3	3.5	21.0
■Carlton Cmtns		561	−5	574	350	1,036	3.7	18.8
6¹⁄₂ p Pf		88	−1	90	61	143.4	9.8	—
Central ITV		1325		1348	480	354.2	2.9	38.8
Chiltern Radio		140		164	120	9.09	1.9	—
✲City of Lon PR		40		58	35	3.08	10.3	9.0
✲Clarke Hooper	†	36		75	36	7.75	16.3	12.8
Colorgraphic		54		108	54	9.22	‡	6.2
■✲Craton Lodge		2		2¹⁄₄	1³⁄₄	8.25	—	—
■✲Crown Comms		28		*60	22	17.1	—	—
Daily Mail A		£69¹⁄₄		£69¹⁄₂	£37	343.3	2.3	21.4
■EMAP	†	256	−4	268	179	359.4	3.6	19.8
Euromoney		610	+2	613	338	122.8	4.9	18.4
Fitch RS	‡	45		61	29	3.00	‡	27.8
6p Cv Pf '07		27		30	11	1.18	25.0	—
✲ GWR		260		268	195	7.74	1.0	35.1
■Gold Greenlees		224		226	63	38.3	4.9	10.3
Goodhead	‡	46		61	26	6.89	‡	—
Grampian TV A	†	145		151	59	22.9	3.8	11.3
✲Greenwich Comm		7		8	4	0.49	—	—
■HTV		69	−1	71	33	47.7	7.2	15.9
Harrington K'bride	L	148		148	125	14.0	4.1	♦
Haynes Publ	†	165		178	105	16.7	2.0	18.4
Headline Book		180		181	116	20.0	2.2	♦
Holmes March		22		*100	22	5.37	20.0	♦
Home Counties		180	−1	205	160	18.0	6.1	9.6
Independent f£	†	328		340	213	119.8	5.0	13.5
■Intl Bus Comms		5	+¹⁄₄	6¹⁄₂	1	7.60	—	—
Johnston Press	†	293		298	158	79.1	2.3	16.9
LWT 3.9375p Pf	u	270		279	80	239.2	2.6	19.3
■Lopex	‡	45		80	31	10.2	‡	4.7
MMI		16		24	16	1.39	10.4	7.0
Warrants		5		9	5	0.09	—	—
Maxwell Comm		35#		241	1	228.2	—	—
✲Metal Bulletin		208		208	106	19.1	4.9	♦
✲Metro Radio		184		185	124	31.3	3.6	27.5
Midlands Radio		105		108	62	14.1	3.2	30.3
Mirror Group	R	125#		130	86	501.0	7.0	11.2
■More O'Ferr		243	−1	*285	160	77.7	7.6	♦
News Corp A$		807	+32	807	134	2,948	0.5	13.7
■News Int Spec Div		350	+3	358	85	604.3	1.8	—
Novo	‡a	72		103	62	7.03	‡	—
Osprey Comms	‡	15		49	15	2.08	‡	3.5
■Pearson		828	−15	844	590	2,252	3.7	19.0
Ports & Sund	†	370		370	225	44.4	3.0	14.9
Quarto $	†	146		149	87	23.9	4.5	8.8
✲Radio Clyde		313		319	222	27.9	3.5	26.4
■Reed Int	†	525	−17	563	343	2,924	3.8	20.7
■Reuters		1154	−3	1226	673	5,031	2.0	♦
■Saatchi		16	−¹⁄₂	*31	9¹⁄₄	252.3	—	—
Scottish TV	h	764		778	257¹⁄₂	181.5	2.5	23.8
■✲SelecTV		20¹⁄₂		*27¹⁄₂	7⁷⁄₈	22.1	—	63.3
■Shandwick	Ma	28	−1	145	28	23.1	18.0	1.7
■Southern Radio		46		92	42	13.0	—	—
✲Southnews	‡	67	+4	74	44	10.2	‡	—
✲Sterling Pub	‡	41	+1	77	18	11.6	‡	12.3
Sunset & Vine		193		195	110	10.2	2.4	22.7
TSW	s	46		86	41	9.79	9.4	12.6
■✲TV—am	a	87	−1	217	77	57.8	26.4	♦
■TVS Ent	‡	4¹⁄₄		31¹⁄₂	3¹⁄₂	2.87	‡	0.2
7.4pc Pf '08		26		59	20	13.0	—	—
Thames TV	‡	183		352	172	90.7	‡	10.2
Thomson		775	−20	875	715	4,323	4.3	13.2
✲Trans World		68		*88	46	27.1	—	—
■✲Trilion		8		21	7	4.55	—	—
Trinity Intl		270		272	179	151.2	4.0	12.5
Tyne Tees	H	295	−9	322	230	30.6	6.6	8.3
Ulster TV	†	194	−1	197	116	20.4	4.6	44.8
■Utd News	†	371	−6	418	278	736.6	7.5	15.6
■WPP		92	−1	231	31	49.9	—	2.5
■ Warrants		8		17	1¹⁄₂	0.41	—	—
8¹⁄₄ p Cv Pf		38	−1	52	16¹⁄₂	81.3	28.9	—
Watmoughs	H	415	+1	*420	294	136.3	3.4	18.3
Yorkshire TV		160		312	148	56.4	10.0	7.4

Source: Financial Times (12 March 1992).

appropriate for a change of ownership to a potentially unsuitable owner to be hindered by the use of a dual ordinary share structure).

Other companies in the list are significant in having more than one type of security listed. This is because such companies – TVS Ent(ertainment) and WPP in Example 5.2 – have a more complex capital structure than just ordinary shares, with two or more kinds of equity capital. Most of the types of equity capital other than ordinary shares fall into one of three categories: preference shares, convertible preference shares, and warrants. Preference shares, as described in Chapter 4, are a form of equity with a fixed dividend, with no right to put the company into liquidation in the event of non-payment of the preference dividend. As well as in the type of dividend they receive, they also differ from ordinary shares in that they do not carry the right to vote in General Meetings and may not even have a vote in the event of a takeover. This can be serious, since if preference shareholder approval is not required for a takeover bid to be successful, preference shareholders may find themselves left out in the cold, with no bid for their shares at all. Convertible preference shares and warrants will be discussed in more detail in Chapter 7, after options have been described. As far as votes are concerned, however, warrants are unlikely to carry any voting rights, whereas recent issues of convertible preference shares, for example, the 8 1/4% convertible preference shares issued by WPP, would have voting rights in the event of a takeover or a reconstruction and such voting rights would ensure that this type of shareholder is not penalised by major changes to the company.

Fixed interest securities, whether company- or government-issued, have a specified maturity or spread of redemption dates. Ordinary share capital, however, like most preference share capital, is usually irredeemable. Ordinary shares thus have an indefinite life, unless the company is wound up, voluntarily or involuntarily, or there is some scheme to reduce the share capital, or the company is taken over. So, except when the company is forced into liquidation, the voting shareholders have a say in whether their shares should be repaid or acquired.[7].

The attraction of ordinary shares is their limited liability and possible unlimited returns. An investor in fully paid ordinary shares can never lose more than 100% of his investment but his return on the shares can be far greater than this.[8] Fixed interest securities have specified income, in the form of the periodic coupon and the repayment on maturity. Although the holding period rate of return can vary according to changes in price of the fixed interest security, the returns on fixed interest securities will on

---

[7] Although, if 90% of a company's shares have been acquired or are held by another company, the remainder can be compulsorily purchased if 100% control is desired.

[8] This is why the probability distribution of returns on shares is not quite normal; returns can never be less than -100% but can exceed $+100\%$.

average be less volatile than those on ordinary shares, where both the income *and* the future share price are uncertain.

Because of this extra volatility of share price and income, and hence of holding period return, shares are in general riskier than fixed interest securities. As a result, ordinary shareholders require a risk premium for taking on this additional risk, that is, a return in excess of the return on less risky investments, such as gilts. We saw in Chapter 2 that risk could be measured by the standard deviation of the probability distribution of returns. In fact, in Chapter 8, we shall find that the relevant measure of risk for an ordinary share is its risk *relative* to other shares and to the stock market as a whole, since shares are not usually held in isolation but as part of a diversified portfolio.

Methods of issue

There are two types of issue of equity, which can be defined as primary and secondary. In a primary issue, shares are listed on the Stock Exchange for the first time[9] and in a secondary issue new shares in a company are added to those already listed on the Stock Exchange by means of rights issues, takeovers, or scrip issues.[10]

Primary issues

Companies cannot issue shares via the Stock Exchange unless they are listed and have thereby satisfied the listing requirements of the Stock Exchange, for example as to size and profit record[11] and paid their listing fee. The rationale for such a primary issue, or flotation as it is sometimes called, is usually that a privately held company has grown to such an extent that the owners want the ability to raise further capital through the issue of shares and also feel the need to take some profits by selling part of their shareholdings on the open market. However, in the 1980s, a new source of

---

[9] Although, as we shall see below, some shares issued in privatisations were listed in their pre-nationalisation days. One example is Rolls Royce, nationalised in 1971 and privatised in 1987.

[10] A scrip issue is often referred to as a capitalisation or bonus issue.

[11] For full details of existing requirements, see the *Stock Exchange Yellow Book* published by the Stock Exchange. For a briefer description of both the main stock market and Unlisted Securities Market requirements, see Chapter 1, pp. 8–10 and p. 20.

flotations came from the massive privatisation programme carried out by successive Conservative governments. These companies were often utilities, such as British Telecom and British Gas, which had a long track record of offering a service at a low cost rather than of attempting to maximise shareholder wealth. Other privatisations were simply the sale of shares in companies which had previously been listed on the Stock Exchange but which had been bought by the government when they, or companies which owned the shares, experienced financial difficulties. Examples of this are the Rolls Royce and BP privatisations.

Such flotations are normally carried out by merchant banks on behalf of the company or government in the form of an offer for sale at a fixed price agreed between the issuer, the merchant bank, and the broker to the issue who advises on market sentiment. Primary issues are normally underwritten by the merchant bank. In other words, if potential investors are not interested in the offer for sale at the agreed price, and do not fill in application forms included with the offer document describing the company's past and prospects for the future, the merchant bank (and other financial institutions to whom it has sub-underwritten) contract to buy any new shares not taken up by investors at the agreed price. In this way, the company can be sure of receiving the new funds whatever happens to the stock market during the offer period. The underwriters charge a fee for underwriting and sub-underwriting which, under the UK system, is around 2–5% of the amount of the issue but can be substantially more for new issues as large as international as Eurotunnel or Eurodisney.

If an offer is oversubscribed, as many primary issues and privatisations were in the 1980s, the issuing company and their financial advisers can choose what is known as an *allotment policy*. The normal mechanism is to divide applications into bands according to the number of shares applied for and to allot percentages of the total available to each band. In this way, preference can be given to large or small applicants as desired. Before the privatisation programme, it was normal to favour large bidders since this reduced the administrative costs of maintaining the shareholder register. With privatisations, however, the government attempted to encourage small shareholders by favouring the smallest bidders. An example could be:

Bids for up to 100 shares   Allotted in full

Bids for between 100
and 300 shares   50% of bids allotted

Bids for over 300 shares   20% of bids allotted

As Example 5.1 earlier in this chapter shows, however, the long-run trend away from direct private ownership of shares was not halted by this.

Successful applicants simply sold their shares at a profit to the investing institutions as soon as the shares were quoted on the market – a process known as 'stagging' a primary issue.

An offer for sale which is oversubscribed is considered to be a success although too much unsatisfied demand reflected in the shares immediately trading at a substantial premium to the offer price could imply that the shares were sold too cheaply. An alternative method of primary issue which aims to maximise the amount of money raised by the sale of the shares is the new issue by tender. In this case, would-be investors bid the price that they are prepared to pay for the shares and those with the highest bids get the shares. This method does not require underwriting, thereby saving the issuer fees, but does expose the issuer to the risk of selling the shares at an unsatisfactory price or, if a minimum share price to be tendered is imposed, to having a rump of shares unsold. The other disadvantage is that it requires investors to be confident of the price they are prepared to pay for the shares since there will be no quick profits in the form of a premium over the offer price, as is the case in a fixed price offer. A variant of the new issue by tender method allows investors to bid either a particular price of their choice or the average price at which the shares are allotted. In this way, the government was able to use the new issue by tender method for one or two privatisations without frightening away the less sophisticated investor. However, most new issues, whether privatisations or not, use the fixed price method in order to maximise interest in the new issue.

Secondary issues

Secondary issues occur when an already listed company seeks to raise additional risk capital via an issue of shares or when, in a takeover, new shares in the bidding company are issued to the shareholders of the company being acquired, in compensation for the sale of their shares to the bidding company.

(i) NEW FUNDS

Additional equity funds for companies listed on the Stock Exchange are usually raised by means of rights issues, where existing shareholders are entitled to subscribe for new shares at a fixed price, usually below the existing price, in proportion to their existing shareholdings. General offers for sale by companies whose shares are already listed (as opposed to companies coming to the Stock Exchange for the first time, as was discussed above) are severely restricted in order to protect existing shareholders from what is known as 'dilution of equity'.

For example, suppose the ordinary shares of Crumbly Cakes plc are quoted at 100p. A rights issue of one for four is announced, with the subscription price set at 80p per share. Mrs Tooth holds 1,000 shares and is therefore entitled to purchase 250 new shares at 80p each. She will then hold 1,250 shares and these shares should be worth, other things being equal, their previous market value plus the new funds invested:

1,000 shares at 100p $\qquad$ = £1,000

New funds invested: 250 at 80p = $\underline{\quad£200}$
$\qquad\qquad\qquad\qquad\qquad\qquad$ £1,200

Ex rights price $\qquad = \dfrac{£1,200}{£1,250}$

$= \mathbf{96p}$

So, in most cases, a rights issue will cause the share price to fall after the issue, in the case of Crumbly Cakes plc from 100p to 96p. This will affect comparison with the year's high and low prices for the shares and, in Example 5.2, an asterisk next to the 1991/92 high and low prices, as with Crown Comm(unication)s, for example, indicates that these have been adjusted to take account of a rights issue during the period. Of course, the announcement of a rights issue may be contemporaneous with the announcement of a profitable project (for which the funds are needed) and lead to an increase in the value of the company by greater than the amount raised by the rights issue. A famous example of this was the 1989 rights issue by Polly Peck (now defunct) to raise money for its acquisition of the non-US Del Monte brand names. The Polly Peck shares rose by one third on the announcement of the rights issue.

If Mrs Tooth does nothing, her shares would in this case fall in value from £1,000 to £960. So, in the case of a rights issue, action must be taken, either to take up the rights to buy new shares or to sell the rights to someone else.[12] These rights will be worth approximately the difference between the subscription price and the price of the share after the rights issue:

----

[12] The management of the company may arrange to sell any shareholders' rights not taken up and to distribute the proceeds of the sale to those shareholders. In such instances, the shareholders may take no action if they so wish without financial loss. However, in cases where the amount is small, the management may sell the rights not taken up for the benefit of the company.

Ex rights price   = 96p

Subscription price = (80p)

Value of one right = **16p**

However, if Mrs Tooth sells her rights, she will have reduced her level of investment and percentage holding in Crumbly Cakes plc. A third alternative is for Mrs Tooth to sell just sufficient of her existing shares to be able to take up the rights without having to invest 'new' money. She would then maintain the level of her investment at £1,000.

Rights issues are usually underwritten by a merchant bank. In other words, if investors such as Mrs Tooth choose not to take up their rights (for example, if the share price falls below the subscription price on the new shares and the rights thus become worthless), the merchant bank, and other financial institutions to whom it sub-underwrites, contract to buy any new shares for which the rights have not been taken up. In this way, the company can be sure of receiving the new funds, whatever happens to its share price between the offer date and the closing date of the issue. An alternative to underwriting is a 'deep-discount' rights issue, where the subscription price is set so far below the current share price that there is no risk that the share price will fall below the subscription price during the three weeks or so of the issue period. In this way, the costs of underwriting, usually around 2½% of the funds raised, can be avoided. However, deep-discount issues are not as common as underwritten rights issues, since to raise the same amount of money as with a conventional rights issue, more new shares would have to be issued. If, as is usual, dividends per share are maintained at pre-rights issue levels, a deep-discount rights issue would involve companies in substantially increased dividend payments.

(ii) TAKEOVERS

Company *A* can choose how to offer to pay for its acquisition of company *B*. It can pay in cash or issue some new securities. The most common type of security used in such offers is ordinary shares, since one risky security is replaced by another. The shareholders of company *B* can then decide whether to sell any shares received and reinvest elsewhere or whether to retain the shares and hold an investment in company *A*. The possible advantage of shares over cash to the shareholders of company *B* is that, by holding on to the company *A* shares they receive, they can delay any crystallisation of capital gains tax.

(iii) SCRIP ISSUES

A scrip issue of shares is one where new shares are issued to existing shareholders, in proportion to their existing holdings (as for a rights issue) but where no payment is required. In the case of both takeovers and rights issues, the value of the company issuing the shares changes. In the case of scrip issues, there should be no fundamental change in the value of the company. An example of a scrip issue could be where Crumbly Cakes issued one new share free for each two existing shares held. No money would change hands. Mrs Tooth would then hold, instead of 1,000 shares, 1,500 shares. Since the value of the company would remain the same, other things remaining constant, each share would be worth

$$\frac{£1,000}{1,500} = 67\text{p}$$

and Mrs Tooth's total investment in Crumbly Cakes would still be worth £1,000. An *accounting* change would take place in the sense that, in the balance sheet, the share capital would be increased and the reserves reduced, by the amount of the scrip or 'capitalisation' issue.

One may ask why companies make scrip issues. One reason is to reduce the share price, since UK company share prices are usually below £5. It can be seen, for example, in Example 5.2 that only nine UK media company shares (excluding convertibles) are quoted at prices greater than £5. However, this convention for low share prices is disappearing, particularly for internationally traded UK shares, because shares in the US, Europe and Japan traditionally have much higher quoted share prices than in the UK.

Another reason for a scrip issue is that it provides a method of paying non-cash dividends. If Crumbly Cakes announces a 'scrip dividend' of 1/20 new share for each existing share held, what effect will this have on Mrs Tooth's investment?

Existing holding	1,000 shares
Scrip dividend $\frac{1}{20} \times 1,000$	50 shares
Ex dividend holding	1,050 shares

Again, no money has changed hands and the value of the company should therefore remain the same. Mrs Tooth's ex dividend holding must still be worth £1,000, and so the ex scrip share price will be £1,000/1,050 = 95.25p.

Mrs Tooth has not received any cash dividend. She can, however, sell her scrip entitlement of fifty shares at 95.25p if she wants income from the shares. She would thus realise approximately £47.50 and might be liable to capital gains tax on the proceeds. Mrs Tooth would then be left with 1,000 shares worth £952.50. (She could, of course, sell part of her existing holding if she wished, without a scrip issue, and achieve the same effect.)

If Crumbly Cakes had chosen to pay a cash dividend, say, of 4.75p per share, instead of making a scrip issue, Mrs Tooth would have received £47.50 dividend (on which she would be liable for income tax[13]) and be left with shares worth, ex dividend, 100p − 4.75p or 95.25p per share, giving the same total of £952.50.

So, a scrip issue may affect the tax position of the investor differently from dividends, and alter the balance sheet of the company, but it does not change the fundamental value of the company or the value of Mrs Tooth's investment. Of course, if the company announces some other news at the same time as a scrip or rights issue, such as increased profits, or the issue is felt to be telling the market something about the company's future prospects, the ex-scrip or ex-rights price may be greater than the theoretical price calculated in the above examples.

Summary measures for ordinary shares

We saw in Chapter 2 that the two most important measures for any security were its expected return and its risk. Risk could be measured by standard deviation and expected return by the expected holding period return,

$$HPR = \frac{D_1 + (P_1 - P_0)}{P_0}$$

where P_0 was the cost of the security, D_1 the expected income to be received during the period, and P_1 the expected value of the security at the end of the period.

In Chapter 3, we looked at surrogate measures for the holding period return on gilts and other fixed interest securities, the interest yield and the redemption yield. The interest yield is given by

$$\text{Interest yield} = \frac{D_1}{P_0}$$

---

[13] The amount of capital gains tax and income tax to which Mrs Tooth is liable will depend on her individual tax position.

and is a measure of the income yield from the security, ignoring the capital gain or loss element, $(P_1 - P_0)/P_0$, because P_1 cannot be determined with certainty during the life of the gilt. However, P_1 is usually known with certainty at maturity, since it must then equal its redemption value. Thus, an estimate of total holding period return can be made, provided the gilt is assumed held to maturity, and this return, converted into an annual average, is termed the redemption yield.

In the case of ordinary shares, any estimate of expected holding period return is subject to much greater uncertainty. Since there is usually no fixed redemption date or redemption value for shares, P_1 is not known for *any* point in the future. Also, D_1 is not certain since the size of the future dividend D_1 is at the discretion of the company and depends on future profitability. Alternative summary measures have to be used for ordinary shares.

The extract from the *Financial Times* shown in Example 5.2 on p. 130 gives, as well as details of the previous day's closing share price, the year's highest and lowest prices for the share and the market capitalisation of the company, the two major summary measures for ordinary shares. These are the gross dividend yield and the price–earnings ratio. In Monday's edition of the *Financial Times*, the *net* dividend and the dividend cover are also given. The dividend cover is described in an Appendix to this chapter, on p. 159.

Dividend measures

The dividend yield is the equivalent for ordinary shares of the interest yield for gilts. It is merely the income element of the holding period return, D/P_0, ignoring the capital gain or loss term, $(P_1 - P_0)/P_0$.

Dividends on UK company shares are usually paid twice yearly, in the form of an interim and a final dividend. The value of these dividends is determined by the Board of the company, subject to shareholder approval, and is usually announced only a few weeks before payment. So future dividend payments are unknown until shortly before they are paid. The dividend yield given in the *Financial Times* refers to *last* year's *known* interim plus final dividends and not the *unknown* dividends for *next* year. The dividend yield calculated is thus D_0/P_0 and not D_1/P_0 and represents part of the historic rather than the expected holding period return. In the case of gilts, D_1 is always equal to D_0 and so D_1/P_0 is known with certainty. With ordinary shares, there is no guarantee that D_1 will exceed D_0 or even equal D_0, although the company may drop hints about expected future dividends, for example:

> In respect of the financial year ending 1 April 1989, the Directors expect, in the absence of unforeseen circumstances, to recommend a single dividend, payable in August 1989, of 5.0p net per Share.[14]

A tentative indicator of future dividends can be found in the symbols under Notes next to the company names in Example 5.2. These attempt to give an idea of trends in dividend payments – an indication of what D_1 will be relative to the D_0 given. For example, the symbol † shows that the most recent interim dividend (the first half of D_1) has been raised relative to last year's interim (or resumed), and the symbol ‡ shows that the interim dividend has been reduced or passed.

Thus the investor might expect, looking at Example 5.2, a raised total dividend next year for, say, Abbott Mead and a reduced dividend for R. S. Fitch. Letters in the Notes indicate a specific dividend calculation such as the letter G next to Addison (Group) which denotes, in this case, a dividend calculation allowing for a scrip or rights issue which was pending at the time.

The dividend yield is given *gross* in the *Financial Times*, although dividends on UK company shares are declared and paid *net* of personal income tax at the basic rate. The calculation of gross as opposed to net dividend is to aid comparison with other types of security, since, for example, interest yields and redemption yields on gilts are also quoted before income tax.

The present system of tax on dividends has been in operation since 1973. Known as the 'imputation tax system', it was designed to render a company's liability to corporation tax the same, whether or not it paid dividends. Example 5.3 gives an example of two identical companies, one paying a dividend and one not, to show how the total amount of corporation tax paid is the same for both companies.

If a company pays a dividend to its shareholders, it remits to the Inland Revenue a tax payment equivalent to income tax on the gross dividend at a reduced rate. This rate is to be 20% from 5th April 1994, falling from a rate of 25% during most of the 1980s. At 20%, the tax payment will be 20/100 of the gross dividend and 20/80 of the net dividend.[15] The net dividend is received by the shareholder who is then only liable to additional tax if he pays tax at greater than the basic rate. If he is liable to tax at the basic rate, he simply retains the net dividend. If he (or an institution such as a pension fund) is not liable to income tax, he may claim a refund, equivalent to 20/80 or 25% of the net dividend from 1994. The company offsets its dividend tax

---

[14] From the British Steel new issue prospectus (1989).

[15] There is an interim rate of 22.5% for the 1993/94 tax year.

Example 5.3　Impact of dividend policy on corporation tax liability

	Company A £000	Company B £000
Profit before tax	1,000	1,000
Corporation tax at 33%	(330)	(330)
Profit after tax	670	670
Net dividend paid	0	160
Advance corporation tax (ACT) paid on dividend (currently $^{20}/_{100}$ of gross, or ¼ of net, dividend)	0	40
Gross dividend paid	0	200
Tax paid		
ACT	0	40
Mainstream corporation tax	330	290
TOTAL TAX PAID	330	330

payment, known as advance corporation tax or ACT, against it total corporation tax bill and so pays 33% regardless of whether or not it pays a dividend.[16]

For example, in Example 5.2, Euromoney is shown to have paid a total net dividend for its last financial year of 22.5p per share. This was equivalent to a gross dividend of

$$\frac{100}{75} \times 22.5 = 30.0p$$

at the then ACT rate of 25%, and the shareholder was deemed to have paid the difference between 30.0p and 22.5p in income tax. The gross dividend yield, D_0/P_0, was

$$\text{Gross dividend yield} = \frac{30.0}{610}$$

$$= \mathbf{4.9\%}$$

and this is given in Example 5.2 in the next-to-last column.

---

[16] This simple exposition ignores companies with no liability to mainstream corporation tax against which ACT can be offset, for example, companies making a loss. In such a case, a dividend payment will render the company liable to additional tax which can only be offset when the company becomes profitable again.

In Chapter 3, we saw that the interest yield on a gilt was a function of its coupon – a low coupon gave a low interest yield and a high coupon a high interest yield. The interest yield gave no indication of the total return to be expected on a gilt, that is, the return including a capital gain or loss on disposal. Similarly, with ordinary shares, dividend yield is no measure of the total expected return, which will consist of both income and any capital gain. The companies shown in Example 5.2 have gross dividend yields on ordinary shares varying between 0 and 26.4%. These yields will be more a reflection of company dividend policy than company profitability.[17] So, as with interest yield, we find gross dividend yield an incomplete measure of expected return.

The accounting profit reported after deduction of tax, interest on any corporate borrowings and preference share dividends is known as the earnings available to ordinary shareholders. These earnings, divided by the number of shares in the company, give the earnings per share (*eps*). It is up to the company directors to decide how much of these earnings will be paid out as dividends. For example, in recent years, companies making losses or reduced profits have sometimes chosen to maintain the same level of dividend, out of past earnings, rather than reduce it in line with current earnings. Any earnings not paid out are termed retained earnings and can be reinvested by the company to yield future profits although, of course, a company with a high-dividend policy and low retained earnings can finance future investments with borrowings or a new equity issue instead.

Example 5.4 compares the holding period return of two companies with identical earnings, prospects and risk but with different dividend payout policies.

In this idealised example we can see that company X pays out all the period's earnings as dividends. Since it has no retained earnings, the value of the company would in theory remain unchanged, with $P_1 = P_0 = 100p$. Company Y pays a smaller dividend of 10p per share, retaining 40p per share within the company. Company Y should therefore be worth 40p per share more at the end of the period, so $P_1 = 140p$. Both companies yield the same holding period return, with company X's being provided in the form of dividend and company Y's partly from dividend and partly from capital gain on the share. Of course, in practice, company X and company Y could differ in their investment policies; for example, company Y might invest its 40p per share retained earnings profitably and company X might not borrow an equivalent amount to invest. In this case, company Y's share price would increase by more than 40p to reflect its increased future profits. However, if investment policy were the same for these two companies, dividend policy would be irrelevant. In this example, both companies have identical prospects and risk, and identical earnings of 50p per

---

[17] Although an unusually high dividend yield indicates a low share price and hence a company in difficulties.

Example 5.4   Impact of dividend policy on HPR

	Company X	Company Y
No. of issued shares	100	100
Share price, P_0	100p	100p
Earnings for ordinary shareholders	£50	£50
Per share	50p	50p
Net dividend	£50	£10
Per share	50p	10p
Retained earnings	0	£40
Per share	0	40p
Share price, P_1	100p	140p
$HPR = \dfrac{D_1 + (P_1 - P_0)}{P_0}$	$\dfrac{50 + (100 - 100)}{100}$	$\dfrac{10 + (140 - 100)}{100}$
HPR	**50%**	**50%**

share, and so should yield the same total return to the investor. Thus earnings and not dividend yields are indicators of total returns. Unfortunately, as we shall see below, earnings figures as reported in company accounts are not good indicators of future profitability.

Despite the difficulties surrounding the measure of dividend yield, it does, as with the interest yield, provide some indication of the *current* level of income from a share. This can be useful to investors who are liable to different tax rates on their dividend income and on their capital gains from shares. Pension funds, paying tax on neither, should be indifferent to the dividend yield on shares.[18] A private investor, on the other hand, will compare his marginal tax rate on dividends with his marginal tax rate on capital gains. In most countries, capital gains are taxed more lightly (or not at all) compared with income and some investors will therefore prefer shares with a low dividend yield. However, in the UK, the top rate of income tax is currently the same as the capital gains tax rate (40%) although capital gains tax is only payable on realised gains and there is an allowance for inflation. So, in the UK, there is no strong bias towards low income yield shares.

As was mentioned earlier, an additional problem that the dividend yield has, compared with the interest yield, is that dividends are expected to grow whereas interest payments generally are not. However, in cases where companies try to maintain a stable dividend policy, some attempt

---

[18] Although see Chapter 12, p. 361, for a discussion of why this is not so in practice.

can be made to estimate future dividends from past dividends. For example, a company could maintain a regular 5% growth in dividend or always pay out a constant proportion of earnings. In this latter case, it would be said to have a constant dividend payout ratio, where this is equal to

$$\text{Dividend payout ratio} = \frac{dps_0}{eps_0}$$

We can see from Example 5.4 that company X has a dividend payout ratio of 50p/50p = 100%, whereas company Y's ratio is 10p/50p = 20%.

The reciprocal of the dividend payout ratio is termed the dividend cover:

$$\text{Dividend cover} = \frac{eps_0}{dps_0}$$

What does dividend cover tell us? From our example, we see that company X has dividend cover of one and company Y dividend cover of five times. A dividend cover of one in the case of company X would seem to imply that a downturn in earnings might force company X to cut its dividend next year. On the other hand, a dividend cover of five in the case of company Y would appear to imply that company Y can afford to maintain the present level of dividend payments in the future even if it suffers a severe drop in earnings. The major problem with the use of dividend cover for such conclusions is that the level of a company's earnings may give a very misleading picture of its ability to pay dividends. Dividends are paid out of cash flow whereas the earnings figure is an accountant's calculation which includes non-cash items such as depreciation. Also, dividends may be paid out of reserves on the balance sheet but not out of share capital or share premium account. So, a company may have high reported earnings and yet have insufficient cash or share reserves to maintain its dividend payments.

As we shall see in the next section, any measure which uses reported earnings is subject to difficulty of interpretation. See also the Appendix to this chapter for further problems in calculating dividend cover. Because of these difficulties, as of March 1992, the *Financial Times* ceased to show dividend cover as one of its summary measures for ordinary shares.

Price–earnings ratio

One of the two summary measures provided in Example 5.2 is concerned with dividends – the gross dividend yield. And yet, we have seen that dividend measures provide inadequate estimates for holding period return. The problem lies in the fact that, for any ordinary share, future earnings, dividends and share prices are unknown. The only information available concerns the current share price and past earnings and dividends.

The second summary measure given in Example 5.2 is the price–earnings or *PE* ratio, which uses two known figures, the current share price divided by the latest earnings per share. Thus,

$$PE_0 = \frac{P_0}{eps_0}$$

Because they are ratios, the dividend yield and dividend cover can be used for comparative purposes, unlike the net dividend per share. This use for comparison also holds true for the *PE* ratio and is its major attraction. For example, the *PE* ratios of the ordinary shares in the Media sector are given in the last column of Example 5.2. They range from 10.2 to 63.3 and, because they are ratios, questions such as 'Why is Home Counties' *PE* ratio almost double that of Lopex?' can be asked.

What does the *PE* ratio tell us? That investors are willing to pay 9.6 times last year's reported earnings for Home Counties compared to 4.7 times Lopex's reported earnings. In some sense, Home Counties' earnings could be said to be more expensive and this could be because they are expected to grow faster than those of Lopex in the future. Example 5.5 gives a possible scenario for the two companies. Because, in this scenario, Lopex's earnings are expected to grow more slowly than those of Home Counties, the time taken to earn the share price is the same in both cases, five years. Home Counties appears more 'expensive' because it has a much higher expected growth rate.

So, the comparison of *PE* ratios is an attempt by the investor to use currently available information to find out something about the future expected growth in earnings.

Unfortunately, the expected growth rate in earnings is not the only factor affecting a company's price–earnings ratio. For example, the *PE* ratio will also be affected by the uncertainty surrounding future earnings.

Example 5.5   Explanation of differences in PE ratios

	Company	
	Home Counties	*Lopex*
PE_0	9.6	4.7
P_0	180p	45p
eps_0	18.8p	9.9p
Possible expected annual growth rate in *eps* (%)	32	4
Number of years for cumulative *eps* to equal share price	5	5

So, Home Counties and Lopex could have the same *expected* growth rate, but the variability (standard deviation) of the predicted earnings growth could be higher for Lopex than for Home Counties, either due to a riskier business activity or higher gearing, or both. Because of the greater certainty attached to Home Counties predicted earnings growth, it would be more highly valued than Lopex with its riskier future earnings. So Home Counties could have a higher *PE* because its future earnings are less risky than those of Lopex. Similarly, as we shall see later, dividend payout policy also affects a company's *PE* ratio.

Before we go on to discuss how the *PE* ratio can be used to estimate expected holding period return, several problems which arise when using the *PE* ratio must be mentioned. Firstly, companies which are to be compared may well have different year ends. For example, the *PE* ratio for company *X* could be determined from 1993 earnings whereas the *PE* ratio for company *Y* could be calculated from earnings for the year ended 28 February 1993, almost twelve months earlier. The earnings for the most recent period could be higher due to inflation, reducing *X*'s *PE* ratio relative to *Y*'s. Alternatively 1993 could have been a recessionary period, with many companies' earnings unduly depressed, giving *X* an unnaturally high *PE* ratio relative to *Y*.

This cyclicality problem can be emphasised in another way. Suppose Crumbly Cakes plc trades on a *PE* of 5 and, when its latest earnings are announced, these are declared to be only half those of the previous year. However, the company confidently expects to recover from the downturn and return rapidly to its normal earnings level. Because of this, the share price does not fall and the *PE* ratio doubles to 10; and yet, Crumbly Cakes has not become a high-growth company overnight. An extreme example is when a company declares zero earnings. Should it have an infinitely high *PE* ratio? So, two companies could have high *PE* ratios for completely different reasons, one because it is a high-growth share and the other due to a sudden – but believed temporary – plunge in profits. One way of getting round this problem is to 'normalise' the earnings, that is, to calculate the *PE* ratio using an earnings figure which the analyst believes to be a reflection of the trend in earnings rather than the peaks or troughs. Another method of avoiding this problem is to compare *industries* rather than to compare individual companies. This is because companies in an industry are subject to the same economic cycles and commonly have the same year end. Also, because the *PE* ratios in Example 5.2 are weighted averages for each industry, anomalies caused by individual companies are reduced. Example 5.6 shows the *PE* ratios for each sector or industry.

In the fifth column of Example 5.6 we can see that the average *PE* ratio for the Electricity industry is 8.94 whereas the average for Stores in 17.91. So, Stores are either considered to be companies offering good potential for growth or are recovering from a cyclical downturn. The Electricity industry, on the other hand, has less growth potential.

Example 5.6   PE ratios

FT-ACTUARIES SHARE INDICES

© The Financial Times Ltd 1991. Compiled by the Financial Times Ltd in conjunction with the Institute of Actuaries and the Faculty of Actuaries

EQUITY GROUPS & SUB-SECTIONS — Figures in parentheses show number of stocks per section	Thursday October 24 1991						Wed Oct 23	Tue Oct 22	Mon Oct 21	Year ago (approx)
	Index No.	Day's Change %	Est. Earnings Yield% (Max.)	Gross Div. Yield% (Act at 25%)	Est. P/E Ratio (Net)	xd adj. 1991 to date	Index No.	Index No.	Index No.	Index No.
1 CAPITAL GOODS (181)	805.68	−0.9	9.53	6.03	13.11	30.83	813.07	813.68	819.23	706.18
2 Building Materials (23)	972.42	−1.4	7.61	6.41	17.31	41.32	986.07	987.74	988.69	954.69
3 Contracting, Construction (30)	1057.59	−0.6	8.57	6.95	16.06	49.81	1064.46	1062.69	1057.66	1145.45
4 Electricals (11)	2489.54	−0.4	8.78	5.30	14.43	84.23	2498.86	2494.38	2519.93	1880.00
5 Electronics (25)	1704.82	−0.7	11.21	5.59	11.28	50.62	1717.30	1725.40	1743.41	1574.12
6 Engineering-Aerospace (8)	355.62	−0.4	15.76	7.30	7.66	16.48	357.12	355.49	355.53	418.61
7 Engineering-General (43)	483.25	−0.4	10.16	5.25	12.11	16.55	485.28	485.48	487.80	360.66
8 Metals and Metal Forming (9)	427.71	−6.6	15.35	8.28	7.91	17.48	430.26	430.76	435.60	399.59
9 Motors (12)	336.01	−1.5	7.07	7.17	19.36	14.65	341.21	340.25	348.20	276.46
10 Other Industrial Materials (20)	1559.50	−1.1	8.11	5.23	14.66	56.92	1576.90	1579.09	1594.05	1160.51
21 CONSUMER GROUP (190)	1539.11	−1.0	7.42	3.62	16.67	33.59	1555.14	1549.66	1555.30	1197.35
22 Brewers and Distillers (22)	1924.67	−0.7	8.01	3.49	15.20	38.33	1937.26	1932.93	1932.55	1510.07
25 Food Manufacturing (19)	1193.06	−2.0	9.50	4.19	13.02	29.98	1216.93	1221.27	1218.48	1014.79
26 Food Retailing (17)	2424.49	−0.9	9.07	3.35	14.40	50.36	2445.77	2460.35	2464.98	2283.05
27 Health and Household (23)	3714.50	−1.5	5.44	2.55	21.08	61.57	3771.27	3732.13	3768.85	2439.46
29 Hotels and Leisure (24)	1321.43	−1.5	7.71	5.33	16.03	45.61	1341.13	1329.63	1336.16	1202.38
30 Media (26)	1497.36	−1.4	7.19	4.74	18.17	44.30	1519.26	1523.72	1539.90	0.00
31 Packaging, Paper & Printing (17)	758.46	−0.9	7.41	4.34	16.39	22.51	765.48	765.40	764.95	484.19
34 Stores (33)	1015.64	+0.3	7.32	3.65	17.91	19.48	1012.47	1004.88	1005.60	792.49
35 Textiles (9)	635.97	−0.3	7.27	4.89	17.45	15.49	637.74	637.08	637.27	421.56
40 OTHER GROUPS (110)	1248.84	−1.1	9.62	5.19	13.07	35.79	1262.78	1266.94	1274.96	967.85
41 Business Services (12)	1386.24	−1.2	7.70	4.71	16.15	34.95	1403.46	1405.44	1412.68	0.00
42 Chemicals (21)	1420.57	−2.2	7.10	5.09	17.39	48.39	1452.94	1453.70	1454.39	996.84
43 Conglomerates (11)	1465.88	−2.1	9.87	7.15	12.27	38.76	1497.46	1493.21	1498.92	1298.15
44 Transport (13)	2292.51	−1.4	7.46	4.94	16.60	68.02	2325.13	2333.33	2336.85	1875.89
45 Electricity (16)	1204.95	−1.2	14.58	5.40	8.94	27.53	1219.76	1226.95	1241.57	0.00
46 Telephone Networks(4)	1522.27	......	9.85	3.98	13.29	28.34	1522.00	1538.77	1551.51	1060.68
47 Water(10)	2325.09	+0.4	17.56	6.62	6.30	118.37	2315.98	2310.70	2347.47	1963.61
48 Miscellaneous (23)	1839.68	−1.5	5.32	5.36	26.05	69.91	1868.22	1862.89	1872.86	1524.41
49 INDUSTRIAL GROUP (481)	1265.71	−1.0	8.53	4.58	14.63	34.28	1278.90	1278.23	1284.76	1007.11
51 Oil & Gas (19)	2409.77	−1.5	10.85	5.77	12.18	93.60	2445.74	2447.66	2465.41	2313.48
59 500 SHARE INDEX (500)	1363.49	−1.1	8.81	4.73	14.27	38.99	1378.47	1377.97	1385.37	1114.06
61 FINANCIAL GROUP (91)	771.30	−1.4	−	6.06	−	31.43	782.27	782.73	791.18	686.65
62 Banks (9)	910.31	−1.6	4.58	5.86	41.31	37.46	925.23	923.63	937.77	730.22
65 Insurance (Life) (7)	1432.98	−0.9	−	5.91	−	63.68	1446.45	1449.77	1456.88	1281.63
66 Insurance (Composite) (6)	574.44	−2.4	−	7.64	−	30.72	588.64	590.79	596.18	583.67
67 Insurance (Brokers) (9)	1108.36	−0.7	7.41	6.12	17.66	43.14	1116.41	1116.07	1120.45	862.19
68 Merchant Banks (7)	474.92	−0.2	−	4.45	−	13.08	476.03	472.85	476.08	347.88
69 Property (36)	872.76	−0.9	6.24	5.33	22.72	23.78	880.72	884.27	893.27	938.85
70 Other Financial (17)	257.31	−0.8	11.11	7.14	11.30	10.86	259.26	260.35	261.06	244.57
71 Investment Trusts (70)	1225.05	−0.9	−	3.53	−	27.02	1230.04	1227.43	1231.28	1016.36
99 ALL-SHARE INDEX (661)	1221.71	−1.1	−	4.86	−	36.63	1235.40	1235.05	1242.46	1009.72

	Index No.	Day's Change	Day's High (a)	Day's Low (b)	Oct 23	Oct 22	Oct 21	Oct 18	Oct 17	Year ago
FT-SE 100 SHARE INDEX‡	2528.3	−32.8	2569.7	2524.1	2561.1	2559.5	2575.7	2601.1	2588.7	2088.7

Source: *Financial Times* (24 October 1991).

In fact, companies in the Store sector have a higher average *PE* ratio than the average *PE* ratio for the stock market as a whole. The *PE* ratio for the stock market can be represented by the *PE* ratio of the 500 Share Index, shown in Example 5.6 as 14.27.

However, a major problem with the *PE* ratio, which affects its use in any context, is the quality of the earnings per share figure. Firstly, as already noted, the *eps* is an accounting approximation to an economic determination of income. It is difficult to know how well accounting earnings reflect the economic profits of a company and how a historic earnings figure can indicate the extent to which future cash flows will be affected by economic changes. Economic profits, by definition, can only be assessed by taking a view of the future. Accounting profits are the results of calculations based on conventions in which such a view takes only a limited part and which also depend on personal judgements.

Secondly, different companies use different accounting practices to arrive at their earnings figures, and so the earnings and hence *PE* ratios may not be comparable. For example, suppose company *F* and company *G* are identical in all respects save in their method of accounting for depreciation. Example 5.7 shows how they will have different earnings per share and *PE* ratios whilst remaining, in all economic respects, identical.

Thirdly, the earnings per share figure is fraught with problems in its calculation due to the current tax system on dividends. Earnings can be calculated either on a 'net' basis, representing earnings which allow for the actual tax charge incurred by the company, or on a 'nil' basis, where an earnings figure is determined independent of the company's dividend policy. For most companies, the 'nil' and 'net' *eps* and *PE* ratio calculations will give the same numbers, but for some companies, for example those with substantial overseas earnings, the payment of a dividend will mean unrelievable ACT (since ACT can only be offset against mainstream corporation tax due on *UK* taxable profits), giving a lower 'net' *eps* than 'nil' *eps*.

Example 5.7   Impact of different accounting practices for depreciation on eps and PE ratios

	Company F £m.	Company G £m.
Earnings before depreciation and tax	1,000	1,000
Depreciation*	(100)	(300)
Tax[†]	(300)	(300)
Earnings after tax	600	400
Number of ordinary shares (b.)	10	10
Share price	40p	40p
Earnings per share (*eps*)	**6p**	**4p**
PE ratio	**6.7**	**10.0**

* Company *F* uses straight-line depreciation (10% p.a.); company *G* uses accelerated depreciation (30% of balance p.a.).
[†] Since the same tax allowances for fixed assets will apply to both companies, their actual tax liabilities will be the same.

Example 5.8 Difference between 'net' and 'nil' earnings

		International Irrigation plc £m
Profit before tax		100
Overseas tax at 50% (giving relief from mainstream corporation (tax)		(50)
Profit after overseas tax		50 *
Unrelieved ACT on dividend		(8)
Profit after tax		42 †
Gross dividend	40	
ACT due (20% × 40)	(8)	
Net dividend paid		32
Retained earnings		10

* 'Nil' earnings.
† 'Net' earnings.

For example, in Example 5.8, International Irrigation plc earns profits entirely overseas, but because it pays a dividend it incurs additional tax.

In this example, if International had 100 million shares in issue, the 'nil' *eps* would be 50p and the 'net' *eps* 42p. If the share price were 500p, the 'nil' *PE* ratio would be 10.0 and the 'net' *PE* 11.9. The *Financial Times* publishes *PE* ratios calculated by the 'net' method. However, the dilemma of which *eps* figure to use is admitted by bracketing *PE* ratios where the difference in *PE* ratio calculated by the two methods differ by 10% or more. Also, certain sectors, such as mining, do not have *PE* ratios given at all, since the problems of dividend policy, accounting differences and tax render the *PE* ratios in these instances 'meaningless'.

Despite these fundamental problems with both the meaning of the *PE* ratio and its use for comparative purposes, the *PE* ratio is still commonly used as a summary measure by investors and their advisers, as evidenced by its appearance, however qualified, in the *Financial Times*. Also, the most recent publication by the Accounting Standards Board which discusses earnings per share states that: 'although no one figure will encapsulate a period's results, it is recognised that some users favour having a starting point for their analyses. For this purpose earnings per share should be calculated on profit attributable to ordinary shareholders of the company'.[19]

---

[19] *Financial Reporting Exposure Draft*, para. 68 (December 1991).

This attitude towars the *PE* ratio's usefulness lies behind the accounting profession's concern over providing clear guidelines for the calculation of earnings per share – despite the fact that there is no empirical evidence to show that a company's past earnings per share can successfully be used to predict its future earnings.[20]

Estimate of Holding Period Return

We saw in Chapter 2 that the two most important measures describing a share were its expected holding period return and its risk, measured by the standard deviation of the expected returns. The two summary measures discussed so far, gross dividend yield and the *PE* ratio, have not proved of much help in estimating either risk or return. We have to find alternative means.

The simplest way to express a one-period expected holding period return is

$$\text{Expected } HPR = R = \frac{D_1 + (P_1 - P_0)}{P_0} \tag{5.1}$$

where D_1 is the expected income to be received during the period, P_1 the expected value of the security at the end of the period, and P_0 the cost of the security.

If the share is held for n periods or years, in each of which income is received, as we saw in Chapter 2 (Example 2.5, p. 37) equation (5.1) could be rearranged and extended to give

$$P_0 = \frac{D_1}{(1 + R)} + \frac{D_2}{(1 + R)^2} + \ldots \frac{D_n}{(1 + R)^n} + \frac{P_n}{(1 + R)^n} \tag{5.2}$$

where P_n is the value of the security at the end of n years and D_i the income to be received in the ith year. We also saw that, since P_n could be viewed as the present value of the future dividends from year $(n + 1)$ onwards, the equation for P_0 could be written as the present value of *all* future dividends.

$$P_0 = \frac{D_1}{(1 + R)} + \frac{D_2}{(1 + R)^2} + \ldots + \frac{D_n}{(1 + R)^n} + \ldots \tag{5.3}$$

---

[20] See Brealey (1983) ch. 5.

In equation (5.1), R represents the one-period expected holding period return. In equations (5.2) and (5.3), R is the expected *annual* rate of return whatever the holding period. Yet, we saw in Chapter 3 when considering the redemption yield, R, for gilts that there was no reason why R should be the same in year 1 as it is in year n, since interest rates and required rates of return will vary according to time. So, equation (5.2), for example, should be written:

$$P_0 = \frac{D_1}{(1 + R_1)} + \frac{D_2}{(1 + R_2)^2} + \ldots + \frac{D_n + P_n}{(1 + R_n)^n} \qquad (5.4)$$

However, in the case of ordinary shares, the future P_n and all the future D_i are uncertain and must be estimated. So, the approximation inherent in using R for all years instead of R_i is less important (since R must of necessity be a rough estimate) than in the case of gilts, where the D_i and P_n (at redemption) are known for certain and an accurate assessment of the implicit R_i can be made.

Dividend valuation models

Equations (5.2) and (5.3) are known as dividend valuation models for shares. How can we use them to estimate the expected annual holding period return R?

If we look at equation (5.2), we know P_0 and so we need to estimate the dividend stream, $D_1, D_2, \ldots, D_n$ expected during the holding period and the end-of-period share price, P_n. The holding period can be as long or short as desired and will probably reflect how far into the future the investor feels able to predict the cash flows, D_i. This type of dividend valuation model, given in equation (5.2), is known as a *finite horizon model*, since we consider the cash flows up to a finite horizon in year n.

The dividend stream must be estimated from knowledge of the company's dividend policy and from expectations concerning the company's future prospects, since dividends ultimately depend on the cash flows generated by the company. Even if the company has a declared dividend policy, for example a constant percentage growth or constant payout ratio, it will not be able to maintain this policy if insufficient cash flow is generated.

How can P_n be estimated? It represents the company's share price in n years' time and its value will depend on market views at time n of all future cash flows attributable to the share beyond year n. Since it is impossible to estimate with any degree of accuracy such a share price n, one method would be estimate the *PE* ratio and earnings per share *n* years hence, because

$$P_n = eps_n \times \frac{P_n}{eps_n}$$

so,

$$P_n = eps_n \times PE_n$$

The investor may, despite the problems inherent in the use of *PE* ratios and earnings per share which were discussed earlier, feel more confident about estimating the future earnings per share figure and *PE* ratio than their product, the future share price, P_n.

The *PE* ratio of a company will vary according to expected future growth and risk, and the stage of the economic cycle prevailing. These must be considered from the point of view of year *n*. The earnings per share figure in year *n* will also depend on many factors – the company, the industry and the economy as a whole. It has been found, for example,[21] that around 21% on average of changes in company earnings can be attributed to industry factors and a further 21% to economy-wide factors. Of course, earnings will also reflect accounting conventions and policies, and will thus be even more difficult to forecast correctly than cash flows. Unfortunately, as has already been mentioned, there appears to be no strong trend in earnings, so that a study of past earnings cannot be relied upon to give a good prediction of the future pattern of earnings.

As a result of the problems of estimating P_n, either directly or indirectly through PE_n and eps_n, the alternative method for estimating *R* is to use equation (5.3), obviating the need to estimate P_n. In other words, we consider an infinite horizon model. Since it would be a Herculean task to estimate with any degree of accuracy *all* the future dividends the company will ever pay, simplifying assumptions concerning future dividends must be made. For example, if it can be assumed that all future dividends will grow by a constant percentage, *g*, equation (5.3) becomes

$$P_0 = \frac{D_1}{1 + R} + \frac{D_1(1 + g)}{(1 + R)^2} + \frac{D_1(1 + g)^2}{(1 + R)^3} + \ldots$$

which simplifies to[22]

---

[21] See Brealey (1983) p. 95.

[22] Using the formula for the sum to infinity of an infinite geometric progression,

$$S = a + ar + ar^2 + \ldots ar^n + \ldots = \frac{a}{1 - r}$$

$$P_0 = \frac{D_1}{R - g} \qquad (5.5)$$

Rearranging gives

$$R = \frac{D_1}{P_0} + g \qquad (5.6a)$$

or

$$R = \frac{D_0 (1 + g)}{P_0} + g \qquad (5.6b)$$

This is known as Gordon's growth model.

To use Gordon's growth model, all that is needed to estimate R is last year's dividend, D_0, the current share price, P_0 and the expected dividend growth rate, g. For example, if Battered Biscuits plc has a current share price of 60p, paid a (*gross*) dividend last year of 3p per share, and is expected to increase its dividend by 5% each year, we find from equation (5.6b) that

$$R = \frac{3 (1 + 0.05)}{60} + 0.05$$

$$= 0.05 (1 + 0.05) + 0.05$$

$$= 0.0525 + 0.05$$

$$R = 10.25\%$$

The gross dividend should be used in the Gordon Growth model to yield a gross holding period return R. This should be borne in mind when comparing share returns with, say, the redemption yield on gilts which is quoted gross in the *Financial Times*.

The assumption of constant growth in expected dividends is a simplification of reality. Problems can arise using this model if the company currently does not pay any dividends but is expected to do so in the future, or if it is a small, rapidly growing company with a high dividend growth rate, say 25% per annum. We can see that, in equation (5.5), if g is large, R will not be much greater than g, and so the denominator will be very small, giving a very large (or, when $g = R$, infinite) share price. Since we do not see companies with infinitely large market values traded on the Stock Exchange, we can assume that the very high growth rates currently experienced will not last for ever. This leads us to another form of finite horizon model.

$$P_0 = \frac{D_1}{(1 + R)} + \frac{D_2}{(1 + R)^2} + \ldots + \frac{D_n}{(1 + R)^n} + \frac{D_n (1 + g^*)}{(R - g^*)(1 + R)^n} \quad (5.7)$$

where $D_1, \ldots, D_n$ can be assumed to grow at, say, g per annum, but after year n, the dividend growth rate will be a smaller g^*.

An alternative way of using the dividend valuation model is to transform it into an earnings model. Since the dividend payout ratio is defined to be

$$K_i = D_i/eps_i$$

we can write

$$D_i = K_i \, eps_i$$

and equation (5.3) becomes

$$P_0 = \frac{K_1 \, eps_1}{(1 + R)} + \frac{K_2 \, eps_2}{(1 + R)^2} + \ldots \frac{K_n \, eps_n}{(1 + R)^n} + \ldots \quad (5.8)$$

This type of model allows the investor to forecast future earnings instead of dividends. However, some assumption still has to be made about dividends. It could be assumed, for example, that the dividend payout ratio will remain constant, say at $K = 40\%$. So, equation (5.8) would become

$$P_0 = \frac{K \, eps_1}{(1 + R)} + \frac{K \, eps_2}{(1 + R)^2} + \ldots + \frac{K \, eps_n}{(1 + R)^n} + \ldots \quad (5.9)$$

where $K = 0.4$.

If the same simplification of constant growth is applied to earnings as was applied to dividends, we get

$$P_0 = \frac{K \, eps_0 (1 + g)}{(1 + R)} + \frac{K \, eps_0 (1 + g)^2}{(1 + R)^2} + \ldots + \frac{K \, eps_0 (1 + g)^n}{(1 + R)^n} + \ldots$$

$$= \frac{K \, eps_0 (1 + g)}{(R - g)} \quad (5.10a)$$

or

$$P_0 = \frac{K \, eps_1}{(R - g)} \quad (5.10b)$$

This is the same as Gordon's growth model, since the assumption of constant growth g in earnings and a constant dividend payout ratio must also give constant growth g in dividends. So, the constant growth version of the dividend valuation model can either be used by forecasting dividend growth explicitly or by forecasting both earnings growth and a dividend payout ratio. Unfortunately, as we saw earlier, the evidence is that there is in practice no such trend in earnings growth which means that the simplifying assumption of constant earnings growth (as well as constant dividend payout and constant dividend growth) must be viewed as an approximation to reality.

Before we leave the earnings version of the dividend valuation model, let us take a further look at equation (5.10a). If we divide both sides by eps_0, we get

$$PE_0 = \frac{K(1 + g)}{(R - g)} \tag{5.11}$$

The left-hand side of the equation is simply the PE ratio and the equation, written in this way, allows us to see exactly which factors affect the PE ratio. The term g reflects earnings growth, K shows how much of earnings is paid out as dividends, and R, the holding period return, gives an idea of the riskiness of the share (since the higher the required R, the riskier must be the share). We can now see that the PE ratio will be greater, the higher the earnings growth (as we saw in Example 5.5), but also the higher the dividend payout ratio and the lower the risk of the share. So, despite the limitations of the model, it does allow us an insight into the factors that are likely to affect the value of a share.

All the above methods of estimating holding period return, whether from finite or infinite horizon models, require estimates of future dividends, earnings or share prices. Each model is based on the same fundamental equation for the value of a share, equation (5.2), which simply states that the current value of a share, given by its share price, must be equal to all the future cash flows attributable to that share discounted by the required rate of return given its risk.

Figure 5.1 shows a small sample of the large number of different share valuation models which can be derived from equation (5.2). The choice of model will depend on the investor's subjective estimate of which variables he can best forecast, for example dividends or earnings, growth rates or future PE ratios.

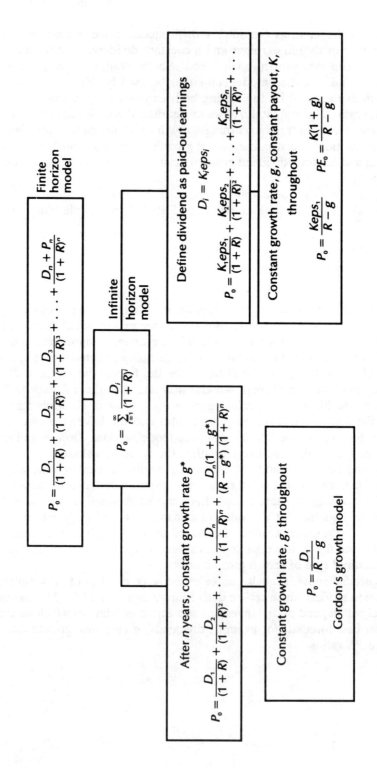

Figure 5.1   Alternative share valuation models

Risk

Whichever model is employed to estimate the expected holding period return, R, it is useful to think of R as being made up of a basic return required on a riskless investment, say, a very short-term gilt, plus a premium for the uncertainty of the future cash flows. Thus we can write

$$R = R_F + \text{risk premium} \tag{5.12}$$

where R_F is the riskless return, which will change as interest rates and hence required rates of return change. This serves as a useful check to any estimates of R; the figure calculated should always be greater than the redemption yield on gilts because of the greater risk of holding shares.

Of course, the expected holding period return on a share cannot be calculated in isolation from its risk which can be measured, as we saw in Chapter 2, by the standard deviation of the probability distribution of returns. How should the standard deviation be assessed? Strictly, we need to estimate not only all expected future cash flows but the probability distributions of all such flows. This would in practice be a daunting task. Luckily, the risks attached to particular shares have been found in general not to change rapidly over time so that risk can usually be fairly adequately measured by the standard deviation of past returns.

Thus, given the expected *HPR* and risk of, say, two shares being considered as potential investments, the investor can, given his attitude to risk and return (utility function), decide which share he prefers. However, if the investor is considering adding a share to his existing portfolio, knowledge of the expected *HPR* and standard deviation of each share is not sufficient for the investor to make his decision. Each share cannot be considered in isolation but must be considered in the light of its impact on the portfolio as a whole. This 'portfolio' approach will be considered in more detail in Chapter 7, where we will see that the return on a share reflects only that part of the risk of the share which is common to the stock market as a whole. The remaining risk on any share can be avoided through diversification, by holding a portfolio of shares. This portfolio approach will also provide an alternative method of deriving the required rate of return of a share and of measuring its risk, known as the capital asset pricing model. This method is based on measuring each share's risk and return relative to the stock market as a whole and offers a different, but not incompatible, means of estimating R from that offered by any of the versions of the dividend valuation model. It would thus be prudent to estimate the expected *HPR* using one of the valuation models described above *and* the capital asset pricing model described in Chapter 9. If the returns obtained from the two methods are approximately the same, more confidence can be placed on the estimates.

Fundamental analysis

In practice, many investment analysts do not use these share valuation models to determine the expected holding period return but prefer to use them to derive estimates of what P_0 should be, given an *assumed* holding period return, R. This is done to determine what they believe to be the '*intrinsic*' value of the share. As we shall see in Chapter 10, trying to determine an intrinsic value for a share presupposes that the current share price, P_0, is in some sense an incorrect value for the share and that the fundamental analyst is better able to value the share than the market as a whole. These assumptions are clear in the following definition of intrinsic value: 'the value that the security *ought* to have and will have when other investors have the same insight and knowledge as the analyst'.[23] If the intrinsic value, say P_0^*, obtained from a share valuation model exceeds the actual price P_0, the share is considered undervalued and it is recommended for purchase. If the intrinsic P_0^* is less than the actual P_0, the share is considered overvalued and recommended for sale. This method of valuing shares, known as 'fundamental analysis', is the most common form of analysis carried out by City analysts and is discussed in greater detail in Chapter 10. Estimates of future earnings and dividends are still needed, but P_0^* is the unknown as opposed to R.

Thus, estimates of R must be found from other sources. In practice, either the capital asset pricing model estimate of the required rate of return, R, described in Chapter 9, is used, or an arbitrary risk premium, based on intuition or judgement, is added to the current yield on gilts, as in equation (5.12), or it is assumed that the average rate of return achieved over some holding period in the past is a good estimate of the future *HPR*. However, the historic *HPR* is unlikely to be a good estimate of the future *HPR* as earnings and dividends will of course change over time as, more importantly, will the riskless rate of return, R_F, even if the risk *premium* remains constant. The basic premise for fundamental analysis is that the market is not 100% efficient – in the sense that some of the securities sold on it will later prove to have been wrongly priced and that greater returns than expected given the shares' risk can be made from spotting such share bargains. Far more time is spent in the City on such activities as fundamental analysis than on calculating the 'fair' rate of return on a share bought at a fair price, given the risk. Chapter 10 will describe in more detail such commonly used investment techniques as technical and fundamental analysis, and consider whether, for the ordinary investor, such activities are likely to be worthwhile.

---

[23] From Lorie and Hamilton (1973) p. 114.

Summary

This chapter has examined ways in which ordinary shares and associated securities are valued. The major characteristics of ordinary shares and their methods of issue were described as well as measures used to compare equities – dividend yield, dividend cover and *PE* ratios. The advantages and disadvantages of these measures were discussed, the major disadvantage being that none of them provided an estimate of total holding period return. The chapter then described how the expected holding period return could be derived from estimates of future earnings or dividends, this model being known as the dividend valuation model. All the different versions of the basic model require subjective estimates of future income from the share and these estimates depend on a multitude of factors, including company, industry and general economic influences. The major use to which these valuation models are put in practice is not, in fact, to determine expected holding period return, but, *assuming* a value for *R*, to determine an intrinsic share price to see whether the share is undervalued or overvalued and should be bought or sold.

Appendix: calculation of dividend cover

Dividend cover is defined to be the earnings per share divided by the dividend per share. It is a measure of the ease with which a particular company can make dividend payments. A dividend cover of more than 3 implies that the dividend payout is low compared with profits; a dividend cover of less than one implies that the company is using reserves to maintain its dividend. However, note that dividends are paid with cash flow and not with accounting profits in the shape of earnings and so the dividend cover can be misleading.

Another problem with the computation of dividend cover is the decision on whether to use net or gross dividends in the denominator. The simplest way to calculate dividend cover is to divide the *eps* by the *gross dps*. However as we saw on p. 148 when looking at *PE* ratios, there are different types of *eps*, and the preferred *eps* will depend on the type of comparison between companies being made. For example, the *Financial Times* uses the 'net' *eps* figure for its calculations of *PE* ratios. However, the *eps* figure used for dividend cover calculations is the 'full distribution' *eps*. This attempts to measure the maximum amount of earnings available for the payment of a *gross* dividend (i.e. *net* dividend plus associated ACT). The *Financial Times* therefore defines dividend cover to be *'full' eps/gross dps*.

Note: The use of different measures of *eps* for *PE* ratio and dividend cover calculations in the *Financial Times* is the reason why, for many companies

$$\frac{P_0}{PE_0 \times \text{gross } dps_0}$$

(an indirect method of calculating $eps_0/gross\ dps_0$) does not equal the dividend cover shown in Monday's edition of the *Financial Times*.

Problems

1. Mr Foot is assessing his investments. He holds £5,000 nominal of gilt-edged stock, Treasury 9½% 1999 and 5,000 25p ordinary shares of Royal Bank of Scotland. The *Financial Times* gives him the following information on his investment:

	Price £	Interest yield %	Gross yield %	Redemption yield %	PE
Treasury 9½% 1999	98²¹⁄₃₂	9.63		9.74	
Royal Bank of Scotland 25p shares	1.82		6.2		14.9

   (i) What is the current value of Mr Foot's investments and what annual *gross* income (i.e. before income tax/tax credit) do they provide?
  (ii) What does the term 'gross yield' mean for Royal Bank of Scotland shares and how is it calculated? It is lower than either the interest or redemption yield on the gilt-edged stock. Does this mean that Royal Bank of Scotland shares give a lower return?
 (iii) Explain why investment in a share such as Royal Bank of Scotland is said to be riskier than investment in a fixed interest government security. How can risk be measured?

2. (i) Bloomington's Boutiques plc has a share price of 68p. It paid a gross dividend of 5p per share last year and is expected to pay 5.5p per share next year. Assuming the dividend is expected to grow at a constant rate in perpetuity, what is the return on the share? (**Hint:** use Gordon's growth model.)
   (ii) There are 1,000,000 Bloomington's ordinary shares in issue and Bloomington's is expected to earn £11,700,000 after tax next year. Calculate the expected earnings per share, *PE* ratio, gross dividend yield and dividend cover. Explain the significance of each of these ratios.
  (iii) Suppose the current gross redemption yield on gilts is around 10%. This is higher than Bloomington's gross dividend yield. Does this mean that Bloomington's can raise share capital more cheaply than the UK government can borrow in the gilt market?
   (iv) How would you decide whether to buy Bloomington shares? What further information would you require?

3. Blue Boxes plc has just announced a rights issue of 2m. new shares. The

pre-announcement share price was 145p and the rights issue involves the issue of one new share (for every existing three shares held) at a price of 115p.

   (i) What will be the theoretical ex rights price and the value of the 'rights'?
  (ii) How much new money will be raised (before transaction costs)? What will those transaction costs consist of?
 (iii) Mr Blair already holds 3,000 shares. Outline the main alternatives available to him. Can Mr Blair simply do nothing without financial loss?

4. You are given the following information from the *Financial Times* on two companies in the Electricals section:

	Share price p	Gross yield %	PE
Cable & Wireless	543	2.9	18.7
Racal	56	8.8	6.0

   (i) How would you explain the differences in *PE* ratio?
  (ii) How would you choose which share to purchase from the above information?

5. The reverse yield gap is the gross redemption yield on gilts less the gross dividend yield on shares. If the gross redemption yield is, say, 10% and the gross dividend 4%, the reverse yield gap is 6%. What does this imply about the return on equity relative to the return on gilts?

6. Advanced Electronics Corp. expects to pay a dividend of 20p per share at the end of the present year. The dividend is then expected to grow at a 15% rate for three years, then at a 10% rate for the next three years, and at 5% for ever more.
   (i) What value would you place on the share if a 9% rate of return were required?
  (ii) Would your valuation change if you expected to hold the shares for only three years?

7. How would you expect inflation to affect the value of your equity investments?

Financial futures

Introduction

In the earlier chapters of this book, we introduced the major types of securities, bonds and ordinary shares. We now cover an increasingly important element of investment, namely *derivatives*. Derivatives are instruments based on the underlying securities of bonds and ordinary shares which enable investors to reduce risk or enhance returns on these securities. Chapter 6 will concentrate on futures contracts and Chapter 7 on options.

One phenomenon of stock markets since the 1970s is their increasing volatility – the tendency of the market to move up or down in a random, unpredictable manner. Such volatility makes it difficult for investors to predict with accuracy the likely return on an investment. Investors run the risk of making short term losses on their portfolios even though their long-run expectations are for a reasonable return. The last quarter of 1987, which included the Crash of 19 October, taught investors that shares in particular can go down as well as up. So, there is a need for financial products which can protect or hedge the investor against the ill effects of market volatility, and the years since the early 1970s have seen the development of futures and option instruments designed to do just this.

The simplest hedging instrument is the *forward* contract in which two parties agree to effect a transaction at some date in the future, at a price agreed on the day the forward contract is entered into. An example given in Chapter 2 was of a commodity forward contract, in which the grower of cocoa agreed in advance a price and a date at which to sell the next cocoa crop to the chocolate manufacturer, with the cocoa and money changing hands on the pre-determined future date at the pre-determined price. The most common forward contract traded today is the currency forward contract, and its characteristics and the reasons for its continued success are described in Chapter 11 on International Investment.

When it comes to instruments which offer the ability to hedge the risks inherent in Stock Exchange securities rather than in commodities or foreign currencies, financial *futures* contracts, rather than financial *forward* contracts, are preferred.[1] Futures contracts, as mentioned in Chapter 2, are exchange-traded forward contracts which are standardised in terms of their quantity, quality and settlement dates. The advantage of trading through an exchange is that the risk of default by a counterparty to a futures contract is transferred to the futures exchange (in return for deposits called 'margins' from buyers and sellers). Frequent trading in forward contracts involves the determining of the credit risk of a wide range of counterparties and smaller would-be hedgers may be excluded as too risky. Frequent trading in futures contracts involves the setting up of a single deposit or margin account with a broker to the exchange.

Another advantage of standardised futures contracts over tailormade forward contracts is that futures markets encourage liquidity in the market for the hedging or trading instrument. Instead of there being a wide range of different forward contracts, which are difficult to trade since they will not necessarily appeal to all traders, only a few futures contracts on any instrument can be traded, forcing all the trades to be on those contracts. With liquidity created by traders speculating on movements in the futures price, hedgers have the ability to buy and sell futures at any time with ease. However, they lose the advantage offered by forward contracts of being able to hedge the exact quality, quantity and time period they wish.

Financial futures originated in the United States in the early 1970s. Although the first contracts were not actively traded, successful currency futures were introduced on the Chicago Mercantile Exchange (CME) in 1972 and interest rate contracts on both the Chicago Board of Trade (CBOT) and the CME in 1975.[2] The first European exchange was the London Financial Futures Exchange (LIFFE) established in 1982 and,

---

[1] The term *financial* futures contract is applied to futures contracts which hedge stock market and currency risks in order to differentiate from those futures contracts designed to hedge commodity risks.

[2] Notice how the financial contracts were set up by exchanges which already specialised in meat and grain futures contracts.

since then, there has been rapid growth in both Europe and the Far East in financial futures exchanges. LIFFE is the European futures exchange with the widest range of futures contracts since it was able to establish sucessful futures contracts not only on UK interest rate and equity risks but also on German, Italian, and Swiss risks before Continental European futures exchanges were fully developed.

The remainder of the chapter begins with a description of the major characteristics of financial futures contracts and, in particular, those based on short- and long-term interest rate instruments and those based on equity securities. Currency futures are only referred to briefly since the more successful currency forward contracts are described in Chapter 11. The following section describes how the main LIFFE futures contracts are priced. Finally, the ways in which futures contracts can be used as surrogates for the underlying securities for trading and investing purposes is considered, as are the ways of hedging interest rate risk and equity risk using futures contracts.

Description of financial futures

Growth of financial futures

Essentially, a futures contract is a deferred spot contract, where a spot contract is the normal purchase or sale for immediate delivery of, say, a security such as a bond. The futures contract can therefore serve two purposes: the first is as a substitute for the spot contract since, whether a security is bought for immediate settlement or for settlement six months later, once the later settlement date has been reached, the investor in either case holds the underlying security; the second is as a hedge, since the spot purchase of a security can be offset by the sale of a futures contract, neutralising the risk of holding the security.

There are several factors which have contributed to the phenomenal growth of financial futures markets since the 1970s and to their appeal to both traders and hedgers. First, financial futures markets are often more liquid than the underlying securities markets. For example, there are 83 gilts for the investor to choose from if he wishes to invest in the UK gilt market compared with only one futures contract on the gilt. Investors wishing to buy gilts or alter the size of their exposure to the gilts market can do so more quickly and easily via the futures market than via the cash gilts. This liquidity creates low transaction costs which enhance the attraction of using the futures markets as a 'synthetic' or alternative way into the underlying securities. Because of this liquidity in financial futures markets, financial futures prices usually 'lead' cash prices. In other words, if traders and investors can more quickly and efficiently alter their exposure to cash securities via the futures market, the futures price will move faster than the underlying cash security prices and will be a better short-term guide to market sentiment.

A second attraction of financial futures markets is that they offer traders a cash efficient means of taking a position in a market. Futures are traded on margin, which means that the trader only has to invest a fraction of the market value of an underlying security in order to be fully exposed to price rises or falls on that security. The margining system therefore allows traders a geared exposure to equity or interest rate risk. However, the gearing effect of the margining system also means that investors can quite quickly lose 100% of their investment, which is unlikely if they invest in bonds or shares directly.

Another advantage of the margining system is that credit risk is reduced by the futures exchange interposing itself between the two counterparties to any trade. So, if Mr Bull buys a futures contract from Mr Bear, Mr Bull will have the futures exchange as his counterparty and Mr Bear will also have the futures exchange as *his* counterparty. In fact, neither Mr Bull nor Mr Bear are aware of each other at all. All that they have to do is satisfy the exchange that they are creditworthy to do the transaction. Instead of having to have lengthy talks with each other on their financial strength, they each place a deposit or initial margin with the exchange which is usually equal to the maximum price movement of the futures contract in any one day. In this way, the maximum loss the futures exchange can incur is one day's adverse price movement on either Mr Bear's or Mr Bull's position, and this one-day loss is covered by the initial margin placed by each of them with the exchange. The futures exchange then requires daily settlement of any losses and records daily credits of any profits to accounts by means of 'variation margin'. When Mr Bull, for example, wishes to realise his profits or limit his losses in the futures position, he simply sells the futures contract at the then prevailing price and closes out his account. The counterparty in this case will not necessarily be Mr Bear, who may still wish to retain his futures position. If Mr Bull has made a profit, it will already be in his account; if he has made a loss, he will have already covered it by variation margin payments into his account.

A further advantage of financial futures contracts is that they offer both the trader and the investor the ability to take a short position in the underlying security, that is, to sell something they do not have. The trader, for example, may think the market is going down. By selling futures contracts and buying them back later after the price has fallen, he will be able to make money in a bear market. Similarly, the investor can use futures contracts to limit exposure to a particular securities market or indeed to sell short a particular market. Suppose a pension fund manager holds an equity portfolio which closely resembles the UK stock market in its composition. If he thinks that the UK equity market is going to fall and wishes to turn his portfolio into cash, he can either sell all his shares (which may take time and depress share prices anyway if his portfolio is large) or he can simply sell stock index futures against his portfolio. (Stock index futures are futures contracts whose price is based on a stock market index, in the case of the UK, the FT-SE 100 Share Index.) If he is right, the loss incurred on his equity portfolio will be counterbalanced by a profit on his financial futures position. Alternatively, he can sell *more* futures contracts than his share portfolio is worth. In this case, he would be like the trader and effectively have a 'short' position in shares.

Also, stock index futures contracts allow small investors and traders to gain *short-term* exposure to a stock market without having to buy a port-folio of shares, and to earn the average rate of return on a stock market instead of holding a small number of shares which may outperform or underperform the market as a whole. However, by the expiry date, the small trader or investor who had bought futures contracts would have to decide whether to then buy shares, stay in cash, or whether to buy new futures contracts with a later expiry date (known as 'rolling forward' his position).

As we have seen, financial futures markets are used by both traders and investors. A third category, arbitrageurs, is vital to the well-being of these markets. Arbitrageurs seek to make money by exploiting anomalies be-tween the prices of futures contracts and of the underlying cash securities. It is difficult to estimate the importance of each of these three types of participant although it is definitely the case that traders dominate in terms of volume. This may at first sight seem to imply that futures markets are only for speculators and not for investors seeking to hedge interest rate or equity risk. However, it is the traders who accept the risk which the hedgers wish to offset. Further, it is the traders who provide the liquidity and depth to the financial futures markets by always being willing to buy or sell futures contracts and the arbitrageurs who ensure that futures are correctly priced relative to the underlying cash securities. This creates a market in which would-be hedgers can hedge in an efficient manner.

Types of financial futures contracts

There are currently four major types of financial futures contract which are based on the major cash markets: futures contracts linked to short-term interest rates; futures contracts linked to long-term interest rates via long-term government bonds; futures contracts linked to equity markets via stock market indices; and currency futures contracts based on forward exchange rates. We will not describe currency *futures* contracts in this section since, in London in particular, the forward currency market is dominant; indeed, LIFFE closed down its currency futures contracts in 1990 since they had failed to achieve sufficient volumes to offer viable competition to the already established forward currency market. We will describe the *forward* currency market in Chapter 11 and restrict ourselves here to the three types of short-term interest rate, long-term bond and equity-linked futures contracts currently traded on LIFFE and shown in Example 6.1.

At present on LIFFE, there are six bond futures contracts, six short-term interest rate futures contracts, and one stock market contract. Example 6.1 lists the details of these contracts as given in the *Financial Times* of 5 August 1992, showing the closing prices for 4 August 1992.

The heading above each table shows the title of each contract, the nominal value of each futures contract, and the unit of trading. For example, the UK gilt futures contract has a nominal value of £50,000 and the unit of trading is one 32nd of 100%. This is because gilt prices are quoted in multiples of 32nds of 1%.[3]

Under the actual futures prices are given the estimated volume figures and what is known as the 'open interest' for the previous day. If we look at the volume figures for each of the thirteen contracts listed in Example 6.1, we can see that, not surprisingly, the domestic futures contracts on UK gilts, on the short-term sterling interest rate, and on the FT-SE 100 Index are among the most successful in the list in volume terms. However, the volumes traded on both the German government bond futures contract and on the short-term deutschemark interest rate (Euromark) futures contract are higher than their UK equivalents, reflecting the march stolen by LIFFE on the German futures exchange which only opened in 1990 and the large number of European banks based in London wishing to trade in and hedge interest rate risk in the benchmark European currency of the deutschemark.

(i) SHORT-TERM INTEREST RATE FUTURES CONTRACTS

All six LIFFE short-term interest rate contracts are based on three-month money market rates, for example the short sterling contract is based on the three-month sterling inter-bank rate for a £500,000 deposit and the three-month eurodollar contract is based on the three-month eurodollar interest rate for a $1 m. dollar deposit. Such futures contracts effectively fix the cost of borrowing or lending money for three months starting on the expiry date of the futures contract. The futures contract is then equivalent to an

---

[3] See Chapter 3, p. 66.

Example 6.1   LIFFE financial futures contracts

LONDON (LIFFE)

9% NOTIONAL BRITISH GILT *
£50,000 32nds of 100%

	Close	High	Low	Prev.
Sep	96-29	97-12	96-22	97-06
Dec	97-05	97-05	97-05	97-14

Estimated volume 38402 (32936)
Previous day's open int. 65074 (64049)

US TREASURY BONDS 8% *
$100,000 32nds of 100%

	Close	High	Low	Prev.
Sep	104-31	105-05	104-28	104-22
Dec	103-26			103-17

Estimated volume 452 (403)
Previous day's open int. 3452 (3591)

6% NOTIONAL GERMAN GOVT. BOND *
DM250,000 100ths of 100%

	Close	High	Low	Prev.
Sep	86.94	87.06	86.78	86.93
Dec	87.42	87.52	87.28	87.46

Estimated volume 49077 (43041)
Previous day's open int. 116278 (119726)

6% NOTIONAL LONG TERM JAPANESE GOVT.
BOND Y100m 100ths of 100%

	Close	High	Low
Sep	105.04	105.07	104.96
Dec	104.52		

Estimated volume 868 (404)
Traded exclusively on APT

9% NOTIONAL ECU BOND
ECU 200,000 100ths of 100%

	Close	High	Low	Prev.
Sep	97.05			96.85
N				
A				

Estimated volume 0 (0)
Previous day's open int. 0 (0)

12% NOTIONAL ITALIAN GOVT. BOND (BTP) *
LIRA 200m 100ths of 100%

	Close	High	Low	Prev.
Sep	94.18	94.85	93.90	93.59
Dec	94.71	95.00	94.64	94.09

Estimated volume 38652 (30781)
Previous day's open int. 35876 (38563)

THREE MONTH STERLING *
£500,000 points of 100%

	Close	High	Low	Prev.
Sep	89.64	89.71	89.61	89.67
Dec	89.76	89.83	89.74	89.80
Mar	90.11	90.17	90.10	90.13
Jun	90.41	90.44	90.35	90.44
Sep	90.62	90.69	90.61	90.69
Dec	90.69	90.76	90.68	90.76

Est. Vol. (inc figs. not shown) 31908 (24944)
Previous day's open int. 237327 (236574)

THREE MONTH EURODOLLAR *
$1m points of 100%

	Close	High	Low	Prev.
Sep	96.54	96.54	96.52	96.50
Dec	96.17	96.17	96.14	96.09
Mar	96.07	96.08	96.04	95.97
Jun	95.72	95.72	95.69	95.58

Est. Vol. (inc. figs. not shown) 865 (1606)
Previous day's open int. 28884 (29400)

THREE MONTH EUROMARK *
DM 1m points of 100%

	Close	High	Low	Prev.
Sep	90.17	90.20	90.15	90.17
Dec	90.31	90.37	90.30	90.34
Mar	90.64	90.70	90.62	90.67
Jun	90.94	91.01	90.92	90.98
Sep	91.17	91.23	91.15	91.22
Dec	91.33	91.42	91.33	91.44

Estimated volume 33963 (30224)
Previous day's open int. 353639 (353650)

THREE MONTH ECU
ECU 1m points of 100%

	Close	High	Low	Prev.
Sep	89.13	89.16	89.10	89.08
Dec	89.40	89.44	89.38	89.37
Mar	89.90	89.94	89.90	89.87
Jun	90.36	90.36	90.33	90.33

Estimated volume 1472 (671)
Previous day's open int. 11679 (11467)

THREE MONTH EURO SWISS FRANC
SFR 1m points of 100%

	Close	High	Low	Prev.
Sep	91.42	91.53	91.42	91.55
Dec	91.63	91.74	91.63	91.75
Mar	91.92	92.03	91.93	92.07
Jun	92.20	92.33	92.20	92.37

Estimated volume 9269 (7915)
Previous day's open int. 45992 (45936)

THREE MONTH EUROLIRA INT. RATE
LIRA 1,000m points of 100%

	Close	High	Low	Prev.
Sep	85.93	86.20	85.66	85.47
Dec	86.60	86.90	86.55	86.07
Mar	87.14	87.60	87.04	86.78
Jun	87.40	87.48	87.48	86.98

Estimated volume 5810 (3612)
Previous day's open int. 22498 (21913)

FT-SE 100 INDEX *
£25 per full index point

	Close	High	Low	Prev.
Sep	2418.0	2460.0	2414.0	2445.0
Dec	2461.0	2498.0	2467.0	2489.0
Mar	2496.0		2524.0	

Estimated volume 9738 (9528)
Previous day's open int. 47639 (47214)

° Contracts traded on APT. Closing prices shown.

---

exchange-traded forward agreement to borrow or lend money for a future three-month period at an interest rate fixed today. For example, a December short sterling futures contract purchased in September fixes in *September* a three-month interest rate starting in *December*. The futures price reflects the forward interest rate[4] for the period of the loan, December to March in the three month short sterling example.

The one somewhat unusual characteristic of short-term interest rate contracts is that they are *not* priced in terms of interest rates. This is because traders prefer prices to go up on good news and prices to go down on bad news. This is not the case with interest rates since falling interest rates are normally viewed as good news and rising interest rates as bad news. So, in order to please traders, interest rate futures are priced as 100 *minus* the interest rate.

The open interest for each contract is the total number of financial futures contracts outstanding, that is, the number of all the long (purchases) positions which is also the number of all the short (sales) positions.[5] The open interest figure reflects the number of futures contracts which have been bought or sold and held open, in contrast to the volume figures which include day trades. 'Day traders' buy and sell futures contracts intra-day, preferring not to keep a highly geared position open overnight.

For example, from Example 6.1 we can see that the September three-month sterling futures contract closed at 89.64 and the December contract at 89.76. For three-month sterling futures, traded on LIFFE, the last trading day for a particular maturity month is always the third Wednesday of the relevant month. Thus, the three-month forward rate implied in the September contract would start on the third Wednesday in September, in this case 16 September, and the equivalent start date for the December contract would be the third Wednesday in December, 16 December in this example. The forward rate implied by the September contract is 100–89.64=10.36% and the forward rate implied by the December contract is slightly lower at 100–89.76=10.24%. Convention has it that the interest rate implied by the futures price is the borrowing rate. Since the normal spread between borrowing and lending rates for three-month £500,000 loans is 1/8%, the implied forward lending rate for the same period would be the borrowing rate less 1/8% or 0.125%. So, for example, from Example 6.1, the September three-month lending rate is 100–89.64−0.125 = 10.235%.

The smallest price move permitted by the exchange on a particular futures contract is known as the 'tick size' of the futures contract. For example, the tick size of the short sterling contract is 0.01% or 1 basis point of 1%. So, the minimum price which the December short sterling futures

---

[4] For a quick revision of forward interest rates, see Chapter 4, pp. 108–12.

[5] The open interest number is always announced one day later because it takes longer to compile than the price and volume figures.

contract could experience on trading would be from, say, the 89.76 quoted in Example 6.1 to 89.77 or 89.75. This can be translated into a profit or loss per tick if the nominal value of the futures contract is taken into account. In the case of the short sterling futures contract, the nominal value per contract is £500,000. 1 basis point of 1% of £500,000 is £50; but, the contract is for three months, whereas the price is based on annual interest rates. This gives a value per tick of £50/4 = £12.50. So, if the price moves up three ticks, the buyer of ten short sterling futures contracts would be better off by 10 × 3 × £12.50 = £375.

The expiry months for the short sterling contract follow a March/June/September/December cycle, as do all the other futures contracts traded on LIFFE. Notice that there are more expiry months quoted for the short sterling contract than for any other LIFFE futures contract. Traders and hedgers using this contract in August 1992 could choose an expiry date as early as September 1992 and as late as December 1994.[6] Thus, the three-month forward rate can be locked in for around eighteen months ahead, offering a range of hedging opportunities to the investor worried about short-term interest rate risk. However, the LIFFE three-month sterling contract is limited by comparison with the three-month eurodollar futures contract traded on the CME, which has expiry dates stretching out more than four years ahead.

(ii) BOND FUTURES CONTRACTS

Long-term interest rate futures contracts are generally contracts on government bonds in the currency concerned. Bond futures contracts differ from short-term interest rate contracts in that they are *not* cash settled; sellers of bond futures contracts deliver, instead of cash, one of a range of bonds to buyers of the bond futures contracts. Since no one bond is issued in large enough size to prevent a speculator being able to 'corner' the market in the bond, futures exchanges avoid the 'cornering' problem by allowing a number of bonds to be deliverable. For example, for the UK gilt futures contract in August 1992, all gilts within the maturity range 2003 to 2009 years were deliverable against the contract and, at that time, there were nine gilts in issue which fell into that category, with coupons ranging from 8% to 13½%, maturities ranging from 2003 to 2009, and prices ranging from £91$\frac{1}{32}$ for Treasury 8% 2009 to £128$\frac{10}{32}$ for Treasury 13½% 2008.[7]

If no adjustments were made, investors would always choose to deliver £50,000 nominal of Treasury 8% 2009, the gilt with the lowest price, rather than, say, £50,000 nominal of Treasury 13½% 2008. LIFFE overcomes this

---

[6] Not all the contracts are quoted in the *Financial Times*.

[7] Notice that the range of deliverable gilts changes over time.

problem by adjusting the price paid by the buyer of the gilt future to reflect the market price of the particular gilt which is delivered to him. LIFFE does this by applying a different conversion factor or price factor to the price which must be paid for each gilt. For example, the conversion factor on the expensively priced Treasury 13½% 2008 for the December 1992 futures contract is 1.3155523, reflecting a market price well above par. So, if Ms Golden wishes to sell £50,000 nominal of Treasury 13½% 2008 through the gilt futures contract for settlement in December 1992,[8] and sells in August at the closing price quoted for the December contract in Example 6.1, she will fix in advance a selling clean price for each £100 nominal of the gilt of £97⁵/₃₂ × 1.3155523 = £97.15625 × 1.3155523 = £127.81, plus accrued interest. If, on the other hand, Ms Golden chose to deliver £50,000 of Treasury 8% 2009, with a conversion factor of 0.9143034, she would receive, in December, for each £100 nominal of the gilt, a clean price of £97⁵/₃₂ × 0.9143034 = £88.83, plus accrued interest. In either case, the purchaser of the gilt will have to pay a price for the gilt commensurate with its value.

(iii) EQUITY INDEX FUTURES CONTRACTS

Equity index futures contracts are contracts on the basket of ordinary shares which make up the particular index. Although there are a number of equity index futures contracts traded world-wide, for example the successful US S&P 500 index futures contract traded on the CME, LIFFE only has one equity index futures contract on the UK equity index represented by the FT-SE 100 index. This index was specially designed to be the basis of a futures contract: it has only 100 shares to enable the trader or arbitrageur to replicate the futures contract with a portfolio of the underlying shares. Since it is made up of the 100 largest shares by market capitalisation, it also moves quite similarly to the broader FT-All Share Index which has 750 shares in it. Fund managers holding portfolios resembling the FT-All Share Index can therefore use the FT-SE 100 Index to hedge their portfolios.[9]

In practice, delivery of the 100 shares representing the FT-SE 100 share index in the correct proportions would be difficult for most sellers of equity index futures contracts. As a result, the FT-SE 100 Share index futures contract is cash settled. Notice how there is no nominal amount underlying

---

[8] The settlement for gilt futures is on any business day during the expiry month (in this case December 1992) at the option of the seller of the gilt futures contract and hence of the deliverer of the gilt. Also, the seller of the gilt futures can choose which of the deliverable gilts he will actually deliver.

[9] The Appendix to Chapter 10 on Efficient Markets briefly describes how the FT-SE 100 share index differs from the other stock market indices commonly used to measure the performance of the UK stock market. It is likely that LIFFE wil also begin trading on an FT-SE 350 share index designed to more closely mirror the stock market as a whole.

Example 6.2   LIFFE short sterling, long gilt and FT-SE 100 futures contract specifications as of August 1992

	Contract		
	Short sterling	Long gilt	FT-SE 100
Unit of trading	£500,000 nominal	£500,000 nominal notional Gilt with 9% coupon	£25 per full index point
Delivery months	Mar, Jun Sep, Dec	Mar, Jun, Sep, Dec	Mar, Jun, Sep, Dec
Quotation	100 minus rate of interest	per £100 nominal	Index points
Minimum price movement:			
Tick size	0.01%	£1/32	0.5
Tick value	£12.50	£15.625	£12.50
Contract standard	Cash settled	Any gilt on list of deliverable gilts as published by LIFFE	Cash settled against average FT-SE 100 Index between 10.10 and 10.30 a.m. on Last Trading Day
Initial margin requirements*	£400	£625	£2,000

* These are frequently changed by LIFFE.
Source: LIFFE.

the FT-SE 100 futures contract unlike, say, the £500,000 nominal value of the short sterling contract. With an equity index futures contract, a complex basket of shares, held in different amounts to reflect their relative market values, underlies the futures contract. So the equity index futures contract is priced at £25 per index point. For example, if Ms Golden chose to buy one equity index futures contract for December 1992 delivery at the closing price of 2461 quoted in Example 6.1, she would be buying into a portfolio of shares currently worth 2461 × £25 = £61,525. The tick size for the FT-SE 100 share index futures contract is 0.5 of an index point, equivalent to £25/2 = £12.50. So, if the futures price rose 10 index points or 20 ticks, Ms Golden's position would be in profit by 20 × £12.50 or £250. Example 6.2 lists the major characteristics of the three UK futures contracts: short sterling, long gilt, and FT-SE 100.

From Example 6.2, we can see that LIFFE defines a different time and method of settlement for each type of futures contract. However, in many cases, the termination of a futures contract is straightforward and does not involve settlement on expiry; most contracts are not held to expiry and hence delivery does not take place. So, for example, the buyer of 10 gilt futures contracts with a December 1992 expiry date would simply sell his futures contracts before December, to close out his position and prevent delivery being forced on him by a seller of gilt futures contracts. Similarly, a seller of gilt futures contracts would buy them back before the delivery month was reached. However, in the few cases in which the futures contract is kept open until expiry, some futures contracts (such as short sterling and the FT-SE) are cash settled and others (such as the long gilt) entail physical delivery of securities. Notice that the futures price on expiry (sometimes called the Exchange Delivery Settlement Price, or EDSP) is defined in all cases to be the underlying asset price or 'cash' price. In this way, LIFFE ensures that the futures price always converges to the underlying cash price on expiry.

Pricing financial futures

Pricing short sterling futures

Financial futures contracts are deferred cash contracts and so, unlike options, they are simple to value. For three-month interest rate futures contracts, we have seen how they are the forward rates implied by spot rates from now to the beginning and end of the three months in question. So, for example, with a three-month futures contract with expiry in exactly ninety days' time, the implied forward rate would be $_3f_6$ where:

$$(1 + r_2 \times 180/365) = (1 + r_1 \times 90/365)(1 + {_3f_6} \times 90/365)$$

and r_1 and r_2 are the three- and six-month spot rates respectively.[10]

For example, if we are on 16 September, and the futures contract expires in 90 days' time, on 15 December, we can write, with three-month and six-month spot rates at 10% and 11% respectively,

$$(1 + 0.11 \times 180/365) = (1 + 0.10 \times 90/365)(1 + {_3f_6} \times 90/365)$$

Solving this equation, we obtain

$$_3f_6 = 11.71\%$$

---

[10] Notice how the formula uses simple interest rates for periods of under twelve months, unlike the formulae for gilts in Chapter 4. These assumed compound interest rates, since periods of more than one year were involved.

The futures contract should therefore be priced at 100–11.71 or 88.29. This is known as the 'fair' futures price.

Thus, given spot money market interest rates, forward interest rates and hence futures rates are predetermined. Any difference between the *fair* futures price and the *actual* futures price rate would lead arbitrageurs to enter the market in order to profit from the mis-pricing. The constant threat of arbitrage will therefore keep the futures price in what is known as its 'arbitrage channel' – the implied forward price plus or minus the transaction costs of doing the arbitrage.

Pricing stock index futures

Turning to futures contracts on bonds and on equity indices, these can be priced by considering what happens on expiry. At that point, we have seen how futures prices are defined to converge to the underlying security prices. So, before expiry, the difference in price between a futures contract and the cash security price is equal to the difference in what is known as the 'cost of carry'.

Let us consider the price of the stock index futures contract as quoted in Example 6.1. The closing price on 4 August 1992 for the December futures contract on the FT-SE 100 share index was 2461 whilst the closing price for the index itself was 2407.5, implying a premium for the futures index price over the cash index price of 2.2%. And yet, on the expiry date in December 1992, the futures price must equal the cash price.

Why is the futures price trading at a 2.2% premium? Because it is cheaper to buy the futures contract on the FT-SE 100 share index and hold it to expiry than to buy the 100 shares underlying the index and hold them for the same period. Buying shares implies a cash outflow which has an implied interest cost; on the other hand, buying shares provides a dividend income which can be offset against the interest cost of the shares. Since the interest rate on the money used to buy shares usually exceeds the dividend yield expected from holding shares, the cost of carrying shares is positive. In contrast (ignoring the impact of margin accounts), futures have a zero cost of carry. No money need be borrowed to buy futures contracts and no dividend income is received in return for buying futures contracts. Thus, the difference in price between the equity index futures and cash prices is the borrowing cost minus the dividend yield. As an example, we use the December 1992 contract with the cash index and futures prices as given in the *Financial Times* dated 5 August 1992. Example 6.3 calculates whether or not the futures price is fair, given the underlying cash index price and the cost of carrying the cash shares.

Both methods imply that the futures price was 0.1% cheap. However,

Example 6.3   Determining the Fair Price of a Stock Index Futures Contract

Date	5 August 1992
Futures prices	2461
Cash index price	2407.5
Interest rate	10.40% p.a.
Expected dividend income*	38.38 or 1.594% of 2407.5
Number of days to futures settlement	138

* Estimated by Bloomberg from declared dividends not yet paid and from estimated dividends payable during the period to expiry of the futures contract.

Determining the fair price of the futures contract

Method (1)

Determine the cost of carry

Cost of carry = Interest cost over period − expected dividend yield over period
  = 0.104 × 138/365 − 0.01594
  = 0.03932 − 0.0159
  = **2.34%**
Premium of futures index price to cash index price
  = (2461/2407.5) − 1
  = **2.22%**

Method (2)

Determine the fair futures price

Fair futures price = Cash price + interest cost − cash dividends expected
Fair futures price = 2407.5 + 2407.5 × 0.1040 × (138/365) − 38.38
  = **2464**
Actual futures price = **2461**

given that transaction costs in switching between cash and futures prices are substantially higher than 0.1%, the index futures contract was fairly priced, being higher than the cash index price by the cost of carry (allowing for transaction costs).

If the futures price were not fairly priced with respect to the underlying cash price, an arbitrage opportunity would arise. For example, suppose that, on 5 August 1992, the futures contract was trading at 2490 and the cash index at 2407.5. What would the arbitrageur do? He would buy the shares underlying the cash index at an index-equivalent price of 2407.5 and simultaneously sell the futures contract at 2490. By doing so he would lock in a profit since, assuming the same interest rate charge and expected dividends as in Example 6.3, his costs per futures contract would be 2407.5 × (1 + 0.1040 × 138/365) − 38.38 = 2464 and his revenue per futures contract would be 2490, leaving a gross profit per futures contract of 26 ticks or, at £25 per tick, £650. However, transaction costs would need to be deducted from the gross profit to determine the net proceeds. As a result, only arbitrageurs with access to large amounts of cash, and hence with low percentage transaction costs, could take advantage of any futures pricing anomalies. Indeed, the opposite arbitrage is more complex: if the futures price is below the fair price, say at 2430 in this example, the arbitrageur would wish to buy the futures and sell short the cash securities. In the UK stock market, only certain participants can sell short securities, in particular market makers, and thus take advantage of futures mis-pricing.

However, the equity fund manager, who wishes to hold a portfolio which resembles the FT-SE 100 Share Index *does* have shares to sell from his portfolio and so is not restricted by any limitations on short selling. He can take advantage of cheap futures contracts to switch out of cash shares into the futures contract, switching back to cash shares on expiry of the futures contract or earlier if the futures price moves back to its fair level. What impact does such switching have on his portfolio's returns? It offers the fund manager the opportunity to earn more than the index return on his portfolio with no additional risk.

Pricing bond futures

Exactly the same valuation technique applies to all futures and forward contracts: they differ from the value of the underlying cash instrument by the cost of carry. In the case of bond futures, there is one complication. Since a number of bonds can be delivered, (the choice of bond is at the option of the seller), determination of the fair price of the futures contract must assume that a particular bond will be chosen. In practice, this is less difficult than it sounds since there is always one bond which is 'cheapest to deliver'.

As we saw earlier, there is a wide range of gilts deliverable into the LIFFE gilt futures contract. We also showed how the price paid by the gilt futures purchaser on settlement was adjusted to reflect the value of the particular gilt for which the cash was paid. Gilts with high coupons were relatively more expensive than gilts with low coupons and had higher conversion factors.

However, the relative prices of all the deliverable gilts vary all the time, as do their redemption yields, and yet the conversion factors for each of these gilts assume that the gross redemption yield at which they will all be priced on delivery is both flat and equal to 9%. This is done by assuming that the notional gilt underlying the futures contract is priced at par and thus has a redemption yield of 9%. This yield is then applied to all the deliverable gilts to price them on the expected date of delivery of the futures contract and the ratio of the price determined to the 100 of the notional gilt determines the conversion factor.

Example 6.4   Determination of the Cheapest to Deliver Gilt

Gilt	Price £	Conversion factor	Gross redemption yield %
T 13½% 2008	128$\frac{10}{32}$	1.3155523	9.42
T 12½% 2005	120$\frac{31}{32}$	1.2412503	9.41
T 11¾% 2007	115$\frac{9}{32}$	1.1809062	9.41
T 10% 2003	105¼	1.0681802	9.23
T 9½% 2004	102$\frac{10}{32}$	1.0360234	9.17
T 9½% 2005	102$\frac{11}{32}$	1.0368092	9.16
T 8% 2009	91$\frac{1}{32}$	0.9143034	9.03
T 9% 2008	99$\frac{22}{32}$	0.9999282	9.03

Example 6.4 shows the deliverable gilts for the December 1992 gilt futures contract. It gives their prices, conversion factors, and gross redemption yields. In this case, the Treasury 13½% 2008, with an actual gross redemption yield of 9.42% will be the cheapest to deliver on an assumed gross redemption yield of 9%. Thus, the gilt futures contract will be closely linked to the price of this particular gilt – until changes in relative gilt prices make another gilt the 'cheapest to deliver'.

Using financial futures

Trading

Financial futures contracts are most frequently bought by traders who buy or sell futures contracts in order to profit from a view that the market will either go up or go down. With the range of currently available LIFFE contracts given in Example 6.2, traders can take a view on short-term interest rates in six currencies via the short-term interest rate contracts, on long-term interest rates in six currencies via the government bond contracts, and on the UK equity market via the FT-SE 100 Share Index contract.

The advantages to traders of using futures contracts rather than, say, three-month Treasury bills for exposure to short-term interest rates, or equity index futures contracts instead of a portfolio of shares for exposure to movements in stock market prices, are low transaction costs, speed of trading, liquidity (essential to the trader who may wish to close out his position at any time to lock in a profit or limit a loss) and, most importantly, gearing provided by the margining system.

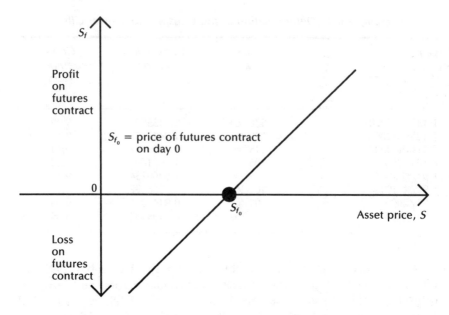

Figure 6.1   Profit and loss profile of futures contract

As a simple example, suppose that Mr Fish believes that long-term interest rates are due to rise over the next week after poorer than expected trade figures have been announced. He expects long gilt prices to fall and the price of the gilt futures contract to fall. He therefore sells 10 gilt futures (say, the December futures shown in Example 6.1 at the closing price of 97–05 or 97$\frac{5}{32}$, and expects to be able to buy them back at a lower price soon after the trade figures have been announced. Note that Mr Fish is able to sell futures contracts in order to exploit a bearish view of a particular market, in this case the gilts market. Unless he were a gilt market maker, he would not otherwise be able to do so since he could not sell short gilts he did not own.

Suppose that the initial margin required on the position is £625 (as shown in Example 6.2) and that, a week later, the gilt futures contract *has* fallen 9/32nds as a result of the trade figures announcement to 96–28. Since the tick size for the gilt futures contract is 1/32nd and the tick value is £15.625, Mr Fish will have made a profit on ten contracts of $9 \times £15.625 \times 10 = £1,406.25$ or 225% of his initial margin investment of £625.

However, Mr Fish could have been wrong and the gilt futures contract could have gone up. The potential loss on simple futures trading is unlimited, since the futures contract moves on a 1 to 1 basis with the underlying cash market. This is shown in Figure 6.1 which plots the profit or loss on a futures contract assuming price moves in the underlying asset.

Profit and loss profile of a futures contract

For example, in the case of the LIFFE gilt futures contract, for every one tick or one 32nd price move in the cheapest to deliver gilt (at that time the Treasury 13½% 2008), the futures contract will move the same number of ticks in the same direction. However, because of the gearing effect, the trader can lose far more than his initial margin. Unlike shares, there is no downside risk limit of a loss of 100% of the investment. For an initial margin of £625, the trader could lose five or ten times that amount with ease. For this reason, simple trading is normally very short term and often intra-day, to reduce the risk of large swings in price. Also, traders may put a stop loss order on their positions, so that the trade is closed out once a certain futures price has been reached, limiting the loss to a manageable quantity. However, in volatile markets or around the announcement of volatile figures, futures prices may jump (as they did in the Crash of 1987) and the futures price may jump right over the stop loss price set by the trader. It is for this reason that most small investors who wish to trade in a geared way in the securities markets do so via options, described in Chapter 7. Although selling options can be of similar risk to selling futures, *buying* options limits the potential loss to a maximum of 100%.[11]

Hedging with financial futures

The main purpose of hedging by an investor is to protect the future value of his portfolio. So, if an investor holds a portfolio of cash, shares and bonds, he will take out a hedge to protect the future sale price of his portfolio. A financial futures hedge is similar in principle to a forward hedge for cocoa. A financial futures hedge locks in a future sale price for a holder of securities and a cocoa forward hedge locks in a future sale price for a grower of cocoa.

In Chapter 7, we will look at the role of options as a possible hedge for the investor.[12] The main difference between futures and options as hedging alternatives is that the futures contract offers certainty but does not offer the upside potential of options. So, if the hedger of an equity portfolio sells futures contracts against his position and then sees the stock market go up rather than down as he had feared, he cannot take advantage of that upswing. He has locked in an effective selling price: if the stock market

---

[11] See Chapter 7, p. 193.

[12] See Chapter 7, pp. 210–17.

goes up, he will have to buy back his futures position at a loss and the loss on the futures hedge will balance the gain on his portfolio. Entering into a futures contract *obliges* the hedger either to go through with cash or physical settlement (depending on the type of futures contract) or to do a counterbalancing trade on the futures market – in this example to buy back the number of futures contracts he has sold. With bought options, there is no *obligation* to go through with exercise or even to do a counterbalancing trade. The hedger can write off the cost of the option and walk away from his hedge. For that reason, options are a more expensive way of hedging than are futures. As we saw in the section on pricing financial futures, futures are simply priced as the underlying cash instrument plus the cost of carry. Hedging via a futures trade is thus free insurance. Hedging via options, which offer more flexibility, is not.

Determining the hedge ratio

We now turn to the problem of how many futures contracts to use as a hedge. The simplest type of futures contract is the short-term interest rate futures contract. Suppose that Ms Ball runs a pension fund portfolio which is due to receive a £1 million cash inflow in mid-December 1992. She would like to place the cash on three-month deposit when it is received but is concerned that, between August and December, interest rates will fall to below the forward interest rate level implied in the three-month short sterling futures contract. The December short sterling futures contract closed at 89.76 on 4 August 1992 and this implies a lending rate of $100 - 89.76 - 0.125 = 10.115\%$. In order to lock in this rate, Ms Ball must *buy* two short sterling contracts since their nominal value is £500,000 each. She must buy the futures contracts in order to lock in the lending rate because, if interest rates *do* fall before expiry of the futures contract, the settlement price of the futures price on expiry will have risen, creating a gain on the futures hedge to compensate for the lower interest rate to be received on the £1 million deposit Ms Ball actually makes.

If Ms Ball wished to hedge the interest rate on a *six*-month deposit from mid-December, she would have to adjust her short sterling hedge in order to reflect the greater cash loss she would incur on the six-month deposit when compared with the three-month deposit if interest rates fell. The loss would be twice as great (if interest rates fell in parallel) and so she should buy *four* short sterling contracts in this case.

In the same way, a futures hedge of a bond portfolio must take into account the relative volatility of the bond portfolio and of the bond futures contract. We saw earlier how the bond futures contract will move 1 to 1 with the particular gilt which is deemed to be the 'cheapest to deliver'. So, before hedging a bond portfolio by *selling* bond futures,[13] the interest rate volatility of the bond portfolio must be compared with the volatility of the cheapest to deliver bond.

Let us suppose for simplicity that Ms Ball, as part of the pension fund for which she is responsible, holds £200,000 nominal of the Treasury 13½% 2008, currently the cheapest deliver to bond. If this is the only bond which needs to be hedged, the hedge ratio (the number of futures contracts which need to be sold to create a hedge) is simply the ratio of the nominal values of the gilt futures and the amount to be hedged adjusted for the conversion factor of the cheapest to deliver bond. There is no need to adjust for volatility differences, since the bond futures contract moves 1 to 1 with the cheapest to deliver gilt. Thus, Ms Ball would need to sell:

$$\frac{\text{Nominal value of CTD gilt held} \times \text{Conversion factor}}{\text{Nominal value of gilt futures contract}} \quad (6.1)$$

$$= \frac{£200,000 \times 1.3155523}{£50,000}$$

$$= 5.3 \text{ futures contracts}$$

if she were using the December gilt futures with which to hedge. In practice, only round numbers of futures contracts can be traded and so Ms Ball would have to slightly underhedge by selling 5 December gilt futures contracts.

If she wished to hedge another gilt with the gilt futures contract, Ms Ball would have to carry out an adjustment to reflect the relative volatility of the gilt she wishes to hedge and of the cheapest to deliver gilt which drives the volatility of the gilt futures contract. As we saw in Chapter 4,[14] the interest rate volatility of a gilt can be measured by its duration. In fact, equation (4.3) on p. 101 gave us a formula for estimating a price change dP given the duration D of a bond and its redemption yield:

$$dP = -D \times P \times dR/(1 + R) \quad (6.2)$$

What Ms Ball wishes to do is to make sure that the sterling price move on the gilt which she holds is exactly offset by the price move in the gilt futures contract. What she therefore needs to do is to convert her gilt holding into an equivalent risk holding in the cheapest to deliver gilt and *then* use the

---

[13] Note how this is the opposite trade to that recommended for short sterling futures. This is because we are here dealing with fixed income securities rather than floating rate deposits and fixed income securities go *up* in value when interest rates go down.

[14] See Chapter 4, pp. 98–103.

hedge ratio in equation (6.1) above to determine the appropriate number of December gilt futures contracts to sell.

Suppose Ms Ball held, on 4 August 1992, £200,000 nominal of Exchequer 15% 1997 priced at £120⅝ and yielding 9.84%. We know that, at that time, the cheapest to deliver gilt was priced at £128⁵⁄₁₆ and yielding 9.42%. The durations of the gilts were 3.82 and 6.57 for the Exchequer 1997 and the cheapest to deliver gilt respectively.

Let us consider the impact of a 1% rise in redemption yield on Ms Ball's portfolio. Using equation (6.2), £200,000 nominal of Exchequer 15% 1997 would fall:

$$dP = -3.82 \times £200,000 \times (120.625/100) \times 0.01/(1.0984) \qquad (6.3)$$

$$= -£8,391$$

The cheapest to deliver gilt would fall:

$$= -6.57 \times H \times (128.3125/100) \times 0.01/(1.0942) \qquad (6.4)$$

$$= -0.077 \times H$$

where H is the nominal amount held of the cheapest to deliver gilt. Equating (6.3) to (6.4) gives $H = £108,901$. Thus, Ms Ball could view her portfolio as being equivalent, in interest rate risk terms, to £108,901 nominal of the cheapest to deliver gilt. She could then use the normal hedge ratio formula in equation (6.1) to calculate the number of gilt futures contracts to sell. In this case, it would be

$$\frac{£108,901 \times 1.3155523}{£50,000}$$

$$= 2.9 \text{ gilt futures contracts}$$

However, the method used to translate Ms Ball's holding of Exchequer 15% 1997 into cheapest to deliver equivalent gilts assumes that both gilts would experience the same change in redemption yield if interest rates moved. This assumption is more risky the further away on the yield curve the gilt to be hedged is from the cheapest to deliver gilt. A hedge of a short or medium gilt with the gilt futures contract will be more exposed to the risk of different yield changes than with the hedge of a long-dated gilt.

Turning finally to equity index futures, let us now assume that Ms Ball has a well-diversified UK equity portfolio worth £500,000 and that she wishes to lock in a sale value for December 1992 of 2461, the closing price on 4 August 1992 of the December FT-SE 100 share index futures contract.

The number of FT-SE 100 share index futures contracts is determined by the ratio of the market value[15] of the equity portfolio to the amount of equity exposure inherent in one equity index futures contract, which is £25 times the cash value of the equity index concerned. In this example, we have a hedge ratio of:

$$\frac{£500,000}{£25 \times 2407.5}$$

$$= 8.3 \text{ futures contracts}$$

Thus, Ms Ball would sell 8 FT-SE 100 share index futures contracts to hedge the equity element of her portfolio. If her portfolio differed in characteristics from the FT-SE 100 share index, she might choose to adjust the hedge ratio accordingly.[16]

Summary

Ten years ago, investors could afford to ignore the then relatively new market in derivatives, and financial futures in particular. Since then, the derivatives markets have experienced phenomenal growth, in Europe and the Far East as well as in their home market of the US. Now, financial futures and options have become an integral part of the investor's tools with which he can adjust the risk and return profile of his portfolio in order to protect against heightened interest rate risk, currency risk, and equity market risk.

Financial futures contracts have found widespread appeal among both hedgers and traders. Indeed, the liquidity in the major financial futures markets is such that the futures price leads the underlying cash instrument's price as a market indicator. Contributing to the popularity of financial futures markets are their liquidity, low transaction costs, simplified credit risk, and the way they can be used by traders to create short positions and by hedgers to neutralise interest rate, currency, or equity market risk. Financial futures have also helped fund managers in a number of areas, in particular, trading and hedging stock market risks. Chapter 7 looks at options in more detail.

---

[15] Rather than the ratio of the *nominal* values, as was the case for gilts.

[16] We shall see in Chapter 9 that a measure of equity portfolio risk known as beta can be used to adjust the hedge ratio. For example, a portfolio with a beta of 1.5 would require 1.5 times as many futures contracts to be hedged against market movements.

Problems

1. (i) What are the main differences between forward and futures con-
        tracts?
    (ii) What are the advantages to the trader of using futures contracts?
    (iii) What are the advantages to the hedger of using futures contracts?

2. The following information is printed in the *Financial Times* for 22 July
    1992.

9% NOTIONAL BRITISH GILT
£50,000 32nds of 100%

	Close	High	Low	Prev
Sep	98-22	98-24	98-07	98-15
Dec	98-29			98-21

Estimated volume 30628 (56194)
Previous day's open int. 65068 (65327)

   (i) What is a government bond futures contract, such as this contract on
        a 9% Notional British gilt?
   (ii) Explain the meaning of the £50,000 32nds of 100%. By how little can
        the gilt futures price move and what value per contract does that
        imply?
   (iii) Explain the terms 'estimated volume' and 'open int'.
   (iv) Suggest a reason why the December contract is trading at a premium
        to the September gilt contract.

3. It is 15 June 1993. The following prices are quoted in the *Financial Times*
    of that day for the September 1993, December 1993, and March 1994 short
    sterling futures contracts. The date in brackets is the settlement date in
    the relevant month for each contract.

Expiry	*Price*
Sep 1993 (15)	89.75
Dec 1993 (15)	89.98
Mar 1994 (15)	90.33

   (i) Calculate the implied three-month borrowing and lending rates start-
        ing from 15 September 1993, 15 December 1993, and 15 March 1994.
   (ii) If the three-month spot interest rate is 10.00–10.125% and the six-
        month spot interest rate is 10.20–10.325%, calculate the arbitrage
        channel for the September 1993 contract. The spot rates given are for
        lending (lower rate) and borrowing (higher rate). Use common sense

to work out the two arbitrages, one of which derives a lending rate for the futures contract and the other a borrowing rate.

4. Mr Wishful buys 20 bond futures contracts with a nominal value of US$100,000 each and a tick size of ¹⁄₃₂nd of 1%. The initial margin callable is $1,500 per contract. The purchase price is 101–03 (101³⁄₃₂). At the end of the first day, the futures contract is priced at 100–29; at the end of the second day, the futures contract is priced at 100–20; and at the end of the third day, Mr Wishful closes his position out by selling the 20 futures contracts at a price of 100–26. Calculate:
   (i) the overall loss in dollars;
   (ii) the variation margin on each of the three days;
   (iii) the balance on the margin account at the end of the three days.

5. Miss Cricket has a large portfolio of UK shares, whose returns are closely correlated to the returns on the shares underlying the FT-SE 100 Share index. The current level of the FT-SE 100 Share index is 2250, the short-term interest rate is 12% p.a., the expected dividend yield 4% p.a., and the FT-SE 100 futures contract due to expire in exactly three months' time is standing at 2260.
   (i) Should Miss Cricket be holding shares or should she switch to the futures market to gain exposure to the UK equity market?
   (ii) What difference would it make if selling shares and buying them back involved Miss Cricket in round trip transaction costs of 1.75%?

6. Does a perfect hedge lock in the current spot value of an instrument for future settlement?

7. Mr Barclay wishes to hedge £450,000 nominal of Conversion 9½% 2005 by selling gilt futures contracts against his position. The Conversion 9½% 2005 is currently trading at £103–19 (103¹⁹⁄₃₂) with a redemption yield of 9.01% and a duration of 7.57. The cheapest to deliver gilt at the time is Treasury 13½% 2004–8 which is priced at £130–04 with a redemption yield of 9.21% and a duration of 6.64 (assuming redemption in 2004).
   (i) Estimate the nominal value of the cheapest to deliver gilt which has the same interest rate risk as Mr Barclay's current portfolio.
   (ii) Estimate the number of gilt futures contracts which Mr Barclay should sell.

8. Miss Bountiful is considering switching 50% of her £3 million equity portfolio into gilts. She would like to do an immediate futures sale in order to be able to take her time over selling the shares. If the cash value of the FT-SE index is currently trading at 2415.6, how many FT-SE 100 Share index futures contracts should she sell?

Options

Introduction

In this chapter, we introduce options. The ability to buy and sell options on a wide variety of instruments has been the most interesting development for investors of the past decade. Options offer the investor the ability to create a wide variety of risk and return alternatives from the same underlying security. Options allow investors to take a view not only on prices in a market but on the volatility or risk of that market. Options also form the basis of all the securities we have already come across. Options are the building blocks of investment. An understanding of futures and options, or 'derivatives' as we saw in Chapter 6, is of importance to both private and institutional investors.

Although options on ordinary shares have existed in the UK since the seventeenth century, interest in options on shares listed on the UK Stock Exchange took off in the 1980s following the opening of the traded options market in 1978. Advances in the techniques of valuing options have also encouraged trading in options and the creation of a whole range of securities which have options embedded in them, the most common of which is convertible unsecured loan stock.

Options on securities offer their holders the right to buy (*call* options) or sell (*put* options) the securities at a fixed price at some time in the future, which can range from a few weeks to months for traded options to several years for options embedded in bonds. At present, LIFFE offers investors and traders options on 67 UK listed shares; options on the FT-SE 100 Share Index; options on government bond futures, including gilts; options on currencies; and options on short-term money such as the three-month sterling contract.

Early growth in UK traded options was not as rapid as had been widely expected. Hopes had been high given the huge success of the Chicago Board Options Exchange. However, reasons for the initial relative lack of success in the UK seem to have been tax disadvantages for institutional investors (disadvantages which have now been removed) and a perception by institutional investors and private investors alike that options were a risky investment.

This concept of options as risky and speculative is not a recent one. Dealing in options was officially banned on the London Stock Exchange from 1734 to 1860 and again from 1939 to 1958. The first ban was as a result of speculation leading to the South Sea Bubble which burst in 1720.[1] The second was imposed as part of general restrictions on share dealings during wartime but, despite pressure from would-be dealers in options, was only relaxed nearly twenty years later in 1958. The idea that options are used for speculation also appears to be confirmed by the fact that the biggest options market in the world (which includes equity index options) is based in Chicago, the home of commodity markets with their tradition of speculation,[2] rather than in New York, the site of the New York Stock Exchange. Options are similar to futures in that only a small amount of money need be spent initially to gain exposure to a large underlying securities position. This, as we shall see later in the chapter, can lead to

---

[1] The South Sea Bubble was a rush of share speculation which was concentrated on the shares of the South Sea Company. This company was granted a monopoly in the South Seas by the British government in return for taking over the entire British government debt. Its share price during the Bubble rose from £86 to £1,100.

[2] Cornering a commodities market, for example the famous squeeze on silver by the Hunt brothers in 1980, has been a popular pastime over the years.

large percentage gains or losses and this type of trading activity will clearly attract speculators.

Options also have the property of becoming completely worthless, if the security price has moved contrary to the purchaser's expectations by the expiry date of the option. A share, for example, only becomes completely valueless if the company's liabilities exceed its assets so as to have nothing for the shareholders on a winding up. In contrast, a put or call option can become worthless whatever the solvency of the underlying asset.

It is these characteristics of options which lead to the view that options are speculative investments. What is often not appreciated is that options enable the investor to vary the risk element in shares in *both* directions. In other words, the investor may either increase *or* decrease expected return and risk by trading in options. For example, institutional investors such as insurance companies which, as we shall see in Chapter 12, are generally considered to be risk averse in their attitude to investment, are frequent sellers or 'writers' of call options. By simultaneously holding shares and writing call options on those shares, they can reduce their risk to less than that of simply holding the shares.

Another major difference between traded options and futures and the types of securities we considered in earlier chapters is that traded options do not represent direct claims on the assets of the borrower. An ordinary shareholder, for example, holds the right to some fraction of the earnings and assets of the company whereas a traded call option holder merely has the right to buy shares in the future (shares which are already in issue) representing only a potential claim on the company's assets. An ordinary shareholder holds a security issued by the company, providing funds for the company in return for future income. A traded option holder has no relationship with the company whose shares he has an option to buy or sell. He has simply entered into an agreement with another party, the option seller or 'writer', concerning the possibly future purchase or sale of shares at a predetermined price. The writing of such option contracts has no impact on the company's issued share capital and neither the writer nor the purchaser has any direct relationship with the company. However, options attached to or embedded in other securities are *not* indepedent of the issuer. For example, warrants attached to bonds and convertible unsecured loans stock are two kinds of embedded options which, when exercised, are exercised against the issuer which then issues new shares to the holder.

This chapter begins with a description of options, concentrating on individual share options as the main example. Options on other securities will also be described, but only briefly. The chapter goes on to compare the differences between buying call options on shares and buying the underlying shares themselves. We find that the purchase of a call option contract involves a smaller initial outlay than the purchase of the underlying shares, with a smaller potential loss in money terms but a greater risk overall. Put options are then described, as are various combinations of options (and options with shares) which can increase or reduce risk and expected return. This, combined with an understanding of the various factors which affect the value of options, allows us to derive an option valuation model, known as the Black–Scholes model. The reader is then shown how to use this model to value traded options. The final section of the chapter discusses the new types of security now being issued, which include embedded options in the form of convertibles or index-linked bonds, and to which option valuation techniques can be applied.

It should be noted that the option valuation model *looks* difficult to use and it is, probably, the most complex model in this book. However, in practice, this is irrelevant since the calculations can be done by a very simple computer program. All that is needed is an understanding of the factors affecting the value of an option. The computer will do the rest.

Description of options

The purchase of a *call* option on an ordinary share entitles the holder to buy the share, on or before some fixed date in the future, at a fixed price. The fixed date is known as the exercise or expiry date and the fixed price as the exercise or striking price. A *put* option, on the other hand, entitles the holder to *sell* an ordinary share on or before the expiry date at a fixed price. Puts or calls which offer the holders the option to exercise *before* as well as on the expiry date are known as American options. European options entitle the holders to exercise their options to buy or sell only *on* the expiry date itself. Traditionally, in the UK, options were of the 'European' type. However, the traded options market has been based on the US options markets and so traded options purchased via the UK Stock Exchange are of the 'American' type.[3]

Example 7.1 gives details on London traded options provided daily in the *Financial Times* on the market statistics page.

Information on traditional, European-styles options is also provided by the *Financial Times* on the same page, below the traded options, as can be seen in Example 7.1. The terms of traditional options, such as the date they are set up, are not standardised as for traded options. In fact, traditional options can be arranged at any time, with the expiry date usually fixed at three months from the date of the contract and the exercise price traditionally fixed around the prevailing offer price for the share.[4]

---

[3] Because a traded option is an American (as opposed to a European) option, the holder has the right to exercise throughout the life of the option. We shall see later that the holder is more likely, in fact, to sell rather than exercise before expiry.

[4] Plus a small premium representing the interest cost to the writer of financing the option for three months.

Example 7.1   Details of London traded options

LONDON TRADED OPTIONS

Column 1

Option		CALLS Apr	Jul	Oct	PUTS Apr	Jul	Oct
Alld Lyons	550	41	52	68	4½	16	22
(*583)	600	9	25	43	24	40	46
	650	3	10	23	69	79	85
ASDA	25	7	9	10	1	2½	4
(*30)	30	3	5½	6½	7½	5	6½
	34	1½	–	–	5½	–	–
Brit. Airways	220	28	33	40	2	8½	12
(*245)	240	10½	20	29	5½	17	21
	260	3	11½	20	18	29	32
SmKl Bee- cham A	800	45	75	100	6½	23	34
(*837)	850	13	45	69	27	45	57
Boots	390	30	39	50	3½	12	15
(*419)	420	8	19	31	12	24	29
B.P.	240	12	19	22	3	9	14
(*248)	260	3	10	13	14	20	24½
British Steel	60	10½	12	13½	1	2½	7½
(*69)	70	3	6	8	3	7	8
Bass	525	13	33	47	13	27	33
(*527)	550	6	19	36	29	40	50
C & Wire	500	39	57	71	7	15	20
(*537)	550	8	28	43	28	32	43
Courtaulds	500	23	36	51	7	21	28
(*513)	550	3	15	30	39	52	57
Com. Union	390	22	40	46	3½	11	17
(*409)	420	6	22	29	17	24	32
Fisons	330	15	29	41	7½	23	28
(*338)	360	5	17	29	29	40	45
GKN	330	19	32	38	3½	11	17
(*346)	360	4	16	23	19	25	33
Grand Met.	850	45	78	97	7	21	33
(*885)	900	15	48	68	31	42	54
I.C.I.	1250	38	92	112	17	38	58
(*1273)	1300	14	64	87	44	64	82
Kingfisher	460	32	42	53	4½	15	22
(*487)	500	10	22	33	21	37	42
Ladbroke	200	15	25	32	4½	8½	13
(*210)	220	5½	14	21	13	18	23
Land Secur	360	21	26	30	5	15	17
(*376)	390	5	10	15	17	35	36
M & S	300	8	18	28	10½	16	20
(*300)	330	2	7	15	32	36	38
Sainsbury	390	13	24	34	7	15	21
(*396)	420	2	12	21	30	34	38
Shell Trans.	460	9	29	36	9	17	24
(*460)	500	1	10	17	41	44	48
Storehouse	110	7½	13	17	4	9	12
(*114)	120	2½	8	13	9	15	19
Trafalgar	110	12	17	21	4	11	15
(*119)	120	6	12	16	7	17	21
Utd. Biscuits	390	17	35	47	3	9	14
(*405)	420	4	17	29	19	24	28
Unilever	850	40	72	100	5	16	25
(*883)	900	15	42	67	27	37	47
Ultramar	220	8	14	–	13	–	–
(*217)	240	2	66	–	28	–	–

Option		CALLS May	Aug	Nov	PUTS May	Aug	Nov
Brit Aero	300	29	43	51	10	17	26
(*316)	330	13	27	36	26	30	41
	360	5	15	24	49	54	62

Column 2

Option		CALLS May	Aug	Nov	PUTS May	Aug	Nov
BAA	500	57	67	81	4	12	16½
(*548)	550	21	35	50	18	31	36
	600	5	13	30	55	63	67
BAT Inds	650	42	61	70	11	24	35
(*677)	700	15	33	44	35	48	60
	750	5	16	26	77	82	92
BTR	390	37	48	54	4½	7½	11½
(*418)	420	14½	27	34	13	19	23
Brit. Telecom	300	25	31	34	7½	12	15
(*314)	330	10	16	18	22	28	30
Cadbury Sch	420	38	53	63	6	12	16
(*446)	460	14	28	40	24	29	34
Eastern Elec	200	25	30	33	8	15	17
(*213)	230	9	–	–	23	–	–
Guinness	525	33	–	–	14	–	–
(*540)	550	22	38	50	27	32	38
GEC	200	12	15	19	5	10	12
(*205)	220	3½	7	10	17	24	24
Hanson	200	20½	23	26	2½	5	7½
(*216)	220	7½	12	15½	9	14	16½
LASMO	180	19	29	35	8	13	16
(*190)	200	8½	18	25	18	23	27
Lucas Inds	110	8	13	16	5½	8	12
(*111)	120	4½	8	11	12	13	17
P. & O.	360	37	50	54	8	15	24
(*383)	390	19	34	37	21	28	40
Pilkington	120	10½	15	19	5½	9½	12
(*125)	130	6	9½	14	10½	15	17
Prudential	200	24	32	34	4	6½	8½
(*219)	220	11	18	23	10	14	17
R.T.Z.	550	38	57	70	12	18	25
(*572)	600	12	30	43	37	43	49
Scot. & New	420	39	50	55	6	16	19
(*450)	460	14	26	34	21	34	40
Tesco	240	18	25	31	5	9	12
(*254)	260	6½	14	19	14	18	22
Thames Water	330	30	32	39	11	22	28
(*343)	360	18	21	27	26	45	48
Vodafone	330	8	16	26	23	28	30
(*343)	360	3	7½	15	50	51	51

Option		CALLS Jun	Sep	Dec	PUTS Jun	Sep	Dec
Abbey Nat.	260	18	24	31	7½	11½	14
(*265)	280	9	14	21	19	22	24
	300	4	7½	14	36	36	37
Amstrad	25	8½	10	11	2	3	4½
(*31)	30	5½	8	8½	4½	5½	7
	35	3½	5½	6½	7½	8½	9½
Barclays	300	22	29	34	14	21	22
(*303)	330	9	15	20	32	39	41
Blue Circle	240	21	27	33	9	14	18
(*255)	260	9	17	23	20	25	28
British Gas	240	15	22	26	8	10½	15
(*250)	260	6	12	15½	21	23	26
Dixons	200	20	25	31	9	13	16
(*210)	220	11	15	21	18	24	26
Eurotunnel	390	40	60	75	22	30	35
(*402)	420	27	42	60	40	47	50

Column 3

Option		CALLS Jun	Sep	Dec	PUTS Jun	Sep	·ct
Glaxo	750	59	82	106	33	51	59
(*762)	800	34	58	80	60	75	84
Hillsdown	160	13	17	21	8	11	13
(*169)	180	5	8	12	22	23	25
Lonrho	80	13	18	24	12	15	20
(*82)	90	8½	16	21	17	24	24
Midland Bk	330	36	40	49	13	17	19
(*346)	360	15	23	32	26	29	30
National Power	180	29	37	38	6	12	15
(*202)	205	15	20	–	16	24	–
Reuters	1050	87	118	148	39	52	60
(*1085)	1100	62	89	122	65	75	83
R. Royce	140	24	28½	31	3½	5½	7
(*157)	160	10	16	19½	9½	13	15
Scottish Power	80	12	15	17	8	12	15
(*82)	90	7½	9	13	14	20	22
Sears	90	11	13	14	5	6½	8½
(*96)	100	5	6½	8½	12	13	14
Forte	200	18	22	27	8½	11	13
(*213)	220	7½	13	17	21	22	23
Thorn EMI	719	67	71	–	10	22	–
(*764)	769	34	40	–	28	46	–
TSB	120	9½	13	16	5	8	9
(*122)	130	4½	7½	11	11	14	15
Vaal Reefs	50	7	7½	9	3	5	5
(*552)	60	2½	4	5	9	11	12
Wellcome	1050	88	125	157	44	60	71
(*1086)	1100	61	100	130	70	85	98

EURO FT-SE INDEX (*2435)

	2225	2275	2325	2375	2425	2475	2525	2575
CALLS								
Apr	235	190	146	107	74	47	29	17
May	249	206	165	128	96	69	49	31
Jun	264	–	183	–	114	–	63	–
Sep	315	–	235	–	165	–	110	–
Dec	345	–	275	–	210	–	155	–
Mar	375	–	305	–	242	–	177	–
PUTS								
Apr	6	11	19	27	46	69	102	140
May	14	20	30	42	60	82	110	143
Jun	20	–	36	–	65	–	112	–
Sep	38	–	57	–	85	–	125	–
Dec	47	–	70	–	100	–	135	–
Mar	50	–	70	–	100	–	135	–

FT-SE INDEX (*2435)

	2300	2350	2400	2450	2500	2550	2600	2650
CALLS								
Apr	168	127	90	59	40	22	14	8
May	186	147	110	83	58	39	25	15
Jun	202	163	133	104	75	52	35	24
Jul	217	182	147	120	92	70	50	36
Dec †	285	–	225	–	165	–	115	–
PUTS								
Apr	13	22	35	59	90	128	170	220
May	24	34	49	70	98	133	170	220
Jun	31	41	56	76	106	138	173	221
Jul	40	50	65	86	110	138	178	220
Dec †	70	–	100	–	140	–	200	–

April 9 Total Contracts 41,847
Calls 27,932 Puts 13,915
FT-SE Index Calls 15,272 Puts 7,062
Euro FT-SE Calls 528 Puts 615
Eurotrack 100 Index Calls 0 Puts 0
*Underlying security price. † Long dated expiry mths
Premiums shown are based on middle prices.

Source: Financial Times (10 April 1992).

Traded options are created on a rota system, with options always having nine-month lives and being created at three-monthly intervals. Options on some shares, for example BP, will be in the January, April, July and October series, whereas options on other shares, such as British Telecom, will belong to the February, May, August and November series, or to the March, June, September and December series, as for Barclays. Only three out of four options in a series will exist at any one time; for example, in Example 7.1, there are no February options in GEC since February is more than nine months from the date of the table. The actual expiry date on a traded option is usually the second Wednesday in the last Stock Exchange account to fall within the nine-month period.

Another difference between traditional and traded options is that traded options are created with more than one exercise price around the current share price, with at least one below and one above. For example, we can see from Example 7.1 that BP call options have exercise prices of 240p and 260p, with a current share price of 248p (shown with an asterisk below the name). Commission charges are also different between traditional and traded options, with commission being charged, at the same rate as for shares, on the *exercise price* of traditional options, and commission being paid on the option price (plus a fixed charge) for traded options.[5] The unit in which traded options are bought and sold is a *contract*, usually representing options on 1,000 shares. The total number of contracts traded on 9 April 1992,[6] given in Example 7.1, was 41,847. This compares with 27,993 ordinary share bargains on that date.

Purchase of call option contract or shares?

We now examine the effect of buying a call option contract. We suppose Mr Choice buys one Sainsbury call option contract with an exercise price of 390p per share and due to expire in July. The price quoted for such a contract in Example 7.1 is 24p per share, equivalent to 24p × 1,000 = £240 for the contract. The current Sainsbury share price is 396p and so the option will entitle Mr Choice to buy Sainsbury shares at below the current market price. Such an option is termed 'in the money' since Mr Choice could buy the option, immediately exercise his right to buy the shares at 390p, then sell them at 396p to make 6p per share, before any transaction costs. Call options such as the 420p July Sainsbury contract, where the exercise price exceeds the current share price, are referred to as 'out of money'. Obviously, for an 'in the money' call option to be traded, its value

---

[5] See Appendix 1 (p. 415) for details of these transaction costs.

[6] The day before the *Financial Times* edition shown in Example 7.1.

must exceed the profit which could be made on immediate exercise. For example, the option purchased by Mr Choice is worth 24p per share, compared to the 6p per share profit which could be made if the shares were exercised immediately.

We ignore for the moment the alternatives that Mr Choice has of selling the option unexpired or exercising his option *before* expiry and assume, for simplicity, that he holds the option until expiry. How will Mr Choice decide whether or not to exercise his option on expiry? If the Sainsbury shares are quoted at the expiry date of the option at less than 390p, there will be no point in exercising the option, since it would be cheaper for Mr Choice to buy the shares in the marketplace than at the exercise price of 390p. His total loss on the contract, if the option is not exercised, will be 24p × 1,000 = £240, a 100% loss on his investment in the option. However, if the Sainsbury shares are quoted at more than 390p on the expiry date, the exercise price will be less than the market price and it will benefit Mr Choice to exercise. When he has exercised his option, he can then decide whether to keep the Sainsbury shares he has acquired or immediately sell them. Suppose the Sainsbury share price on expiry is 420p. If Mr Choice immediately sells the shares, he will make a profit of 30p per share (420p – 390p). However, he paid 24p per share for the right to exercise at 390p and this must be deducted from the 30p per share to arrive at his actual profit:

Cost of option contract (1,000 at 24p)	(£240)
Cost of exercise (1,000 at 390p)	(£3,900)
	(£4,140)
Proceeds on sale (1,000 at 420p)	£4,200
Profit before transaction costs	£60

Of course this profit of £60 would be reduced by the transaction costs incurred by Mr Choice. These are excluded from our analysis to simplify the exposition. Note that it would still pay Mr Choice to exercise if the Sainsbury share price on expiry were only, say, 400p, since he would be able to make 10p per share by exercising his right to buy the shares and selling them to offset against the 24p per share cost of the option.

By purchasing a call option, Mr Choice has limited his maximum potential loss to the cost of the option, £240. His potential profit, however, is unlimited and will depend on the Sainsbury share price when he exercises the option. For it to be worthwhile to exercise, the Sainsbury share price must be greater than the exercise price, in this case 390p.

Example 7.2 compares the alternative investment strategies of buying a call option contract on 1,000 Sainsbury shares as opposed to buying the

Example 7.2   Purchase of call option or shares

	S = 370p	S = 420p
1. Call option on 1,000 shares (exercise price X = 390p)		
Cost of option	(£240)	(£240)
Cost of exercise	(0)	(£3,900)
Proceeds on sale	(0)	£4,200
Net profit/(loss)	(£240)	£60
Holding period return	−100%	+25%
2. Buy 1,000 shares		
Cost of shares	(£3,960)	(£3,960)
Proceeds on sale	£3,700	£4,200
Net profit/(loss)	(£260)	£240
Holding period return	−7%	+6%

1,000 shares themselves at the current market price of 396p. Two possible Sainsbury share prices on the exercise date are considered, $S = 370p$ and $S = 420p$, and, again, transaction costs are ignored.

Example 7.2 is unrealistic since it assumes that, if Mr Choice bought an option which expired in the money, he would exercise his right to buy the shares and would then immediately sell them to realise his profit. In practice, he would merely sell the options back just before exercise, to save the bother and cost of actual exercise. However, the numbers (barring transaction costs) would be the same.

Example 7.2 highlights the three fundamental differences between buying a call option on shares and buying the underlying shares themselves. Firstly, the investment outlay required for a call option is smaller, in this case £240 as opposed to £3,960 for the shares. Secondly, the downside risk in *money* terms is smaller for a call option. The maximum amount Mr Choice can lose on his option is £240, by leaving the option unexercised. However, Mr Choice can lose much more in money terms on the shares themselves if the price falls substantially below his purchase price. In this example, Mr Choice would lose £260 from holding shares if the share price fell to 370p. Thirdly, the *percentage* gain or loss given by the holding period return is greater on an option purchase than on share purchase. Relative to the amount invested, Mr Choice stands to make a greater percentage gain or loss on the option than on the shares. This implies, from our knowledge of the relationship between expected return and risk, that the purchase of a call option is riskier than the purchase of the underlying shares.

Graphical presentation of options

Call option

Figure 7.1(a) illustrates the potential gain or loss to Mr Choice on the Sainsbury option just before expiry, depending on the underlying share price, S, and the exercise price, $X = 390\text{p}$. We can see that Mr Choice makes a loss on his option investment unless the share price, S, reaches 414p, equal to the exercise price, X, of 390p plus the cost of the option, C, of 24p. Beyond that, his profit amounts to $(S - X)$ per share minus the cost of the option, C, giving a profit of $S - (X + C)$.

Figure 7.1(b) shows the equivalent gain or loss on the underlying shares. This is simply the difference between the cost of the share, in this case, 396p, say S_0, and the share price on expiry, S.

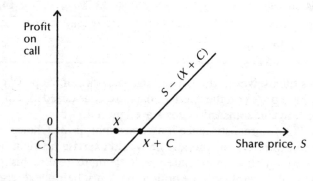

Figure 7.1(a)   Profit on a call option just prior to expiry

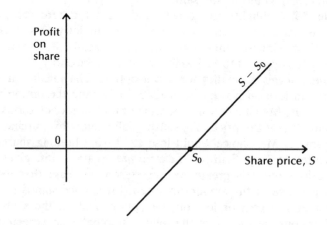

Figure 7.1(b)   Profit on underlying share just prior to expiry

Put option

A put option can be analysed graphically in exactly the same way as a call option. Figure 7.2 shows that the holder of a put will make money on his investment if the share price on expiry is *less* than the exercise price (by at least as much as the cost of the put), since he can then sell at the exercise price, X, and buy back immediately at the lower market price, S. Thus, the holder of a put makes money on a share price fall without actually having to hold shares. All that he has to do on exercise is buy the shares at the share price, S, and immediately sell them for the higher exercise price, X, to make his profit.

For example, look at the August British Telecom put option in Example 7.1 with an exercise price, $X = 300p$. This put is valued at $P = 12p$ with the share price at 314p. In this case, P is 'out of the money' since the shares could be sold in the market at 314p compared with only 300p if the put were exercised. The put is still worth 12p, since there is the possibility that the share price could fall further before the expiry date and the put be worth exercising. If Mr Choice bought the British Telecom put now at 12p, he would make a profit on expiry if the British Telecom share price fell to below the exercise price of 300p *minus* the cost of the put, $P = 12p$, that is, to below 288p. Suppose the British Telecom share price on expiry were 280p. Mr Choice would make the following profit on his investment in the British Telecom put option.

Proceeds of exercise at 300p per share
for 1,000 shares   =   £3,000

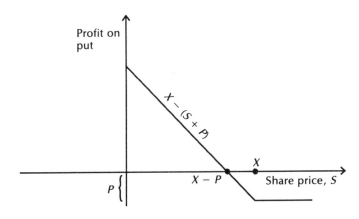

Figure 7.2   Profit on put option just prior to expiry

less: cost of acquiring shares at 280p per share	(£2,800)
less: cost of put option (1,000 × 12p)	(£120)
Profit before transaction costs	**£80**

Buying a put is a way of selling shares 'short', that is, selling shares that you do not have in the expectation that you will be able to buy them back at a lower price before you have to deliver. Short selling is allowed in the US but not in the UK. However, the potential losses from buying puts and short-selling are different. The short-seller is obliged to buy shares for delivery whatever they may cost whereas the put option holder does not have to exercise his right to sell. This limits the put option holder's losses to the cost of the option whereas the short-seller's losses are potentially unlimited.

Combinations of options

This graphical way of looking at options also allows us to examine combinations of different options, all based on the same underlying share. For example, the simultaneous purchase of a put and a call option on a share, with the same exercise price and expiry date, called a 'straddle', would lead to the profit pattern shown in Figure 7.3 on expiry.

Since the holder of a straddle will make money if the share price moves substantially up *or* down, an investor in a straddle would be someone who believed that the future price changes in that particular share, whatever their direction, had been underestimated by the market (as reflected in the market price of the straddle).

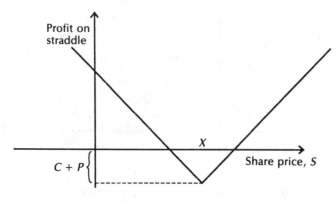

Figure 7.3 Profit on straddle just prior to expiry

Other types of option combinations include a 'strip' (the purchase of two puts plus one call) and a 'strap' (two calls plus one put). The number of possible variations is vast, allowing different amounts of risk to be borne, by speculating on or hedging against a variety of possible share price movements.

Use of options to hedge risk

As well as combining different types of option to speculate on share price movements, we can combine options with shares to *reduce* the risk to the investor of substantial price changes in the share. It will be remembered from Chapter 2 that options were mentioned, along with forward or futures contracts, as a means of hedging risk. And yet we have seen that options are risky investments, with possible returns on, say, a call option ranging from a 100% loss to unlimited positive returns. However, options can be used to hedge risk provided they are combined with investment in the underlying shares.

For example, suppose that Miss Pick buys shares in Axe plc and simultaneously sells or writes a call option contract in Axe shares. By writing a call option contract we mean that Miss Pick effectively sells a call option contract to an investor. Suppose, for example, that the Axe share price is currently 100p and that the exercise price of the call option is to be 110p with nine months to expiry. Suppose also that Miss Pick sells the call option contract for 20p per share. (This 20p is known as the *premium*.) Miss Pick will therefore receive 20p × 1,000 = £200 if she sells a call option contract for 1,000 Axe shares. Now, if the share price never exceeds 110p during the life of the option, the purchaser of the option will not exercise the option and Miss Pick will be left with a clear profit of £200. However, if the option is exercised, Miss Pick will be obliged to sell 1,000 Axe shares at the exercise price of 110p, whatever their market value. If Miss Pick did not already hold 1,000 Axe shares, her written call contract would be 'uncovered' since she would have to buy the shares needed in the market. If she already held the necessary Axe shares, her written call contract would be 'covered'. Note, however, that whether or not her written call contract is covered, her loss per share if the call option is exercised will still be the same, the difference between the current share price, S (the price at which she could have sold the share if there had been no contract) and the exercise price, X (the price at which she is obliged to sell the share) *less* the premium she has already received.

Figure 7.4 illustrates the effect on Miss Pick of buying Axe shares, of writing a call contract and of combining the purchase of Axe shares with the writing of a call option contract just prior to expiry.

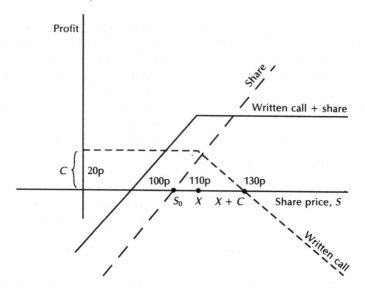

Figure 7.4   Profit just prior to expiry on combination of share purchase and written call option

For simplicity, we look at the profit per share. The impact of this particular combination, compared to simply buying the shares, is to increase the profit if the share price, S, is low on expiry and to reduce the gain if the share price is high on expiry. The break-even point is when the share price on expiry, S, is equal to the exercise price, X, plus the premium received, C, in this case, 110p + 20p = 130p. Thus, the risk of holding shares and writing call option contracts is *lower* than the risk of simply holding shares and, as mentioned in the introduction to this chapter, this combination is frequently employed by risk averse financial institutions.

In fact, if Miss Pick could alter the number of shares and the number of written call contracts in her investment portfolio as she wished, she could actually hedge risk completely not only at expiry but throughout the life of the option contract. So, whatever happened to the share price, the value of her shares *plus* the written contracts would remain constant. For example, suppose that, for every 1p change in the Axe share price, the value of a call option on the share changed by ½p. Miss Pick would then write call options on two Axe shares for every Axe share she held. Every time the share price went up by 1p, Miss Pick would lose 1p on her written call options leaving no change in the value of her portfolio. Similarly, when the Axe share price fell by 1p, Miss Pick's two written call contracts would gain 1p. As a result, the value of her combination of shares and written call options would remain the same, whatever happened to the Axe share price. Miss Pick would thus be perfectly hedged against any change in share price. Unfortunately, the relationship between the value of a call option and a share changes as the share price changes and over time (as we shall see when we examine in the next section the factors affecting the value of call options). So the 'hedge' ratio (as the ratio of the number of written call options needed to hedge changes in the price of one share is called[7]) will change all the time. However, if it were possible for Miss Pick continuously to alter the ratio of the number of written call options to the number of shares, thus ensuring a certain outcome whatever happened to the Axe share price, she would be able to hedge completely all the risk of her investment in Axe shares, provided the price changes for the share were relatively small.

Despite the complications encountered in practice for completely hedging risk by using options, it is this property of options which enables us to value them. However, before deriving an exact valuation model for options, we first need to consider which factors will affect their value.

Valuing options

Factors affecting value of call option

We now consider the factors which will affect the value of a call option. We can see from Figure 7.1 on p. 194 that the value of a call, C, is greater the greater the underlying share price, S. Also, the call option will be worth more, the lower the exercise price, X. This can be seen to be true in practice by looking at Example 7.1 on p. 190 where the BP July option contract is worth 19p per share with an exercise price, X, of 240p and only 10p per share with $X = 260$p.

Similarly, the longer the call option has to expiry, the more valuable it will be, since there will be more time for the share price to rise. So, in Example 7.1, the BP call contract with $X = 260$p is worth 3p, if expiry is in April, and 13p if expiry is six months later in October. An important corollary to this is that it usually does not pay an investor to exercise a call option before the expiry date, since, even if the current share price, S, exceeds the exercise price, there is still time for S to increase even further. Since shares are expected to have positive returns, share prices must be expected to rise over time (unless there is a dividend imminent).[8] Therefore, the holder of a traded option will usually do better if he wishes to realise his investment before the expiry date by selling his option than by

---

[7] This ratio (of ½ in this example) is also known as the 'delta' of the option.

[8] We know that the expected holding period return on a share consists of any dividend plus an expected capital gain. If there is to be no dividend during the holding period, the share price must be expected to rise. See, also later in this section and in the valuation sections of this chapter, for more comments on the problem of dividends.

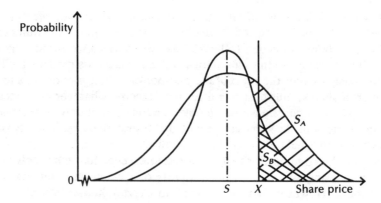

Figure 7.5   Effect of variability of share price on call option value

exercising it before expiry. For example, with the Sainsbury July call option contract with $X = 390\text{p}$, Mr Choice will do better by selling his contract for 24p per share than by exercising, buying and selling the shares, and making 6p per share. The 18p premium, known as the 'time' value element of the option, reflects the potential gain from a further expected rise in the share price in the time remaining to expiry.

Two other factors affect the value of a call option. Firstly, the prevailing rates of interest influence the call's value. The purchaser of a call option acquires the right to buy something in the future. By not having to buy the shares now, he is in effect saving money which he could invest until (possibly) needed at expiry. So, the higher the prevailing interest rate, the more valuable the option. In fact, the relevant interest rate affecting the value of a call option is, rather surprisingly, the *risk-free* interest rate, R_F. This is because we saw that if Miss Pick combined written call contracts on shares with the shares themselves in a suitable hedge ratio, she could completely hedge all the risk of her investment. Whatever happened to the share price, her return from the combination of written call contracts and shares was certain and risk-free. So, since investment in call options *can be* risk-free (if it is correctly combined with the underlying shares) the rate of return required on such call options will be the risk-free rate.

Secondly, the more risky the underlying share, the more the option is worth. Figure 7.5 considers two shares, A and B, where A is riskier due to the greater standard deviation or volatility, V_A, of its share price probability distribution. Suppose that these shares currently have the same share price, S, and that identical call options can be bought on each, with exercise price, X. If X is greater than the prevailing share price on each share when the investor buys the call options on A and B (the options are 'out of the money'), he must hope that, on expiry, the share prices, S_A and S_B, will exceed X. That eventuality is more likely in the case of A, since there is a greater possibility that S_A will exceed X than S_B exceed X, as evidenced by the greater shaded area in Figure 7.5. In the case of put options, it will be the downside risk (also measured by the variance or standard deviation in a normal probability distribution) which affects its value. So again, the higher the risk of the share, measured by the standard deviation, the higher the value of the put option.[9]

It is worth emphasising at this point that, when valuing options, we are concerned with share *prices* and not share returns. The future share *price* is relevant, since this is what determines the future return on the option. Dividends are not paid to option holders and are only of interest in so far as they affect the future share price. (Share prices usually fall when shares go ex-dividend.) At this stage, we assume for simplicity that no dividends are paid during the life of the option, although we shall relax this assumption later.

Option valuation model

Knowing the five factors which affect the value of a call option – the share price, S; the exercise price, X; the time to expiry, t; the risk-free interest rate, R_F; and the risk of the underlying share measured by its standard deviation or volatility, V – all that remains is to combine these into a formula for the value of the call option, C.

The valuation model most commonly used is one formulated by Black and Scholes, using the technique we considered for Miss Pick of combining written call contracts with the purchase of shares in such a way as to obtain a totally risk-free, hedged investment. Using the hedging strategy devised for Miss Pick, Black and Scholes obtained the formula for the value, C, of a call option:

$$C = S\,N(d_1) - PV(X)\,N(d_2) \tag{7.1}$$

where S is the underlying share price, X the exercise price, $PV(X)$ the present value of the exercise price payable on expiry (discounted to the present by using the risk-free rate of interest) and $N(d_i)$ the value of the cumulative normal probability distribution with a mean of 0 and an area under the curve of 1, evaluated at d_i. The d_i are functions which depend on the five factors, S, X, t, R_F and V.[10] Although equation (7.1) looks

---

[9] We shall see in Chapter 9 that, when considering investing in a share, only part of the total risk of the share is relevant, the part known as beta or market risk, since the remainder can be diversified away. However, when considering investing in options, the *total* risk or volatility is relevant since the value of the option depends on the *total* price movements of the share.

[10] For further explanation of the relevance of the $N(d_i)$ and the Black–Scholes model generally, see Jarrow and Rudd (1983). However, note that $N(d_i)$ is the hedge ratio of the number of shares per call option (½ in Miss Pick's example) known as the delta of the option.

Example 7.3   Determining a lower bound for C

Investment portfolio	Value at expiry date	
	$S_1 \geqslant X$	$S_1 < X$
Portfolio A		
Buy call for C	$S_1 - X$	0
Invest $PV(X)$	X	X
	$\overline{S_1}$	$\overline{X}$
Portfolio B		
Buy share for S	$\underline{S_1}$	$\underline{S_1}$

complex, it becomes much more comprehensible if, for the time being, we ignore the $N(d_1)$ and $N(d_2)$. By doing this, we get

$$C = S - PV(X) \tag{7.2}$$

In fact, the equality in equation (7.2) only holds at the date of expiry. However, it represents a lower bound for the call option value at any point in its life. We can show that this is so by considering two alternative investment portfolios, as in Example 7.3.

Portfolio A consists of buying a call option with an exercise price of X at a cost of C and of investing risk-free sufficient money, denoted $PV(X)$, which, with interest, will be worth X by the expiry date. If the share price on expiry, S_1, is greater than or equal to the exercise price, X, the call option will be worth the difference, $S_1 - X$, and the risk-free investment will be worth X, giving a total of S_1. If the share price is less than X, on expiry, the call option will be worthless and the value of portfolio A will simply be X.

Portfolio B consists only of the underlying share, purchased for S, which must be worth S_1 on the expiry date, by definition. Thus, if S_1 is greater than or equal to X on expiry, portfolios A and B will have identical values. However, if S_1 is less than X on expiry, the value of portfolio A will be greater than the value of portfolio B, since X is greater than or equal to S_1, in that case.

Since in both cases the value on expiry of portfolio A 'dominates' the value of portfolio B, the cost of portfolio B must be less than or equal to the cost of A, which may yield a higher value on expiry. Thus,

Cost of $B \leqslant$ Cost of A

$$S \leqslant C + PV(X)$$

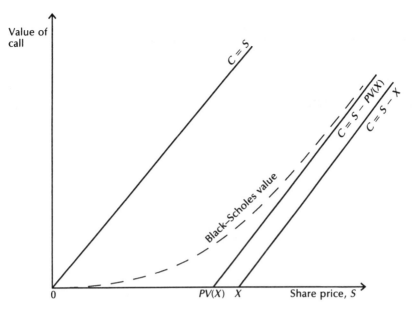

Figure 7.6   Limits on value of call option

or,

$$C \geqslant S - PV(X) \tag{7.3}$$

We can now see that $S - PV(X)$ is a lower bound for the value of a call option at any point in its life, as predicted by equation (7.2).

In fact, we also know an upper bound for the value of a call option since the value of C can never exceed the value of the underlying share, S. For example, if the exercise price were zero, the value of the option would at most be the value of the free gift – the share. If the exercise price were positive, there would be a cost to acquiring the share and the value of C would be less than S.

The solid lines in Figure 7.6 represent the upper and lower bounds that we have derived for C. The dotted line shows the value of C as given by the Black–Scholes formula in equation (7.1). This diagram shows the value of C at a particular point in time, say T, where there remains a period t to expiry. However, we can see that, as C approaches expiry, it must become less valuable since there is less time for the share price to increase. Thus, the dotted line will get closer and closer to the lower bound, $S - PV(X)$, as the option moves to expiry. Simultaneously, the value of $PV(X)$ will approach X as the expiry date nears, and so the right-hand bound, $S - PV(X)$, will move towards the value $S - X$. On expiry, provided $S \geqslant X$, the call option will be on the boundary itself, since it will then be worth exactly $S - X$. Prior to expiry the option is worth more than the lower limit (as we saw with the Sainsbury July option worth 24p), given the potential for the share price to rise further.

Using the Black–Scholes formula

Valuing a call option

The use of the Black–Scholes formula to obtain an exact value of C requires either a good calculator and some probability distribution tables or, more simply, a computer program which can be used interactively.

If a computer program is used to value options, the program will request details on the current asset price, the exercise price, the time remaining to expiry, the volatility of the asset price distribution, and the risk-free rate of interest for a period equal to the time to expiry of the option. In the case of options on shares, it will also ask for the dividend yield on the shares. This is because if a share pays dividends which option holders do not receive, the potential profit on exercise is reduced by the present value of the dividends to be paid. The Black–Scholes formula discussed in the previous section ignored this aspect; the Appendix to this chapter gives the Merton formula which represents a Black–Scholes value adjusted for the assumption that the share in question has a constant dividend yield. An alternative method is simply to deduct from the share price the present value of any dividends expected to be paid on the share during the time to expiry of the option.

Example 7.4 shows the inputs for and the Black–Scholes value[11] of Mr Choice's July 390 Sainsbury call option.

Example 7.4   Black–Scholes valuation of call option using a computer program

Input	
Share price	396p
Exercise price	390p
Risk-free rate of interest	10.75%
Time	0.2822 years
Volatility	20.62%
Dividend yield	2.5%
Output	
Value of call option	25.33p

---

[11] Strictly speaking, using the Merton version of Black–Scholes.

The share price and exercise price were as given in Example 7.1. The risk-free rate of interest of 10.75% was the mid-price between the inter-bank bid and offered price as given in the *Financial Times* of the same day for three-month money. (The actual time to expiry was just over three months – from 10 April 1992 to 22 July 1992.) The expiry date of 22 July 1992 for this particular option was as determined and published by LIFFE; equity option expiry dates are variable since they are determined by the closing dates for stock market accounts in each month. The volatility figure for Sainsbury was provided by a real time analytics software package called Bloomberg and represents the annualised standard deviation or volatility of returns of Sainsbury shares calculated from their daily price movements in the previous 30 days. Any periodicity (daily, weekly, or monthly) and number of days can be used to determine the volatility number. In this example, we have elected to use the most popular calculation method of daily data for the previous 30 days for input into the computer program. The Appendix to this chapter gives the manual method for calculating the Black–Scholes value of the July Sainsbury call option with an exercise price of 390p.

If we compare the value of the Sainsbury call option found using the Black–Scholes model of 25.33p with the actual market price (given in Example 7.1) of 24p, we can see that the two values are quite close, with a difference of only 1.33p. One reason for the small discrepancy in valuation could be that the assumptions underlying the Black–Scholes model are not appropriate for realistic option valuation. For example, although we have not derived the Black–Scholes formula from first principles, we are aware of one of the major assumptions – that written calls and shares can be combined in such a way as to produce a perfect hedge against changes in share price thoughout the life of the option. We saw with Miss Pick that this was hardly feasible in practice; in any case the transaction costs would be enormous. Other assumptions which might not be robust are the particular model of share price behaviour underlying the model[12] and the fact that traded options are American rather than European, allowing the investor to opt for early exercise if he so chooses. However, the difference in value between the market price of the option and its Black–Scholes value is small and is more than swamped by the bid–ask spread on the options. The *Financial Times* publishes the mid-price between the two. In practice, option market makers would have quoted the Sainsbury July 390

---

[12] For example, this assumes that the continuously compounded rate of return on the share in any given time period is normally distributed and that interest rates are constant over the life of the option. (For further details, see Hull, 1991, Ch. 10.) The other major option valuation model used in the markets is the binomial model which is also described in Hull (1991). It is numerical- rather than calculus- driven and has certain advantages when pricing American-style options (puts in particular). However, prices derived from the binomial model do not differ significantly from those derived using Black–Scholes when valuing the simpler traded call options such as described here.

call at 22p–26p, a 4p spread, removing any potential anomalies between the Black–Scholes value and the market value.

Valuing a put option

Since the values of call options, put options, and the underlying shares are related, the Black–Scholes model can also be used to value put options. We can find the relationship between the values of put and call options by returning to the concept of the two alternative portfolios, A and B, this time with portfolio A consisting of a share and a put option P and portfolio B of money on deposit, again PV(X), and a call option C. Example 7.5 shows the values of these two portfolios on expiry.

This time the two portfolios have identical values on expiry whichever value of S prevails. Their initial costs must therefore also be identical, giving

$$S + P = C + PV(X) \tag{7.4}$$

So, once the value of either a call or a put is known, the price of the other (provided it has the same exercise price and time to expiry) can be found from equation (7.4). Calculations by hand or using a computer program as we did earlier can give the investor the Black–Scholes value of either type of option without difficulty. Example 7.6 shows the input and output values from a computer program for a BP October 240 put option. The model value of 12.93p is, as for the Sainsbury call option, close to the market price given in Example 7.1 of 14p.

Example 7.5   Relationship between put and call values

Investment portfolio	Value at expiry date	
	$S_1 \geqslant X$	$S_1 < X$
Portfolio A		
Buy share for S	S_1	S_1
Buy put for P	0	$X - S_1$
	$\overline{S_1}$	$\overline{X}$
Portfolio B		
Buy call for C	$S_1 - X$	0
Invest PV(X)	X	X
	$\overline{S_1}$	$\overline{X}$

Example 7.6   Black–Scholes valuation of put option using a computer program

Input	
Share price	248p
Exercise price	240p
Risk-free rate of interest	10.75%
Time	0.5507 years
Volatility	25.74%
Dividend yield	9.0%
Output	
Value of put option	**12.93p**

The role of volatility

We have seen that most investors and traders in the markets use Black–Scholes (or variants) for their option valuation models. There thus appears to be substantial agreement on how to price equity call and put options. However, it may still be the case that Mr Choice regards, for example, the Sainsbury July 390 call as 'cheap' and that another investor regards it as expensive. How can this happen?

By allowing for disagreement, not over the model but over the inputs. Given that there is little room for argument over the share price, the exercise price, the risk-free rate of interest, the time to expiry, and the dividend yield, any difference of opinion between investors must stem from differing expectations concerning the future volatility of the share. In Example 7.4, we used a volatility estimate derived from a particular set of historical data for Sainsbury, but we have no means of knowing that this is the volatility which the Sainsbury share price will experience between 10 April and 22 July 1992. Mr Choice may feel that the Sainsbury share price is likely to be more volatile over that period than it had been the previous month. Other investors may hold the opposite view.

The fact that the only option valuation model input over which the investor can argue is that of volatility has an interesting implication. If the Black–Scholes model is the industry standard for option valuation, as it appears to be in practice, the model can be used to provide not the value of a call option but the market's best estimate of the likely volatility of a share during the period to expiry of the option. Thus, the market price of the option becomes the input into the model and the volatility or standard deviation the output. For example, if we use the data in Example 7.4 to find the volatility of Sainsbury shares, by inputting the market price of the July 390 call option of 24p we obtain an implied volatility of 18.87%.

This ability to determine implied volatilities from option prices has led to a new method of trading and investing in securities. If Mr Choice is bullish about Sainsbury shares and also has a view on their future volatility, he can choose an option strategy to suit his view. For example, if he thinks that volatility will be higher than the 18.87% implied in the July 390 call option price of 24p, he will buy the option, since the option will become more valuable (all other things remaining the same) the higher the actual volatility of the share. Similarly, if he is comparing several alternative options on the same share, he might choose to buy the option with the lowest implied volatility since this is effectively the best value for money. On the other hand, if he believes that the Sainsbury share will be *less* volatile than implied in the call option prices, he may well consider an alternative investment strategy which involves *selling* options. If Mr Choice has no view on prices but a view on increased or decreased volatility in the future, he could buy or sell a straddle (a strategy referred to earlier on p. 196 of this chapter).

The importance of volatility in option pricing means that the investor always has to be aware of his view both on prices *and* on volatility. For example, if Mr Choice thinks that prices are going to fall and he wishes to make money out of this, he has two choices, assuming that he has no underlying equity portfolio position. He can either buy a put option, which involves a money outlay and makes money if the share price falls, or he can sell a naked call,[13] which brings in a limited amount of money in the form of the option premium if the price stays stable or falls but loses potentially unlimited amounts of money if he is wrong and the price rises instead. This is because the seller or writer of options has the *obligation* to deliver if the buyer of the call option chooses to exercise his right to buy. In this case, Mr Choice would lose money since he would have to buy shares in the market at a higher price in order to sell them at a lower, fixed price to the call option buyer. Figure 7.7 highlights the different profit profiles of the two alternative strategies if he holds the options positions to expiry.

However, what Figure 7.7 does not make clear is the volatility strategies implied by each alternative. This will be of importance if Mr Choice decides to unwind his strategy *before* expiry. Buying a put option involves being long of volatility; selling a call option involves being short of volatility. So, Mr Choice will make more money by buying a put option when compared with selling a call option if the price falls sharply and the market for the share becomes more volatile – as happened during the Crash of 1987. Buyers of put options before the Crash benefitted from both the price drop *and* increased implied volatility when they came to sell their put

---

[13] 'Naked' because he has no underlying equity position. The next section considers alternative option strategies for the investor already holding shares.

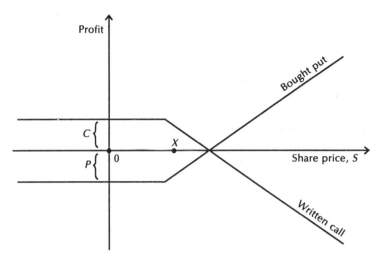

Figure 7.7   Comparison of bought put and sold call strategies

options after the Crash. On the other hand, Mr Choice would make more money from a sold call option position if the price stays stable or falls a little and the market for the share stagnates, with reduced volatility. In that case, Mr Choice could buy back his option at a relatively cheaper price reflecting the reduced implied volatility as well as the lower share price.

Finally, notice that the implied volatility in put and call options on the same share for the same maturity and the same exercise price may be different. For example, for the Sainsbury July 390 options, the call has an implied volatility of 18.9% and the equivalent put an implied volatility of 26.5% So, relative cheapness will also enter into the equation when deciding whether to buy or sell calls or puts. It is quite common for puts to be priced at higher volatilities than calls; institutional investors, with equity portfolios, are frequent writers of call options, thus depressing their price relative to equivalent put options. Traders, looking for value, will therefore prefer to buy call options rather than puts when this suits their view of the future share price.

One further point, particularly relevant to put options, which must be borne in mind when using the Black–Scholes model is that the formula actually gives the value for a European option, that is, one which can only be exercised on maturity. In the same way as the problem of dividends is ignored in the basic Black–Scholes option valuation model, the assumption that the option is European is made in order to simplify the option sufficiently to be able to value it at all! However, this difficulty is not insuperable. We can see that the 'American' London traded options must be worth at least as much as equivalent European ones because of their additional right to exercise before expiry. However, they may be worth no more than European ones since we saw earlier that it was usually more profitable either to sell the option or to hold the option to expiry rather than to exercise before expiry. For example, the call option held by Mr Choice was worth 24p unexercised compared to 6p exercised. This was because of the 'time' value of the option. So the Black–Scholes formula which gives the value of European options will usually also give the value of American options provided there are no complications such as dividends. If a dividend is due before expiry, however, the investor may do better to exercise before the share goes ex dividend and collect the dividend rather than wait till expiry to exercise and thus forfeit the dividend payment. So, in the case of an option on a dividend-paying share, such as the BP 240 put expiring in October considered above, the option must be valued twice, first assuming that it will be exercised on expiry and, second, that it will be exercised before the shares go ex dividend. It may be that the option will be more valuable if exercised before the shares go ex div and thus, in this case, an American option will be more valuable than an equivalent European option.

Hedging strategies

As we have mentioned throughout this chapter, options can be used to reduce risk as well as to increase risk through their gearing characteristic. We are now in a position to summarise the basic hedging strategies using options, and to compare them with the futures hedging strategies encountered in the last chapter.

To do this, we will use, for variety, a different type of option to the individual share options used up to now in this chapter, and one for which there is an equivalent futures contract. This type of option is an option on the FT-SE 100 Share Index and prices are given in Example 7.1 on p. 190, following on from the prices for individual share options but above the traditional option prices. The FT-SE 100 Index is an arithmetic index on the top 100 shares by market capitalisation listed on the UK stock market and described in more detail in an Appendix to Chapter 9.

Notice that there are two tables of FT-SE 100 option prices, one headed Euro FT-SE Index and the other simply FT-SE Index. The first table gives European option prices and the second American option prices. In order to prevent confusion, they have different exercise prices. European style options are traded as well as the more usual American style because UK fund managers like to sell options and, when they do, they wish to avoid early exercise against them, and we saw in the last section that early exercise might be in the interests of the option holder depending on the underlying dividend pattern and on the level of interest rates. By selling European-style options, fund managers can be sure that there will be no early exercise. However, the trading volume on the European style FT-SE 100 Index options is currently substantially below that of its American-style counterparts. For example, in Example 7.1, the volume of call options traded for 9 April was 15,272 for the FT-SE 100 Index calls and only 528 for the Euro FT-SE calls.

Fundamentally, options on a stock market index, such as on the FT-SE 100 Index can be treated in a similar way to individual equity options. They can be valued in the same way and trading and hedging strategies can be adopted with either type of option. Also, since LIFFE (which was responsible for the index options) and LTOM (which was responsible for individual equity options) merged in 1991, the way in which such options are paid for and margined is identical. Essentially, both types of option are premium paid for buyers of options (that is, the entire option premium is paid up front) and margined for sellers of options. Additionally, if several trades in individual equity options and index options are done, margin credits and debits can be netted off. The same risk measurement system for the calculation of margins is used for both types of option.[14]

Options on the FT-SE 100 Index differ from options on individual shares in two main ways. FT-SE 100 Index options are cash settled on expiry whereas exercise of an individual share option involves the exchange of cash for actual physical shares. Exercise of FT-SE Index options does not involve the transfer of portfolios of 100 shares. There are also consequent technical differences. For example the expiry day is different – the third Friday in the month for FT-SE 100 Index options and two days before the last day of the closest Stock Exchange Account[15] for individual equity options. Example 7.1 also shows that there is a greater number of exercise prices and exercise dates available for options on the FT-SE 100 Index. Indeed, the FT-SE 100 Index American-style options operate on a June and December cycle plus a monthly cycle so that the nearest *four* calendar months are always available for trading.[16]

Secondly, options on the FT-SE 100 Index are not acquired on a fixed number of stock index units; rather, as for the FT-SE 100 Index futures contract described in Chapter 6, options are acquired on a notional sterling

---

[14] For further details, see the LIFFE/LTOM publications on margining and settlement and see also Chapter 6, p. 165, on futures margining. Note, however, that FT-SE 100 Index options are options on the cash index and not options on the futures contract.

[15] Technically, the Stock Exchange Account falling wholly within the relevant expiry month.

[16] The European-style options operate on a March, June, September, December cycle plus a monthly cycle which ensures that the nearest *three* calendar months are always available for trading.

amount of the contract which varies with the level of the index. For example, if 100 call options were bought on the FT-SE 100 Index at the level of 2435 quoted in Example 7.1, the underlying value of the shares in which the option buyer has an interest would be

$$100 \times 2435 \times £10$$

$$= £2.435 \text{ m.}$$

Notice that the point size for FT-SE Index options is £10 compared with £25 for the futures contract on the same index. This point size is also important when determining the cost a particular option trade. For example, if Ms Bush decided to buy 100 2450 June calls quoted at 104 in Example 7.1, she would pay

$$100 \times 104 \times £10$$

$$= £104,000$$

for an exposure to a portfolio worth £2.435 m.

Returning to our hedging strategies, we will now look at the position of an investor, Mr Maze, who is holding a diversified portfolio of shares worth in total £200,000. We assume, for simplicity that the behaviour of this portfolio will mirror that of the FT-SE 100 Share Index; in other words, if the index goes up or down by 10%, Mr Maze's portfolio will also rise or fall by 10%.

Essentially, Mr Maze has four ways of hedging his portfolio: selling his shares; selling index futures against the portfoliio; selling index call options; or buying index put options. Each of these strategies, labelled (A)–(D), is shown graphically in Figure 7.8 as is the strategy of doing nothing, labelled (E).

(A) SELLING SHARES

This is the most radical hedging strategy of the four alternatives since the transaction costs related to the sale of the shares will be high. Also, should Mr Maze change his mind at a later date, and wish to re-enter the stock market, his transaction costs will be even higher and, whilst reassembling his portfolio of shares, he may miss a sudden surge in share prices.

The cash return earned by Mr Maze if he sells his shares will simply be the rate of interest on the £200,000, which we assume to be 10% per annum for simplicity.

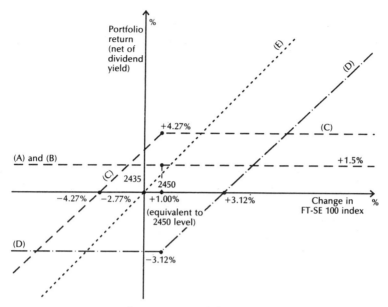

Figure 7.8 Alternative portfolio hedging strategies

(B) SELLING INDEX FUTURES

By selling index futures, as was shown in detail in Chapter 6, Mr Maze would effectively neutralise his exposure to the equity market. For every 1 per cent fall in the value of his share portfolio, the sold futures hedge would rise 1 per cent, maintaining the total value of his investment at £200,000. However, by selling futures rather than shares, Mr Maze would save on transaction costs and would retain the flexibility to re-enter the market whenever he wished, simply by reversing the futures hedge or by allowing the futures contract to expire.

In contrast to the strategy of selling shares, by selling index futures Mr Maze would retain an exposure to the *income* from his portfolio, since he would still receive the dividend income from the shares he had not sold. However, the proceeds from the sale of the futures contracts would not be received until the expiry date of the futures contract and so, unlike strategy (*A*), Mr Maze would not receive any interest income under strategy (*B*). Since, on the futures expiry date, Strategy (*A*) and Strategy (*B*) are equivalent, in order to equalise the returns from these two strategies, the futures price will differ from the cash index level, as was shown in Chapter 6, by the interest yield minus the dividend yield, adjusted for the time to expiry.

In Figure 7.8, all strategies bar the sale of the shares allow Mr Maze to receive the dividend yield. We therefore show an annual return for

Strategy (*A*) and Strategy (*B*) of the interest yield of 10% minus the dividend yield of, say, 4% to give an annualised 6% or 1.5% over the three-month option period.

(C) SELLING INDEX CALLS

We now turn to one of the two hedging strategies which uses options. By using options instead of futures to hedge his share portfolio, Mr Maze retains some exposure to the equity market rather than neutralising his exposure by selling shares or futures contracts against the portfolio. For example, if we look at Strategy (*C*) in Figure 7.8, by selling or writing calls against his share portfolio, Mr Maze chooses to enhance his portfolio return (compared with holding an unhedged portfolio) if the index level stays at around the same level or falls, but also chooses to cap his return potential if the index rises. So, incorporating options into a portfolio alters the risk and return profile of the returns for the investor.

Notice that, when looking at portfolio hedging, Mr Maze would seek to hedge the full value of the portfolio with options and not use the delta hedging techniques employed by Miss Pick. Miss Pick, you will recall, was seeking a continuous hedge.[17] whereas the portfolio hedger, in this case Mr Maze, is usually trying to hedge his portfolio for a specified time period such as three months or one year.

We assume, for the purposes of this example, that Mr Maze is seeking to hedge his portfolio up to the end of June by using the nearest to 'at the money' June options available. With the cash index at 2435, Mr Maze chooses the 2450 exercise price American-style June options.

Since the exposure from selling one index call option is 10 × the current index level, to write calls against a £200,000 share portfolio, Mr Maze should sell

$$\frac{£200,000}{2435 \times 10}$$

$$= 8.21$$

or, rounding, 8 index call option contracts.

Using the prices given in Example 7.1 for the June 2450 FT-SE 100 Index option contracts, Mr Maze would receive a premium of 8 × 104 × £10, or £8,320 (ignoring transaction costs).

If we compare the hedging strategy of writing calls with the other strategies shown in Figure 7.8, we can see that selling shares or futures is

---

[17] Also known as a dynamic hedge, namely a hedge with protects the hedger from each price move.

best if the index falls by more than 2.77% (4.27%−1.5%) and doing nothing is best if the index rises by more than 4.27%. However, if the index falls by less than 4.27% or rises by more than 4.27%, then writing call options against his portfolio turns out to be the best strategy for Mr Maze. The percentage number, 4.27%, is derived by calculating the price of the June 2450 index call option of 104 given in Example 7.1 as a percentage of 4.27% of the cash index value of 2435.

So, if Mr Maze thought that the stock market was going to drift sideways over the next three months, he could earn 4.27% during the period up to expiry (equivalent to $(1.0427)^4 - 1 = 18.21\%$ per annum) by writing calls. However, if the market rises, he will limit his return to 4.27% when it could have been more. If the market falls, he will add a 4.27% cushion to the fall but will suffer if the market falls by more than the size of the cushion.

Notice that, if Mr Maze thinks the market will move sideways, he probably also thinks that the market will not be volatile. We saw in the previous section in this chapter that if the investor thinks market volatility will be low he should sell options. This is exactly what Mr Maze is doing by writing calls. However, this point highlights the fact that using options to hedge a portfolio forces the investor to take a view both on price and on volatility.

(D) BUYING INDEX PUTS

The second hedging strategy to involve options is to buy puts. In this example, Mr Maze would buy 8 2450 June FT-SE 100 Index puts, quoted at 76 in Example 7.1, costing a total of 8 × 76 × £10, or £6,080 (ignoring transaction costs). The puts are cheaper than the equivalent calls because the calls are slightly in the money with the index at 2435 and the exercise price of these options at 2450.

If we look at Strategy (D) in Figure 7.8, we notice a rather startling phenomenon. Buying puts as a hedging strategy is *never* optimal, whatever the percentage rise or fall of the index. And yet, buying puts is the most common hedging strategy. Why? Because it gives the best profit profile for the investor who cannot afford the risk that the index will fall (and so cannot adopt the unhedged strategy, Strategy (E)) and yet wants to take advantage of a market rise (and hence cannot adopt the capped profit strategy of writing calls, Strategy (C)). In effect, by buying a put, such an investor is buying insurance. If the market falls, Mr Maze has the right to make a 'claim' and to lock in a minimum value for this portfolio of £193,920 (£200,000 – the cost of the put options of £6,080); if the market rises, he has the right not to exercise the put options and to write off the cost of the insurance against the rise in value of his portfolio.

One element which can be varied is the type of put option used to hedge the portfolio. The shorter the time period which is hedged, the cheaper the option. But also, the lower the exercise price, the cheaper the put option. Looking at Example 7.1, we can see that the 2350 June FT-SE 100 put option is priced at 41 instead of 76 for the 2450 puts, equivalent to 1.68% of the index value of 2435 compared to 3.12% for the 2450 puts. However, the downside protection is not so good. The market has to fall by another 100 points before the protection implied by the 2350 put options kicks in. Nevertheless, cheap options are a popular form of portfolio hedge. They are known as 'catastrophe insurance' and are used by institutional fund managers to try and protect against sudden market falls such as happened in the US and UK in 1987 and 1989 and in Japan in 1990.

An alternative way of reducing the cost of buying puts is to sell calls against them. For example, again looking at Example 7.1, the 2550 June FT-SE 100 calls are priced at 51. Mr Maze could buy the 2450 puts and sell the 2550 calls for a net cost of 8 × (76 − 51) × £10, or £2,000. This is substantially less than the full cost for the 2450 puts of £6,080, but the disadvantage is that the upside potential of the portfolio is capped at an equivalent index level of 2550. Yet again, the type of put hedge preferred by Mr Maze would involve his taking a view on market prices and volatility.

Volatility also plays a part in Mr Maze's choice of hedging strategy. Buying puts is for the more cautious investor who cannot make up his or her mind whether the market is going up or down. It is, the investor believes, going to do one or the other and not remain static. If the investor is right and it falls dramatically or rises fast, the volatility of the market is likely also to increase, giving an investor such as Mr Maze a windfall gain if he sells his put options before expiry when they still have some time value (related to volatility) left. This was exactly what happened to investors, during the Crash of 1987, who had bought put options to protect themselves against a market fall. On 19 October, their put options rose in value as the market fell but they went up far more than the change in intrinsic value as the volatility used to determine their value also rose dramatically. Notice that a hedge which involved buying a put and then selling a call at a higher exercise price would neutralise the impact of volatility changes on the hedge. In this case, Mr Maze would be long of volatility with the put option and short of volatility with the call option, and these would cancel each other out.

One final point on using put options to hedge a share portfolio. The shape of Strategy (D) in Figure 7.8 looks strangely like a call option profile. This comes from the equality we derived in equation (7.4):

$$S + P = C + PV(X)$$

Buying puts and holding shares is equivalent to investing the present value of the exercise price in cash and the rest in call options. This latter strategy is sometimes referred to as a 90–10 strategy, since approximately 90% of the portfolio is in cash and 10% of the portfolio invested in index call options if the investor has a one year time horizon. There are advantages to the 90–10 strategy in that transaction costs are much lower than those associated with putting together a portfolio of shares and then buying put options to hedge it. However, the share plus put strategy does allow the investor the opportunity to buy shares which are likely to behave differently from the FT-SE 100 Index and which will outperform the index, whether the index goes up or down. Investors with no such stock selection skills are likely to be better off with the 90–10 alternative.

Securities with embedded options

The ability to value options, using a model such as the Black–Scholes model above, is not only of use for traded options. It also enables us to value other securities which have options embedded in them, for example, convertible unsecured loan stock, bonds with warrants attached, and bonds whose principal amount is linked to a stock market index.

The variety of corporate securities has increased dramatically in the past decade, particularly those issued in the Eurobond market. Based on the 'plain vanilla' bond, which can be valued in exactly the same way as the government bonds described in Chapters 3 and 4 (except for credit risk), many variations on a theme have been issued. They are often hybrids between debt and equity, such as convertible unsecured loan stock, and can be quite complex to value, even with the aid of the Black–Scholes model and a personal computer. Or they may be bonds which offer the issuer or the investor certain additional rights. These rights, such as the investor's right to 'put' or sell the bond back early to the issuer at par, can also be valued using option valuation techniques.

In the remainder of this chapter, we briefly describe four types of embedded option: convertible unsecured loan stock; bonds with warrants; equity index-linked bonds; and investor put and issuer call options.

Convertible unsecured loan stock

Convertible unsecured loan stock (or CULS for short) lies somewhere between straight debt and equity in terms of risk for the investor and it has been this compromise in terms of risk and return which has given it its popularity. Companies with high debt–equity ratios and consequently unable to issue more debt in the markets were able to issue CULS. Also, investors, worried about equities after the Crash of 1987 and yet unwilling to give up the profit potential inherent in equities, were happy to invest in convertible debt, which offered the comparatively greater security of fixed interest debt if the ordinary shares did not do well combined with the possibility of switching into shares at a later date if they did do well.

In order to gain an understanding of how convertibles work and how they can be valued, we will examine one particular convertible, the Carlton Communication 6.5% Net Cumulative Convertible Redeemable Preference Shares 2005–2010. Notice that these are technically preference shares rather than bonds, which has implications for the dividend (being paid net of ACT rather than gross for unsecured loan stock) and for the rights of the holders in the event of a liquidation. In all other respects, this issue is equivalent to a convertible unsecured loan stock.

From Chapter 3, we know the significance of the 6.5% coupon and the redemption dates 2005–2010. Carlton Communications have contracted to pay the holders of the convertible 6.5% per annum (in two semi-annual instalments) for each £100 nominal of the convertible held and, provided the stock remains unconverted, to continue to do so until redemption some time between 2005 and 2010. The choice of redemption date in the period 2005 to 2010 is up to Carlton Communications and this choice gives Carlton Communications what is known as an 'option to call' the stock and, in fact, this option can be valued using the option valuation model described earlier in this chapter.

What the coupon and redemption dates do not tell us is that a holder of the Carlton Communications convertible has the right on any 31 March between 1991 and 2005 to exchange his or her convertible preference shares for ordinary shares, receiving in this case 10.336 ordinary shares for every £100 nominal of the convertible preference shares. This figure of 10.336 is known as the 'conversion ratio' and the nominal amount of convertible preference shares given up per share, in this example £100/10.336 = 967p, as the 'conversion price'. However, on 9 January 1992, the convertible was trading at £85 per £100 nominal. This made the *effective* conversion price for Carlton Communications £85/10.336 or 822p, compared with a share price on that date of 503p. This can also be viewed as a conversion premium of (822–503)/503 or 63% over the ordinary share price. In other words, buying the shares by means of the convertible preference shares instead of buying the Carlton Communications shares direct would involve an investor in paying a premium of 63%.

So, why buy convertibles? Because, convertible preference shares also offer the holder an income advantage over the purchase of straight equity. Holders of the convertible preference shares will receive a fixed dividend whereas holders of the ordinary shares will receive a variable (lower) dividend. However, for most healthy companies, ordinary share dividends are expected to grow and, at some point in the future, the income advantage will switch to the ordinary shareholders, at which point it will be optimal for the convertible holders to convert.

For example, in the case of Carlton Communications, buying £100 nominal of the convertible preference shares would give the right to 10.336 shares, trading on 9 April at 503p. This values the convertible at 10.336 × 503p = £51.99, substantially below the then market price of the convertible of £85. However, holders of the convertible would receive 6.5% net dividend whereas the gross dividend yield on the shares was at that time 3.9%. By forecasting dividends for each year up to 2005, and by discounting the benefit of the preference dividend over the increasing dividend stream back to current prices, the investor can decide in which year it will be optimal to convert (when his income from the shares exceeds his income from the preference shares) and can value the convertible by adding the net present value of the income advantage to the equivalent share value of £51.99. For example, assuming 15% per annum dividend growth would make conversion optimal in 2002. Discounting the income advantage between 1992 and 2002 back to 1992 values would give an income advantage of 270.25p per share at a 10% discount rate. For each £100 nominal of convertible preference shares, the income advantage would be 10.336 × 270p or £27.93. Thus, the total value for the convertible is £51.99 + £27.93 = £79.92, equivalent to a discount of £5.08 or 6.0% to the market price. Depending on the dividend forecast and the required discount rate, some investors may view the convertible as cheap equity whereas others may view it as an expensive form of equity. Example 7.7 shows, for the Carlton 6.5% convertible preference shares, a variety of dividend growth assumptions and their effect on the optimal conversion date and on the value of the convertible.

This concept of convertibles as equity plus an income advantage represents the traditional way of viewing convertibles and is still used in the City. A more modern method would be to use option valuation techniques which take into account the value inherent in the *option* to convert; the traditional method assumes that investors always do convert.

The modern method views a convertible as a straight bond or preference share plus the option to convert into shares at a fixed price. For this reason the coupon on a convertible is lower than that on a straight bond to reflect the value of the embedded option. Unfortunately, the options inherent in convertibles are somewhat more complex than those we encountered trading on LIFFE. There are several reasons for this. First, there are a variety of possible conversion dates ranging in the case of Carlton Communications from 1991 to 2005 instead of just one on traded equity or equity index options. This multiple exercise date problem is exacerbated by the need to adjust for dividends over the entire option period. We saw in Example 7.7 above just how sensitive the convertible value is to the dividend growth assumption using the traditional valuation method. This disadvantage also applies to the option method of valuing convertibles.

Example 7.7   Valuing a convertible as shares plus income advantage

---

Carlton Communications 6.5% Net Cumulative Convertible Preference Shares 2005–10

Value as at 9 January, 1992

Assumptions:

Convertible price £85 per £100 nominal
Share price 503p
Conversion terms 10.336 shares per 100 nominal
Net dividends paid of 6.1p on 28 August 1991 and 9.4p
payable on 7 August 1992
Net dividend of 6.5% per annum payable on 1 January and 1 July
Conversion dates 31 March in any year from 1991 to 2005
Discount rate for income advantage calculation of 10%
Value per £100 nominal

Value of shares £	Dividend growth rate (%)	Optimal conversion year	Income advantage £	Total value £	Premium (disc) to conv. price (%)
51.99	10	2005	34.90	86.89	2.2
51.99	15	2002	27.93	79.92	(6.0)
51.99	20	2000	23.33	75.32	(11.4)
51.99	25	1998	20.29	72.28	(15.0)
51.99	30	1997	18.00	69.99	(17.7)

Source: James Capel, *The Convertibles White Book* (January 1992).

A second disadvantage when applying the Black–Scholes model to convertible valuation is the determination of the exercise price. With a traded option, the exercise price is fixed. With a convertible, the exercise price is the value *at conversion* of the fixed income security given up. This value will change depending on the interest rates prevailing at the *estimated* optimal conversion date. Interest rates will clearly affect the exercise price of the option and yet the Black–Scholes model specifically assumes that interest rates are fixed during the life of the option.

As a result of these complications, simple Black–Scholes option valuation models cannot be applied to the valuation of convertibles. Valuation software can be bought but it is as yet too expensive for the retail investor. Convertibles are still valued, in the UK at least, by the traditional method.

Bonds with warrants

The eurobond market[18] has seen the invention of a very wide range of bonds – from plain vanilla to such exotic creations as 'heaven and hell' bonds, for example! Banks have been expert in designing bonds in order to tempt the investor. Bonds with warrants are an example of this and were devised in the 1980s to raise money for companies, often Japanese, which were not well enough known in the euromarkets to raise money via plain vanilla issues. Warrants are exactly the same in concept as options in that they offer the investor the right to buy shares at some date or dates in the future at a fixed price. The warrants issued with eurobonds were seen as sweeteners which would be of interest to investors wishing to gain a leveraged way into the seemingly ever-rising Japanese stock market. The warrants were detachable from the bonds, allowing investors to choose the level of risk they wished to bear – straight bonds, warrants, or a combination – unlike convertibles which are an inseperable mixture of debt and options.

One major difference between the options embedded in convertibles and warrants and the traded options discussed earlier in the chapter is that embedded options usually involve the issuing of new shares by the company when the embedded options are exercised. This creates what is known as dilution of the equity, by creating more shares, but has a positive effect on total earnings by either extinguishing the interest liability on the convertible or by receiving exercise payments on the warrants. Thus, the effect on earnings per share when exercise of the embedded options takes place can be positive or negative, depending on the number of shares issued relative to the money taken in. The other major difference between embedded options and traded options is that the embedded options usually have much longer lives[19] than the three or nine month traded options described earlier.

A typical Japanese bond plus equity warrant was that issued by Best Denski in 1986 in US dollars. The bond had a low 3% coupon and a five-year maturity; the warrants allowed the purchase of 636 shares at an exercise price of ¥1,423.3 and a fixed exchange rate of ¥181.05. This was because the bond was denominated in US dollars but the shares were traded in Japan and priced in yen. In order to protect investors from currency fluctuations, the exercise price was effectively fixed in dollars. However, to a dollar-based investor, the potential profits on exercise of the warrants would naturally depend on the yen/dollar exchange rate as well as

---

[18] Already referred to in Chapter 3 in the section on eurobonds, pp. 117–18.

[19] We saw in the Carlton Communications example that the conversion period lasted from 1991 to 2005, namely 15 years.

the yen value of the shares.[20] The exercise price was fixed at 2% over the share price on issue, and the issue price of the combined bond plus warrants package was $5,000. When the warrants were sold off, the bond became a straight bond, albeit with a low coupon and hence selling at a substantial discount to par. The warrants were bought by investors eager to invest small amounts with high potential returns in Japanese shares.

In the 1980s, Japanese companies were quick to take advantage of this low cost funding; some companies managed to raise money at an interest cost of less than 1%. However, there was the prospect of substantial dilution when the warrants expired in the early 1990s. This risk evaporated with the crash in Japanese share prices in early 1990 which wiped out the likelihood of investors wishing to exercise the many warrants that they held and led to a fall in popularity amongst investors of bonds with such warrants. Nevertheless, bonds with warrants attached have retained their popularity in other markets.

Equity-linked bonds

Taking the desire to issue bonds which appeal to investors to its limits, companies now issue bonds with embedded options linked not to their own share price but to a stock market. The issuer does not bear the risk of this: the bank arranging the issue will normally take that risk and offer instead a fixed liability to the issuer. The attraction to the issuer is that, by issuing bonds which have features to risk–return profiles which appeal to investors, the company may be able to reduce its cost of funding by a few basis points. The larger the bond issue, the more important the basis point savings.

An example is the issue by Nordic Investment Bank in October 1991 of a three-year zero coupon bond in pesetas. On maturity, the investor would receive an amount, in pesetas, equal to the *maximum* (for a par value of 100) of 100 and $100 + 0.9 \times (FIEX_m - FIEX_0/FIEX_0$ where $FIEX_m$ is the level of the Spanish stock market index known as the FIEX on maturity of the bond and $FIEX_0$ is its level on the issue date. At the date of the issue, the value of the zero coupon bond was 72.38% of the face value, leaving a value of 25.62% for the embedded option on 90% of the face of the bond[21] since the option element plus the bond element add up to the issue price of 98% of face value. This implies a 'gearing' on the option of 3.5 times, determined from 90/25.62 where the higher the gearing, the greater

---

[20] The reader will find more on currency risk in Chapter 11 on International Investment.

[21] 90% of the face value of the bond since there is a factor of 0.9 in the redemption formula.

the potential percentage gains and the lower the effective cost of the option. Investors looking at this bond would determine the implied volatility of the option (assuming a dividend pattern for the shares in the FIEX index) and then decide whether it was cheap or dear. The advantages to the investor are that it may be a relatively cheap way to gain leveraged exposure to the Spanish stock market when compared with borrowing money and buying cash shares with all their associated transaction costs and monitoring costs. There are now a whole variety of warrants issued by banks and companies in order to offer investors this type of investment. However, the Nordic Bank warrant is embedded in a bond and so is *less* risky rather than *more* risky than a pure equity investment. Since it is combined with a zero coupon bond, the investor is guaranteed at worst his or her money back (with no interest) and this may be an attractive risk–return profile to investors tempted by the attractions of equity but concerned about the downside risk, particularly when entering a relatively small stock market.

Investor put and issuer call options

One further example of embedded options is the call and put options written into the terms of corporate bonds. There are two main kinds – investor put and issuer call options – and we have seen one example of an issuer call option in the Carlton Communications convertible described on p. 218. By having a redemption period from 2005 to 2010 rather than a single redemption date, Carlton Communications reserves the option to choose when to redeem the bond. This will be a function of interest rates. If, say in 2005, the coupon on the bond is higher than the required coupon and yield on a replacement bond, Carlton Communications will exercise its option to redeem the bond in that year; if not, it will choose to keep the bond in issue. Some bonds have longer call options, with the issuer having the right to call the bond back only a few years after issue. In such cases, investors may receive more than par value for their bonds, but it is usually the case that investors lose out with an issuer call option.

Investor put options have become relatively popular in recent years, particularly in the case of risky companies which found it difficult to issue fixed income securities without offering investors some added protection. One example of such a put option is that attached to the Saatchi & Saatchi 6.75% Convertible Preference Shares 2003 issued in June 1988, when Saatchi & Saatchi needed further finance to fund a series of acquisitions. Example 7.8 gives details of the put option.

This security was the classic debt–equity hybrid. Investors could convert into equity or convert into debt by exercising their put option, thereby

Example 7.8   Investor put option

Saatchi & Saatchi 6.75% Convertible Preference Shares 2003: extracts from prospectus

Conversion: Convertible after 1 October 1989 and prior to the close of business on 8 July 2003 at 441 pence per Ordinary share, representing a premium of approximately 10 per cent, over 401 pence, being the middle market quotation of the Ordinary shares as at the close of business on 16 June 1988.

Investor put option: Each Preference Share may be redeemed at the option of the holder on 15 July in each of the years 1993 to 1998 (inclusive) at its nominal value together with such amount of special dividend as will give an annual compound redemption yield of approximately 9.98% per annum.

Source: Saatchi & Saatchi.

ensuring a full market yield to maturity on their investment, without the lower coupon usually associated with convertibles: in this example, they could have their cake and eat it. In fact, by 1991 the share price of Saatchi & Saatchi had fallen to such a point that it became clear that all holders of the £176 m. issue *would* exercise their put option and it also became clear that Saatchi & Saatchi did not have sufficient financing capability to pay all the holders the promised principal return and the 9.98% per annum yield in July 1993, the firm conversion date. This potential liability from the inclusion of the put option in the terms of the convertible preference shares triggered a restructuring of the entire company.

Summary

This chapter has described the market in options. A call option offers the investor the right to acquire a share on or before a particular date at a fixed price. A put option offers the holder the right to sell a share at a fixed price on or before the expiry date. Options traded on LIFFE, the London International Financial Futures Exchange, were described, in particular individual equity options and options linked to the FT-SE 100 equity index.

Investment in options was compared with investment in the underlying shares themselves and it was found that combinations of different options or combinations of options with ordinary shares allowed the investor to increase or reduce return and risk relative to the return and risk of simply holding ordinary shares. Upper and lower limits to the value of a call option were found and factors affecting the value of a call option discussed. This led to an explicit valuation model for call options, the Black–Scholes model, which is commonly used by traders in the options markets. A discussion on how to apply the Black–Scholes model to value both call and put options, and of the role of volatility in option pricing, then followed.

The remainder of the chapter looked at how to use options for hedging portfolios and then concluded with a look at securities which have options embedded in them and which, although more complex than simple traded options, can be viewed and valued in the same way. The four types considered were convertibles, bonds with warrants, equity-linked bonds, and investor put and issuer call options.

Appendix: calculation of value of call option without computer program

If the value of the call option is to be determined manually, we must know the exact formula.

The simple Black–Scholes formula, with no adjustment for dividends, is:

$$C = S \, N(d_1) - X \, e^{-R_F t} \, N(d_2) \tag{A.1}$$

where

$$d_1 = \frac{\ln (S/X) + (R_F + V/2)t}{\sqrt{Vt}} \tag{A.2}$$

and

$$d_2 = d_1 - \sqrt{Vt} \tag{A.3}$$

We use $e^{-R_F t}$ for the present value of the exercise price, X, since the Black–Scholes model assumes that all returns are continuously compounded. Notice that V is the *square* of the standard deviation of returns, that is the variance of returns.

In order to adjust for dividends on shares, we will use the Merton formula, which assumes continuously paid dividends with a dividend yield of q. The Merton value for a call option is then

$$C = S \, e^{-qt} \, N(d_1) - X \, e^{-R_F t} \, N(d_2) \tag{A.4}$$

where

$$d_1 = \frac{\ln (S/X) + (R_F - q + V/2)t}{\sqrt{Vt}} \tag{A.5}$$

and

$$d_2 = d_1 - \sqrt{Vt} \tag{A.6}$$

We now input the values of the variables into equations (A.5) and (A.6) for input into equation (A.4). We know, for the Sainsbury July 390 call, that

$$S = 396$$
$$X = 390$$
$$t = 0.2822$$
$$V = (0.2062)^2 = 0.04252$$
$$R_F = 0.1075$$
$$q = 0.025 \text{ (or 2.5\%)}$$

Substituting these values into equations (A.5) and (A.6) we get

$$d_1 = 0.4067$$
$$d_2 = 0.2972$$

Example 7A.1 on p. 227 shows an extract from cumulative normal distribution tables which enable us to determine $N(d_1)$ and $N(d_2)$. (See also a graphical representation in Figure 7A.1.) We find from Example 7A.1 that

$$N(d_1) = 0.6578$$
$$N(d_2) = 0.6167$$

Substituting into equation (A.4) for $N(d_i)$ gives

$$C = 396 \times e^{-0.025 \times 0.2822} \times (0.6578) - 390e^{-0.1075 \times 0.2822} (0.6167)$$
$$C = 258.65 - 233.32$$
$$C = \mathbf{25.33p}$$

This is the same value as was found using the Merton formula in a computer program (although there may sometimes be differences due to the accuracy of the normal distribution tables used in either case).

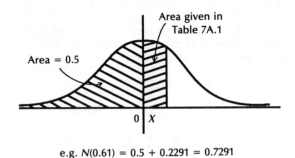

e.g. $N(0.61) = 0.5 + 0.2291 = 0.7291$

Figure 7A.1 *Areas under the standard normal distribution function with mean of 0 and total area of 1*

Example 7A.1 Areas under the standard normal distribution function
$$\int_0^z f(z)dz$$

z	0.00	0.01	0.02	0.03	0.04	0.05	0.06	0.07	0.08	0.09
0.0	0.0000	0.0040	0.0080	0.0120	0.0160	0.0199	0.0239	0.0279	0.0319	0.0359
0.1	0.0398	0.0438	0.0478	0.0517	0.0557	0.0596	0.0636	0.0675	0.0714	0.0753
0.2	0.0793	0.0832	0.0871	0.0910	0.0948	0.0987	0.1026	0.1064	0.1103	0.1141
0.3	0.1179	0.1217	0.1255	0.1293	0.1331	0.1368	0.1406	0.1443	0.1480	0.1517
0.4	0.1554	0.1591	0.1628	0.1664	0.1700	0.1736	0.1772	0.1808	0.1844	0.1879
0.5	0.1915	0.1950	0.1985	0.2019	0.2054	0.2088	0.2123	0.2157	0.2190	0.2224
0.6	0.2257	0.2291	0.2324	0.2357	0.2389	0.2422	0.2454	0.2486	0.2517	0.2549
0.7	0.2580	0.2611	0.2642	0.2673	0.2704	0.2734	0.2764	0.2794	0.2823	0.2852
0.8	0.2881	0.2910	0.2939	0.2967	0.2995	0.3023	0.3051	0.3078	0.3106	0.3133
0.9	0.3159	0.3186	0.3212	0.3238	0.3264	0.3289	0.3315	0.3340	0.3365	0.3389
1.0	0.3413	0.3438	0.3461	0.3485	0.3508	0.3531	0.3554	0.3577	0.3599	0.3621
1.1	0.3643	0.3665	0.3686	0.3708	0.3729	0.3749	0.3770	0.3790	0.3810	0.3830
1.2	0.3849	0.3869	0.3888	0.3907	0.3925	0.3944	0.3962	0.3980	0.3997	0.4015
1.3	0.4032	0.4049	0.4066	0.4082	0.4099	0.4115	0.4131	0.4147	0.4162	0.4177
1.4	0.4192	0.4207	0.4222	0.4236	0.4251	0.4265	0.4279	0.4292	0.4306	0.4319
1.5	0.4332	0.4345	0.4357	0.4370	0.4382	0.4394	0.4406	0.4418	0.4429	0.4441
1.6	0.4452	0.4463	0.4474	0.4484	0.4495	0.4505	0.4515	0.4525	0.4535	0.4545
1.7	0.4554	0.4564	0.4573	0.4582	0.4591	0.4599	0.4608	0.4616	0.4625	0.4633
1.8	0.4641	0.4649	0.4656	0.4664	0.4671	0.4678	0.4686	0.4693	0.4699	0.4706
1.9	0.4713	0.4719	0.4726	0.4738	0.4738	0.4744	0.4750	0.4756	0.4761	0.4767
2.0	0.4772	0.4778	0.4783	0.4788	0.4793	0.4798	0.4803	0.4808	0.4812	0.4817
2.1	0.4821	0.4826	0.4830	0.4834	0.4838	0.4842	0.4846	0.4850	0.4854	0.4857
2.2	0.4861	0.4864	0.4868	0.4871	0.4875	0.4878	0.4881	0.4884	0.4887	0.4890
2.3	0.4893	0.4896	0.4898	0.4901	0.4904	0.4906	0.4909	0.4911	0.4913	0.4916
2.4	0.4918	0.4920	0.4922	0.4925	0.4927	0.4929	0.4931	0.4932	0.4934	0.4936
2.5	0.4938	0.4940	0.4941	0.4943	0.4945	0.4946	0.4948	0.4949	0.4951	0.4952
2.6	0.4953	0.4955	0.4956	0.4957	0.4959	0.4960	0.4961	0.4962	0.4963	0.4964
2.7	0.4965	0.4966	0.4967	0.4968	0.4969	0.4970	0.4971	0.4982	0.4973	0.4974
2.8	0.4974	0.4975	0.4976	0.4977	0.4977	0.4978	0.4979	0.4979	0.4980	0.4891
2.9	0.4981	0.4982	0.4982	0.4982	0.4984	0.4984	0.4985	0.4985	0.4986	0.4886
3.0	0.4987	0.4987	0.4987	0.4988	0.4988	0.4989	0.4989	0.4989	0.4990	0.4990

Reprinted from Copeland and Weston, *Financial Theory and Corporate Policy*, Addison-Wesley Publishing Company, Inc. By permission of the publishers.

Problems

1. XYZ shares are currently quoted at 105–107p. An investor wishes to buy a three-month traded call option contract on 1,000 shares. Explain what a 'call option' means and under what conditions the investor should exercise his option. The call option is priced at 12p per share and the exercise price is 115p.

2. (i) Suppose it is early September and an investor believes the annual results of International Manufacturing, due shortly, will cause a sharp rise in the share price. The shares can be bought at 320p or the October traded options, with an exercise price of 280p, at 50p. If his prediction is correct and the shares rise to 350p while the options rise to 70p, what profit will he have made (allowing for transaction costs) if:

(a) he has bought 2,000 shares,

(b) he has bought two October 280p call option contracts for 1,000 shares each?

(ii) Using your results from part (i), discuss the advantages of buying options rather than shares.

3. (i) Use the Black–Scholes model to determine the value of a European call option with an exercise price of 40p and a maturity date six months from now, if the current share price is 30p, the volatility (standard deviation) of the share price is 40% and the risk free rate 10%.

(ii) What would the call option be worth if the current share price were (a) 40p or (b) 50p?

4. (i) Use the Black–Scholes model to value a six-month European put option on a share currently priced at 20p, with an exercise price of 30p, a risk-free rate of 8% and the volatility (standard deviation) on the share equal to 36%.

(ii) How good an estimate of the value of an *American* put option would you expect the Black–Scholes model to give if the put option were substantially

(a) 'in the money'

(b) 'out of the money'?

5. Look at actual trading prices of Sainsbury traded call options to see if they behave as the theory would predict, e.g.

(i) Follow some Sainsbury options as they approach maturity. Do their prices behave in the way you would expect?

(ii) Compare two Sainsbury call options with the same maturity but different exercise prices. Which call option has the highest value?

(iii) Compare two Sainsbury options with the same exercise price but different maturities. Which option is worth more?

(iv) Use the Black–Scholes model to value any Sainsbury call option with the shortest maturity. Does your answer give the same as the market price? If not, why do you think you get a different answer?

(v) What complications would have to be taken into account if you applied the Black–Scholes model to valuing longer maturity traded call options, say, for example, with an exercise date over six months away?

6. (i) Which variables affect the value of a call option on a share? Derive boundaries within which the value of a European call option must lie.

(ii) Show how an option and a futures contract can be used to hedge risk. How does an option differ from a futures contract?

7. Brick Bat plc, with 10 m. ordinary shares priced at 80p (15 May 1992), has just paid a final net dividend at 4.6p per share. The interim dividend, paid six months ago, was 2p net. Brick Bat plc is issuing, in the form of a right issue, 10½% Convertible Unsecured Loan Stock 2001–6. Each shareholder will be entitled to buy £1 of convertible unsecured loan stock for each eight ordinary shares held. The loan stock can be converted on 15 May in any year 1993–2001 and, on conversion, the holder will receive 75 ordinary shares for each £100 nominal of convertible unsecured loan stock.

  (i) Miss Ball holds 100,000 Brick Bat ordinary shares. How much convertible unsecured loan stock is she entitled to purchase?
 (ii) If Miss Ball does not wish to put any new money into the company, how many of her existing Brick Bat ordinary shares will she have to sell to provide sufficient cash to take up her right to the convertible unsecured loan stock in full?
(iii) Assume Miss Ball has taken up rights as in (ii). She wishes to maximise her income and decides to convert when the income to be received from the shares in the form of dividends exceeds the interest from the loan stock. In which year will Miss Ball convert if dividends grow by 10% per annum? Assume Miss Ball pays tax on income at the basic rate of 25%.
 (iv) Discuss the factors that Miss Ball would consider when deciding whether to invest in convertible unsecured loan stock.

PART II
INVESTMENT STRATEGY

Portfolio theory

Introduction

In Chapter 2 we discussed how to measure the most important character-istics of a security, its return and its risk. We decided that, for each secur-ity, investors would compare the expected return from a range of probable outcomes with the risk of the security, as measured by the standard deviation of the probability distribution of returns.[1] So, investors would only need to consider expected returns and standard deviations when choos-ing securities for their investment portfolios. They would, since they were assumed risk averse, choose those securities which offered the most return for a given level of risk or the least risk for a given level of return.

However, we did not consider the effects of *combining* securities; we only looked at how to compare them. We did get an inkling that combining them into a portfolio might be sensible when we looked at ways of reducing risk, in particular, pooling. Pooling was concerned with *independent* invest-ments. The problem with securities is that they are not independent. If the

---

[1] The variance, V, of a probability distribution of returns measures its total dispersion. The standard deviation, S, is the square root of the variance. If the probability distribution of returns is normal then either V or S is a sufficient measure of the risk of the security in question.

FT-SE 100 Share Index[2] goes up, an investor will expect most company shares to show an upward trend, whether or not they are in the FT-SE 100 Share Index. There are market influences, such as changes in interest rates or tax rates, which will affect the prices of all securities to a greater or lesser extent. We shall see that, despite this common market influence, with the few assumptions about investor behaviour described above, it still makes sense to combine securities even if their returns are related. In fact, portfolio theory, as it is known, shows that it is foolish to hold only one security. An investor can always get more return for his risk by holding a portfolio with at least two and possibly many more securities in it.

Portfolio theory enables the investor, given a set of securities to choose from, to decide which combinations of these securities, or portfolios, give him the best return for the risk involved. He can then choose the portfolio which has the optimal risk–return relationship for him, depending on his individual circumstances. For example, an individual investor on the stock market may prefer a high-risk, high-return portfolio whereas a pension fund manager may choose a lower-return portfolio because he feels unable to accept more than a certain level of risk. Each investor will end up with what is known as an *efficient portfolio* (which provides the best return for the risk involved); but each investor will probably hold a different efficient portfolio according to his individual risk–return preference.

We shall see in Chapter 9 that, with a few additional assumptions such as the existence of a risk-free security, a model which is simpler to use than portfolio theory can be derived, known as the capital asset pricing model. However, the additional assumptions inherent in the CAPM, as it is known, are less realistic than those underlying portfolio theory. For this reason, portfolio theory is still widely used. For example, in the chapter on International Investment, Chapter 11, we find that there is no world-wide risk-free security. Because of this, the CAPM cannot easily be extended to an international framework. However, we find that portfolio theory offers us a suitable model for determining optimal international portfolios.

This chapter now goes on to explain how the results of portfolio theory were obtained and what they mean in practical terms to the investor. Some mathematics is involved, since the reader needs it to understand implications of the theories, but this is kept to a minimum.[3] The initial part of the chapter considers a portfolio of only two securities and shows how an investor can decide on a combination of these two securities which is optimal for him, given his utility function. The result is then extended to any number of securities. The chapter concludes with the general implications of portfolio theory for investment and with the problems inherent in its use.

---

[2] See the Appendix to Chapter 10 for a description of share indices, including the FT-SE 100 Share Index.

[3] For more advanced discussion of portfolio theory and the CAPM, see Elton and Gruber (1991).

Portfolio theory

In order to understand how combining securities together into a portfolio can reduce risk, we shall start by looking at the simplest case, where two securities are combined, and then extend the results to any size of portfolio. Suppose the investor is considering securities A and B, which have the characteristics detailed in Example 8.1.

The investor could choose which of these securities he prefers if he calculates the utility he would derive from the risk–return relationships of each security. However, what would happen if, instead of buying A or B, he bought both A and B, say in proportions W_1 and W_2 such that $W_1 + W_2 = 1$?

If we call the resulting combination of A and B, portfolio P, what can we say about P's expected return and risk?

Firstly, the expected return of P is simply:[4]

$$E(R_p) = W_1 E(R_A) + W_2 E(R_B) \tag{8.1}$$

That is, the expected return of P is the weighted average of the expected returns of A and B. For example, if the investor had half his portfolio in A and the other half in B, we would have $W_1 = W_2 = \frac{1}{2}$.

So,

$$E(R_p) = \frac{1}{2}E(R_A) + \frac{1}{2}E(R_B)$$

$$= \frac{1}{2} \times 10\% + \frac{1}{2} \times 25\%$$

$$E(R_p) = 17.5\%$$

Example 8.1   Portfolio of two securities

	% Return	
Probability	*Security A*	*Security B*
0.25	20	45
0.50	10	25
0.25	0	5
1.00		
Expected return	$E(R_A) = 10\%$	$E(R_B) = 25\%$
Variance of returns	$V_A = 50\%$	$V_B = 200\%$
Standard deviation of returns	$S_A = 7.1\%$	$S_B = 14.1\%$

[4] For a more detailed discussion of the properties of expected values and standard deviations in this context, see Markowitz (1991).

The variance of any security, as we saw in Chapter 2, can be written as

$$V_i = S_i^2 = \sum_{i=1}^{i=n} (R_i - E(R))^2 p(R_i) \tag{8.2}$$

which is just the sum of the probabilities of each return (R_i) multiplied by the square of the difference of each R_i from the expected return $E(R)$.

In exactly the same way, the variance of the portfolio return can be written

$$V_p = S_p^2 = \sum_{i=1}^{i=n} (R_{pi} - E(R_p))^2 p(R_{pi}) \tag{8.3}$$

If we allow for the fact that P is made up of $W_1 A + W_2 B$ in (8.3) we get

$$V_p = W_1^2 S_A^2 + W_2^2 S_B^2 +$$
$$2W_1 W_2 \sum_{i=1}^{i=n} (R_{Ai} - E(R_A)) (R_{Bi} - E(R_B)) p(R_i) \tag{8.4}$$

This expression for the variance of P is not quite the weighted average of the variances of A and B, S_A^2 and S_B^2, as was the case for the expected return of P. In equation (8.4), the expression for the variance of P includes a complex-looking term at the end which describes the relationship between the returns of A and B. This term (excluding the proportions $2W_1W_2$) is called the *covariance* of returns of A and B and is written COV_{AB}:

$$COV_{AB} = \sum_{i=1}^{i=n} (R_{Ai} - E(R_A)) (R_{Bi} - E(R_B)) p(R_i) \tag{8.5}$$

What does the covariance of returns between two securities mean? In each state of the world (expressed by different probabilities $p(R_i)$), the return is compared with its expected value for both securities. If the return on A is greater than its expected value and the return on B in the same state of the world is greater than *its* expected value, then that term in COV_{AB} will be positive, and similarly, if the returns on A and B are less than their expected values in the same state of the world. So, if two securities do well (better than expected) or badly (worse than expected) in the same state of the world, they will have a positive covariance. If the returns of A and B are on different sides of the expected value, for each state of the world, covariance will be negative. If they are sometimes on the same side of the expected value and sometimes on different sides, the signs will cancel out to give a covariance of around zero.

The correlation coefficient, written $CORR_{AB}$, is defined to be the covariance divided by the product of the standard deviations of A and B:

$$CORR_{AB} = \frac{COV_{AB}}{S_A S_B} \tag{8.6}$$

The reason for bothering to define the correlation coefficient is that it can only take values of between -1 and $+1$. It is merely another way of expressing the amount of covariance between the returns of two securities which has the property that it can never be greater than 1. If two shares' returns move together in perfect unison, they will have a correlation coefficient of $+1$. If they move in exactly opposite directions, $CORR_{AB}$ will be equal to -1.

If they are totally independent, so that if they move together it is by chance, they will have $CORR_{AB} = 0$.

Rearranging equation (8.6) to give

$$COV_{AB} = CORR_{AB}S_AS_B$$

and substituting for COV_{AB} in equation (8.4), we get

$$V_p = W_1^2S_A^2 + W_2^2S_B^2 + 2W_1W_2S_AS_BCORR_{AB} \tag{8.7}$$

This is a quadratic equation in S. We now investigate what effect on the variance of the portfolio, V_p, different values of the correlation coefficient will have.

Perfectly correlated securities

First, let us look at the securities A and B described in Example 8.1. We can calculate the covariance and hence the correlation coefficient from the information we have:

$$COV_{AB} = \sum_{i=1}^{i=3} (R_{Ai} - E(R_A)) (R_{Bi} - E(R_B)) \, p(R_i)$$

$$COV_{AB} = (0.20 - 0.10)(0.45 - 0.25) \times 0.25 + (0.10 - 0.10)$$
$$(0.25 - 0.25) \times 0.50 + (0 - 0.10)(0.05 - 0.25) \times 0.25$$

$$= 0.10 \times 0.20 \times 0.25 + 0 + -0.10 \times -0.20 \times 0.25$$

$$COV_{AB} = 0.01$$

So,

$$CORR_{AB} = \frac{COV_{AB}}{S_AS_B} = \frac{0.01}{0.071 \times 0.141}$$

$$\mathbf{CORR_{AB} = 1.0}$$

This means that the returns of the two securities A and B move perfectly in unison which was intuitively obvious from looking at Example 8.1.[5] Substituting $CORR_{AB} = +1$ into equation (8.7) we get

$$V_p = W_1^2 S_A^2 + W_2^2 S_B^2 + 2W_1 W_2 S_A S_B \tag{8.8}$$

or

$$V_p = (W_1 S_A + W_2 S_B)(W_1 S_A + W_2 S_B) \tag{8.9}$$

because multiplying out the terms in (8.9) gives us (8.8). Taking positive square roots of both sides,[6] with S_p the square root of V_p

$$S_p = W_1 S_A + W_2 S_B \tag{8.10}$$

Equation (8.10) tells us that, when $CORR_{AB} = +1$, the standard deviation of P is the weighted average of S_A and S_B. So, when two securities are perfectly positively correlated, the risk and expected return of any combination of these two securities are just the weighted averages of the constituent securities' risks and returns.

In Figure 8.1, any combination of A and B, with particular values of W_1 and W_2, will be on the straight line joining A and B. No particular advantage has been gained by combining A and B in this case.

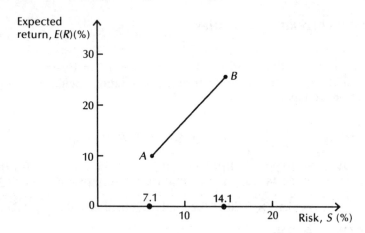

Figure 8.1   Possible combinations of A and B when $CORR_{AB} = +1$

---

[5] In fact, the returns of securities A and B are related by a linear equation

$$R_B = 0.05 + 2R_A$$

which shows that they move exactly together.

[6] The standard deviation is defined to be the *positive* square root of the variance.

Let us look again at equation (8.7):

$$V_p = W_1^2 S_A^2 + W_2^2 S_B^2 + 2W_1 W_2 S_A S_B CORR_{AB} \tag{8.7}$$

If $CORR_{AB} = +1$, the right-hand side of the equation is the square of the weighted average of the standard deviations. What happens if $CORR_{AB}$ is less than $+1$? The right-hand side of the equation must be *less than* the weighted average and so the risk of the portfolio must be less than the weighted average of the risk of its constituent securities.

This implies that, provided two securities are not perfectly positively correlated, advantages can be gained by combining them. We look first at two specific cases, where $CORR_{AB} = 0$ and $CORR_{AB} = -1$.

Unrelated securities

Suppose that $CORR_{AB} = 0$. In this case, the two securities A and B are completely unrelated. They are not affected by any common factors and any similar movements will be due to chance.

Equation (8.7) becomes

$$V_p = W_1^2 S_A^2 + W_2^2 S_B^2$$

Suppose the investor holds two identical securities (each with standard deviation of 10% and expected return of 10%) in equal proportions.
We get

$$V_p = \frac{1}{4} \times 0.01 + \frac{1}{4} \times 0.01$$

$$V_p = 0.005$$

$$S_p = 7.1\%$$

The standard deviation of the combination is less than that of the individual securities. This result gives us the principle of pooling discussed in Chapter 2.[7] To be more general, if each security had the same standard deviation, S, the risk of the portfolio would be

$$V_p = \frac{1}{4} \times S^2 + \frac{1}{4} \times S^2$$

$$V_p = \frac{1}{2} S^2$$

---

[7] Risk can be reduced by pooling insurance against unrelated events. See Chapter 2, p. 56.

Taking square roots of both sides,

$$S_p = \frac{S}{\sqrt{2}}$$

For n securities held in equal amounts, we would get the following result:

$$S_p = \frac{S}{\sqrt{n}} \tag{8.11}$$

As we discussed in Chapter 2, events such as houses being destroyed or the deaths of individuals are in the main unrelated and so any two insurance policies covering such eventualities would have returns which were un-correlated, that is, have a zero correlation coefficient. As a result, the risk of holding a portfolio of n such insurance policies would be S_p, as in equation (8.11), which would be substantially less than the sum of the risks, S, on the individual policies. The independence between events insured, reflected in zero correlation coefficients, represents the rationale behind the principle of pooling. Unfortunately, the returns of securities quoted on the Stock Exchange are not independent in the same way.

Perfectly negatively correlated securities

In this case, $CORR_{AB} = -1$. The returns of each security react in exactly opposite ways in each state of the world. An example could be company A selling ice cream and company B selling umbrellas. If the weather is fine, A will do well and B badly and, if the weather is poor, A will do badly and B well. Equation (8.7) becomes

$$V_p = W_1^2 S_A^2 + W_2^2 S_B^2 - 2W_1 W_2 S_A S_B$$

This is also a perfect square and can be written

$$V_p = (W_1 S_A - W_2 S_B)(W_1 S_A - W_2 S_B)$$

The square root can be taken to give

$$S_p = |W_1 S_A - W_2 S_B| \tag{8.12}$$

where the two vertical lines require the absolute value, that is, whichever square root has a positive value.

Example 8.2   *Portfolio of two securities*

Probability	% Return	
	Security A	Security B
0.25	20	5
0.50	10	25
0.25	0	45
1.00		
Expected return	$E(R_A) = 10\%$	$E(R_B) = 25\%$
Variance of returns	$V_A = 50\%$	$V_B = 200\%$
Standard deviation of returns	$S_A = 7.1\%$	$S_B = 14.1\%$

In fact in this particular case, W_1 and W_2 can always be found to give $S_p = 0$ in equation (8.12). In other words, a riskless portfolio can always be found when combining two perfectly negatively correlated securities.

For example, suppose we have two securities A and B as described in Example 8.2. (Note that they are as in Example 8.1 with the returns of B reversed.) If we choose equal proportions of A and B so that $W_1 = W_2 = \frac{1}{2}$, we will get

$$E(R_p) = \frac{1}{2} \times 10\% + \frac{1}{2} \times 25\%$$

$$E(R_p) = \textbf{17.5\%} \text{ as before for } CORR_{AB} = +1.$$

However the risk of the combination will be substantially reduced:

$$S_p = |\tfrac{1}{2} \times 0.071 - \tfrac{1}{2} \times 0.141|$$

$$S_p = \textbf{3.5\%}$$

This combination is shown as point P in Figure 8.2.

In what proportions must we hold A and B to get a riskless portfolio P, with $S_p = 0$? Equation (8.12) must be set to zero so that

$$0 = W_1 S_A - W_2 S_B$$

Rearranging,

$$W_1 S_A = W_2 S_B$$

$$0.071 W_1 = 0.141 W_2$$

$$W_1 = 2W_2$$

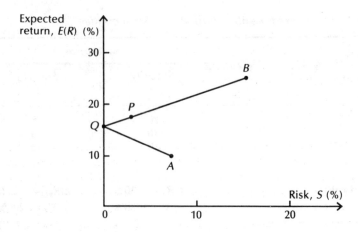

Figure 8.2   Possible combinations of A and B when CORR$_{AB}$ = −1

We must choose $W_1 = \dfrac{2}{3}$, $W_2 = \dfrac{1}{3}$

and in this case the expected return of P would be

$$E(R_p) = \frac{2}{3} \times 10\% + \frac{1}{3} \times 25\%$$

$$E(R_p) = 15\%$$

This is a riskless portfolio, so the investor is *certain* of getting a return of 15% whichever state of the world prevails. In this case of perfectly negatively correlated securities, the investor has been able to remove risk altogether whilst still achieving a return in between those expected of *A* and *B*. This riskless portfolio is shown as point *Q* in Figure 8.2.

Small positive correlation between securities

What implications do the above results have for the investor? If he can find two securities which are not perfectly positively correlated, that is, which have $CORR_{AB} < +1$, then he can combine them into a portfolio and expect to get the weighted average of their expected returns with less than the weighted average of their risk. In other words, he will have reduced risk without sacrificing return. Provided two securities do not have $CORR_{AB} = +1$, he can always do better than just holding one risky security.

The less correlated the returns of two securities, the more the investor can reduce risk by combining them. If he can find two securities which have $CORR_{AB} = -1$, he can reduce his risk to zero whilst still getting a weighted average of expected returns.

Unfortunately, risky securities are not usually negatively correlated or even independent since they are subject to common influences. The correlation coefficient between two securities will probably be small and positive, for example $CORR_{AB} = 0.3$.

If we substitute a value of 0.3 for $CORR_{AB}$ into equation (8.7), we get

$$V_p = W_1^2 S_A^2 + W_2^2 S_B^2 + 2W_1 W_2 S_A S_B \times 0.3$$

This is not a perfect square and so gives a *curve* of possible combinations rather than a straight line. This curve is shown in Figure 8.3 with A taken, as before, to have an expected return of 10% and a standard deviation of 7.1% and B an expected return of 25% and a standard deviation of 14.1%. If, for example, we assume equal proportions of A and B are held, we still get

$$E(R_p) = \frac{1}{2} \times 10\% + \frac{1}{2} \times 25\%$$

$$E(R_p) = 17.5\%$$

but risk is reduced to less than the weighted average:

$$V_p = \frac{1}{4} \times 0.005 + \frac{1}{4} \times 0.02 + 2 \times \frac{1}{2} \times \frac{1}{2} \times 0.071 \times 0.141 \times 0.03$$
$$V_p = 0.0078$$
$$S_p = 8.8\%$$

This particular combination is shown as P on Figure 8.3.

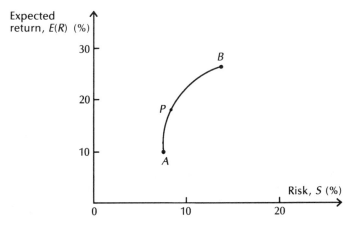

Figure 8.3   Possible combinations of A and B when $CORR_{AB} = 0.3$

We have shown how the investor can reduce risk by holding different combinations of two securities instead of just one on its own. It is likely that the securities he will consider will provide a curve of possible combination as in Figure 8.3. The investor then has to decide which point on the curve *AB* he prefers, that is, which portfolio maximises his utility. To show how this can be done we first discuss how indifference curves can be derived for each investor from knowledge of his utility function. These indifference curves will then be used to determine the investor's *optimal* portfolio.

Indifference curves

As we saw in Chapter 2, each investor has a utility function which quantifies his attitude towards risk and return at different levels of wealth. If we consider a risk averse investor, his utility of wealth function will describe a curve as in Figure 8.4.

This curve implies a certain trade-off relationship between risk and expected return. For example, we found in Chapter 2 that Mr Black, armed with his utility function, could distinguish between two securities which offered different expected returns and different risks.

An investor's risk–return trade-off can be expressed more directly by using the utility function to determine the investor's indifference curves.

For example, if the investor requires 10% return for accepting a standard deviation of 12% and for each additional 3% of standard deviation he requires an additional 4% of return, we can draw his 'indifference curve' – by identifying the risk–return combinations between which he is indifferent. From the above information we know that he is indifferent between a security which offers 10% expected return and has $S = 12\%$ and a security which offers 14% and has S 3% higher at 15%. If we plot these and other points on a graph we will get a curve I_1 as shown in Figure 8.5. We know that I_1 will curve upwards because we are dealing with a risk averse investor who requires more return for taking on more risk – as measured by standard deviation. Each investor will have a different curve, although of the same basic shape, because each investor will differ in how he trades risk and return.

In fact each investor will have an infinite number of parallel indifference curves I_1, I_2, I_3 and so on. He will be indifferent between any point on I_1, say between A and B, but he will *not* be indifferent between a point on I_1 and a point on I_2. Compare points A and A_2. Both have the same risk but A_2 has a higher expected return. The investor will obviously prefer to be on I_2 rather than I_1. In fact, he will aim to get on the highest possible

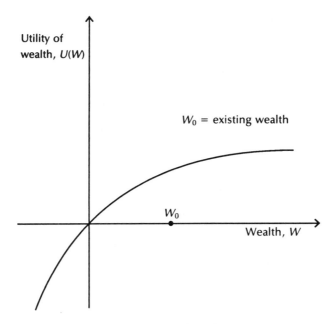

Figure 8.4   Utility curve of a risk-averse investor

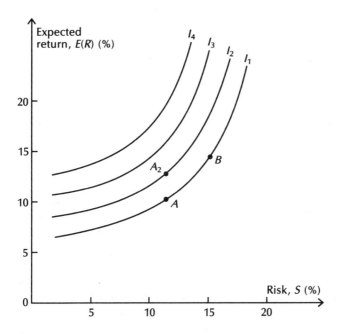

Figure 8.5   Risk-averse investor's set of indifference curves

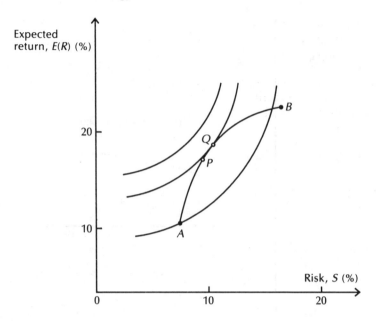

Figure 8.6   Optimal combination of A and B where CORR$_{AB}$ = +0.3

indifference curve, in order to maximise his utility, but once there he will be indifferent to where he is on that curve.

Once the utility function of an investor is known, his indifference curves can be drawn. These curves are used in deciding which portfolio the investor should choose to maximise his utility. Suppose A and B are the only securities the investor can buy and that they are as described in Figure 8.3 with CORR$_{AB}$ = 0.3. Any combination of securities A and B lies on the curve AB. If the investor plots his indifference curves on this graph, as is done in Figure 8.6, we can see that he would prefer A to B because A is on a higher indifference curve than B.

We also know that the investor could do better than buying A on its own by investing in P, a portfolio containing equal quantities of A and B and with a standard deviation of 8.8%, as described earlier. However, the investor can maximise his utility in this case by investing in portfolio Q. At this point, one of his indifference curves is a tangent[8] to the curve AB. This is the highest indifference curve he can reach (any higher one would not touch a portfolio on AB) and so Q must be his optimal portfolio.

So, unless securities A and B are perfectly positively correlated, an investor can always reach a higher indifference curve and hence achieve greater expected utility (a better risk–return trade-off) by investing in a combination of the two securities.

---

[8] A tangent is a line or curve which only touches another line or curve at one point.

Extension to *n* securities

We can extend all the above results that we have shown hold for two security portfolios to any size of portfolio. If we assume that we have a combination of *n* securities, it can be shown[9] that the resultant portfolio has an expected return and variance as follows:

$$E(R_p) = \sum_{i=1}^{i=n} W_i E(R_i) \tag{8.13}$$

$$V_p = \sum_{i=1}^{i=n} W_i^2 S_i^2 + \sum_{\substack{i=1 \\ i \neq j}}^{i=n} \sum_{j=1}^{j=n} W_i W_j COV_{ij} \tag{8.14}$$

Although daunting to look at, equation (8.13) says, as for two securities, that the expected return of the portfolio is the weighted average of the expected returns of the constituent securities. Similarly, equation (8.14) is the sum of the variance terms $W_i^2 S_i^2$ plus the sum of the covariance terms COV_{ij}.[10] Equation (8.14) looks complex because, in order to be able to calculate the variance of the portfolio, V_p, we not only have to know the variance of each of the *n* securities, S_i^2, but also the covariance (COV_{ij}) or correlation coefficient ($CORR_{ij}$) of *each pair of* securities. With the two security case, we only had one covariance term. With the *n* security case we have many more covariance terms $[(n^2 - n)/2]$.[11]

However complicated the equations for *n* securities look, the same basic results hold. For example, as with two securities, the risk of any combination of *n* securities will be less than the weighted average constituent risks unless *each pair* of securities is perfectly positively correlated, an extremely unlikely event. Having decided that a portfolio of securities should always be held rather than one security on its own, we again face the problem of deciding which combination of these *n* securities is optimal for the investor.

Suppose $n = 10$, that is, the investor has ten securities to choose from. He has a choice of ten different portfolios with only one security in them, 45 portfolios with two securities in them, right up to one portfolio with ten securities in it. In fact he has a choice between 1,023 possible portfolio

---

[9] For proof of these results, see Markowitz (1991) or Elton and Gruber (1991).

[10] Note that

$$COV_{ij} = CORR_{ij} S_i S_i = S_i^2$$

(since $CORR_{ij}$ must equal 1). So equation (8.14) consists only of covariance terms with the special cases where $i = j$ separated out.

[11] See p. 250 below for an explanation of how we calculate this.

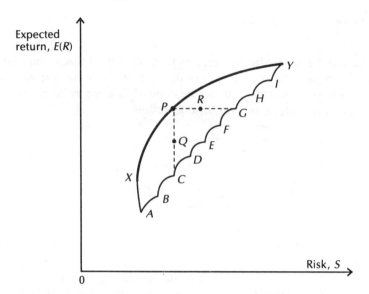

Figure 8.7   Opportunity set with ten securities

combinations of the securities[12] and, of course, an infinite variation in the proportions in which he can hold the securities in each possible portfolio.

If we draw these possible portfolios on a graph, as in Figure 8.7, we find that they all fit into a shape which resembles an umbrella. This is because each pair of the *n* securities is likely to have a small positive correlation coefficient and so the possible combinations of each pair of securities will lie on a *curve* joining the securities. This will give the serrated edge *AB*, *BC* and so on. Combinations of more than two securities will similarly lie on curves inside or on the umbrella. All possible portfolios are said to make up the 'opportunity set' available to the investor.

The curve *XY* is called the 'efficient frontier'. This means that all the portfolios lying on the curve joining *X* and *Y* are efficient in the sense that they are superior to any portfolios in the opportunity set. A portfolio can always be found in *XY* which has a higher return for the same risk or a lower risk for the same return than any other possible portfolio *not* on *XY*. For example, *P* offers a higher expected return than *C* or *Q* for the same risk and *P* offers a lower risk than *G* or *R* for the same expected return.

---

[12] The formula for the number of possible combinations of *m* securities out of a choice of *n* securities is

$$nCm = \frac{n!}{(n-m)!m!}$$

where *n*! represents the multiple of all numbers from 1 to *n*. For example, $6! = 6 \times 5 \times 4 \times 3 \times 2 \times 1$.

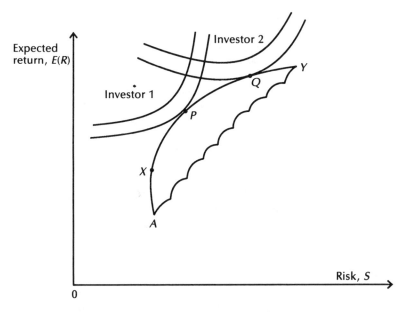

Figure 8.8 Optimal portfolio from ten securities for investors with different utility functions

How does the investor choose between efficient portfolios on *XY*? He simply draws his indifference curves and, as in Figure 8.8, chooses the point where his indifference curve is tangent to *XY*. So investor 1 would choose portfolio *P* as optimal and investor 2, portfolio *Q*.

Investors 1 and 2 would probably choose different portfolios from the same efficient frontier because they no doubt have different attitudes to the relationship between risk and return (although both risk averse) which will be reflected in different utility functions and indifference curves. Also, investor 2 may not even have the same opportunity set and efficient frontier as investor 1, because he may have different views on the expected returns and risks of the ten securities in question. This would lead him to a different umbrella altogether.

Practical implications for the investor

Portfolio theory therefore allows the investor, given a set of securities, to choose the particular combination of securities which will maximise his utility. How is this done in practice? For each security, the investor has to estimate its expected return $E(R_i)$, its variance V_i, and its covariance COV_{ij} or correlation coefficient $CORR_{ij}$ with every other security in the set. For

Example 8.3   Determination of optimal three-security portfolios

Security	Expected return (%)	Standard deviation (%)	Covariances (%)
A	6	4	$COV_{AA} = 16$ $COV_{AB} = 12$ $COV_{AC} = 16$
B	8	6	$COV_{BB} = 36$ $COV_{BC} = 12$
C	10	8	$COV_{CC} = 64$

example, suppose the investor is considering three securities, A, B and C, whose characteristics are detailed in Example 8.3.

The section between vertical lines is called the variance–covariance 'matrix'.[13] Variances are just a special case of the covariances COV_{ij} where $i = j$. (For example, $COV_{AA} = CORR_{AA}S_AS_A = S_A^2 = V_A$.) So we need n expected returns, n variances and just under half the matrix of covariance items (since $COV_{AB} = COV_{BA}$), giving $(n^2 - n)/2$ covariances. In the case of Example 8.3, we need a total of nine values, three expected returns, three variances and $(9 - 3)/2 = 3$ covariances.

Given these figures, the portfolios on the efficient frontier can be calculated (equivalent to the curve XY in Figure 8.8) and some are shown in Example 8.4. With this example, the efficient portfolios can be calculated manually but for any larger number of securities a computer program is needed.[14]

How will the investor choose between these efficient portfolios? If he knows his utility function he has two choices. He can either calculate the utility he will get from each efficient portfolio and choose the one which offers him the highest utility or he can plot his indifference curves against the efficient frontier and choose the portfolio where the tangent indifference curve touches the efficient frontier (as in Figure 8.8).

In practice, the investor will probably not know his utility function nor be able to plot his indifference curves. What he can do is specify a minimum acceptable level of expected return or a maximum acceptable level of risk. For example, he could require his portfolio to have minimum risk given an expected return of at least 8.5% – pension funds, for instance may have the objective of doing at least as well as inflation – or be unwilling to accept a higher level of risk than 20% measured by variance –

---

[13] A matrix is simply a rectangular array of numbers of symbols. Matrices allow multiple equations to be solved more simply than ordinary algebra. Covariances are often expressed in matrix form since this helps computation of, for example, the efficient frontier or the optimal portfolio.

[14] Details on how the efficient frontier can be calculated using graphical analysis (by hand), calculus or quadratic programming can be found in Elton and Gruber (1991).

Example 8.4   Some efficient portfolio combinations of A, B and C

	Proportions held of A,B,C			Expected return $E(R_p)$ (%)	Standard deviation S_p (%)
	W_A	W_B	W_C		
(1)	0.46	0.33	0.21	7.5	4.3
(2)	0.41	0.35	0.24	7.7	4.4
(3)	0.3	0.4	0.3	8.0	4.6
(4)	0.13	0.48	0.39	8.5	5.1
(5)	−0.19[15]	0.63	0.56	9.5	6.1

the investor may be acting as trustee for someone who cannot afford to lose more than a certain amount. If the former requirement held, portfolio (4) in Example 8.4, which yields an expected return of 8.5%, would be chosen as optimal. If the latter restriction held, portfolio (2), with a standard deviation of 4.4%, would be preferred.

Size of optimal portfolio

The investor, given a set of n securities, can now choose the combination of those securities which is optimal for him. It may include only two securities or it may include all n, depending on the correlations of the securities. The question that the investor will now no doubt ask is how many securities should he consider in the first place? What would n be? He knows that he should diversify to gain the benefits of risk reduction, but to what extent? The small investor will be particularly concerned to know the answer to this question since he will have higher transaction costs the more securities he buys.

We now examine what happens to the risk of a portfolio as we increase its size. If we look at the equation for the variance of a portfolio of n securities, equation (8.14), we can see that

$$V_p = \text{weighted variance terms} + \text{weighted covariance terms}$$

If we assume that the n securities are all held in equal amounts, that is, $W_i = 1/n$ for each i, it can be shown that the variance terms diminish in

---

[15] In this example, we have allowed negative amounts of securities to form part of the portfolio – in other words, it is assumed that securities can be sold short (p. 196). In practice, this may not be possible. However, the computer program used to determine the efficient frontier can be adjusted to incorporate the requirement that all $W_i \geqslant 0$.

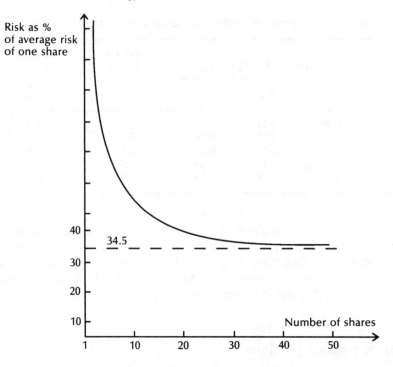

Figure 8.9   The effect on risk of number of securities in portfolio

Source: Solnik (1974). By permission of the *Financial Analysts' Journal*.

importance as we increase n. For larger n, the risk of the portfolio will depend on the average covariance between the securities. Obviously, as n becomes large enough to include all securities in the stock market, so the risk of the portfolio will become the risk of the stock market.

How quickly does the risk of a portfolio decrease and tend towards the average market risk as we increase n? Experiments have been carried out on different sizes of *randomly* selected portfolios of UK shares.[16] Portfolios from one to fifty securities were chosen and the *average* risk of each size of portfolio calculated. This average risk was then expressed as a percentage of the average risk of holding only one share. The results are as shown in Figure 8.9.

We can see from Figure 8.9 that average risk decreases fast as we increase the number of securities held from one upwards. Each time another security is added, risk is reduced by a smaller amount, and no matter how many securities are held, risk cannot be reduced on average to

---

[16] See Solnik (1974). It must be noted that standard deviations of past returns for a particular period were used. Somewhat different results would be achieved if a different period were to be examined.

below 34.5% (in this particular study) of the risk of holding only one share. This reinforces the view we already held that there is a certain amount of risk common to all shares quoted on the UK stock market which cannot be diversified away. This is intuitively obvious since if an investor held all quoted UK shares, he would not be holding a riskless investment!

These results have two major implications for investors. Firstly small investors need only diversify by holding ten to fifteen shares to have substantially reduced risk from holding one share and to have removed most of the non-market risk from their portfolios. For example, by holding ten randomly selected shares in equal amounts, an investor may, on average, diversify away 90% of the shares' non-market risk. Secondly, institutional investors do not need to hold vast numbers of securities to be diversified. The extra reduction in risk gained by holding 150 rather than fifty securities is very small and may well be more than outweighed by the additional transaction and monitoring[17] costs involved in holding the extra 100 shares.

So far, in discussing how many securities the investor should hold, we have considered *naïve* diversification (randomly chosen securities held in equal amounts) and *average* levels of risk for different sizes of portfolios. This misses the more dramatic reductions in risk which can be achieved by carefully selecting securities and then calculating efficient frontiers. It may be that two negatively correlated shares could be found, in which case a minimum risk portfolio would include only those two shares. If another share were added it would add risk. So, on a *naïve* diversification policy, at least ten shares should be held to reduce risk to near the average market risk level, whereas a careful examination of covariances could lead to a smaller efficient portfolio.

Problems with portfolio theory

When portfolio theory was first discussed in the 1950s, it was not widely accepted by analysts and investors. There were two main reasons for this. Firstly, if n securities are to be considered, estimates of the value of n expected returns, n variances and $(n^2 - n)/2$ covariances have to be made. As can be seen from Example 8.5 overleaf, the number of figures required soon gets extremely large and computers in the 1950s and 1960s were slow and expensive to run.

Secondly, the investment research departments were usually organised on an industry basis and who was to determine the covariance of returns of

---

[17] By monitoring costs, we mean the cost of keeping up to date with all information on the shares.

Example 8.5   Comparison of data requirements for different sizes of portfolio

Number of securities	3	30	300
Number of data items required for calculation of efficient frontier	9	495	45,450

a timber company with those of a shoe retailer? In any case, the only way such variances and covariances could be estimated was by looking at past data and assuming that underlying factors affecting the securities would be the same in the future so that values based on past frequencies could be used for future probabilities. This was relatively straightforward for returns and variances but calculations were messy for covariances.

One further potential problem with portfolio theory is that it is only a one-period model. Investors usually consider investment policy for several years (or periods) ahead and wish to maximise their expected utility of wealth at the end of the whole period. However, it can be shown that, if certain assumptions concerning the utility function of the investor are made,[18] the investor will maximise his overall expected utility by considering each period separately. Thus, he can use the portfolio theory approach in each individual period.

So, despite the problems in using portfolio theory which derive from the cumbersome nature of the required input data, as computers evolved and acceptance of more quantitative techniques in investment analysis grew, portfolio theory began to be used in determining optimal portfolios.

Portfolio theory does offer a framework for each investor to determine his optimal portfolio from inputs which he can derive subjectively or from past data. For example, the theory can be applied to net of tax returns, thus allowing for the particular tax position of the investor. This would lead to different portfolios for each investor even if they started off with the same expected *gross* returns and risk for each security. Also, as was mentioned in the introduction to this chapter, portfolio theory can be applied to the determination of optimal portfolios in an international context. If the expected returns, risks and correlation coefficients are estimated in sterling terms (again usually relying to some extent on past data), optimal international portfolios can be found for UK investors. Similarly, if the returns and risk data are calculated in DM terms, optimal international portfolios for German investors can be determined. Finally portfolio theory can also be applied successfully to the asset allocation problem, namely what proportions of equities, bonds, cash and, say, property to have in a particular portfolio.

---

[18] For example, if the utility function is a logarithmic one, $U = f(ln(W))$.

Summary

This chapter has looked at how the investor can decide on an optimal *portfolio* of securities. It was discovered that not only should the expected return and risk (measured by standard deviation) of each security be considered, but also its correlation or covariance with the other securities in the portfolio.

Since most shares quoted on the UK stock market are correlated positively, but less than perfectly, with each other, combining them into a portfolio will actually reduce the risk to the investor to less than the weighted average of the individual risks of the securities. However, the expected *return* on a portfolio is equal to the weighted average of the expected returns of the constituent securities. So, it will always pay the investor to diversify, provided the securities in his portfolio are not perfectly positively correlated.

The investor, knowing his utility function and indifference curves, can then find a portfolio which is optimal for him from the efficient frontier of portfolios, that is, from those portfolios which offer the best expected returns given their risk. This method of finding the optimal portfolio is termed 'Markowitz' diversification, and involves careful consideration of all the securities and how they relate to each other. The investor can also reduce risk by going for 'naïve' diversification where he simply invests equal amounts in randomly selected securities. 'Naïve' diversification will reduce risk substantially, but will involve a portfolio with more securities and a worse risk–return ratio than the more rigorous 'Markowitz' diversification.

Problems

1. Shares *A* and *B* have the following characteristics:

	E(R) (%)	S (%)	CORR$_{AB}$
A	10	10	0.5
B	20	20	

(i) Calculate the expected return and risk of the portfolio consisting of
  (a) ¼A, ¾B
  (b) ½A, ½B
  (c) ¾A, ¼B

(ii) Plot these portfolios on a graph of expected return against risk. Which proportions of *A* and *B* do you think will maximise expected return given the risk?

2. The expected returns and variance–covariance matrix of 3 shares are given below:

	E(R) (%)	COV$_{ij}$		
A	8	25	100	150
B	10	100	120	180
C	12	150	180	300

(i) Calculate the expected return and variance of equally weighted portfolios of
(a) *A* and *B*
(b) *A* and *C*
(c) *B* and *C*
Why is the variance of the *B, C* portfolio greater than the variance of the *A, B* portfolio?
(ii) Calculate the expected return and variance of a portfolio consisting of equal amounts of *A, B* and *C*. Compare with the two security portfolios.

3. Suppose two shares *P* and *Q* have perfectly negatively correlated returns.

	E(R) (%)	S (%)
P	13	25
Q	18	40

(i) What will be the expected return and risk of an equally weighted portfolio?
(ii) What portfolio weights for *P* and *Q* will lead to a perfectly hedged portfolio?
(iii) Plot your results on an expected return and risk graph.
(iv) Can you suggest any securities whose returns might, in practice, be negatively correlated.

4. Mrs Peach intends to invest in three securities, *J, K* and *L*, each with expected return of 15% and variance of 150%. The three securities all have returns which are totally uncorrelated with each other.
(i) What will be the expected return and risk of Mrs Peach's portfolio if she holds the three securities in equal amounts?
(ii) What if Mrs Peach puts 40% in *J*, 40% in *K* and 20% in *L*?
(iii) Estimate the weights for *J, K* and *L* which would lead to a minimum risk portfolio for Mrs Peach.
(iv) Would Mrs Peach be right to go for a minimum risk portfolio?

5. 'Three hundred equities, if they are rightly chosen, are sufficient as a selection ground for most portfolios. I feel that increasing the number of shares under consideration to an unmanageable number is no way of diversifying.' Does this statement conflict with the results of portfolio theory?

The capital asset pricing model

Introduction

We saw, towards the end of Chapter 8, that finding an optimal portfolio using portfolio theory requires a computer program and a rather large variance–covariance matrix. This has hindered general acceptance of portfolio theory, despite its usefulness. We also saw, in the section called 'Size of Optimal Portfolio', that however much we diversify and however many securities are included in the portfolio, risk cannot be reduced, using a naïve diversification policy, to less than a certain amount. This is because as we hold more and more securities, we end up holding the whole stock market, and thus bearing the risk of that stock market, which cannot be diversified away. This concept of undiversifiable market risk, as it is known, is fundamental to the development of the more rigorous capital asset pricing model (or CAPM), which is described in this chapter. The CAPM shows that the risk of any security can be divided into two parts – the element which reflects that undiversifiable market risk and an element which is specific to the share and which can be diversified away when the share is held as part of a large portfolio.

The CAPM is a much stronger model than portfolio theory, in that it not only prescribes optimal portfolios for investors but also derives an equation relating the expected return and risk of any security.

For example, if we consider the optimal portfolio prescribed by the CAPM and compare it to that derived by portfolio theory, we find that the CAPM, with further assumptions about the market in which securities are traded, including the introduction of a risk-free security, shows that all investors will hold, not different portfolios derived from different opportunity sets, but different amounts of the *same* portfolio. The portfolio of securities which all investors will hold is the market portfolio, that is, the portfolio consisting of all securities in the market. Each investor will adjust to his particular risk–return requirements by combining his holding of the market portfolio, M, with positive or negative amounts of the risk-free security. For example, the individual investor wishing to take on more risk than the stock market for shares offers will borrow money and invest further in M. This will increase the risk of his investment through 'gearing up'. In contrast, a more cautious investor, not wishing to bear all the risk of ordinary shares, will put only a small part of his money into M and will invest the rest in risk-free securities, for example Treasury bills.

The relationship between the risk and return of any security, which is found in the CAPM, is an equally strong result. The equation, known as the securities market line, shows that there is a *linear* relationship between the risk and expected return of any security but that the risk for which the investor is to be rewarded by return is *not* the total risk (represented by the standard deviation or variance of returns) but only a proportion of it – that element referred to earlier which reflects the undiversifiable market risk. Any risk arising from holding the share on its own and not as part of a diversified portfolio will not be rewarded.

The implications of the CAPM for investment decision-making are far-reaching. Investors who assume that securities are valued according to the CAPM will not attempt to select investments according to techniques such as fundamental analysis (mentioned in Chapter 5), but will simply select securities on the basis of the risk and expected return predicted by the CAPM. Such investors will expect only a 'fair' return for the risk they bear, as opposed to fundamental analysts who expect to earn better than average returns from their share selection skills. These differing investment strategies are discussed in greater depth in Chapter 10.

The chapter starts with the empirical basis of the CAPM, the market model. The assumptions underlying the CAPM are then introduced and the results of the CAPM are derived. A whole section is then devoted to how the results of the CAPM can be applied in practice, for example how the notion of market risk, called beta, should be used, and the chapter concludes with a discussion of more complex models than the CAPM which are currently being used, including arbitrage pricing theory.

Market model

It was inevitable that a simplification of portfolio theory would be proposed, especially given the fact that securities do seem to be subject to
common influences – we have noted their tendency to move up or down
together. Sharpe (1963) postulated that the returns of securities, which we
have seen are usually positively correlated, were only so related because of
their common 'market' response. This led him to suppose that the expected
return of any security could be expressed as a linear function of the
expected return of the market as a whole. (The expected return of the
market could be approximated by using the return on a suitable stock
market index.) This would lead to an equation of the form

$$E(R_i) = a_i + b_i E(R_m) \tag{9.1}$$

for each security i, where $E(R_i)$ was the expected return on security i, a_i
and b_i were constants specific to that security and $E(R_m)$ the expected
return on the market as a whole. In practice the return R_i would not
necessarily turn out to be equal to its expected value, $E(R_i)$, and so, if past
data on returns were used, an equation of the form

$$R_i = a_i + b_i R_m + e_i \tag{9.2}$$

would be found where R_i and R_m were the actual returns for security i and
the market as a whole, and the residual term, e_i, was the difference
between the actual and expected result. The expected value of e_i would be
zero. Such a model obviously has quite strong assumptions. It presupposes
that the *only* common factor affecting all securities is the return on the
market.[1] Other common influences such as industry factors or economic
influences affecting only some securities are ignored.

Obviously, it would be nice if Sharpe's market model worked in the real
world but, as yet, we have no theoretical foundation for such a model.
However, as we shall see in the next section, such a market model can be
proved theoretically if certain additional assumptions are made about the
stock market and investor behaviour.

---

[1] Mathematically, this is expressed by requiring the covariances between all values of e_i to be
$0 : COV(e_i, e_j) = 0$ for all i, j. Sharpe's model also requires $COV(e_i, R_m) = 0$ for all i which
means that the size of the error term e_i is unaffected by the size of the market return.

Advantages of the market model

How does this market model help us? It radically reduces both the number of variables needed to determine efficient portfolios and the calculations to find these variables. For each security to be considered, all that is needed is a_i, b_i and the variance of the error term $V(e_i)$. These can be calculated using regression[2] by plotting actual past values of R_i and R_m against each other, as in Figure 9.1.

For example, monthly returns[3] over the past five years could be plotted. The intercept of the line fitted to the points by regression would give a_i, the slope of the line b_i, and the variance of the error terms would be calculated from the regression analysis by the computer. It must then be assumed that these values will hold in the future for each security. If any specific changes are anticipated, a_i, b_i and $V(e_i)$ can be subjectively estimated. The variance of the market V_m and its expected return $E(R_m)$ must also be estimated. In all, a total of only $3n + 2$ data items are required for an n-security portfolio. For example, with 30 securities, portfolio theory requires 495 data items and the market model 92.

The expected return and variance of any portfolio P are then simply

$$E(R_p) = a_p + b_p \, E(R_m) \tag{9.3}$$

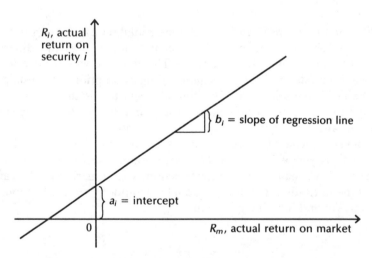

Figure 9.1   Calculation of coefficients in $R_i = a_i + b_i R_m = e_i$

---

[2] Regression (of Y on X) is used to plot a *line of best fit* through a set of points by minimising the sum of the vertical distances of the points from the line. It is an attempt to find a linear relationship between two variables, using empirical data.

[3] Return = dividends received plus any capital gains or losses.

$$V_p = b_p^2 V_m + \sum_{i=1}^{i=n} X_i^2 V(e_i) \tag{9.4}$$

where a_p and b_p are the weighted averages of the constituent securities' a_i and b_i and the X_i are the weightings.

$$a_p = \sum_{i=1}^{i=n} X_i a_i$$

$$b_p = \sum_{i=1}^{i=n} X_i b_i$$

and

$$\sum_{i=1}^{i=n} X_i = 1$$

The attractions of the simpler model are obvious.

Capital asset pricing model (CAPM)

Assumptions of the model

The market model's attempt at explaining security returns is attractive in its simplicity but we have as yet no theoretical foundation for believing that we can cut corners in this way. Portfolio theory, provided we accept its assumptions and the fact that it is a one-period rather than a multi-period model,[4] leads to some interesting results. However, to get any further we need to introduce some *additional* assumptions:

(1) a perfect securities market; that is, perfect competition in a frictionless securities market which is also in equilibrium;[5]

(2) all investors agree on a period under consideration for investment

---

[4] The one-period model restriction means that all investment decisions must be made at the beginning of the period and no changes can be made during the period. (A multi-period model would allow changes at the beginning of each period and so perhaps achieve greater utility.) The period considered can be as long or short as desired. But see p. 254 for a reconciliation of the multi-period and single-period models.

[5] The underlying assumptions for a perfect frictionless market are:
  (i) no taxes, no transaction costs and no restrictions on short-selling (selling shares you do not have);
 (ii) information is free and simultaneously available to all investors;
(iii) securities are infinitely divisible (can be bought in any quantity) and they all have a market price;
(iv) no individual can affect the market price by buying or selling securities;
 (v) investors are all rational, expected utility maximisers.

purposes (say, one month or one year) and have identical expectations regarding the probability distributions of security returns for that period;

(3) unlimited amounts of money can be borrowed or lent by all investors at the risk-free rate. If inflation exists, it is fully anticipated in interest rates.

Assumption (1), which requires the absence of such possible distorting factors as taxes and transaction costs, is obviously unrealistic and far from the 'real world'. However, if too many realities are introduced into a model at an early stage, no analysis of the basic return relationships of securities or of how investors behave can be made. The validity of the model can be tested empirically[6] and, if necessary, complexities can be added at a later stage.

Assumption (2) is important since the CAPM requires investors to have the same opportunity set of portfolios and the same efficient frontier. Portfolio theory does not require this – each investor can derive his own set of efficient portfolios, map his own indifference curves on to them and choose his own optimal portfolios without concerning himself with other investors' beliefs.

Assumption (3) is also crucial to the derivation of the CAPM, because the existence of risk-free lending and borrowing extends the range of opportunities available to the investor. Before we continue, what do we mean by 'risk-free'? We mean without any of the risks described in Chapter 2. Suppose the investor buys government fixed interest securities (equivalent to lending money free of default risk); he may still be subject to inflation risk and interest rate risk. The former is dealt with in this instance by the assumption that inflation is fully anticipated in interest rates. The latter can be avoided if a zero coupon[7] fixed interest security is chosen which matures exactly at the end of the period in question.

In practice, the security which most clearly satisfies the conditions is a Treasury bill, a default-free government security bought at a discount to par and always paying exactly par at maturity. Treasury bills are also shorter-term securities than gilts, thereby reducing interest rate risk and inflation risk to a minimum.

However, even if a relatively risk-free asset can be found in which to invest, the assumption that any investor can also *borrow* money at the risk-free rate is more difficult to envisage being possible in the real world.

---

[6] In other words, the model can be tested to see if it reflects what actually happens in the stock market.

[7] A zero-coupon bond is one which pays no interest during its life. The price is therefore low to allow the required return to be made entirely through capital gain.

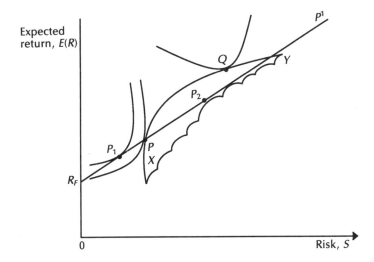

Figure 9.2   Optimal portfolios with risk-free borrowing and lending

Results of CAPM

Given these assumptions, over and above those needed for portfolio theory, we now have the capital asset pricing model (or CAPM), from which we can derive interesting results both as to how the risk and return of securities are related and as to how investors should behave.

First of all, we can say that all investors face the same opportunity set of risky securities and portfolios and the same efficient frontier, XY, as shown in Figure 9.2. They may, however, choose different optimal portfolios according to their different indifference curves, for example P and Q.

The introduction of the risk-free borrowing and lending possibilities widens the alternatives available to each investor. For example, the investor who initially chose P can now, as well as choosing P, also move up and down the line $R_F PP^1$. If he borrows money at the risk-free rate of interest, R_F (or 'gears up'), he can move along PP^1, say to P_2, having increased the risk of his investment in P by using some borrowed money. If he lends, he can move along $R_F P$ say to P_1, having reduced the amount of his investment in the risky portfolio P and hence his overall risk.

In fact, the possibility of moving up and down $R_F PP^1$ enables the investor to increase his utility by moving to a higher indifference curve. For this particular investor, if he lends and moves to P_1, he will have reached a higher indifference curve and thereby increased his utility.

Let us look at other alternatives available to our investor. He does not have to restrict himself to portfolio P which was optimal without the

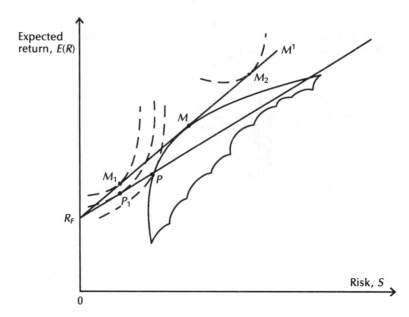

Figure 9.3   Optimal portfolio with risk-free borrowing and lending

borrowing and lending possibilities. It can be seen from Figure 9.3 that he would do better still by investing in portfolio M and then lending until he reached M_1 on the line R_FMM^1. M is the point on the efficient frontier where the line from R_F is a tangent to the frontier.

In fact, it can be shown that *every* investor would maximise his utility by choosing portfolio M and then moving up or down R_FMM^1 until he reached the point where R_FMM^1 touched his indifference curve, M_1 in the case of one investor, M_2 in the case of another. So every investor will hold some proportion of M and either positive amounts of R_F (lend) or negative amounts of R_F (borrow).

What will M be? If all individuals hold M in equilibrium, M must be the total of all risky assets in the market place. So individuals will hold small amounts of all risky securities in proportion to their market values. If they want higher risk than that offered by the market, they will borrow to buy more of M and move to the right up R_FMM^1. If they want less than the market risk, they will hold less M and lend some money at R_F (say, buy Treasury bills).

The model we have built up from our assumptions has told us how investors ought to behave. The staggering result is that all investors should hold not different portfolios, but different amounts of the *same* portfolio M combined with positive or negative amounts of money invested at the risk-free rate. Unlike portfolio theory which expects each investor to hold his own tailor-made portfolio, the CAPM says we should hold the same security portfolio made up of all risky securities in the market in proportion

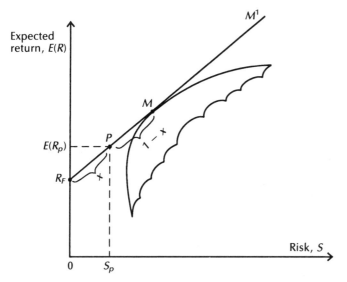

Figure 9.4   Capital market line

to their market value – not ten or fifteen shares but several thousand securities.

The CAPM does not stop there. It also tells us about return and risk. Suppose an investor holds a portfolio P on the line $R_F M M^1$, made up of fraction x of M and fraction $(1 - x)$ of R_F, as in Figure 9.4.

The expected return on his portfolio will be

$$E(R_p) = R_F(1 - x) + xE(R_m)$$

Rearranging gives

$$E(R_p) = R_F + x(E(R_m) - R_F) \tag{9.5}$$

The variance of this portfolio will be

$$V_p = x^2 V_m$$

because the variance of a risk-free investment in R_F must be zero, giving

$$S_p = xS_m$$

So,

$$x = \frac{S_p}{S_m} \tag{9.6}$$

Substituting for x in (9.6), we get

$$E(R_p) = R_F + (E(R_m) - R_F) \frac{S_p}{S_m} \tag{9.7}$$

Equation (9.7) is known as the *capital market line* and expresses the expected return of a portfolio which lies on $R_F MM^1$ in terms of its risk, S_p. This equation is useful if we are dealing with efficient portfolios lying on the capital market line,[8] but we would like an expression relating the return and risk of *any* security, not just of portfolios lying on $R_F MM^1$. In fact, equation (9.7) can be used to derive the required expression for the expected return of any security in the market:

$$E(R_i) = R_F + (E(R_m) - R_F) \frac{COV_{im}}{S_m^2} \tag{9.8}$$

Equation (9.8) is known as the *securities market line* since it relates the expected return of any security to its risk. This equation is similar to the capital market line but instead of expressing $E(R_i)$ in terms of its standard deviation, S_i, we see that the return of a security is a function of its covariance with the market, COV_{im}.

If we consider a risk-free security, COV_{im} will be zero[9] and so $E(R_i)$ will be equal to R_F. If the security is risky, a premium will be required over and above the risk-free rate, which will increase with the covariance of the security with the market. $(E(R_m) - R_F)/S_m^2$ is sometimes called the unit market price of risk. For each 1% increase in COV_{im}, the expected return required of the security will increase by the market price of risk.

This has serious implications for the investor when considering adding a security to his portfolio. The only risk for which he will be rewarded will be the *covariance* of the security with the market and not its total risk measured by variance or standard deviation. This can be seen more clearly if we simplify equation (9.8). If we let $\beta_i = COV_{im}/S_m^2$ (different for each security i) the equation can be written

$$E(R_i) = R_F + \beta_i (E(R_m) - R_F) \tag{9.9}$$

or

$$E(R_i) = a_i + b_i E(R_m)$$

---

[8] Any portfolio lying on $R_F MM^1$ must be efficient in the sense that it must be perfectly positively correlated with the market portfolio M (because it is joined to M by a straight line).

[9] Since $COV_{im} = S_i S_m CORR_{im}$ and S_i, the standard deviation of a riskless security must be zero.

where a_i is equal to $R_F - \beta_i R_F$ and b_i is equal to β_i.

This looks like the market model that Sharpe suggested might hold. We have shown that, under certain conditions, it does hold and that the return of a security depends on its relationship to the market return. β_i is a measure of sensitivity to the market and it is for this sensitivity that the holder of the security is rewarded. The market portfolio M will have a β of 1; this can be seen by substituting $\beta_i = 1$ into equation (9.9). Securities with βs less than 1 will be less risky than the market as a whole and yield less return. For example, companies in stable industries such as food manufacturers, whose profits and hence returns vary less than the average, will have shares with low βs. Securities with high βs, greater than 1, will be those of companies in cyclical industries, such as construction, with returns fluctuating more than the market average. For example, Example 9.1 on p. 268 shows Asprey plc to have a low β of 0.73 and Associated British Ports to have a higher β than average of 1.22.

How do we calculate the β (or beta as it is more usually written) of an individual security? Ideally, we would need to look at the future to determine beta. If, as with standard deviation, we assume that a past figure will be a good surrogate for the future, we can, as for the market model, plot historical returns R_i against R_m, as in Figure 9.1. β_i will then be the slope of the regression line

$$R_i = \alpha_i + \beta_i R_m + e_i \tag{9.10}$$

where e_i is the error term of the regression.

Taking the risk from both sides of equation (9.10), we get the variance of the return, V_i, on the left-hand side. On the right-hand side, there is no risk to α_i since this is a constant. We therefore obtain, for V_i,

$$V_i = \beta_i^2 S_m^2 + S^2(e_i) \tag{9.11}$$

since using variance as a measure of risk always involves squared terms.

Equation (9.11) splits the total risk of a security, measured by its variance, into two parts – risk relative to the market, measured by the sensitivity factor β_i, and specific risk or diversifiable risk, $S^2(e_i)$. The latter risk is called diversifiable because it can be diversified away. We saw when looking at portfolios of n securities that risk was quickly reduced to market risk as n increased. The risk specific to individual securities could easily be reduced through diversification. This will become clearer when we have looked at a numerical example in the next section.

So, what the securities market line, equation (9.8) or (9.9), tells us is that the holder of a security is *only* rewarded for the risk, sometimes known as systematic or β risk of his security, and not for his diversifiable risk. In other words the market assumes all investors hold diversified portfolios and thus have diversified away the specific risk of securities, $S^2(e_i)$.

Example 9.1   Extract from the London Business School Risk Measurement Service

SEDOL Number	Company Name	S.E. Industry Classification	Market Capit'n	Market-ability	Beta	Vari-ability	Specific Risk	Std Error	R-Sq'rd	Qty Ab Return	Ann Ab Return	Ann Act Return	Gross Yield	P/E Ratio	Price 30:00:90
32393	ANGLIAN WATER PLC	WATERWRK	902	0 Fa						23			6.7	7.3	306
32218	ANGLIA SECURE HOMES PLC	CONSTRCT	11	0 Ab	1.23	61	54	.23	23	-26	-47	-67			34
32069	ANGLIA TELEVSN 'A' N.V.	LEISURE	91	OTAb	1.08	41	33	.16	36	-1	-7	-23	6.0	7.4	207
36577	ANGLO EASTERN PLANTATION	RUBBER	15	4 a	.68	38	35	.17	17	11	-33	-37	4.0	33.0	66
32810	ANGLO GROUP PLC	FIN.TRST	66	.1 g	1.08	54	47	.24	23				3.7	6.3	198S
198789	ANGLO IRISH BANKS CP PLC	BANK	29	2T g	.89	54	49	.22	18	-8	-27	-37	9.3	6.5	48
33608	ANGLO & OVERSEAS TS PLC	INV.TRST	238	.1TAb	1.06	28	13	.07	80	-8	-10	-25	3.7	29.9	207
644936	ANGLO PACIFIC RESOURCES	MINE FIN	13	.8 Ub	1.15	60	53	.22	22	-6	-30	-48	.0	27.4	17
40200	ANGLO-PARK GROUP PLC	PROPERTY	4	1 g						3			13.3	3.1	40
39576	ANGLO SCANDINAVIAN INV T	FIN.TRST	15	3 g						0			8.1		74
41117	ANGLO UNITED PLC	GEN.CHEM	77	0 Ab	.95	44	37	.18	29	-16	-25	-37	6.0	7.5	31
43704	ANSBACHER (HENRY)HLGS PL	MRCH.BNK	114	1 Ab	.79	29	22	.12	40	-9	-0	-6	5.5	17.6	61
915900	ANTARES GROUP PLC	OIL	2	0 g	1.30	64	58	.23	23	-16	-47	-69	.0		3
45562	ANTOFAGASTA HLDGS PLC	OVSE.TRD	132	.5T g	.84	40	35	.16	26	-14	-9	-19	3.9	6.1	440
59206	API GROUP PLC	PACK&PAP	18	1T g	.70	29	24	.12	32	-30	-46	-52	10.6	12.5	85
45874	APOLLO METALS PLC	METALLGY	14	.9 Ug	.76	28	22	.18	37	13	25	18	2.6	14.4	121
45830	APOLLO WATCH PROD PLC	UNCLASS	5	1 Ug	.98	53	50	.28	13	26	-38	-51	6.1	6.0	11
46316	APPLEBY WESTWARD PLC	FOOD RET	11	6 Ug	.93	26	20	.18	42	0	-2	-13	5.3	8.5	203
46134	APPLETREE HOLDINGS PLC	FOOD MAN	13	3 g	1.12	47	39	.19	28	0	-16	-28	8.0	9.1	75
46037	APPLEYARD GROUP PLC	MTR.DIST	37	.6TAb	1.18	41	31	.16	42	-8	-21	-39	13.0	3.6	80
46219	APPLIED HOLOGRAPHICS PLC	UNCLASS	35	.7 Ug	1.00	48	42	.19	23	-19	-6	-19	.0		235
4950	APV PLC	IND.PLNT	227	OTAb	1.01	39	31	.16	35	-22	-23	-37	9.2	6.8	73
46725	AQUASCUTUM GRP PLC 'A'	STR.MULT	54	5T	.90	47	43	.20	18				2.0	31.5	197A
46703	AQUASCUTUM GRP PLC	STR.MULT	19	13T									.7	33.7	555A
46491	ARAN ENERGY PLC	OIL	141	0 b	1.07	43	38	.23	22	32	7	-8		117.4	54
48088	ARCHER(A J) HLDGS PLC	INS.BRKR	20	1 b	.54	22	19	.17	20	-17	-25	-26	13.2	5.0	85
47386	ARCHIMEDES INV TR 'CAP'	INV.TRST	3	6 g	.84	27	20	.11	46	10	-14	-22			230
47364	ARCHIMEDES INV TR 'INC'	INV.TRST	2	8 g									12.1	11.6	193
47524	ARCOLECTRIC HDGS'A N V'	ELECTRCL	2	6 g	.90	47	43	.20	17	-4	-29	-36	3.0	22.3	42
47502	ARCOLECTRIC HLDGS	ELECTRCL	2	14 g									1.2	54.8	103
48657	ARGOS PLC	STR.MULT	655	0 Aa						12			2.4	15.2	221
49241	ARGYLL GROUP	FOOD RET	2253	OTFa	.67	23	18	.10	42	8	15	11	4.1	13.0	238
49456	ARLEN PLC	ELECTRCL	9	.5 g	1.21	49	41	.19	31	1	-45	-64	15.2	14.5	29
686961	ARLEY HOLDINGS PLC	MECH.ENG	2	3 g	1.11	63	59	.25	12	-39	-70	-85		2.9	16
49810	ARMITAGE BROTHERS PLC	FOOD MAN	4	8 g	.89	36	31	.18	26	6	-9	-16	6.2	18.4	112
49661	ARMOUR TRUST LTD	FOOD MAN	9	.1 g	1.29	45	34	.17	42	1	-8	-30	5.1	5.7	32
50878	ARNCLIFFE HLDGS. LTD.	CONSTRCT	5	7 g	.92	41	36	.19	21	-6	-25	-38	8.3	2.7	108
1434	ASB BARNETT KINNINGS PLC	UNCLASS	2	8 Ug	.93	71	69	.29	8	-2	-52	-62	.0		31
57200	ASDA GROUP PLC	FOOD.RET	1337	OTFa	.78	31	25	.13	33	16	-26	-34	5.6	10.9	114
52551	ASDA PROPERTY HLDGS PLC	PROPERTY	35	.8 Ag	1.10	38	28	.15	43	-11	-35	-51	3.8	12.2	62
5500	ASD PLC	SPEC.STL	23	2 Ug	1.15	43	35	.18	33	-7	-6	-20		5.5	78
52841	ASH & LACY PLC	METALLGY	23	1T g	.30	28	27	.13	7	-24	-32	-26	9.5	6.8	90
53491	ASHLEY GROUP PLC	FOOD.RET	127	.2 Ab	1.40	65	56	.23	25	12	27	2	2.0	14.1	90
53372	ASHLEY(LAURA) HLDGS	STR.MULT	120	0 Ab	1.13	43	35	.17	36	35	-12	-30	1.9		60
53673	ASHTEAD GROUP PLC	CONSTRCT	33	.8 Ug	.82	43	38	.19	23	-6	-29	-35	2.7	6.4	183
53941	ASPEN COMMCTNS PLC	UNCLASS	28	1 Ug	.98	36	28	.15	36	-5	-38	-51	5.1	6.6	213
54096	ASPREY PLC	STR.MULT	211	2T*g	.73	36	32	.15	23	-19	-25	-32	2.2	14.1	265
54706	ASSAM DOOARS HLDGS	TEA	20	31T	.40	25	24	.17	11				.7	59.1	2000F
55282	ASSET TRUST PLC	FIN.TRST	13	99	1.08	52	44	.21	26				5.6	12.0	84A
56003	ASSOCD. BRIT. ENG. LTD	OTHINDCP	5	0 g	.93	74	71	.25	8	-5	-9	-21	6.7	7.1	2
56100	ASSOCD.BRIT.FOODS	FOOD MAN	1811	OTFa	.59	22	18	.10	37	13	8	6	3.6	9.6	404
56575	ASSOCD BRITISH CONSLTNTS	UNCLASS	10	8 g	.88	31	28	.26	20	10	-17	-26	6.2	6.7	138
56434	ASSOCD BRITISH PORTS HDG	TRANSPRT	353	OTAb	1.22	34	19	.10	67	10	-19	-38	4.7	8.4	192
57631	ASSOCD ENERGY SERVICES P	ENG.CONT	1	.7 Ug	.90	84	81	.26	6	-4	-71	-82	C		4
58128	ASSOCD.FISHERIES	FOOD.MAN	19	.8T g	.88	34	27	.14	36	12	-29	-40	7 t	11.1	112
57976	ASSOCIATED FARMERS PLC	UNCLASS	2	4 U	.90	32	29	.26	21	-5	-10	-22		48.2	66
58311	ASSOCIATED HENRIQUES PLC	FIN.TRST	17	.5 g	.99	47	47	.27	10				8.2	8.3	535
59143	ASSOCIATED NURSING SVS	HLTH&HSD	8	3 Ug	.68	29	26	.21	16	-18	-14	-19	2.8	4.2	145
68224	ASTEC (BSR) PLC	ELECTRNC	111	OT b	1.33	54	45	.20	31	-3	-0	-21	11.3	19.7	36
60640	ASTRA HOLDINGS PLC	UNCLASS	7	0 Ab	.93	85	82	.27	6	-34	-81	-93	43.3	.6	8
1638	ASW HOLDINGS PLC	SPEC.STL	144	0 Ab	1.04	32	25	.20	37	-7	-0	-14	7.0	5.9	218
4240	A .T.A SELECTION PLC	AGENCY	3	1 Ug	.83	43	39	.19	18	-28	-59	-68	15.9	5.0	21
60509	ATKINS BROS (HOSIERY)	CLOTHING	5	2 g	.82	49	45	.20	15	11	-12	-21	11.9	9.6	135
61535	ATLANTIC RESOURCES PLC	OIL	13	.1 Ug	1.06	69	63	.25	16	1	-38	-53	.0		5
62118	ATLANTIC SECURITIES TRUS	FIN.TRST	8	12 g	.92	34	30	.22	22	-20	-45	-58	.0	69.1	38
61739	ATLAS CONVERTING EQP PLC	IND.PLNT	51	1 Ug	.83	40	36	.19	21	5	45	36	3.1	16.0	635
605740	ATP COMMUNICATIONS GRP P	AGENCY	1	1 Ug	.85	51	47	.21	15	-18	-58	-67	.0	47.8	11
60639	AT TRUST PLC	MECH.ENG	1	0 g	.36	81	75	.26	54	-55	-99	-93			3L
62323	ATTWOODS PLC	UNCLASS	380	OTAb	1.25	37	24	.13	58	9	20	0	2.7	21.4	426
62549	AUDIT & GENERAL PLC	UNCLASS	2	.1 Ug	1.26	72	66	.25	15	-47	-66	-87	23.8	5.6	6
62550	AUKETT ASSOCIATES PLC	AGENCY	7	4 g	.76	25	21	.18	31	-20	-38	-45	10.3	4.6	55
729781	AUSTIN REED GRP PLC'A'	STR.MULT	35	.4TAb	1.00	34	26	.13	44	-4	-24	-38	9.0	8.1	140
729684	AUSTIN REED GRP PLC'ORD'	STR.MULT	10	3 b									3.3	22.1	383
629911	AUSTRALIA INV TRUST PLC	INV.TRST	17	7 g	1.00	36	29	.16	39				5.1	24.2	102U
65601	AUTHORITY INVESTMENTS	FIN.TRST	5	2 g	.98	66	62	.23	13	0	-69	-76		2.1	50S
418885	AUTOMAGIC HLDGS PLC	FOOTWEAR	3	9 Ug	.46	25	23	.12	17	5	-43	-40	15.8	7.4	55
65742	AUTOMATED SECURITY	SECRITY	228	.1TAb	.96	32	24	.13	45	-13	-15	-27	2.9	9.4	209
66176	AUTOMOBILES OF DISTINCTI	MTR.DIST	2	2 3g	.97	56	53	.30	12	-4	-27	-38		110.0	11
66529	AVESCO PLC 'REGD'	LEISURE	17	2 b	1.33	48	36	.18	44	-28	-55	-78	7.1	2.3	28
66552	AVESCO PLC 'BR'	LEISURE	1										2.3	2.3	28
66950	AVONMORE FOODS PLC'A'	FOOD MAN	26	0 Ig						-15			3.8	7.4	66
66701	AVON RUBBER CO PLC	MTR.COMP	66	.2TAb	1.01	35	27	.14	40	-11	-19	-33	7.0	7.3	313
67618	AYRSHIRE METAL PRODUCTS	MECH.ENG	8	.5T g	.76	65	62	.24	7	-9	-36	-43	9.0	3.2	78
67340	BAA PLC	TRANSPRT	1800	0 Fa	1.77	25	17	.11	55	-3	16	10	4.3	9.6	359
70230	BABCOCK INTNL GROUP PLC	MECH.ENG	174	0 Ab	1.19	32	21	.22	57	-3	-11	-30	10.8	5.7	37

Source: London Business School, *Risk Measurement Service* (October–December 1990).

Practical application of the CAPM

How does all this help the investor? In so far as we have derived a theoretical foundation for the market model, so the calculations for determining the risk and return of any portfolio are much simplified. Once the β (or beta) risk and diversifiable risk, $S^2(e_i)$, are known for each security, the risk and return of any combination of securities can be calculated, provided the risk and return characteristics of the stock market are known, as well as the risk-free rate, R_F.

This information is now readily available for all shares quoted on the US, UK and other major stock exchanges. Example 9.1 gives an extract from the London Business School *Risk Measurement Service*, published quarterly, which provides all the information needed to be able to use the CAPM on UK quoted share portfolios. The betas provided in the London Business School publication are derived from historical data (monthly returns for the past five years) using regression analysis. The use of these betas therefore assumes that the shares' past risk characteristics are relevant for the future. This assumption is usually referred to as requiring betas to be 'stationary' over time. Evidence supporting this assumption for both UK and US shares is reasonably strong, in particular for the betas of portfolios rather than of individual shares.[10] In fact, it is always true that the CAPM works better on portfolios of shares than on individual shares. For example, if we compare the standard error terms,[11] in Example 9.1, of Archimedes Investment Trust 'Capital' (which represents a portfolio of shares) with Arley Holdings shares, we can see that the standard error term for the investment trust is much lower, 0.11 compared with 0.25. The standard error is a measure of how much reliance we can place on the beta estimate provided. The lower it is, the more confidence we have in the beta.

Now, suppose that an investor, Miss Divine, holds equal money amounts of the four securities starred (*) in Example 9.1, Apollo Metals, Aran Energy, Armitage Brothers and Ashley Group. The only additional information required for a complete risk–return analysis of her portfolio is the return on the market and the risk-free rate of interest. A way round having to estimate the expected return on the market is to calculate the 'market premium', $E(R_M) - R_F$.

There is considerable argument about what the appropriate 'market premium' or 'risk premium for equities' should be. Historically, the market premium has averaged around 9% over the last 60 years but, in recent

---

[10] See, for example, Blume (1975) and the Editorial to the London Business School, *Risk Measurement Service* October–December 1991.

[11] For a definition of the standard error term, which measures how reliable a beta estimate is, and an explanation of regression analysis applied to beta estimates, see Elton and Gruber (1991).

years, it has been lower. During the 1980s, up to the 1987 Crash, equities experienced a fairly steady bull market whilst interest rates, affecting traditionally stable fixed interest securities, were quite volatile. Investors came to view equities as not much ri.kier than bonds of Treasury bills and reduced the required market premium in their calculations to 6% or sometimes even 3%. The 1987 Crash altered these perceptions somewhat, but it is still common to see numbers below 9%. For the purposes of this numerical example, we will compromise at 7%.

So, all that remains to be estimated is the risk-free rate of interest. We saw in the assumptions of the CAPM that a true risk-free security would be hard to find. Two possible approximation are either a short-term, government-backed security, such as a three-month Treasury bill, to reduce inflation risk and interest rate risk to a minimum, or a longer-term gilt which matches Miss Divine's expected holding period.

Analysing past performance

In fact, the CAPM can be used, as well as for estimating expected return and risk on any portfolio, for the purpose of assessing the past performance of the portfolio. For example, the portfolio performance can be compared with the performance which would have been achieved by following the recommended CAPM strategy of holding a proportion of the market portfolio, M, with a beta of 1, and adjusting to the required level of risk by holding positive or negative amounts of R_F. This CAPM strategy is known as a 'passive' strategy and is discussed in more detail in Chapter 13. A comparison of Miss Divine's portfolio will show her whether or not she was wise to restrict herself to a small, relatively undiversified portfolio, which still has diversifiable (or specific) risk attached, instead of completely diversifying away all specific risk, in other words whether her 'active' strategy beat the passive alternative.

So, let us first examine the past. What were (and will be[12]) the risk characteristics of the portfolio?

The beta of the portfolio is simply the weighted average of the constituent shares' betas:

$$\beta_p = \frac{1}{4} \times 0.76 + \frac{1}{4} \times 1.07 + \frac{1}{4} \times 0.89 + \frac{1}{4} \times 1.40$$

$$\beta_p = 1.03$$

---

[12] Since we assume that the risk characteristics of the securities (and hence the portfolio) derived from past data are also relevant to the future.

If we know that the market risk, S_m, was 20% over the past year,[13] we can calculate the market element of the portfolio's risk, $\beta_p^2 S_m^2$:

$$\beta_p^2 S_m^2 = (1.03)^2 \, (0.20)^2$$

$$= (1.061) \, (0.040)$$

$$= \mathbf{0.042}$$

The other element of risk of the portfolio, the diversifiable or specific risk will be the weighted average of the specific risks of the constituent shares. (Remember that we have to square and add when dealing with risk – we use variances and not standard deviations.)[14] So,

$$(\text{Portfolio specific risk})^2 = S^2(e_p) = \sum_{i=1}^{n} (W_i S(e_i))^2$$

We know that $W_i = \frac{1}{4}$ for each i, giving

$$S^2(e_p) = \frac{1}{16} (0.22)^2 + \frac{1}{16} (0.38)^2 + \frac{1}{16} (0.31)^2 + \frac{1}{16} (0.56)^2$$

$$= \mathbf{0.038}$$

So, the portfolio specific or diversifiable risk is

$$S(e_p) = \mathbf{0.19}$$

Note that the portfolio's diversifiable risk is lower than the diversifiable risk of any of the individual constituents of the portfolio. However, diversifiable risk is still present and represents an unrewarded element of risk according to the CAPM. We shall see below whether or not Miss Divine was rewarded for taking on this unnecessary risk.

To complete the picture of the portfolio's risk, we calculate the portfolio's total risk, V_p, which is the sum of the market element of risk plus the specific risk. From equation (9.11), we can write

$$V_p = \beta_p^2 S_m^2 + S^2(e_p)$$

$$= 0.042 + 0.038$$

---

[13] This can be found by using the standard deviation of a surrogate for the market, say the FT–Actuaries All-Share Index.

[14] This derives from the statistical properties of the variance as opposed to its square root, the standard deviation.

$$V_p = 0.080$$

$$S_p = \sqrt{V_p}$$

$$S_p = 28\%$$

So, we know that the total standard deviation of Miss Divine's portfolio is 28% compared with an equivalent figure for M of 20%. (Note that the standard deviation for each security in the *Risk Measurement Service* is given under the heading 'variability'.)

We can now compare Miss Divine's portfolio's performance last year with what she could have achieved under a CAPM or passive strategy. If we know that the return which could have been achieved on a gilt bought one year ago with one year to maturity was 10%, and the return on the market last year (using the surrogate of the FT-Actuaries All-Share Index) was −13%,[15] we can calculate the return on the benchmark portfolio. Note that the benchmark portfolio is designed to have the same beta risk as Miss Divine's portfolio, that is, a beta of 1.03.

$$R_B = (1 - \beta_p)\, R_F + \beta_p R_m$$

$$= -0.03 \times 10\% + 1.03 \times -13\%$$

$$R_B = -13.7\%$$

We can now compare this with the return Miss Divine actually achieved on her portfolio. We do this by looking at the column labelled 'annual actual return' in Example 9.1 and finding the weighted average of the returns for each of the securities:

$$R_p = \tfrac{1}{4} \times +18\% + \tfrac{1}{4} \times -8\% + \tfrac{1}{4} \times -16\% + \tfrac{1}{4} \times +2\%$$

$$R_p = -1.0\%$$

So, whereas the stock market as a whole did not do well, Miss Divine did better than a CAPM strategy. The diversifiable risk she retained by not holding a diversified portfolio led to her outperforming the benchmark portfolio which had the same amount of beta risk, by $-1.0 + 13.7 = 12.7\%$. This is known as the 'abnormal return' and is given in the *Risk Measurement Service* for each share.

The returns shown above remind us of the meaning of the term 'risk'. According to the CAPM, we expect to earn a premium over the risk-free

---

[15] The one-year gilt 'matches' the one-year holding period and so is relatively risk-free. Last year's R_m can found in the *Risk Measurement Service*.

rate when investing in shares. In fact, the return on the market in the period considered above was actually -13%, was *below* the risk-free rate of 10%. Although we expected to earn more than 10% on the stock market, we actually lost money. However, over a sufficient number of years, we would expect to earn on average, say, 7% per annum more than the risk-free rate. This does not stop us earning much less in some years and much more in others.

Estimating future performance

As far as estimating the *expected* return on her portfolio, all that Miss Divine needs to know is the risk-free rate over her desired holding period. Suppose she again wishes to consider a one-year horizon. She can use the one-year spot interest rate implicit in gilt prices, which can be derived as we saw in Chapter 4, as her risk-free rate. Suppose this is 11%. The market premium can be estimated at 7% again, giving the expected return on the portfolio, $E(R_p)$ as

$$E(R_p) = R_F + \beta_p(E(R_m) - R_F)$$

$$= 11\% + 1.03\ (7\%)$$

$$= \textbf{18\%}$$

Note that Miss Divine can only expect to be rewarded for the element of market risk, measured by the beta of 1.03, of her portfolio. She can expect no additional reward from bearing diversifiable risk.

How to construct a benchmark portfolio

Before we leave this example, let us consider how Miss Divine could follow the recommended CAPM strategy in practice. First of all, she should hold a proportion of the market portfolio. Obviously, it would be difficult in real life for her to hold small amounts of each risky security in issue, in proportion to its total market value, because of the enormous transaction costs involved. She would also have to buy and sell securities continually, as share prices moved, to maintain her weightings.

An alternative strategy would be to buy shares in an index fund, a fund set up specially to mirror the market portfolio as closely as possible. This type of fund restricts itself to shares (although strictly it should include all marketable assets) and it may not contain all the shares in the market, or even, say, all the 655 shares in the FTA All-Share Index (discussed in the Appendix to Chapter 10). This is because a reasonably good approximation to the share market as a whole can be obtained by holding only a few hundred shares. With that number, a beta of 1 can be achieved and there is hardly any specific risk.

Index funds were initially set up in the US where it is estimated that around 30% of institutional investment in equities is now invested in such funds. Index funds have taken off in the UK in the past few years, with an estimated 12% of institutional investors investing in the equity market in this way. Indeed, index funds are now global, with any country's equity market available to investors through funds tailored to the most representative stock market index for that country. Retail products are also being developed so that individual investors, as well as institutional investors, have access to a CAPM or passive investment strategy.

An alternative would be to invest in an investment trust or unit trust (both discussed in greater detail in Chapter 12) with a beta of 1. To achieve a beta of 1.03, Miss Divine would have to borrow a small amount to 'gear up' her investment in the index fund or investment trust.

Another alternative strategy for Miss Divine would be to invest in a portfolio much better diversified than her present one and which has the beta that she requires of 1.03. She would thus avoid having to borrow to reach her required level of risk. In fact, she would not need to hold many more shares than she holds at the moment, since we saw in Chapter 8 that a portfolio equally divided amongst ten shares will on average eliminate 90% of the diversifiable risk of the individual securities.

Miss Divine must therefore be holding her present portfolio either because she has not heard of portfolio theory and the CAPM or because she believes that she can pick shares that will do better than predicted by the CAPM. In other words, she believes that she can 'pick winners'. She appears to have succeeded last year. It remains to be seen whether she will again exceed her expected return of 18% next year. Chapter 10 discusses her chances in the light of the efficiency of the stock market.

Problems with CAPM

We have seen how simple the CAPM is to apply in practice to portfolio investment. And yet, we do not see all investors holding index funds (or investment trusts) with betas of 1 and positive or negative amounts of some risk-free security. In practice, each investor holds a different portfolio of shares, as predicted by portfolio theory but not by the CAPM. So what is wrong with the CAPM?

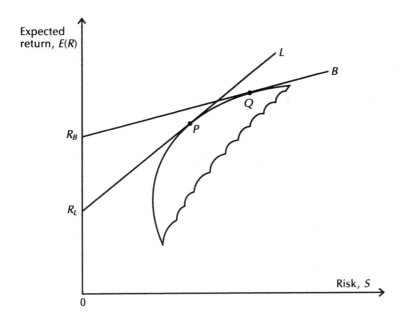

Figure 9.5 Efficient portfolios with different borrowing and lending rates

First of all, we must remember the restrictive assumptions of the model, for example no taxes or transaction costs. The small investor will be unwilling to buy a proportion of all the securities in the stock market when he has only £10,000 to invest although an index fund or investment trust will, as we saw with Miss Divine, offer him a surrogate for *M*. Also, *M* in theory should contain all marketable assets, including the works of art and property we excluded in Chapter 1. For practicalities' sake, a market index including most company shares is used to represent *M* but this excludes a substantial number of marketable assets.

Another problem with the assumptions which immediately springs to mind is that all investors cannot borrow and lend at the risk-free rate. If we assume that the lending rate R_L, is lower than the borrowing rate, R_B, we get the result shown in Figure 9.5. There is no longer only one efficient portfolio *M*. The investor will choose either a point on one of the two lines $R_L P$ and *QB* or any efficient portfolio from the efficient frontier *PQ*. We can see that, with a relaxation of one of the assumptions of the CAPM, we have the result that investors will not necessarily all hold the market portfolio. However, it has been shown that other assumptions underlying the CAPM can be relaxed *without* affecting its major results.[16]

---

[16] For example, the CAPM can still be derived without the need for a risk-free asset. A zero beta security (or combination of securities) can be used instead. See Black (1972).

Alternatives to CAPM

Despite the problems associated with the assumptions underlying CAPM, there are few simple alternatives to the CAPM which can provide estimates of the future expected return on a share. One method, already mentioned in Chapter 5, is to forecast all future dividends to be paid on the share or, more simply, to assume constant growth of such dividends (Gordon's growth model). The assumptions underlying Gordon's growth model are as restrictive as those underlying the CAPM and the CAPM provides an intuitively logical relationship between risk and expected return as well as using market data, albeit historic, rather than subjective forecasts.

Other alternatives to the CAPM are compromises between the single-index approach of the CAPM, where expected return is a function of only *one* factor (namely beta or covariance with the market), and the more computationally complicated portfolio theory. These multi-index models do not have the same theoretical base as the CAPM but start off from the same point. The single-index market model was based on the observation that all share prices tend to move up or down with a market index. Multi-index models are based on the fact that variations in share prices and returns can be traced to other common factors such as industry influences or interest rate changes. For example, it has been shown[17] from a sample of US securities that, on average, 21% of share price movement could be attributed to the market, and a further 21% to industry factors.

Such models can be written in the form

$$E(R_i) = a_i + b_{i1} E(I_1) + b_{i2} E(I_2) + \ldots b_{im} E(I_m) \tag{9.12}$$

where the a_i and b_{ij} are constants and $I_1, I_2, \ldots, I_m$ are the indices used to measure the different influences on share returns. I_1 could be a market index, I_2 an industry index and so on. Equation (9.12) can always be stated so that I_i and I_j are independent of each other $((COVI_i, I_j) = 0$ for all $i, j)$ and this considerably simplifies the computations for calculating efficient portfolios.[18]

Multi-index models are generally derived by putting in possible explanatory factors such as industry or interest rate indices and seeing how well the data can be explained. Historic data are used to calculate the coefficients of the equation and the equation can then be used to forecast expected returns, as with the CAPM. The problem with more complex models, which have more explanatory variables, is that although they explain the historic data better than simpler models (achieve a good 'fit') they may in

---

[17] See Brealey (1983) p. 95.

[18] When considering a portfolio of n securities and m indices, $2n + 2m + nm$ data items are needed for a multi-index model.

doing so include random 'noise' from the data and actually explain less than a simpler model when used on other sets of data. A regression model always involves a compromise between explaining as much variation as possible and running the risk that the 'noise' included will spoil its predictive powers.

A multi-index model which statistically derives the explanatory factors affecting share returns from the actual data (rather than taking economic factors and seeing how well they fit) is that of arbitrage pricing theory. Proposed by Ross in 1976 this provides a theoretical foundation for a multi-index model with independent indices. Firstly, it shows that with the possibility of diversification available to any investor, any non-common causes of risk ('specific' or 'unique' risk) can be diversified away as with CAPM. Secondly, it proves that, if shares are assumed to form an efficient market where no arbitrage profits[19] can be made, the expected return of a share must be a *linear* expression of its sensitivities to the factors affecting it.

So,

$$E(R_i) = a_i + b_{i1}\beta_1 + b_{i2}\beta_2 + \ldots \tag{9.13}$$

where the β_j are the sensitivities of security i to the factors or indices affecting its returns, and the a_i, b_{ij} are constants specific to security i. These indices can be statistically derived from the data rather than by indices suggested by the researcher as in the earlier multi-index models.

Arbitrage pricing theory (or APT as it is known) has gained popularity as the empirical tests of CAPM have come under increasing criticism. It has been shown reasonably successfully[20] that a security's return is an increasing and linear function of its beta but the foundation for such tests has been criticised by Roll who argues that the surrogates used for 'the market' are not good enough and the tests in fact show whether or not the surrogates are efficient portfolios rather than proving or disproving CAPM. The implication of Roll's criticism is, in fact, that the CAPM is untestable. However, empirical testing of the newer APT is hindered by the failure of the model to specify exactly which factors the β_j apply to. Are they interest rate, cyclicality, industry or other factors?

Despite the problems associated with the CAPM and the possible shifts in research emphasis to a multi-index model of the form suggested by the APT, the CAPM is simpler in conception than the newer multi-index models, such as APT. It is therefore unlikely to hold as well as these in the

---

[19] Arbitrage profits are those which can be made without any risk at all – in this case, if there were some securities which were cheaply priced relative to others with the same risk. In efficient markets, where no arbitrage profits can be made, there would be no 'free lunches' of this kind.

[20] For further discussion on both empirical evidence on CAPM and Roll's critique, see Elton and Gruber (1991).

real world but it is computationally simple and easy to understand and apply in practice. Although its results should be treated with caution, it offers a framework for investment decision-making to the investor which 'gut feel' does not.

Summary

We saw in Chapter 8 that portfolio theory provides a basis for determining efficient portfolios for each investor taking into account his risk–return preferences. However, the determination of these portfolios requires a substantial amount of data and calculation and simpler models explaining the risk and return relationship of securities have been put forward which enable a much quicker analysis of portfolios to be undertaken.

The capital asset pricing model (CAPM) provides a theoretically-based single index model. It shows that the reward for holding a risky security is not based on the security's total risk (its standard deviation) but only on its beta, or systematic risk – that risk which remains, assuming the security is held as part of a well-diversified portfolio. The CAPM also shows (unlike portfolio theory which assumes each investor has his individually designed portfolio) that all investors should hold the same market portfolio (all marketable assets) combined with borrowing or lending at the risk-free rate. The only difference between portfolios would be the different proportions held of *M* and risk-free borrowing or lending. However these results can break down if the assumptions underlying CAPM are relaxed.

CAPM allows the expected return and risk of a security or portfolio to be estimated so that alternative investments can be easily compared. Empirical tests of the CAPM have been carried out but criticism of the methodology and a desire for more complete explanations of security returns have led to multi-index models. Arbitrage pricing theory is one such model.

However, the CAPM has gained acceptance, first in the US and now world-wide, as a helpful investment decision-making tool, facilitating the choice of portfolios for the investor, whether investing hundreds or millions of pounds.

Problems

1. (i) If the expected return on a share is 15%, when the risk-free rate is 10% and the expected return on the market is 20%, what is the share's beta?

(ii) Suppose you know that shares A and B are correctly priced according to the capital asset pricing model. Share A is expected to have a return of 19.8% and has a beta of 1.2. A return of 17.1% is expected on share B, which has a beta of 0.9. Derive the securities market line.

(iii) Suppose that the following securities market line was derived for last year

$$E(R) = 10 + 9\beta$$

You see that two unit trusts X and Y achieved returns of 17 and 20% with betas of 0.8 and 1.3 respectively. Can you say anything about their performance?

2. Sharpe postulated that a portfolio's expected return and risk could be expressed as in equations (9.3) and (9.4)

$$E(R_p) = a_p + b_p E(R_m) \tag{9.3}$$

$$V_p = b_p^2 V_m + \sum_{i=1}^{i=n} X_i^2 V(e_i) \tag{9.4}$$

where the X_i are the proportions in which securities are held.

(i) What is the main argument behind the market model?

(ii) How many data items are needed using the market model for a ten-security portfolio compared with portfolio theory?

(iii) As the size of the portfolio is increased (n gets larger) which *part* of the risk, V_p, will become dominant and why? What will happen to the overall risk V_p?

3. (i) Shares with betas below one are sometimes referred to as 'defensive' whereas those with betas above one are known as 'aggressive' shares. Which industries do you think will have defensive shares and which aggressive? Can you think of any shares which might have a negative beta?

(ii) You are trying to construct two well-diversified portfolios, one with a beta of 0.6 and one with a beta of 1.4. How would you go about constructing these portfolios?

4. Mr Quick has inherited the following portfolio from a great-aunt:

Share	Number of shares	Current share price p	Beta	Specific risk (%)	Annual abnormal return (%)
African Mountains Corp.	1,000	28	0.77	34	−39
Board Timber Co.	2,000	41	1.22	28	−23
Millers Mechanical Engineering	1,000	40	0.80	67	−33

(i) What is the beta of the portfolio? Given a risk-free rate of 12% for the next twelve months, and an expected market premium $(E(R_m) - R_f)$ of 9%, what should Mr Quick *expect* to earn next year?

(ii) Calculate the total risk and the specific risk of the portfolio. (Suppose the standard deviation or variability of the market index is 10%.) What can you say about the riskiness of the portfolio?

(iii) Explain the meaning of the term 'annual abnormal return'.* Can you explain why it was negative for Mr Quick's portfolio? If the return on the FT–Actuaries All-Share Index was 20% last year and the risk-free rate was 10%, what was the *actual* return on Mr Quick's portfolio? Does the annual abnormal return figure help you say anything about *next* year's expected return?

(iv) Can you make any suggestions to Mr Quick as to how he can improve his portfolio, bearing in mind that he is employed by a rival of Board Timber Co., Pine Panels plc.

5. (i) Explain how you would use the information provided by a Beta Book service to evaluate an individual security, for example, Lennons Group:

(ii) How has the beta of Lennons Group been calculated, and what assumptions underlie its use?

Extract from London Business School Risk Measurement Service

SEDOL No.	Company name	SE industry classn	Market capn	Marketability
521464	Lennons Group	Food Ret.	16	3A

Beta	Variability	Specific risk	Standard error	R^2	Quarterly Ab. return	Ann Ab. return	Act. return
0.82	32	26	0.14	30	10	34	38

Gross Yield	PE ratio	Price
6.9	9.0	50

*Hint: Annual abnormal return is the difference between the actual return and what would have been achieved on a benchmark portfolio with the same beta.

Efficient markets

Introduction

So far, in this book, we have concerned ourselves primarily with how securities can be valued. For example, forward rates in Chapter 4 gave us a method for forecasting future gilt prices and estimating their expected holding period returns. Particular gilts could then be chosen according to investor expectations about future interest rates. Also, in Chapter 5, it was shown how Gordon's growth model could be used to estimate the expected *HPR* on a share, given assumptions concerning the company's future dividend policy. The shares with the best prospects for high returns or those which were considered undervalued could then be acquired. This type of investment strategy, where securities are evaluated and selected on their individual merits, we shall call 'picking winners'.

Chapters 8 and 9, on the other hand, concentrated on the characteristics of securities in the context of a portfolio. For example, portfolio theory suggested that a diversified portfolio of securities should be held, and that securities should be valued not in isolation but in relation to their impact on the remainder of the investor's portfolio. The capital asset pricing model (CAPM) went further and implied that all investors should hold appropriate proportions of the market portfolio M (consisting of all risky securities) combined with an appropriate positive or negative holding of a risk-free security, such as a gilt. Thus, both portfolio theory and the CAPM take the individual risk and return characteristics of each security as given and concentrate on the optimal risk–return profile of the investor's portfolio. Investment strategies based on these models could be termed 'fair return for risk' strategies, by which we mean that the investor following such a strategy expects to get a return on his portfolio which is equal to that predicted by the CAPM, given the level of risk in his portfolio.

The essential difference between the two approaches is that, when picking winners, the investor's underlying assumption is that he can 'beat the market' without incurring extra risk, whereas an investor using, say, the CAPM as a basis for his investment strategy is expecting only to beat the market if he takes on more risk than the market. Gilt and share prices already incorporate market expectations concerning interest rates, dividends, discount rates, and so on. By considering that some securities will offer higher returns than others, allowing for their relative risk, investors trying to pick these winners must be assuming that they know something about these securities that the market *either* does not yet know *or* has not yet incorporated into the share price. The 'fair return for risk' approach, on the other hand, embodied in portfolio theory and CAPM, *accepts* market expectations for *all* securities as the best estimates available, and merely attempts to combine holdings of securities, given their expected return and risk characteristics, in an optimal way for each investor.

This chapter examines these alternative investment strategies both in terms of what happens in practice and what should happen in theory on the basis of given assumptions about investor behaviour. The type of investment strategy to pursue will be shown to depend on how 'efficient' securities markets are. If these markets are efficient, and we shall see later how this can be defined, trying to pick winners will be a waste of time and effort. This is because, in an efficient market, the prices of securities will reflect the market's best estimates of their expected return and risk, taking into account all that is known about them. There will thus be no under-valued securities offering a higher than deserved expected return, given their risk. So, in efficient markets, an investment strategy concentrating simply on the overall risk and return characteristics of the portfolio will be more sensible. If, however, securities' markets are not efficient, and excess returns can be made by correctly picking winners, then it will pay investors to spend time finding these undervalued securities. By 'excess returns', we mean returns consistently[1] achieved which are above those predicted by

---

[1] By 'consistent' or 'long-run' returns we would normally mean returns achieved over a period of years.

the CAPM, given the level of risk incurred.

This concept of markets as efficient or inefficient has caused much emotion and argument in investment circles. This is no doubt partly because, in practice, the great majority of investment advisers act as if markets are 'inefficient' and therefore attempt to make 'excess' profits. If markets are, in fact, fully efficient in the above sense, the rationale on which most investment advice and policy is based can be shown to be invalid.

This debate has become more heated as investment has become more indirect. Individual investors have, in a sense, only themselves to blame if they try to pick winners and are unsuccessful at it. However, if, say, pension fund managers adopt a 'picking winners' strategy when, in fact, securities markets are efficient, beneficiaries of the fund will suffer. Firstly, the turnover of the fund (and hence transaction costs) will be unnecessarily high, as the pension fund managers think they see opportunities to invest in 'winners'. Secondly, the portfolio may well be badly diversified if the managers have concentrated on holding a few potential 'winners'. Thus, unnecessary and unrewarded (according to CAPM) risk will be incurred, to the detriment of the beneficiaries of the fund who may be unable to indicate their disapproval by moving their funds elsewhere.

As the amount of indirect investment has grown, a need to monitor the investment strategy and performance of financial intermediaries, such as pension funds has developed. Given that these institutions could adopt the 'fair return for risk' strategy prescribed by the CAPM, this model offers a suitable benchmark against which to assess their actual investment strategies. In fact, the CAPM has been used to develop a series of performance measures, adjusted for risk, which can be used to assess any portfolio's performance and hence investment managers' ability, if any, to 'beat the market'. Prior to the development of the CAPM, performance was often judged solely on return with little direct account being taken of risk. Even today, tables on investment trust performance show only the cumulative returns on investment for the past five years, with no indication of the riskiness of each of the trusts. Similarly, unit trusts are ranked according to the last, say, five years' return, although some attempt has been made to apply a rudimentary risk-grading scheme to unit trusts.

In view of the current importance of financial intermediaries for Stock Exchange investment, the whole of Chapter 12 is devoted to a description of the major institutions involved and how they affect the investment scene. Chapter 13 considers how performance can be measured using the CAPM. This chapter concentrates on whether or not the securities markets are efficient and discusses the implications of the different levels of efficiency – weak, semi-strong and strong – on investment strategy.

The chapter begins with a description of the random walk theory of share price changes, which was first discussed at the turn of the century and is the precursor of the more modern concept of efficient markets. Three possible strengths of efficient markets are then discussed, with the evidence supporting the validity of each and the implications for investment decision-making outlined. In particular, the implications for technical analysis and fundamental analysis are considered.

An Appendix to this chapter describes the main stock market indices, and considers which indices can most suitably be used as surrogates for the 'market', whether attempting to measure performance from a 'picking winners' strategy or whether holding the 'market' in a 'fair return for risk' CAPM strategy.

Random walk

The efficient markets hypothesis (or EMH as it is known) and its predecessor, the random walk theory, are perhaps the most misundertood concepts in the theory of investment. This is due partly to the back-to-front way in which the theory of efficient markets has evolved and partly to the misleading and emotive statements often ascribed to these theories, for example 'Investment analysis is a total waste of time' or 'No one can beat the market'. The term 'random walk' is also disturbing with its connotations of share prices determined by chance.

The idea that security prices in an organised market might follow a random walk was first put forward by Bachelier in 1900 for commodities traded on the French commodities markets. The term 'random walk', in this context, is used to refer to successive price changes which are independent of each other. In other words, tomorrow's price change (and therefore tomorrow's price) cannot be predicted by looking at today's price change. $P_{t+1} - P_t$ is independent of $P_t - P_{t-1}$. There are no trends in price changes. In the same way as the best place to look for a drunken man previously abandoned in the middle of a field is where he was left, so the best estimate of tomorrow's commodity price is today's. Both the drunken man and commodity prices follow a random walk, being as likely to go in one way as the other.

In the 1950s and 1960s, the random walk theory was also tested on company share prices and, as we shall see, share prices do appear to follow a random walk. One difference to note between share prices and commodities is that, in so far as shares have a positive expected return, share prices will exhibit an upward trend. So, whereas the statement 'The best estimate of tomorrow's price is today's' holds for commodities with zero expected return, it does not hold for shares. In the case of shares, we can say that tomorrow's price change is as likely to be above the price change expected by the market as below it.

Proofs of the random walk theory can take several forms. As with all tests of theories involving *future* expected prices or returns, *past* actual prices or returns are used for the tests (since these are easier to measure). So, for the random walk theory, sets of past share prices are tested for dependence. One such test involves calculating the correlation coefficients of consecutive (or lagged)[2] share price changes over daily and longer intervals. Tests have been carried out on both UK and US share data bases and the serial correlations, as correlation coefficients for time series data are called, have been found to be around zero. For example, Moore (1962) looked at weekly share price changes from 1951 to 1958 on 29 US shares selected at random and found an average serial correlation coefficient of −0.06.

Another intuitive test of the random walk theory is based on one of the standard arguments used against it – that share price charts *do* show trends. For example, again using US share prices, Figure 10.1(a) shows the FTA All-Share Index plotted weekly during 1991/2. This reveals three clear peaks and troughs during the period. However, if a series of price changes is generated randomly (for example, from random number tables) and then, starting from an arbitrary base number, say the same initial value as in Figure 10.1(a), the prices so derived are plotted on a graph, they too appear to have trends and patterns in them. Figure 10.1(b) shows just such a randomly generated graph which exhibits trends which are as clear as those in Figure 10.1(a).

More recent tests of the random walk theory have benefitted from more accurate price series data. Price changes over varying periods of time from intra-day to several years and for individual shares and portfolios of shares have been tested for serial correlation, giving rise to a plethora of results.[3] Although there is now some evidence that the autocorrelations, particularly for longer time horizon price changes, are significantly different from zero, they are still close enough to zero to prevent forecastable trends from appearing in time series of prices and for share price series to look remarkably like 'random walks'.

Model of share price behaviour

That share prices appear to follow a random walk is an interesting result and proving it or attempting to disprove it occupied many researchers throughout the 1960s and 1970s. But what remained to be shown was *why*

---

[2] For example, a comparison of price changes every second or third day. For a discussion of such tests, see Brealey (1983) ch. 1.

[3] For a detailed summary of these tests, see Fama (1991).

Figure 10.1

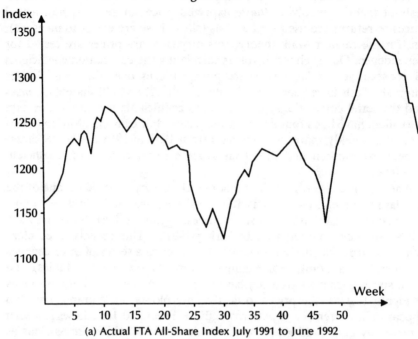

(a) Actual FTA All-Share Index July 1991 to June 1992

Source: Datastream

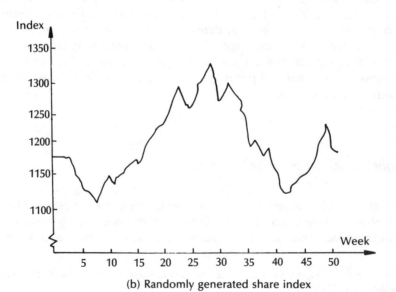

(b) Randomly generated share index

share prices followed a random walk. There was plenty of evidence, but a formal theory was missing. What was needed was a model of share price behaviour to explain the random walk. This gap was filled by a more general model based on the concept of efficiency of the markets in which shares are traded – the efficient markets hypothesis.

If we go back to the idea of a perfect market (which was assumed when deriving the CAPM), with information freely and instantaneously available to all, a homogeneous product, no taxes, perfect competition amongst investors and no transaction costs associated with trading, we can see that, under these conditions, each share will be 'correctly' valued, in the sense that all information will be fully absorbed into the share price and investors will be in agreement that the current share price will be as likely to go up as go down. Thus, the share price can, until new information is released, be considered to be at an equilibrium value. As new items of information about the company's prospects come in, the company's share price will absorb this information and move to a new equilibrium value. It can be shown that, in such a perfect market, successive price changes will be independent and prices will follow a random walk. This follows, firstly because the news inherent in the new piece of information concerning the company may be either good or bad, but it will certainly be *independent* of the last piece of information (otherwise it would not be new) and so the price change towards the new equilibrium value will be independent of the last price change. Secondly, because of the number of traders in the market and the lack of barriers to trading, the information (known to everyone) will be absorbed so quickly that the new equilibrium value will be achieved straightaway.

However, in a market where transaction costs were high enough to deter trading or where information was slow to reach the majority of investors, and speculative dealing by those who had the new information was in some way prevented, it might take several days or weeks for new information to be impounded in the share price. There would then be a trend in the share price as it moved towards its new equilibrium value. In such an imperfect and inefficient market, share price changes would be serially dependent rather than random, and excess returns could be made either by spotting the trends from charts or by trading on new information before it was fully impounded into the share price.

So, a random walk theory for share prices reflects a securities market where new information is rapidly incorporated into prices and where abnormal or 'excess' returns cannot be made from spotting trends or from trading on new information. Of course, we know such securities markets are not in practice *perfect* in the sense of having no transaction costs, no taxes, and so on. We also know that it is an impossible task to make all information immediately available to everyone and to give everyone the ability to interpret instantaneously the information correctly. Nevertheless,

Example 10.1   Efficient markets hypothesis

Efficient markets hypothesis
Prices fully reflect all available information

Weak form	**Semi-strong form**	**Strong form**
Prices fully reflect past prices	Prices fully reflect all publicly available information	Prices fully reflect all information

---

judging from the evidence on random walks, securities markets do appear to be *relatively* efficient at reflecting new information in prices. The question then becomes one of *how* efficient the markets are.

Fama (1970) decided to define different markets in terms of their level of efficiency, where the level reflected the *type* or *scope* of information which was quickly and fully reflected in price. He defined three levels of efficiency, each level designed to correspond with the different types of 'picking winners' investment strategies which were used in practice to try to achieve excess returns.

Example 10.1 shows the three different 'strengths' of the efficient markets hypothesis corresponding to different levels of efficiency. In the weak form of efficiency, each share price is assumed to reflect fully the information content of all past share prices. In the semi-strong form, the information impounded is assumed to include not only that given by all past share prices, which are of course public knowledge, but *all* publicly available information relevant to the share value. This includes, for example, company announcements, brokers' reports, industry forecasts and company accounts. The strong form of the EMH requires all known information to be impounded in the current share price, whether publicly and generally available or not. The strong form will thus include what is known as 'insider' information, for example details of an impending takeover bid known only to senior management of both parties to the bid.

As we saw earlier, markets which are efficient in quickly reflecting new information prevent investors from making excess profits using that information. Thus, in a weak-form efficient market, investors would be unable to pick winners by looking at charts of past share prices or by devising trading rules based on share price movements. In a semi-strong-form efficient market, investors with access only to publicly available information would not be able consistently to make excess profits by buying shares, say on announcement of favourable new information. For example, if an investor decided to buy shares on each announcement of unexpectedly high earnings, this information would be available to all and the share prices concerned would quickly reflect that information and increase. Even if the shares did not reach their new equilibrium values immediately (because it can take time for new information to be fully analysed), the prices at which the investor could buy the shares would be unbiased estimates of these new equilibrium values, as likely to be above as below them. Finally, if the strong form of the EMH held, no investor could generate excess returns whatever information he used, whether a 'new' analysis of the company accounts or a hot tip from the managing director, since in a market with this level of efficiency, share prices would already reflect all information relevant to the shares, whether publicly available or not.

It can be seen from the above that the ability of investors to pick winners and make excess returns using new information is directly related to the speed and efficiency of a market at absorbing that information. So, efficiency can be considered in terms of the 'fair game' concept. A market can be regarded as efficient with respect to a particular set of information if investors using that information are faced with fair game, that is, they receive *on average* the return expected for the risk involved and make no consistent abnormal returns. This can be expressed in the following way. If ϕ_t is defined to be a particular set of information concerning security j available at time t, then any abnormal or excess return achieved at time $t + 1$ on security j can be written $\epsilon_{j,t+1}$ where

$$\epsilon_{j,t+1} = (R_{j,t+1} - (E(R_{j,t+1})/\phi_t)) \tag{10.1}$$

Equation (10.1) shows that the excess return will be the difference between the return actually achieved and the return expected given the risk. The solidus/simply means that the return are achieved or expected *knowing* information ϕ_t at time t.

The EMH does not say that investors will never beat the market and will never make large profits. In other words, $\epsilon_{j,t+1}$ can be large and positive. What it does say is that, on average, over a period of time, investing is a fair game. 'You win some, you lose some.' So, the $\epsilon_{j,t+1}$ will sometimes be positive and sometimes negative, with the result that the sum of the excess returns over a number of periods of time will average zero:

$$\sum_{t=1}^{t=n} \epsilon_{j,t+1} = 0 \tag{10.2}$$

The fair game for investors is an outcome of a market being efficient. *If* a market is efficient, *then* investing is a fair game. This fair game concept is useful in that it allows the different levels of the EMH to be tested. Instead of trying to measure the amount of information impounded in share prices, we can look to see if, by using different pieces of information, excess returns can be made. If they can, the market is not efficient with respect to that information. If they cannot, it is one piece of evidence supporting efficiency, but not a conclusive proof. However much evidence is piled up in its favour, the EMH can never be formally proved, leaving open the possibility that some investor may have an as yet untested way of picking winners consistently over time.

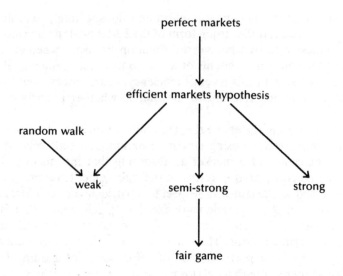

Figure 10.2   Models of share price behaviour

The EMH, as described above, is a more comprehensive model of share price behaviour than the random walk theory, referring not just to past share price movements but to all information pertaining to the share. It is a model which helps us to understand how markets operate in practice and how closely they approximate to theoretically perfect markets. Figure 10.2 places the EMH in perspective relative to the other models of share price behaviour.

In Figure 10.2, the perfect market has the most stringent requirements concerning market behaviour. The attraction of the perfect market is that it is an assumption underlying the major security pricing models, such as the CAPM. In the real world, we know that the conditions assumed in perfect markets do not prevail. There are transaction costs associated with trading in securities and information concerning securities is *not* freely and instantaneously available to all. However, if transaction costs are not excessive, if information is fairly readily available and if there is sufficient competition among investors, markets will be reasonably efficient in the sense that the securities' prices will reflect the information available and reflect it quickly enough to prevent excess returns being consistently made through trading on that information.

It can be seen from Figure 10.2 that the original random walk theory is most closely related to, but slightly stronger than, the weak form of the EMH. This is because the weak form implies that excess profits cannot be made by using past share price information whereas the random walk theory, whilst confirming the uselessness of studying past share prices, also says something about the shape of the pattern of share price movements. For example, it requires successive share price changes to be independent with zero serial correlation. The weak form of the EMH does not require any particular pattern of share price movements. So the random walk theory is stronger than the weak form of the EMH but less extensive than the full EMH.

Technical analysis

Since we have noted that, for the major stock markets of the world, the random walk theory appears to hold, the weak form of the EMH must also hold in practice. Thus, excess profits cannot be made in the long run by using past share price information.

Despite the evidence against them, investment strategies using past share price information do still exist; they are called technical analysis. There are two main types of technical analysis strategies, chartism and mechanical trading rules.

Chartism

Chartists specialise in analysing charts and graphs of share price information, spotting past trends and patterns and using these to forecast future price movements. For example, the shape in the centre of Figure 10.3 is known as a 'head and shoulders' formation. Other commonly occurring patterns include the 'neckline', 'congestion areas' and 'triangles'.

The charts can be plotted in various forms, one of the most common being the 'point and figure' chart, an example of which is shown in Figure 10.4, which emphasises trends (if there are any) in price changes. In point and figure charts, consecutive price increases of at least Yp (where Y is determined by the chartist) are plotted as X in the same column. A price decrease of at least Yp implies a move to the next column where consecutive price decreases of at least Yp are marked with a 0, and so on.

Of course, the difficult part of the analysis is the forecasting of the *future* share price pattern. This is based on study of past patterns, an assessment of whereabouts in a particular pattern the share is at the moment and therefore what pattern will occur in the future. The standard patterns which are believed to exist, such as head and shoulders, triangles or lines (which could all, as we saw earlier, be generated by random numbers) are explained by trading activities in the share. For example, a line, shown in Figure 10.5, is where buyers and sellers are evenly matched. At some stage, trading at this level will cease as would-be buyers or sellers dominate

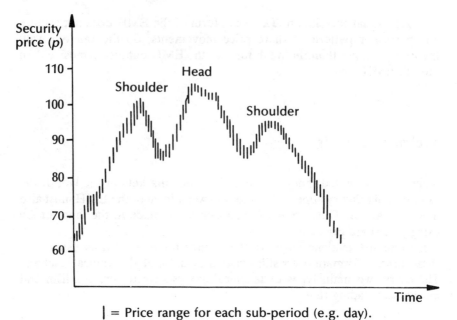

| = Price range for each sub-period (e.g. day).

Figure 10.3   Head and shoulders pattern

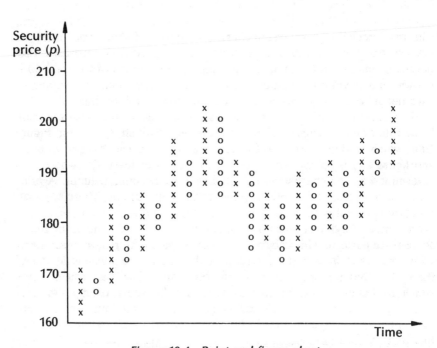

Figure 10.4   Point and figure chart

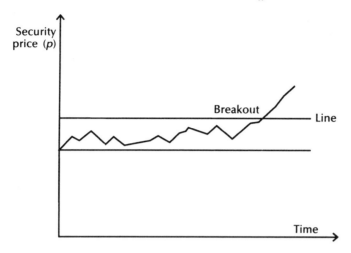

Figure 10.5   Example of line and breakout patterns

at that price level. At this stage, there will be a 'breakout' as in Figure 10.5. It is believed that the longer the share price remains within the line, the bigger will be the breakout.

Notice how chartists are completely uninterested in the fundamental characteristics of a share, such as, for example, the prospects for the company's high technology project in the US. They are concerned only with price movements and also volume of trading in the share.[4] These are then translated into patterns reflecting the elusive 'mood of the market'.

Apart from the evidence already discussed, the problem with this type of analysis is that not only is the imposing of patterns on charts a subjective decision, much more difficult *ex ante* than in hindsight, but also competition amongst chartists will compete the patterns and trends away. To make excess profits, a chartist must therefore be able to spot the pattern before all the other chartists recognise the trend. This will lead to any emerging trends being traded away and the weak form of the EMH being a valid representation of the market.

Another way of using charts is to consider not individual shares but the market as a whole. Stock markets exhibit rising trends (bull markets) and falling trends (bear markets) which are clearly recognisable after the event. If only these trends could be identified *beforehand*. The motivation for chartism is clear! For example, if an investor had bought his share portfolio in January 1987, when the FT-Actuaries All-Share Index was at 835 and sold in October 1987 at 1,215, just before the 'Crash', it is clear that 'excess' profits could have been achieved.

---

[4] The Stock Exchange Daily Official List gives the prices at which shares were traded on a particular day and the number of shares traded at each price.

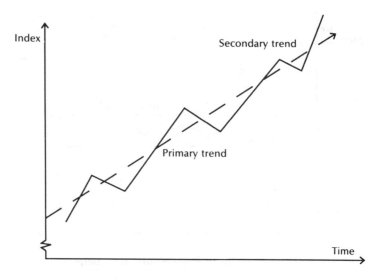

Figure 10.6   Dow Theory

A similar realisation in the US at the end of the nineteenth century led to the Dow Theory. Charles Dow, editor of the *Wall Street Journal*, suggested that the stock market was influenced by three cyclical trends – a primary, long-term trend, a secondary trend lasting months and minor trends lasting days. Bull markets could be identified when successive highs in a suitable market index had been reached after secondary corrections, provided the secondary advances were greater and longer in direction than the second ary downturns. Figure 10.6 gives an example of a bull market trend. A bear market would be identified by exactly opposite trends. Dow used two indices, the Dow Jones Industrial Average started in 1884 (its nearest UK equivalent being the FT Industrial Ordinary Shares Index of thirty shares) and the Transportation Index, mostly railway company shares. Similar trends in both indices had to be noted before a bull or bear market could be confirmed.

In reality, these secondary trends cannot be stringently defined. They cannot be identified objectively before the event, and can turn out after the event to be only minor trends. To confirm this, try covering up half a graph of a suitable share index and then guess, from the first half of the graph, what the market will do next.

Mechanical rules

The other major form of technical analysis attempts to convert subjective impressions of trends or patterns in charts into objective trading rules.

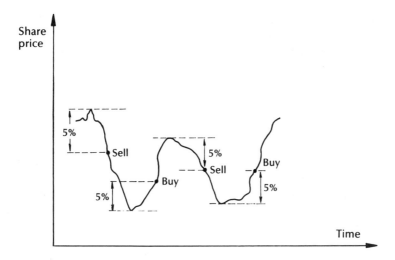

Figure 10.7   Example of filter rule

However objective the rules may sound, they are still based on a theory of share price movement in a weak-form inefficient market.

For example, filter rules are designed to catch the breakout from a line, as shown in Figure 10.5. Within the line, the share is assumed to be trading at around its equilibrium value. As a piece of new information is absorbed, the price will break out towards its new equilibrium value. The filter rule is designed to catch the share at the breakout point as it moves from the old to the new equilibrium value. In an efficient market, this would not be possible, since the price would move too quickly – there would be no trend.

The object of a filter rule is to buy before the share reaches its new, higher value and sell before its new, lower value. The dilemma is which size filter to choose. Figure 10.7 shows a filter of 5%. The wider the filter, the more likely the investor is to trade only on 'true' breakouts, but the later he will be in catching the trend. The smaller the filter, the likelier the investor is to catch the trend early enough. However, he may be misled by false breakouts and his transaction costs will doubtless outweigh any gains he makes from trading in and out of the share as opposed to simply buying the share and holding it.

Another mechanical trading rule often employed is one based on a share's relative strength. This is defined to be $P_t/\bar{P}$, where P_t is a particular share's current share price and $\bar{P}$ the share's average share price over the past x weeks (x is subjectively chosen by the analyst, a common period being twenty-six weeks). The higher P_t relative to $\bar{P}$, the higher the relative strength. Trading on relative strength also assumes serially dependent share price movements, since the idea is that if a share exhibits high relative strength it should be purchased because it will continue to do well.

A typical trading rule is to buy in equal amounts, say, the top 5% of shares ranked by relative strength. As soon as a share's relative strength falls below the relative strength of, say, 70% of the shares, it should be sold and the proceeds reinvested in the new top 5%. Of course the percentages and the time periods can be varied as desired.

Two characteristics of these trading rules should be mentioned. Firstly, where individual shares are concerned, they ignore relative risk, the shares being chosen purely on the basis of past price movements, their fundamental and economic characteristics being ignored. Chartists believe they can afford to do this because they are looking for short-term gains, moving in and out of shares relatively frequently, rather than choosing long-term investments.[5] However, because shares with the biggest price changes will usually be chosen under these trading rules, there may well be an emphasis on shares with higher volatility and therefore higher risk, leading the investor to hold a portfolio which is riskier than he is, perhaps, aware.

Secondly, use of these rules will involve high transaction costs and, perhaps for this reason, are popular with stockbrokers whose commission depends on share turnover. This is no doubt one of the reasons why, when these trading rules have been tested and compared with a simple 'buy and hold' strategy over a period of months or years, the buy and hold strategy has been found to yield higher returns, net of transaction costs.[6]

As was mentioned earlier, no form of the EMH, including the weak form, can conclusively be shown to hold, for any stock market, since it is an impossible task to test every possible trading rule on every possible set of share prices for excess returns. However, the weight of evidence in favour of the weak form of the EMH is generally accepted by academic opinion to be overwhelming, both in the UK and, more particularly, in the US. In the US, legal requirements may place more constraints on investment managers than in the UK; for example, US pension fund managers are required to make investment decisions 'with the care, skill, prudence and diligence . . . that a prudent man . . . familiar with such matters . . . would use'.[7] US investment managers therefore take more account of the results of tests of the EMH than do their UK counterparts. I quote from a US text aimed at US investment managers on the use of technical analysis:

> Thus a situation exists in which a stock selection technique that has been so thoroughly researched – and debunked – that it would no longer be a fitting

---

[5] Although mostly concerned with short-run investment, chartism is also used for the optimal timing of a long-run investment. Market makers, concerned with intra-daily price movements, are the greatest user of charts in the investment world.

[6] Transaction costs are high since, in the UK at least, transfer stamp duty must be paid on each share purchase if the shares are held for a period longer than the account. Notice also that the bid-ask spread on buying and selling shares is an additional cost.

[7] See Section 404(a)(1) of the US Employee Retirement Income Security Act, 1974.

subject for an investment seminar at any leading business school can nonetheless form the basis for an investment management approach just a few blocks away. Unquestionably, employing such analysis is *illogical*. What constitutes imprudence is a matter which, in the final analysis, must be decided by the courts.[8]

However, despite the weight of academic opinion, technical analysis still flourishes in the markets for shares, bonds, and, in particular, foreign currency.[9]

There are probably two main reasons for this. The first is that technical analysis is popular in areas where fundamental information is lacking, in particular with market makers and traders who need help in forecasting minute by minute price movements when no relevant news has been forthcoming. The second is the advent of computerised real time data services; it now takes a few seconds to plot relative strength for a share or to plot bar charts on a gilt index, tempting otherwise rational fund managers to turn to technical analysis as a forecasting tool, even if it is secondary to fundamental analysis in their decision-making process.

Fundamental analysis

In a sense, the semi-strong form of the efficient markets hypothesis is the most interesting of the three forms. As we saw above, there is wide spread agreement that the weak form of the EMH holds and that the use of technical analysis *on its own* is most unlikely to enable anyone consistently to make excess profits.

However, belief in the validity of the semi-strong form in its fullest sense calls into question not just the activities of chartists but the investment strategy of the majority of investment analysts in the City – fundamental analysis – briefly touched on in Chapter 5.

Most investment analysts act as industry specialists, spending their time forecasting future earnings, dividends or returns (according to preference[10]) for the companies within their chosen sector, using anything from a naïve model, such as $eps_1 \times PE_1 = P_1$, to a complex regression model. They do this by studying economic forecasts, industry reports, visiting the company, analysing company accounts and statements and generally forming a view on the company's prospects. This view is usually translated into

---

[8] See Hagin (1979) p. 36.

[9] In 1989, the Bank of England conducted a survey of technical analysis as used in the foreign exchange markets. See the Bank of England *Quarterly Bulletin* (November 1989) pp. 548–51.

[10] We saw in Chapter 5 that although dividends are actual cash flows and earnings are accounting figures, earnings are the more popular variable to forecast (despite their limitations as predictors).

an estimate of what they believe to be the share's intrinsic or 'correct' value (discussed in Chapter 5) which is then compared with the current share price, and generates a 'buy', 'sell" or 'hold' recommendation to clients.

There are over 1,900 members of the Society of Investment Analysts, and many more professional and amateur analysts who are non-members. There are approximately 2,000 UK company equity securities currently listed on the Stock Exchange,[11] of which around 900 have a market capitalisation of under £25m. This leaves approximately 1,100 shares with a market capitalisation of over £25m. to be analysed by *at least* 1,900 analysts. Each major British company will be 'followed' by a good many analysts, who have available to them the same public information, can make the same company visits, and presumably pore over the same company accounts. With this in mind, the semi-strong form of the EMH, which postulates that share prices at any time fully reflect all relevant publicly available information, becomes readily believable. Any new piece of information made public will be so quickly analysed and absorbed into a new market estimate of the company's value that an investor trading on each announcement, say, of unexpectedly good earnings will act too late to be able to make consistent excess returns. Even if the market does not initially fully absorb the new information, the new share price is as likely to be an overestimate as an underestimate of the equilibrium share price reached once the information has been correctly interpreted and impounded.

It is perhaps useful at this point to compare the behaviour of technical analysts and fundamental analysts at the time new information believed to justify a change in price is announced. The fundamental analysts will trade as they evaluate the impact of the announcement. The technical analysts, by looking *not* at the announcement but at the share price and trading volume movements due to the fundamental analysts, will also trade.

The implications of the semi-strong form of the EMH for fundamental analysis, if it closely reflects reality, are far-reaching. Not only does it follow that trading on announcement of new information will not on average and taken over time produce excess returns, but it also implies that the best available indicator of a share's so-called intrinsic value is its current market price. So a fundamental analyst's search for undervalued shares within his sector using publicly available information is a waste of time. For example, a study of the intangible assets of companies could lead an analyst to believe that certain companies were undervalued and others overvalued. However, if the method of valuing intangible assets is publicly available in the notes to the accounts, other analysts will already have impounded whatever additional knowledge was contained in the notes into the share price. Not all analysts and investors need to have fully digested and analysed the details of the accounts. All that is required is for a

---

[11] This includes equity securities listed on the primary and secondary UK stock markets.

sufficient number of analysts and their clients to have traded in the share with that knowledge. Thus, if the semi-strong form of the EMH does hold, no investor or analyst will be able consistently to make abnormal returns from the analysis of such publicly available information.

If the semi-strong form (but not the strong form) is a good approximation to reality,[12] the market value of a share will only be as good an estimate of the share's intrinsic value as the quality of the publicly available information concerning the company permits. If the information available is meagre, the market price of the share will be a correspondingly poor approximation to the share's worth. If, on the other hand, most relevant information is disclosed, the market value will be a good estimate of the share's worth. The implication for those concerned with corporate disclosure and accounting standards is therefore that careful consideration should be applied to *what* information is disclosed rather than *how* it is disclosed, since each new item of information not previously available may improve the market's estimate of the share's worth.

Reasons for fundamental analysis

We shall see later that the empirical evidence regarding the semi-strong form of the EMH as a good approximation to reality in the major stock markets is quite strong. If this is so, why has so much time and effort been devoted – and is still being devoted – to fundamental analysis?

The main reason is probably psychological. Looking at the stock market in hindsight, the investor can see many investments which, had he picked the right ones at the right time, would have made him rich. Abnormally large profits seem only just beyond his grasp. This huge apparent potential for making profits is highlighted by some research carried out by Niederhoffer and Regan. They compared analysts' published forecasts of changes in earnings per share (the favourite variable to forecast, as we saw in Chapter 5) with *actual* changes in earnings per share and actual share price changes. They examined three groups of fifty shares from the New York Stock Exchange. The first group consisted of the shares with the biggest price rises, the next fifty were randomly chosen and the third group of fifty were the worst price performers. The results outlined in Figure 10.8 have two major implications.

Firstly, earnings are very difficult to forecast accurately. We saw in Chapter 5 that earnings appear to follow a random walk (as do share

---

[12] In other words, if all publicly available information is impounded in the share price, but not 'insider' information.

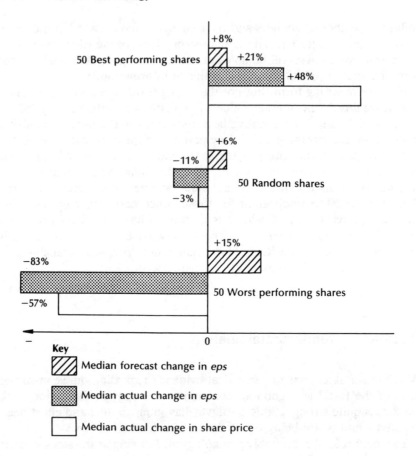

Figure 10.8   Forecast versus actual earnings

Source: Niederhoffer and Regan (1972). By permission of the *Financial Analysts' Journal*.

prices) and so forecasts based on past earnings performance (which, by substituting earnings instead of dividends into the share valuation model to get estimates of *HPR* or instrinsic value, is the most common method used by analysts[13]) are unlikely to do well. For example, in Figure 10.8, we can see that the fifty worst performing shares had a median 15% *increase* in earnings forecast by analysts compared with an actual earnings *decrease* of 83%.

The second point to note from the results in Figure 10.8 is how much money could have been made by analysts who got it right. If an analyst had correctly forecast higher than expected earnings for the top fifty performers and had bought accordingly, he would certainly have made greater

---

[13] See n. 10, p. 297.

than average returns given the risk. This is the motivation behind fundamental analysis.

Figure 10.8 also highlights the kind of investment analysis which will most likely lead to long-run excess returns. What is needed is not simply forecasts of high or low earnings but forecasts which can be assessed relative to market expectations. To be successful at fundamental analysis, the analyst has to forecast better than others in the market (using the same information). Forecasting such variables as earnings per share can be likened to forecasting exchange rates (discussed in Chapter 11). The market estimates of future earnings and future exchange rates are the 'best' estimates but they are not necessarily good estimates. This leaves plenty of apparent potential for excess returns. The question in both cases is how to achieve them and, having done so, how to continue to achieve them consistently over time.

Empirical evidence

Attempts to investigate the validity of the semi-strong form of the EMH have evolved over time. The original method was to investigate whether buying or selling shares immediately following announcements of new information (for example, announcements on dividends, scrip issues, or earnings) could earn investors excess returns over the following weeks or months. The more recent approach to testing the semi-strong form of the EMH has been to concentrate on the speed of reaction of share prices to such announcements by taking advantage of the existence of daily or even intra-day price series.

The problem with testing whether trading on announcement can yield superior returns is that it involves buying the shares on announcement and holding them for, say, a period of a month. It cannot, therefore, be compared, as can trading rules, with a buy and hold strategy. So, the returns from trading on announcement must be compared with the returns expected had no announcement (with its 'new' information) been made, denoted the 'normal' returns. This allows the excess return,

$$\text{Excess return} = (\text{Actual} - \text{Normal}) \text{ return} \tag{10.3}$$

which is usually examined over the period around the announcement date,[14] to be determined.

---

[14] For example, in Fama, Fisher, Jensen and Roll's (1969) study of the effects of scrip issues, they examined the period thirty months before to thirty months after the month of the actual scrip.

How can the normal expected returns be calculated? The only practicable method, which adjusts for risk, is either Sharpe's market model or its theoretical counterpart, the CAPM. Once a share's beta has been estimated, the normal return expected from the CAPM can be written

$$E(R_j) = R_F + \beta_j \left(E(R_m) - R_F \right) \tag{10.4}$$

and from Sharpe

$$E(R_j) = \alpha_j + \beta_j \left(E(R_m) \right) \tag{10.5}$$

The coefficients for equations (10.4) or (10.5), the α_j and β_j, have to be calculated from a set of data different from that actually used in the EMH tests, to avoid using the same data twice and rendering the tests meaningless. Nevertheless, this type of test of the EMH will involve a joint test of both the CAPM and the EMH. In other words, it assumes that the CAPM (or the market model) is an accurate representation of a share's risk-return relationship.

Most studies of such announcements,[15] using this risk-adjusted technique to calculate the normal return, have shown that, on average, the excess returns available from trading on announcement were nil. One reason for this could be that the information provided in the announcement adds nothing new to analysts' knowledge. For example, accurate expectations of dividends may have been formulated long before announcement, or a scrip issue already more than hinted at. However, these expectations are much harder to test since it is difficult to ascertain exactly when they became publicly available.

Despite some well-published anomalies[16], the evidence points to an inability to consistently earn excess returns by trading on announcement. Anomalies could be due to the mis-specification of the CAPM rather than to inefficiencies in the stock markets.

Further support has been given to the semi-strong form of the EMH by more recent tests which have used daily data to show that share prices do move quickly to a new equilibrium value on announcement of new information.[17] The advantage of using daily or even intra-day data is that any misspecification of excess or abnormal returns incurred by using a

---

[15] For example, tests of announcements on earnings, mergers, scrip issues, dividends, and changes in accounting policy. For a more comprehensive survey, see Ball (1990) and Fama (1991).

[16] Such as the 'weekend' effect, the 'January' effect, the 'small firms' effect, and the 'quarterly earnings' effect. Research has shown that excess returns could have been earned from trading strategies based on these effects for particular time periods. For more details on these apparent anomalies, see Kolb (1992) and Fama (1991).

[17] See, for example, Patell and Wolfson (1984) and Brown and Warner (1985).

model such as the CAPM is less likely to affect studies of major events for share prices than when excess returns over weeks or months are estimated. In other words, recent evidence also suggests that the major stock markets adjust rapidly to new information that is publicly available, so that prices change before most people can deal.

Implications of the semi-strong form

The evidence from tests of returns achieved from trading on announcement, or following an adviser's recommendations, point then to the major stock markets being semi-strong form efficient. This would imply that the search for consistent excess returns net of transaction costs through fundamental analysis is a waste of time.

Implications for investors

Such a conclusion is particularly significant for the small investor whose proportionate transaction costs are high. The implication is that the individual investor should not worry about investment analysis. He should simply choose a diversified portfolio of shares and concentrate on his optimum risk–reward ratio and other considerations, such as tax, liquidity and inflation-proofing (which will be considered in greater detail in Chapter 13).

Index funds, set up to mirror rather than to beat the market index, and therefore of interest to investors who wish to choose the diversified portfolio route rather than try to pick winners, have increased rapidly in popularity over the 1980s although they are still more available to investing institutions than to individual investors. However, some unit trust firms do offer individual investors index funds tied to the UK, US, or Japanese stock market indices and new investment products, such as the index-linked bonds described in the last section of Chapter 7, have an index fund element contained within them.

It is difficult for individual investors in practice to ignore fundamental analysis, since they pay for it indirectly through commission to their stockbroker. However, there has been a trend towards a reduction in the amount of stock market research issued to individual investors and towards a low-cost charge for share dealings when no advice is given by the broker. Individual investors no longer have to pay for research that they do not want.

Institutional investors are in an even better position than individual investors since they can deal direct with the market makers and do not have to use an intermediary stockbroker if they do not wish to. However, the market makers still produce investment research which they view as essential in getting institutional business. Institutional investors, at least, do not appear to be convinced by the empirical evidence pointing to the validity of the semi-strong form of the EMH.

Implications for analysts

The implications of the semi-strong form of the EMH are less reassuring for investment analysts than for investors. Their main *raison d'être* is put into question. And yet, if the evidence supports the semi-strong form, why do so many people still manage to make a living out of fundamental analysis? By analysing information and trading (or recommending to clients) on that information, they ensure that share prices fully reflect the information. But if everyone believed the semi-strong form and ignored fundamental analysis, the market would become inefficient.

This paradox, which is not really resolved by the EMH, leads us to consider more recent work on markets for information. These theoretical models[18] attempt, as the EMH does not, to take account of the role of 'information intermediaries', such as fundamental analysts, by assuming assymetry of information. In these models, information is not freely available to everyone since, if this were so, security prices would obviously fully reflect all that information. Instead, they assume that information can be purchased at a cost by any investor and that this information improves estimates of securities' expected returns. Informed investors will thus have valuable information not known to uninformed investors. Asymmetry of information will prevail.

Within this framework, let us consider the role of the fundamental analyst. He acquires information, say by studying publicly available information, but at a cost. For example, there is the opportunity cost of his time and the possible need for qualifications (such as an accounting qualification to be able to understand cash flow statements). The fundamental analyst will then make use of that information by selling it (as a broker) or by trading in the shares himself. Either way, share prices will then reflect that information. This appears to lead us straight back to the paradox inherent in the EMH. If the information acquired at a cost by the analyst is fully reflected in share prices, why should investors buy information or the analyst incur costs when the price will reflect the information anyway?

In order to avoid this problem, the models have to assume that prices do

---

[18] For further discussion on this area of research, see Beaver (1981).

not clearly reflect the information for some reason. For example, they assume that there is a certain amount of 'noise' in share prices, which no amount of information can dispel. When studying share price movements, investors will not be able to tell how much of the price changes are due to information and how much to noise. This assumption allows for an equilibrium situation in which certain investors (and analysts) are informed and others choose to remain uninformed. No investor can improve his expected utility by changing from uninformed to informed. Certain investors will prefer to remain uninformed and to protect themselves by holding a well-diversified portfolio or index fund. Others will prefer to buy information and to use it to 'pick winners'. On average, the cost of acquiring the information will equal the benefit from using it. So, for example, informed investors will not in the long run make excess returns *after* transaction costs which include the cost of acquiring information. Similarly, following the recommendations of an investment strategy based on fundamental analysis will not on average yield excess returns after transaction costs. However, informed investors may do better, on average, than uninformed investors *before* transaction costs, and some may on occasion do better than the average.

Conclusions for analysts

Trying to explain the role of fundamental analysts has led us to consider models which have a stronger theoretical background than the EMH. However, the EMH does have a substantial body of empirical evidence to support it, both at the weak and semi-strong levels.

Although our understanding of exactly how information is impounded into share prices is limited, we can still draw useful conclusions from the EMH for fundamental analysts.

Firstly, it would appear to be a waste of time to study standard, publicly available information and come up with a simple forecast of next year's earnings. What would seem to be a more fruitful approach would be to consider forecasts derived from publicly available information in the light of market expectations already impounded in the share price. Analysts would then be forced to consider whether their forecasts differed from the market consensus and, if so, why.

The second conclusion concerns the identifying of investment analysis ability and its best use. For example, tests by Dimson and Marsh,[19] of UK analysts advising the fund managers of the Prudential insurance company

---

[19] See Dimson and Marsh (1984) for a full description of this research.

have found that the average level of forecasting ability amongst these analysts (measured by the correlation coefficients between forecast returns and actual share price changes) was of the order of 0.08. A coefficient of zero would imply no ability, so a coefficient of 0.08 implies that the average analyst does seem to be able to offer better than a risk-adjusted random choice of shares in which to invest. The question is whether the excess returns generated exceed the cost of acquiring the information from the analyst. In the case of the analysts advising the Prudential, excess returns of 2% after transaction costs would have been generated by following the consensus advice of the analysts consulted. However, the Prudential is the largest single investor in UK equities and will therefore have the lowest transaction costs. The equation would not have such a positive outcome for the smaller investor. So, for the majority of investors, for whom the costs of acquiring information match the benefits, the paradox of fundamental analysis thrown up by the EMH has been to some extent explained away.

In conclusion, the use of such measures as the correlation coefficients between forecast and actual returns mentioned above enables analysts to determine where their strengths and weaknesses lie. It may be that such forecasting ability as they do have is frittered away by analysing too many shares and by wasting time on shares where they have no such forecasting ability. However, the measurement of individual forecasting ability in a quantitative rather than a subjective way is as yet rare in the City. Nevertheless, the implication for analysts is clear. By measuring their abilities, they can decide, for example, whether to adopt a low transaction cost, index fund approach or whether to specialise in sectors where they believe they have a competitive edge.

Strong form

The strong form of the efficient markets hypothesis states that share prices fully reflect *all* knowable information, whether publicly available or not. This would imply that, if only a few people knew something about a company (for example, if only a handful of senior managers and civil servants were aware that the company had just been awarded a lucrative government contract), even they would not be able to make excess profits by trading on this knowledge.

There are far fewer tests of the strong form of the EMH than of the weak or semi-strong form, because of the difficulty in obtaining share trading information on the kind of people likely to have access to non-public information. Such people are known as 'insiders'. However, certain groups of potential insiders can be identified, such as directors and associates of companies and stockbrokers, on whom there is a certain amount of information available. For example, in the US, insiders have long been obliged to register all their share dealings in the companies to which they are insiders and studies of these share dealings have shown that excess returns are possible. Another type of insider dealer is the 'specialist' broker on the New York Stock Exchange who has access to a different kind of non-publicly available information – the orders to buy and sell at particular prices of his clients. The specialist can buy and sell on his own account with no time lag, and tests have shown that he too can, at least occasionally, make excess returns. In the UK, tests on stockbrokers' own trades and newspapers' share recommendations, have also shown excess returns.[20]

An alternative way of testing whether the strong form holds is to examine the behaviour of investing intermediaries or institutions. The economies of scale they can achieve in investment analysis and transaction costs should mean that they, of all investors, stand the most chance of being able to earn consistent long-run returns from publicly available information. Also, the relatively close relationships with the companies in which they invest (due to, for example, company visits) could lead to their obtaining information on these companies which is not generally available. So, examining the performance of such institutions would provide some evidence for and against both the semi-strong and the strong forms of the EMH. Since information on the performance of UK financial institutions is most readily available for unit and investment trusts, these are the institutions which have been studied for evidence of the possibility of long-run excess returns – the ability to pick winners. No such evidence has been found, which provides further support for the semi-strong form. As far as the strong form is concerned, the evidence is less clear-cut, however. If these institutions do not have access to non-publicly available information, a study of their performance is *not* a test of the strong form. In so far as they *do*, the validity of the strong form is supported by the lack of apparent long-run excess returns achieved by investing institutions. However, recent evidence points to excess returns achieved by some investing institutions but counterbalanced by transaction costs and fees charged to clients.[21]

A final point on the strong form of the EMH. Although the evidence appears to be against the strong form, implying that insider dealing can be a profitable activity, the amount of inside dealing must be perceived by the market as a whole to be relatively insignificant or else rational, risk averse, 'outsider' investors would not be prepared to invest in such a market. Indeed, regulation aimed at preventing insider dealing and providing for the rapid disclosure of information is common to all the major stock markets where turnover and investor interest is high. Insiders are more likely to make substantial excess returns in the less developed and less regulated emerging stock markets.

[20] For the brokers' excess returns, see Fitzgerald (1978).

[21] See Hendriksson (1984) and Ippolito (1989) for a survey of US mutual funds.

Summary

This chapter has looked at the level of efficiency of stock markets with respect to information. The more quickly and completely information is impounded into share prices, the less likely that investors will be able to earn excess returns from using that information to pick winners.

The EMH has had a confusing history. It started out as the random walk theory, concerned only with trends in share prices. In its present form, it is concerned with a wide range of information, from past share prices to 'inside' information, and with whether investing in shares is a 'fair game' with respect to each particular set of information.

Fama defined three main levels of efficiency with respect to three types of information. The weak form considers past share prices (as does the random walk theory). The semi-strong form is concerned with all publicly available information and the strong form with *all* information, including information known only to a few insiders.

The evidence in general supports both the weak and the semi-strong forms, but not the strong form. Publicly available information, therefore, appears to be quickly impounded into share prices, so quickly that excess returns, given the risk, cannot consistently be made over a substantial period of time. This result suggests that the use of both chartism and fundamental analysis will not in the long run produce undeserved (in terms of risk) rewards. The role of fundamental analysts appears to be to produce information for a cost which matches any benefits derived therefrom.

The implication of the EMH for investors, in particular 'naïve' investors, is that they can, without needing to analyse or acquire costly information, adopt a 'fair return for risk' strategy, either by holding a well-diversified portfolio or an index fund. Investment analysts, on the other hand, should switch emphasis from a straight 'picking winners' approach to concentrating on analysing shares in the light of market expectations already impounded into share prices and of their ability to select winners. They should also construct share portfolios for investors which take into account the investors' risk–return preferences rather than trying to earn excess returns for everyone, regardless of risk.

Appendix: stock market indices

When we discuss the subject of efficient markets, and the alternative strategies of 'picking winners' to attempt to beat the market or the 'fair return for risk' strategy prescribed by the CAPM, we need to clarify what we mean when we talk about the 'market' and how we measure it in practice.

For example, the 'picking winners' route can involve trying to forecast market movements. Similarly, investment intermediaries may claim to have beaten the 'market'. How do they measure this? Alternatively, the 'fair return for risk' strategy recommended by the CAPM requires investors to hold the 'market' portfolio and betas are measured by comparing security returns with 'market' returns. Again, how is this done in practice?

The 'market' should in theory include all marketable assets, for example works of art and property. In practice, it is confined to the stock market since quoted securities have easily determined market values. So, given that the 'market' for risky assets is usually restricted to shares, how many of them does it include – all of them or a representative sample? Also, how are the share values aggregated into a representative index which can be used for calculating betas, as a benchmark portfolio or as a basis for constructing an index fund?

FT industrial ordinary shares index

The first important UK share index was the *Financial Times* Industrial Ordinary Shares Index, started in 1935 and based on thirty major industrial shares. Similarly, in the US, the most famous index was the Dow Jones Industrial Average, also based on thirty shares, although originally based on eleven shares when started in 1884. The limited size of these indices is a function of their age, since both predate the era of computers, and this limitation has led to their replacement by indices on larger samples of shares as computers have allowed.

The original purpose of both indices was to measure market movements over the short term and not to provide any estimates of market return (they ignore dividends) or to act as benchmark portfolios. Their object was to help predict market trends and to provide measures of market volatility. To this end, the FT 30 Shares Index (as it is known) was constructed as an unweighted geometric mean. All the shares in the index were given equal weighting and the same emphasis was given to a 10% increase in price to 55p of a share quoted at 50p as to a 10% increase in price to 550p for a 500p share. The relative sizes of the companies and the relative share prices were ignored. What counted was the percentage change in share price, that is to say, the share's volatility.

Despite only having thirty shares, the FT 30 Shares Index represents around 25% of the market value of all UK equities. This shows that a small sample mirror movements of the whole market quite effectively. The FT–Actuaries All-Share Index, for example, which includes 655 shares, represents approximately 80% of the total market value of all UK equities.

FT-SE 100 Index

The most popular index is the FT-SE 100 Index, designed to enable futures and options contracts to be linked to the performance of the UK stock market. The FT 30 Shares Index suffered from having too few shares in it to be representative of the market as a whole and, because of its long history, these shares tended to over-represent the manufacturing sector and under-represent the services sector which had grown in the 1970s and 1980s. It was also a geometric index and thus did not reflect a portfolio which could realistically be held by investors. This is vital for an index to which futures contracts are linked since, as we saw in Chapter 6, in order for the futures contract to be correctly priced, investors must be able to carry out arbitrage when there is mis-pricing, say by buying futures and selling the underlying shares when the futures contract is cheap.

The FT-SE 100 Index is a weighted arithmetic index of the top 100 (in terms of capitalisation) companies; it thus mirrors a real portfolio, includes both service and manufacturing companies, and yet has sufficiently few shares to be calculable on a continuous basis.

FT-SE Mid-250 and FT-SE Actuaries 350 Indices

The most recently developed indices are the FT-SE Mid-250 and the FT-SE Actuaries 350 indices. The former is a weighted arithmetic index of the 250 shares below the top 100 in terms of capitalisation. The FT-SE Actuaries 350 index is a weighted arithmetic index of the shares in both the FT-SE 100 and the Mid-250, hence of the top 350 shares.

These indices have been developed as a compromise between the FT-Actuaries All-Share Index (with 655 shares) and the FT-SE 100 Index. They are designed better to reflect movements in the market as a whole than does the FT-SE 100 Index. They are also designed to be calculated on a continuous basis, which the FT-SE Actuaries All-Share Index is not.

Calculating returns on indices

When calculating returns on indices rather than on individual shares, care should be taken as to whether the returns on the index include dividends or not. Most commonly quoted share indices around the world do not include dividends, because they are being quoted to show short-term price movements and not longer-term returns. The exception in Europe is the DAX, the major German index on 30 German shares, which *does* include dividends.

The lack of inclusion of dividends means that indices have to be adjusted before they can be used as true benchmarks for portfolio managers, although the *Financial Times* does produce returns with and without dividends for the FT-Actuaries Indices listed in Example 10A.1. However, when comparing returns on two share indices, say from different countries, which have *not* been adjusted for dividends, a comparison of the returns on the share indices will not give a true picture of either the relative capital gains or the relative holding period returns available in each country unless the dividend yields are also included.

Example 10A.1   FT-Actuaries share indices

FT-ACTUARIES SHARE INDICES

© The Financial Times Ltd 1992. Compiled by the Financial Times Ltd
in conjunction with the Institute of Actuaries and the Faculty of Actuaries

EQUITY GROUPS & SUB-SECTIONS Figures in parentheses show number of stocks per section	Monday June 29 1992						Fri Jun 26	Thu Jun 25	Wed Jun 24	Year ago (approx)
	Index No.	Day's Change %	Est. Earnings Yield% (Max.)	Gross Div. Yield% (Act at (25%)	Est. P/E Ratio (Net)	xd adj. 1992 to date	Index No.	Index No.	Index No.	Index No.
1 CAPITAL GOODS (178)	823.97	-1.3	6.96	5.59	18.63	16.81	834.79	840.34	830.76	801.09
2 Building Materials (22)	909.25	-2.5	6.14	6.16	21.93	25.24	932.52	943.82	934.01	1013.61
3 Contracting, Construction (28)	837.51	-1.0	4.00	7.21	57.01	24.60	846.21	852.54	848.80	1159.27
4 Electricals (8)	2458.56	-1.5	7.01	6.27	18.54	68.82	2494.80	2537.97	2523.54	2259.69
5 Electronics (29)	1963.52	-1.1	8.14	4.34	15.48	9.16	1985.57	1992.08	1973.95	1731.37
6 Engineering-Aerospace (6)	338.03	-0.8	10.78	7.71	11.73	11.27	340.88	347.20	339.38	415.84
7 Engineering-General (44)	511.14	-1.5	7.82	4.67	15.90	9.46	519.12	525.90	523.74	435.43
8 Metals and Metal Forming (8)	310.11	-5.1	0.80	11.16	–	3.60	326.90	335.33	328.39	429.93
9 Motors (14)	343.47	-1.7	7.73	6.84	17.02	10.04	349.29	354.94	355.78	316.10
10 Other Industrial Materials (19)	1773.18	-0.2	6.99	4.66	17.22	34.69	1776.34	1767.89	1736.53	1489.73
21 CONSUMER GROUP (189)	1614.80	-0.6	7.53	3.55	16.32	23.94	1624.09	1638.31	1631.40	1433.55
22 Brewers and Distillers (24)	2064.80	-0.8	8.04	3.59	15.01	29.35	2081.97	2104.93	2099.41	1758.21
25 Food Manufacturing (18)	1249.74		8.65	4.21	14.30	23.82	1250.38	1252.56	1243.21	1151.08
26 Food Retailing (18)	2904.57	+0.5	8.35	3.14	15.68	44.70	2889.33	2890.89	2890.74	2591.75
27 Health and Household (24)	3737.60	-1.3	7.38	2.83	15.45	37.81	3787.65	3860.43	3852.28	3492.83
29 Hotels and Leisure (20)	1276.26	-1.2	6.25	5.30	20.85	23.55	1292.03	1303.97	1294.44	1222.50
30 Media (25)	1546.60		6.25	3.39	19.80	25.88	1545.76	1555.44	1541.25	1361.53
31 Packaging, Paper & Printing (17)	774.35	-2.3	6.66	4.27	18.23	14.67	792.71	801.57	799.03	676.60
34 Stores (33)	1059.22	+0.1	7.14	3.49	18.48	16.22	1058.07	1058.83	1051.30	866.78
35 Textiles (10)	689.74	-0.2	6.71	4.51	18.87	14.72	690.95	697.25	697.57	531.97
40 OTHER GROUPS (116)	1258.24	-0.4	9.92	5.23	12.58	22.32	1263.85	1266.25	1256.43	1192.71
41 Business Services (17)	1400.02	-0.5	6.38	3.69	19.16	20.78	1407.48	1419.28	1408.08	1229.26
42 Chemicals (22)	1459.24	-0.2	7.24	5.00	16.92	32.18	1462.04	1466.26	1456.26	1367.47
43 Conglomerates (11)	1250.77	-0.6	10.32	7.59	12.10	23.62	1258.50	1291.47	1284.08	1390.58
44 Transport (14)	2538.59	-0.1	8.16	4.62	15.01	51.61	2540.18	2577.98	2575.57	2158.15
45 Electricity (16)	1336.77	-1.3	14.20	5.26	8.91	17.21	1332.88	1319.51	1314.81	1161.93
46 Telephone Networks(4)	1366.30	-1.2	11.34	4.83	11.49	21.77	1382.47	1386.25	1377.68	1414.63
47 Water(10)	2832.52	+0.2	15.69	6.12	7.06	86.85	2828.15	2788.13	2752.45	2160.97
48 Miscellaneous (22)	2030.18	-0.6	5.61	4.89	23.84	24.35	2041.81	2016.90	1977.52	1930.20
49 INDUSTRIAL GROUP (483)	1305.09	-0.7	8.18	4.46	15.23	21.88	1313.84	1321.99	1313.18	1203.38
51 Oil & Gas (17)	1937.82	-1.3	7.83	7.34	16.79	63.73	1963.90	2029.93	2011.83	2372.90
59 500 SHARE INDEX (500)	1367.30	-0.7	8.15	4.74	15.37	25.11	1377.37	1389.65	1380.07	1302.18
61 FINANCIAL GROUP (86)	738.41	-0.6	–	6.15	–	20.03	742.78	747.12	734.90	762.60
62 Banks (9)	948.78	+0.1	5.08	5.75	31.15	24.58	947.98	954.85	933.94	848.18
65 Insurance (Life) (6)	1509.88	-1.4	–	5.90	–	44.26	1531.13	1524.83	1496.92	1422.62
66 Insurance (Composite) (7)	526.26	-2.8	–	6.61	–	13.46	541.20	544.60	533.98	654.26
67 Insurance (Brokers) (10)	825.70	-0.8	9.39	7.90	14.01	29.69	832.19	857.33	859.62	1134.88
68 Merchant Banks (7)	479.18	+0.8	–	4.51	–	11.25	475.36	476.10	475.21	414.67
69 Property (32)	639.61	-0.1	9.17	7.17	14.75	19.27	640.02	643.08	642.38	884.83
70 Other Financial (15)	247.45	-0.6	7.34	7.08	18.46	6.63	249.03	249.85	246.41	258.56
71 Investment Trusts (69)	1142.55	+0.4	–	3.93	–	18.86	1137.84	1153.49	1145.42	1179.20
99 ALL-SHARE INDEX (655)	1215.77	-0.7	–	4.89	–	23.55	1224.17	1234.78	1224.88	1172.21
	Index No.	Day's Change	Day's High (a)	Day's Low (b)	Jun 26	Jun 25	Jun 24	Jun 23	Jun 22	Year ago
FT-SE 100 SHARE INDEX‡	2515.8	-18.3	2548.2	2515.6	2534.1	2557.3	2532.6	2560.6	2550.3	2443.6

Source: *Financial Times* (30 June 1992).

Problems

1. You are an investment analyst in the 'electricals' sector for the Cautious Assurance Company. You have been asked to prepare a report for the weekly investment meeting on ABCD Electronic, stating whether the holdings of this share in the various portfolios under the management of Cautious should be increased, maintained at their present level, or reduced.
   Describe
   (i) the information you would require to make a fundamental analysis of the company,
   (ii) how you would determine whether the share was of a 'buy', 'hold' or 'sell' type.

2. (i) To what extent does empirical evidence support the efficient markets hypothesis in its various forms?
   (ii) Discuss the implications of the EMH for stock market investment analysis.

3. Describe a possible mechanical trading rule which you think might lead to possible excess returns. How would you test whether the market is efficient or inefficient with respect to your rule?

4. Mr Dither is undecided between two investment alternatives. His stockbroker has recommended that he invest £10,000 in a portfolio of nine shares and one gilt with an overall beta of 0.9. Mr Dither is also impressed with the Report and Accounts of an investment trust which has the same beta of 0.9. Discuss the advantages and disadvantages of each of these investment alternatives.

5. You have been asked to address a group of pension fund advisers and investment analysts on the subject of efficient markets. Outline the main points you would make.

6. An efficient market implies that the net present value of any security's future cash flow is *zero*, whatever its risk. And yet, finance managers of companies are expected to find *positive* NPV projects to invest in. Is there a contradiction here?

PART III

INTERNATIONAL INVESTMENT AND INVESTING INSTITUTIONS

International investment

Introduction

So far in this book, we have mainly restricted ourselves to securities issued in sterling by a UK company or the UK government. This emphasis is misleading since, as we saw in Chapter 1, over half the market value of securities quoted on the London Stock Exchange is made up of overseas securities,[1] traded in London but not necessarily in pounds and pence. For example, an IBM eurobond may be denominated and quoted in dollars and Deutsche Bank shares will be quoted in German deutschemarks. However, international investment does not have to be made via securities listed on the Stock Exchange in London. Foreign securities such as US

---

[1] Hence its previous, rather confusing name, The International Stock Exchange!

Treasury bonds or Japanese equities which are quoted in markets other than the UK stock market can be bought via brokers based in London or overseas.[2]

Also, indirect investment has long been available through the medium of investment trusts,[3] set up originally in the mid-nineteenth century to enable small investors to invest in such securities as South American railway bonds. In fact, even by buying the shares of UK-based companies, investors may be making another form of indirect overseas investment. For example, around 50% of Hanson Trust's revenues are generated in the United States with the consequent exposure to the US dollar of a large proportion of its earnings.

Prior to 1979, exchange controls were in place which effectively made it difficult for all but the most determined investor to made direct overseas investments in securities. Since 1979, the attitude to international investment has changed dramatically, with the removal of the costs and complications of exchange controls. Most foreign currency investment can now be financed with a straightforward foreign currency purchase. During the 1980s, investing institutions were quick to increase the proportions of their portfolios which were held in overseas securities. By 1992, the typical British pension fund had 20% of its total assets in overseas bonds and equities. This compares with an equivalent figure of under 5% for US pension funds; they have a much shorter history of overseas investment. However, despite their more aggressive international stance, UK pension funds are unlikely to radically increase the proportion of their assets invested in overseas securities. After all, their liabilities are expressed in sterling terms and, even with the threat of a common European currency, they will doubtless restrict the trend towards further overseas investment. UK investors, on the other hand, have also taken advantage of the ability to make overseas investment without restrictions. For example, even the so-called 'balanced funds' which underly portable pensions have a proportion of their assets in non-UK securities. Alternatively, the small investor can make more explicit overseas investments by buying units in unit trusts[4] which are predominantly invested in non-UK bonds or equities: for example, the Norwich Union International Bond Fund or the M&G American Recovery Fund. Thus, he can invest directly or indirectly in specific overseas securities or specific overseas markets.

Despite the ease with which international investments can now be made, there are additional factors, such as exchange risk, not usually relevant when deciding on investment in UK securities, which the investor must take into account. This chapter is designed to give an understanding of the

---

[2] A UK stockbroker will be happy to act as an intermediary but you may find yourself paying two lots of stockbrokers' commission.

[3] Described in more detail in Chapter 12 on Investing Institutions.

[4] Also described in more detail in Chapter 12 on Investing Institutions.

additional risks *and* rewards of international as opposed to domestic investment, as well as an explanation of the techniques required to evaluate
international investment alternatives.

The chapter begins with a discussion of the major factor which differenti-
ates any foreign currency investment from a sterling investment – exchange
risk. This arises from the effects of exchange rate movements on the
returns from overseas investments. Exchange rates can be very volatile,
whether freely floating or linked in some formal way to other currencies.
For example, the US dollar fell from under $1.50 to the pound to just over
$2 to the pound between August 1989 and August 1992. It then recovered
to under $1.50 to the pound by October 1992, after the pound left the
European Exchange Rate Mechanism (ERM).[5]

One of the rationales for sterling belonging to the ERM was to stabilise
sterling exchange rates with other European Community currencies and
hence to reduce exchange risk with these currencies. During the two-year
period of the pound's membership, the sterling exchange rate with the
Deutschemark varied between DM 2.95 and DM 2.79 to the pound.
However, by September 1992, the constraints imposed on sterling by
membership of the ERM forced the UK to leave the ERM and the pound
to fall to around DM 2.45, a depreciation of over 15% from its high within
the ERM.

After a discussion of exchange risk, the chapter then goes on to explain
the workings of the foreign exchange market (in particular spot and forward exchange rates), and the ways of reducing exchange risk by hedging
and matching are outlined. This leads to a discussion of the economic
factors causing exchange rates to change, and hence exchange risk to exist.

The next part of the chapter shows how the underlying concepts of
portfolio theory and the Capital Asset Pricing Model (CAPM) (described
in Chapters 8 and 9), can be extended to cover international investment
decisions. It will be shown that any sterling-based investor should have not
just a domestically diversified portfolio, but an internationally diversified
one. This holds true whether bonds or equities are being considered. The
chapter concludes with a discussion of how to apply portfolio theory
techniques to international investment portfolios in practice.

Exchange risk

What additional factors do we have to consider when making international
investments, factors which do not have to be considered when investing in
sterling securities issued by UK institutions?

---

[5] The European Exchange Rate Mechanism ties exchange rates of currencies belonging to it
to movements within pre-determined bands around a central exchange rate.

Transaction costs, as mentioned earlier, may well be higher, as may the tax burden on any proceeds from the investment. For example, dividends paid on a US share owned by a UK resident are liable to both US and UK tax. However, most countries which allow foreign investors to buy their securities (and some do not)[6] have signed what is known as a double taxation treaty with the UK. Under these tax treaties, each government undertakes not to charge tax on such items as dividends paid to investors who will be liable to equivalent taxes in their own country. Despite these treaties the tax burden on an overseas investment may still be higher than on its UK equivalent for a UK investor.

A third factor to be considered when investing overseas is the risk that, for political reasons, an overseas government may withhold dividends, impose additional taxes or expropriate (for little or no compensation) assets belonging to UK investors. Although unlikely to happen in countries with a long history of political stability as, for example, the US, an uprising in a country such as occured in the former Yugoslav states in the early 1990s could lead to the expropriation of the assets of overseas investors.

Transaction costs, taxes and political risk can all be incorporated into the estimate of the holding period return for any overseas security – transaction costs and taxes directly by adjusting the cash flows and political risk indirectly by altering the probability distribution of returns. However, one other factor, which has a potentially much greater impact on holding period return than do those already mentioned, must be explicitly considered. This is the effect of changes in exchange rates, known as exchange risk, on holding period return. An example will illustrate the potential effect of exchange risk.

Suppose Mr Cook buys 100 shares in Travelog Inc., a US Company, for $50 each[7] and holds them for one year. At the end of the year, Travelog Inc. pays a dividend of $5 per share and Mr Cook sells the shares for $60 each.

The holding period return on his dollar investment, $R_\$$, calculated on each share, is then

$$R_\$ = \frac{60 + 5 - 50}{50}$$

$$R_\$ = 30\%$$

Mr Cook has had to buy dollars to make his investment in Travelog. Also,

---

[6] For example, foreign investment in Thai securities can currently only be made via Thai investment intermediaries. Some more subtle restrictions on foreign investors can also be imposed: for example, foreign investors in most Swiss companies can only buy shares *without* a vote.

[7] As can be seen from the *Financial Times*, shares in US companies trade at higher prices per share than UK companies (although notice how UK 'blue chip' shares such as Glaxo and ICI trade at US-style price levels). Coupled with the fact that brokers like to trade US shares in lots of 100, this reduces the attraction to the small investor of direct investment in US shares.

since he wishes to spend the proceeds of his investment in the UK, he will convert the dollars he receives back into pounds.

If the exchange rate at the time of purchase was £1 = $2, the investment in Travelog would have cost Mr Cook $50/2 = £25 per share, a total of £2,500. Let us now imagine two scenarios for the exchange rate on disposal of the dollar proceeds. In the first, the exchange rate at the end of the year is £1 = $2.50; in the second, the exchange rate is £1 = $1.80.

The holding period return in sterling terms, $R_£$, will thus be:

Scenario (1)

Cost of investment per share = **£25**

Proceeds per share   = $60 + $5

$$= £\frac{65}{2.50}$$

$$= £26$$

So

$$R_{£,1} = \frac{26 - 25}{25}$$

$$\boldsymbol{R_{£,1} = 4\%}$$

Scenario (2)

Cost of investment per share = **£25**

Proceeds per share   = $60 + $65

$$= £\frac{65}{1.80}$$

$$= £36.11$$

So

$$R_{£,2} = \frac{36.11 - 25}{25}$$

$$\boldsymbol{R_{£,2} = 44\%}$$

The change in the exchange rate has had a dramatic impact on the return on investment on the Travelog shares. Whereas, for an American investor, the return would have been 30%, for Mr Cook, who invested sterling and required sterling in return, the return was either 4 or 44%. On any such dollar investment, the probability distribution of returns for Mr Cook will also be affected by exchange risk, involving greater risk than for a US investor.

This is true no matter what the original risk of the investment. If Mr Cook chose to invest in a UK gilt to maturity, his return would be certain in nominal terms. If, however, he invested in a US government bond, his sterling return in nominal terms would vary according to the exchange rate prevailing on the day he realised his investment and converted back to sterling. For example, suppose he bought a US government bond for $960, with a nominal value of $1,000 and a coupon of 6% maturing in exactly one year, when the interest will also be paid. His dollar return would be

$$R_s = \frac{1000 + 60 - 960}{960}$$

$$R_s = \qquad 10.4\%$$

If the exchange rate on purchase was £1 = $2, but on sale was £1 = $2.50, that is, the dollar had depreciated in value against sterling (it took more dollars to buy £1), the sterling return $R_£$ would be

$$\text{Cost of investment} \quad = \frac{\$960}{2} = £480$$

$$\text{Proceeds} \qquad = \frac{\$1060}{2.5} = £424$$

$$R_£ = \frac{424 - 480}{480}$$

$$= \frac{-56}{480}$$

$$R_£ = -11.7\%$$

The positive return in dollars would actually be a loss in sterling terms.

The problem of exchange risk is not as daunting as appears from the above examples, but, before we can discuss how exchange risk may be reduced, we need to know more about how the foreign exchange markets work, in particular the spot and forward markets.

Spot and forward exchange rates

The dollar/sterling exchange rates which we used in the examples were *spot* exchange rates, that is, the price paid today to receive a currency now (on the spot).[8] This is to differentiate from *forward* exchange rates which are prices *agreed* today for payment and delivery at some future date, say one, three or six months from now. Example 11.1 shows an extract from the *Financial Times* giving spot, one month forward and three months forward exchange rates for the major currencies – against sterling and against the dollar. Note that the exchange rates against sterling are in the form of how much £1 will buy in each foreign currency. For example, the sterling/dollar exchange rate is quoted in London, say at $2, that is, how many dollars £1 will buy. In other countries it is usual to quote how much of the domestic currency one unit of foreign currency will buy. For example, in France, an exchange rate for the dollar could be 5 FFr, meaning that $1 (foreign currency) will buy five French francs. The reason for the difference is that, before sterling was decimalised, it was difficult to express how much one US dollar or one French franc was worth in pounds, shillings and pence.

The spot and forward rates quoted in the *Financial Times* come from the prices quoted by traders in the foreign currency market based in London. This inter-bank market, where prices are quoted on screens and trades concluded over the telephone, was estimated to have a *daily* net turnover of $900 b. in 1992, almost as much in daily volume as the IMF countries have in total foreign exchange reserves. An attempt by LIFFE to introduce currency futures contracts with small nominal values to attract the retail trader and hedger was unable to compete with the successful forward currency market already well established in London and these contracts were stopped by LIFFE in 1990. However, both forward and futures currency prices are based on the same valuation principles, discussed below.[9]

Both the spot and forward markets in foreign exchange are efficient in the sense that any discrepancies in pricing which would allow arbitrage profits to be made are quickly adjusted. Any apparent anomalies are due to restrictions in trading, for example restrictions on the purchase or sale of a particular currency or the lack of an active market in the currency. This is not the case for the currencies quoted in Example 11.1.

So, exchange rates are consistent. In other words, it costs the same to buy French francs directly with sterling as it does to buy French francs

---

[8] In fact, delivery on a spot contract is two business days after the transacton is agreed.

[9] See Chapter 2, p. 57 for a discussion of the difference between futures and forward markets, and see Chapter 6 on Futures for a discussion of the general principles underlying all futures markets.

Example 11.1   Spot and forward exchange rates

POUND SPOT - FORWARD AGAINST THE POUND

Jul 21	Day's spread	Close	One month	% p.a.	Three months	% p.a.
US	1.8910 - 1.9150	1.9085 - 1.9095	1.14-1.12cpm	7.10	3.21-3.18pm	6.69
Canada	2.2595 - 2.2795	2.2770 - 2.2780	0.97-0.89cpm	4.90	2.78-2.66pm	4.78
Netherlands .	3.1990 - 3.2100	3.2000 - 3.2100	$\frac{1}{4}$-$\frac{1}{8}$cpm	0.70	$\frac{5}{8}$-$\frac{3}{8}$pm	0.62
Belgium	58.35 - 60.05	58.95 - 60.05	6-1cpm	0.71	12-7pm	0.64
Denmark	10.9260 - 10.9745	10.9325 - 10.9425	$\frac{3}{8}$-1$\frac{1}{8}$oredis	-0.82	1-2$\frac{5}{8}$dis	-0.66
Ireland	1.0655 - 1.0685	1.0655 - 1.0665	0.02pm-0.01pdis	0.06	0.04pm-0.02dis	0.04
Germany	2.8370 - 2.8470	2.8400 - 2.8450	$\frac{1}{4}$pfpm-par	0.53	$\frac{1}{2}$-$\frac{1}{4}$pm	0.53
Portugal	241.50 - 242.95	242.30 - 242.90	79-157cdis	-5.84	147-374dis	-4.30
Spain	182.05 - 182.90	182.20 - 182.50	34-48cdis	-2.70	100-150dis	-2.74
Italy	2157.30 - 2170.40	2158.50 - 2159.50	13-18liredis	-8.62	39-44dis	-7.69
Norway	11.1605 - 11.2055	11.1675 - 11.1775	$\frac{1}{4}$-$\frac{1}{2}$oredis	-0.40	$\frac{1}{4}$-1$\frac{1}{8}$dis	-0.25
France	9.5890 - 9.6255	9.5975 - 9.6075	$\frac{1}{8}$-$\frac{1}{4}$cdis	-0.23	$\frac{1}{8}$-$\frac{1}{4}$dis	-0.08
Sweden	10.3065 - 10.3510	10.3125 - 10.3225	$\frac{3}{4}$-1$\frac{1}{2}$oredis	-1.31	2$\frac{7}{8}$-4$\frac{1}{8}$dis	-1.36
Japan	237.85 - 239.55	238.50 - 239.50	1$\frac{1}{4}$-1$\frac{1}{8}$ypm	5.96	3$\frac{5}{8}$-3$\frac{3}{8}$pm	5.86
Austria	19.93 - 20.02	19.97 - 20.00	1$\frac{3}{8}$-$\frac{1}{4}$gropm	0.49	3$\frac{5}{8}$-1$\frac{3}{8}$pm	0.50
Switzerland .	2.5105 - 2.5335	2.5225 - 2.5325	$\frac{1}{2}$-$\frac{1}{4}$cpm	1.78	1-$\frac{3}{4}$pm	1.38
Ecu	1.3930 - 1.4035	1.3930 - 1.3940	0.09-0.14cdis	-0.99	0.25-0.31dis	-0.80

Commercial rates taken towards the end of London trading. Six-month forward dollar 6.25-6.20pm . 12 Month 11.25-11.15pm

DOLLAR SPOT - FORWARD AGAINST THE DOLLAR

Jul 21	Day's spread	Close	One month	% p.a.	Three months	% p.a.
UK†	1.8910 - 1.9150	1.9085 - 1.9095	1.14-1.12cpm	7.10	3.21-3.18pm	6.69
Ireland†	1.7690 - 1.7900	1.7890 - 1.7900	1.08-1.05cpm	7.14	3.07-3.00dis	-6.78
Canada	1.1890 - 1.1935	1.1920 - 1.1930	0.21-0.23cdis	-2.21	0.56-0.60dis	-1.95
Netherlands .	1.6735 - 1.6970	1.6785 - 1.6795	0.91-0.94cdis	-6.61	2.61-2.66dis	-6.28
Belgium	30.60 - 30.95	30.85 - 30.95	17.00-18.00cdis	-6.80	48.00-51.00dis	-6.41
Denmark	5.7175 - 5.7975	5.7275 - 5.7325	3.72-4.02oredis	-8.10	10.60-11.20dis	-7.61
Germany	1.4820 - 1.5060	1.4880 - 1.4890	0.82-0.83pfdis	-6.65	2.38-2.40dis	-6.42
Portugal	127.05 - 128.40	127.05 - 127.15	134-142cdis	-13.03	360-380dis	-11.64
Spain	95.10 - 96.60	95.45 - 95.55	79-82cdis	-10.12	227-236dis	-9.70
Italy	1127.00 - 1145.50	1130.75 - 1131.25	15.20-17.20liredis	-17.19	40.00-45.00dis	-15.03
Norway	5.8360 - 5.9240	5.8500 - 5.8550	3.55-3.85oredis	-7.59	10.20-10.70dis	-7.14
France	5.0170 - 5.0900	5.0275 - 5.0325	3.05-3.10cdis	-7.34	8.73-8.83dis	-6.98
Sweden	5.3845 - 5.4740	5.4025 - 5.4075	3.78-4.03oredis	-8.67	11.05-11.50dis	-8.34
Japan	124.95 - 125.90	125.20 - 125.30	0.12-0.13ydis	-1.20	0.28-0.30dis	-0.93
Austria	10.4520 - 10.5715	10.5040 - 10.5090	5.80-6.15grodis	-6.82	16.10-17.10dis	-6.32
Switzerland .	1.3070 - 1.3390	1.3230 - 1.3240	0.62-0.64cdis	-5.71	1.78-1.81dis	-5.43
Ecu	1.3520 - 1.3725	1.3705 - 1.3715	0.94-0.92cpm	8.14	2.63-2.60pm	7.63

Commercial rates taken towards the end of London trading. † UK, Ireland and ECU are quoted in US currency. Forward premiums and discounts apply to the US dollar and not to the individual currency.

Source: Financial Times (22 July 1992).

indirectly through the dollar. Example 11.2 shows this for both spot and one month forward rates, using the close of business exchange rates given in Example 11.1. The minor differences which emerge, for example 0.25c for the spot French franc transaction and 0.33c for the forward French franc transaction, would be more than eaten up by the extra transaction costs of buying currency indirectly rather than directly.

Example 11.2   Consistent exchange rates*

---

(1) **Spot**

Direct   £1 buys FFr **9.5975**

Indirect   £1 buys $1.9085
and   £1 buys FFr 5.0275
so £1 buys FFr (1.9085 × 5.0275) = FFr **9.5950**

Difference FFr 0.0025 or **0.25c**

(2) **One-month forward**

Direct   £1 buys FFr (9.5975 + 0.00125 dis) = FFr **9.5988** forward

Indirect   £1 buys $(1.9085 − 0.0114 pm) = $1.8971 forward
and   £1 buys FFr (5.0275 + 0.0305 dis) = FFr 5.0580 forward
so   £1 buys FFr (1.8971 × 5.0580) = FFr **9.5955** forward

Difference FFr 0.0033 or **0.33c**

---

*All rates used are those at close of business and the bid or ask rate is used, whichever is relevant.[10]

As you can see from the example, a forward rate is quoted at a premium or a discount on the relevant spot rate. For example, the French franc is shown in Example 11.2 at a forward *discount* to the US dollar, implying that the French franc is worth less relative to the dollar on the forward market than on the spot. To calculate the forward rate, the relevant (bid or ask) discount must be *added* to the spot rate. So the FFr 5.0580 to $1 forward rate shows the French franc to be worth less than on the spot market where it is FFr 5.0275 to $1.[11] In the case of a premium, as exists for sterling relative to the US dollar in Example 11.1, this must be *subtracted* from the spot rate. This rule cannot be applied in every country since it depends on how exchange rates are quoted; the way exchange rates are quoted in the UK is different from, say, the method employed in Belgium.

Hedging exchange risk

The existence of forward markets in foreign currencies allows exchange risk to be hedged, exactly as the risk of changes in commodity prices or interest rates can be hedged. A UK importer due to pay for goods in

---

[10] For all examples in this chapter.

[11] The figures in brackets next to the forward rates in Example 11.1 show the appreciation or depreciation of forward rates relative to spot rates on an annualised basis. For example, the *average* one month forward depreciation of the French franc relative to the US dollar of 0.03075/5.0300 or 0.611% is multiplied by 12 to give 7.34%.

dollars in, say, one month's time, can fix *now* the amount he will have to pay in sterling terms by buying the dollars forward. Suppose he owes $150,000. He could buy dollars forward, assuming the rates are as in Example 11.1, at a one month forward rate of £1 = $(1.9085 − 0.0114) = $1.8971. In other words, he has contracted now to pay £(150,000/1.8971) = £79,068 in one month's time for dollars to be received at that time which he will immediately use to pay his dollar invoice. Similarly, a UK exporter, due to receive payment in dollars, might sell dollars forward to fix his proceeds in sterling terms.

Hedging exchange risk on equity investments

As we saw earlier, not only traders but also international investors are subject to exchange risk. How can they use the forward markets to hedge exchange risk? Could Mr Cook have eliminated exchange risk and fixed his return on Travelog Inc. shares in sterling terms?

Investment in equities is risky because of the uncertainty of income to be received from the investment. Every such investment has a probability distribution of returns, with one return being the mean or expected return from the investment. The best that Mr Cook could do, without the advantage of perfect foresight, would be to hedge the *expected* return on his Travelog shares. Suppose he had expected the dividend to be $5 per share and the share price on sale $55 per share. He could have financed the cost of $50 per share by buying dollars spot and fixed the expected proceeds in sterling terms by selling $60 per share twelve months forward. If the current spot rate for buying dollars was £1 = $2 and the twelve-month forward rate for selling dollars was £1 = $2.10, Mr Cook could have fixed his *expected* return in sterling terms.

$$\text{Cost of investment per share} \quad \textbf{£25}$$

$$\text{Expected proceeds per share} = \$55 + \$5$$

$$= \frac{£60}{2.10}$$

$$= £28.57$$

$$\begin{array}{c} \text{Expected sterling} \\ \text{return on investment } E(R_£) \end{array} = \frac{28.57 - 25}{25}$$

$$E(R_£) = \textbf{14.3\%}$$

However, suppose the *actual* dollars received at the end of the year were $5 per share dividend and $60 per share (ex div), a total of $65. Mr Cook only sold $60 forward and so would have to sell the remaining $5 at the prevailing sterling/dollar exchange rate. Only if his *actual* return in dollar terms had equalled his *expected* return would he have completely eliminated exchange risk.

In practice, it is even more difficult to use the forward market to hedge exchange risk on risky foreign currency investment. Investments are often held for a period of months or years and the longest liquid forward rates in many currencies are for three months (and some countries, such as Greece, Spain, and Turkey do not have a developed forward market at all). This therefore involves the forward contracts being 'rolled over' every three months. In addition, there are problems in hedging the smaller dividend cash flows as well as the attendant transaction costs of the forward transactions. However, currency hedging of equity positions is becoming ever more popular, as we shall see later in the chapter, since some institutional investors, in particular, are keen to reduce the volatility of their portfolios by hedging exchange risk.

An alternative method of hedging exchange risk is to borrow the currency in which the desired security is denominated. In Mr Cook's case, he would borrow dollars to buy Travelog shares. This method of hedging risk (already discussed in Chapter 2) is known as 'matching', since Mr Cook is matching the currency and holding period of his *asset* (the shares) to the currency and maturity of the *liability* (the debt). Suppose Mr Cook borrowed dollars. To minimise exchange risk, he would borrow sufficient so that, after interest, his debt would equal the expected proceeds from the Travelog shares. Mr Cook expects to get $5 dividend per share and $55 per share on sale, totalling $6,000 for 100 shares. If the interest payable on the loan is 10%, Mr Cook can borrow x, where

$$\$x(1 + 0.10) = \$6,000$$

$$x = \$5,454^{12}$$

At the end of the year, Mr Cook would simply use the proceeds of the Travelog investment to repay the loan (plus interest). Having borrowed $5,454, Mr Cook would owe $6,000 (including interest). The proceeds from the Travelog shares actually turn out to be $6,500, so that the $500 not expected would have to be sold at the prevailing sterling/dollar exchange rate. As with hedging a risky investment in the forward market,

---

[12] This example ignores the problems of what Mr Cook will do with the dollars and the different *risks* of the loan and the shares.

Mr Cook bears exchange risk to the extent that the *actual* proceeds of the investment in Travelog shares are not equal to the *expected* amount of $6,000.

One final method of reducing risk on equity investment can be studied before we consider hedging exchange risk on interest rate investments. We saw in Chapter 6 how stock index futures were futures contracts on equity indices. These exist for most of the major stock markets around the world and can be used as a means of investing in overseas stock markets (and not individual shares, as in the case of Travelog Inc.) with a minimum of exchange risk. Buying exposure to equity markets through futures contracts involves the payment of an initial margin and then a daily marking to market of the position. Suppose, for example, that Mr Wan, a dollar-based investor, decided to buy exposure to the UK stock market by buying stock index futures. If he buys exposure to £120,000 of equities, he might have to put up an initial margin to his broker of £3,000 which he would have to buy at the current dollar/sterling exchange rate. If his position moved into profit immediately and stayed in profit for two weeks, he would not have to make any additional purchases of pounds. If he then sold the futures contracts, say, with a £5,000 profit, the £5,000 plus the initial margin would have to be sold at the then dollar/sterling exchange rate. His total exchange risk would have been limited to risk on £8,000, under 7% of his market exposure. Clearly, the amount of exchange risk borne by an investor in equities using futures contracts will vary according to the size of the initial margin required and to the size of the profit or loss on the position. Investing through futures will, however, significantly reduce the exchange risk of the investment to much the same levels as achieved by using forward contracts or by matching, although reducing exchange risk through futures purchases can only be used for exposure to overseas stock markets rather than for exposure to individual overseas equities.

Hedging exchange risk on interest rate investments

Although investment in most types of risky foreign currency securities cannot be fully hedged against exchange risk, investment in *some* fixed interest securities held until maturity, or money placed on fixed interest deposit, can be fully hedged. The necessary conditions are that the term of the security or deposit is equivalent to a period available on the forward or futures market (say one, three or six months) or the maturity available on a matching loan, and that the proceeds of the investment at maturity are certain in nominal terms.

Let us consider the example of money placed on deposit in eurodollars

Example 11.3   Eurocurrency interest rates

EURO-CURRENCY INTEREST RATES

Jul 21	Short term	7 Days notice	One Month	Three Months	Six Months	One Year
Sterling	$10\frac{1}{8}$ - $9\frac{7}{8}$	$10\frac{1}{8}$ - $9\frac{7}{8}$	$10\frac{3}{16}$ - $10\frac{1}{8}$	$10\frac{1}{4}$ - $10\frac{1}{8}$	$10\frac{5}{16}$ - $10\frac{1}{4}$	$10\frac{11}{16}$ - $10\frac{9}{16}$
US Dollar	$3\frac{1}{4}$ - $3\frac{1}{8}$	$3\frac{5}{16}$ - $3\frac{1}{4}$	$3\frac{5}{16}$ - $3\frac{1}{4}$	$3\frac{3}{8}$ - $3\frac{5}{16}$	$3\frac{1}{2}$ - $3\frac{7}{16}$	$3\frac{13}{16}$ - $3\frac{11}{16}$
Can. Dollar	$5\frac{5}{8}$ - $5\frac{3}{8}$	$5\frac{5}{16}$ - 5	$5\frac{5}{16}$ - 5	$5\frac{1}{4}$ - $4\frac{15}{16}$	$5\frac{1}{4}$ - $4\frac{15}{16}$	$5\frac{5}{16}$ - 5
Dutch Guilder	$9\frac{5}{8}$ - $9\frac{1}{8}$	$9\frac{5}{8}$ - $9\frac{1}{8}$	$9\frac{11}{16}$ - $9\frac{9}{16}$	$9\frac{11}{16}$ - $9\frac{7}{16}$	$9\frac{11}{16}$ - $9\frac{7}{16}$	$9\frac{5}{8}$ - $9\frac{3}{8}$
Swiss Franc	$8\frac{7}{8}$ - $8\frac{5}{8}$	$8\frac{7}{8}$ - $8\frac{5}{8}$	$8\frac{13}{16}$ - $8\frac{11}{16}$	$8\frac{7}{8}$ - $8\frac{3}{4}$	$8\frac{15}{16}$ - $8\frac{13}{16}$	$8\frac{13}{16}$ - $8\frac{11}{16}$
D–Mark	$9\frac{3}{4}$ - $9\frac{5}{8}$	$9\frac{13}{16}$ - $9\frac{11}{16}$	$9\frac{13}{16}$ - $9\frac{11}{16}$	$9\frac{7}{8}$ - $9\frac{3}{4}$	$9\frac{7}{8}$ - $9\frac{3}{4}$	$9\frac{13}{16}$ - $9\frac{11}{16}$
French Franc	$10\frac{1}{8}$ - 10	$10\frac{1}{8}$ - 10	$10\frac{1}{4}$ - $10\frac{1}{8}$	$10\frac{5}{16}$ - $10\frac{3}{16}$	$10\frac{5}{16}$ - $10\frac{3}{16}$	$10\frac{5}{16}$ - $10\frac{3}{16}$
Italian Lira	15 - 13	18 - 17	$17\frac{3}{4}$ - 17	$17\frac{1}{2}$ - $16\frac{3}{4}$	17 - $16\frac{1}{2}$	$17\frac{1}{4}$ - $16\frac{3}{4}$
Belgian Franc	$9\frac{3}{4}$ - $9\frac{5}{8}$	$9\frac{3}{4}$ - $9\frac{5}{8}$	$9\frac{3}{4}$ - $9\frac{5}{8}$	$9\frac{3}{4}$ - $9\frac{5}{8}$	$9\frac{3}{4}$ - $9\frac{5}{8}$	$9\frac{3}{4}$ - $9\frac{5}{8}$
Yen	$4\frac{9}{16}$ - $4\frac{1}{2}$	$4\frac{9}{16}$ - $4\frac{1}{2}$	$4\frac{9}{16}$ - $4\frac{1}{2}$	$4\frac{13}{32}$ - $4\frac{11}{32}$	$4\frac{7}{32}$ - $4\frac{5}{32}$	$4\frac{5}{32}$ - $4\frac{3}{32}$
Danish Krone	12 - $11\frac{1}{2}$	$11\frac{1}{2}$ - 11	$11\frac{1}{4}$ - $10\frac{3}{4}$	$10\frac{7}{8}$ - $10\frac{3}{8}$	$10\frac{7}{8}$ - $10\frac{3}{8}$	$10\frac{7}{8}$ - $10\frac{3}{8}$
Asian $Sing	$2\frac{1}{8}$ - 2	$2\frac{1}{8}$ - 2	$2\frac{1}{4}$ - $2\frac{1}{8}$	$2\frac{3}{8}$ - $2\frac{1}{4}$	$2\frac{5}{8}$ - $2\frac{1}{2}$	$3\frac{1}{16}$ - $2\frac{15}{16}$
Spanish Peseta	$12\frac{1}{2}$ - 12	$12\frac{1}{2}$ - 12	$12\frac{11}{16}$ - $12\frac{3}{8}$	$12\frac{7}{8}$ - $12\frac{9}{16}$	13 - $12\frac{11}{16}$	$13\frac{1}{8}$ - $12\frac{13}{16}$

Long term Eurodollars: two years $4\frac{9}{16}$-$4\frac{7}{16}$ per cent; three years $5\frac{1}{4}$-$5\frac{1}{8}$ per cent; four years $5\frac{3}{4}$-$5\frac{5}{8}$ per cent; five years $6\frac{1}{4}$-$6\frac{1}{8}$ per cent nominal. Short term rates are call for US Dollars and Japanese Yen; others, two days' notice.

Source: *Financial Times* (22 July 1992).

for three months.[13] All eurocurrency interest rates are given in annual equivalents, for comparative purposes. However, they are the simple multiples of, say, the relevant three-month rate. So, to calculate the actual interest payable on a three-month deposit, the annual interest rate given should be divided by 4. Example 11.3 gives an extract from the *Financial Times* of the same day as the exchange rates in Example 11.1, showing eurocurrency rates for deposits and loans with terms up to one year in the major eurocurrencies.

We use the example of a three-month eurodollar deposit to show how an interest rate investment can be completely hedged against exchange risk. To do this, a UK investor will purchase dollars on the spot market, place them in a three-month eurodollar deposit with a fixed interest rate and sell forward the known dollar proceeds on the three-month forward market. We use the data in Example 11.1 and 11.3 and suppose that £100,000 is invested. Example 11.4 shows how the investor can achieve a certain *sterling* return of 10% per annum equivalent despite having made a foreign currency investment.

With Example 11.4 we have shown how short-term fixed interest rate investments, such as eurodollar deposits, can be fully hedged in sterling terms. However, can forward rates be used to hedged fixed interest investments with maturities of longer than one year, such as investments in

---

[13] For a brief description of eurodollars and eurocurrency, see the Appendix to this chapter (pp. 347–8).

Example 11.4   Hedging of exchange risk on fixed interest investment

---

Investment = £100,000

(1) **Use £100,000 to purchase dollars on spot market**

£1 at $1.9085 gives **$190,850**

(2) **Place dollars on one-month eurodeposit**

Three-month eurodollar rate 3⅜% p.a. equivalent to 3⅜/4

$$= \textbf{0.84375\% for three months}$$

Proceeds at end of three months   = $190,850 (1.00844)

$$= \textbf{\$192,461}$$

(3) **Sell dollar proceeds forward**

Three-month forward rate for sale of dollars

$$= \$(1.9095 - 0.0318)$$

$$= \textbf{\$1.8777}$$

Sterling proceeds of investment $= \dfrac{£192,461}{\$/£1.8777}$

$$= \textbf{£102,500}$$

(4) **Calculate holding period return**

$$= \frac{102,500 - 100,000}{100,000}$$

$R_£$ = 2.5% × 4 for annualised rate

$R_£$ = **10.0% p.a.**

---

overseas government bonds? Such securities suffer from the same problem as the foreign equity investments considered earlier: if sold before maturity, their sale price in the foreign currency is unknown and hence only the current value or the expected value can be hedged.

Suppose, for example, that Ms Grun buys a ten-year deutschemark bond with a view to holding the bond for six months, over which period she expects ten-year bond yields in deutschemark terms to fall. If she simultaneously hedges the investment by selling six months forward an amount of deutschemarks equal to the current price plus the coupon to be received, she is effectively exchanging currency risk for yield curve risk. Any change in the deutschemark value of the bond in six months' time (the unhedged element of the investment) will be determined by changes in the ten-year bond yield.

If, however, Ms Grun buys a ten-year deutschemark bond with a view to holding the bond to maturity, there is no uncertainty attached to the sale price (which is par) but there is no forward contract long enough with which to hedge the principal repayment on maturity. There is also the problem of finding long enough forward contracts to hedge each one of the coupon payments to be received over the life of the bond. However, it is now possible for institutional investors to carry out what is known as an 'asset swap' with a bank: this is an agreement between the investor and the bank in which the investor promises to hand over the deutschemark coupons and principal repayment in exchange for equivalent sterling flows at pre-determined exchange rates. This effectively creates a synthetic sterling bond for the investor which may be of a type or maturity not available in the sterling bond markets.

Interest rate parity

In Example 11.4, we showed that the investor, using the eurocurrency and forward currency markets could ensure a completely certain *sterling* holding period return, in this case 10% p.a. equivalent, from a short-term, fixed interest dollar investment. As a result, he should be indifferent between investing in this way in eurodollars and investing in eurosterling, which will also give him a certain sterling holding period return. We can check this from Example 11.3. If the investor had instead placed his money on eurosterling deposit for three months, Example 11.3 tells us that he would have been given interest of 10¼% p.a.

Thus, his three-month return would have been just ¼% per annum different between the two alternatives, equivalent to £62.50 on £100,000. The discrepancy is due to the use of closing prices rather than actual trading prices and to the fact that investing in sterling via the eurodollar market and forward currency market involves two bid–ask spreads rather than just the one bid–ask spread on eurosterling interest rates. So, the returns on the two alternative *sterling* strategies are, after allowing for transaction costs, the same.

This phenomenon of equal returns from equal risk, *hedged* investments in different currencies is known as *interest rate parity*. In a perfect world, interest rate parity would always hold since, if investors could obtain different returns from investing fully hedged in different currencies, they would arbitrage the differences away.[14] Interest rate parity does hold in the eurocurrency markets and in fact, forward exchange rates are determined by comparing interest rate differentials. We can derive the interest rate parity formula as follows:

If the investor places $£Y$ on eurosterling deposit he will earn interest of $R_£$, say, yielding

$$Y (1 + R_£) \tag{A}$$

---

[14] This type of arbitrage, using the forward currency markets and the money markets, is called 'covered interest arbitrage'.

If he buys dollars spot, he will receive

$$Y (X_0)$$

where X_0 is the spot exchange rate.

If he places these dollars on eurodollar deposit for the same period at $R_\$$ interest and sells forward the proceeds at X_f (the forward exchange rate), he will get

$$\frac{Y (X_0) (1 + R_\$)}{X_f} \qquad \text{(B)}$$

Interest rate parity says that the returns from these two equal risk strategies must be equal, so that (A) must equal (B).

Thus,

$$Y (1 + R_\pounds) = Y \frac{(X_0) (1 + R_\$)}{X_f}$$

Y cancels out and rearranging gives

$$\frac{X_f}{X_0} = \frac{1 + R_\$}{1 + R_\pounds} \qquad (11.1)$$

Forward exchange dealers can use equation (11.1) to set forward rates. For example, if the spot dollar/sterling exchange rate is £1 = \$2, and the eurodollar and eurosterling one year interest rates are 5% and 10% respectively, the twelve-month forward rate must be

$$\frac{X_f}{2} = \frac{1.05}{1.10}$$

$$X_f = \$1.91/\pounds$$

Interest rate parity will always hold when currency forward markets and money markets are efficient. Because eurocurrency markets are free, unregulated markets, interest rate parity does hold for the major currencies in the eurocurrency markets as we saw in Example 11.4. However, interest rate parity does not necessarily hold with other types of fixed interest investment which have returns certain in nominal terms (such as UK and US Treasury Bills) or with less internationally traded currencies, since exchange controls, taxes and other government intervention may prevent investors from arbitraging away any differences in return.

The fundamentals of exchange risk

We have seen that the major additional problem in making foreign currency as opposed to sterling investments appears to be that of exchange risk. Although for certain types of short-term, fixed interest investments, exchange risk can be fully hedged, most types of investment in risky foreign currency investments can only be partly hedged against exchange risk, if at all.

Forecasting future exchange rates

Exchange risk is the risk that exchange rates will change and adversely affect the expected sterling return on investments. Of course, if future exchange rates could be perfectly forecast by the investor, exchange risk would no longer be such a problem. He would be able to calculate his expected sterling returns, allowing for forecast changes in exchange rates, and choose those investments which offered him his preferred risk and return characteristics. There are two potential sources of forecasts of future exchange rates. Firstly, and more simply, there may be market consensus forecasts. Secondly, forecasts can be obtained from either studying charts of past exchange rates or by studying the fundamental causes of changes in exchange rates, namely differential inflation and growth rates and balance of payments figures reflecting currency flows.

In Chapter 4, when analysing fixed interest securities, we found that the forward interest rates implicit in the spot interest rate term structure could be used to forecast future spot interest rates. In the simplest case, the expectations hypothesis stated that forward interest rates were the market's best estimates of future spot rates. This leads to the question of whether, in the foreign exchange markets, forward exchange rates are the best market estimates of future spot exchange rates. Can Mr Cook or any investor in foreign currency securities use forward exchange rates to forecast expected future exchange rates?

The empirical evidence appears to show that, on average, forward exchange rates are unbiased estimates of future exchange rates.[15] In other words, the expectations hypothesis holds for exchange rates. Unlike forward interest rates, which appear to include a liquidity or inflation premium in their estimates of future spot interest rates, there seems to be no

---

[15] For a summary of the research in this area, see the section on the efficiency of foreign exchange markets in Levi (1990), ch. 12.

premium to pay for the use of forward markets to hedge exchange risk. Forward exchange rates represent the market's best estimates of future spot rates, without any adjustment needed to include a charge for allowing investors and traders to hedge. The only additional cost to Mr Cook of hedging is the slightly wider bid/ask spreads he has to pay in the forward market. For example, the spread on the close of business one month forward sterling/dollar exchange rate in Example 11.1 on p. 322 is $1.9085 − 0.0114 to $1.9095 − 0.0112 or $1.8971 − $1.8983 equivalent to 0.12 cents, compared with $1.9085 to $1.9095, or 0.10 cents, for the one-month sterling/dollar spot exchange rate.

Having established that there is no bias in the forward exchange rate estimates of future spot exchange rates, the next question to ask is how good these estimates are. If they are perfect estimates, forward rates will provide the investor with the future exchange rates needed to estimate holding period returns and to make investment decisions. Unfortunately, forward rates are in practice fairly poor predictors of future exchange rates and economic forecasting models appear no better at forecasting than the market-determined forward rates.[16] So, if Mr Cook does not hedge exchange risk or cannot fully hedge his risky investments using the forward market, he will experience volatility in his investment returns due to unexpected changes in exchange rates. Forecasting techniques using forward rates or chartist methods are unlikely to help him much.

However, exchange risk is not as great as it seems. Although there is no exact understanding of how exchange rates change, there are certain relationships between exchange rates, interest rates and inflation rates which ought to hold in a world where there are no barriers to trade or investment and which do hold to a lesser extent in the real world. Using these relationships, we can predict in broad terms what will happen in the long run to exchange rates, although shorter–run movements are more difficult to forecast.

Purchasing power parity theory

The first of these relationships is known as the purchasing power parity theory, derived from the law of one price. If a product is freely internationally traded, with negligible transportation costs, the law of one price says that the product should be traded for the same price everywhere. For example, if a McDonald's hamburger or a Mars bar sells for $1 in the US and 50p in the UK, then $1 must be worth 50p and $2 worth £1. The purchasing power parity theory, PPPT for short, extends the law of one price to overall price levels in each country, measured, for example, by a

---

[16] See Levi (1990), ch. 12.

retail prices index. The PPPT is usually expressed in terms of *changes* in exchange rates, and says that, given the assumption of free international trade, the change in an exchange rate over a period will be equal to the relative change in inflation rates of the two countries concerned.

This can be written as

$$\frac{X_1}{X_0} = \frac{P_{f1}/P_{f0}}{P_{d1}/P_{d0}} = \frac{1 + infl_f}{1 + infl_d} \qquad (11.2)$$

where X_0 is the exchange rate at the beginning of the period and X_1 the exchange rate at the end of the period; the P_f and P_d are the price levels in the foreign country and domestic country respectively, and the $infl_f$ and $infl_d$ their equivalent inflation rates during the period. For example, suppose inflation over a period is 8% in the UK and 4% in the US, with the exchange rate at the beginning of the period $1.60 = £1.

We know that

$$P_{f1}/P_{f0} = 1 + infl_f = 1.04$$

$$P_{d1}/P_{d0} = 1 + infl_d = 1.08$$

$$X_0 = 1.60$$

PPPT says that the exchange rate will adjust over the period to give

$$\frac{X_1}{1.6} = \frac{1.04}{1.08}$$

So,

$$X_1 = \textbf{1.54}$$

In other words, the pound would be expected to depreciate against the dollar to £1 = $1.54, reflecting its relatively reduced purchasing power.

PPPT cannot hold exactly as in equation (11.2) since not all goods included in a general measure of inflation are internationally traded. Also, such factors as transportation costs, time lags in price adjustments, government controls and taxes on international trade mean that, although exchange rate changes may in the *long* run be expected to reflect relative changes in purchasing power parity, the PPPT relationship cannot be used for accurate short-run forecasts of future exchange rates. Indeed, the failure of economic indices such as PPPT to explain short-term movements in exchange rates is a major reason why technical analysis and chartism, described in Chapter 10, are popular forecasting techniques for day-to-day exchange rate movements.

International Fisher effect

The PPPT is concerned with the connection between inflation and exchange rates. However, we saw in Chapter 2 that inflation also affects interest rates, with Fisher postulating that interest rates fully take account of *expected* (as opposed to *actual*) inflation. Fisher suggested an expression relating the nominal interest rate, R, and the real interest rate, r, as follows:

$$(1 + R) = (1 + r)(1 + E(infl)) \tag{11.3}$$

where $E(infl)$ is the inflation rate expected over the period.

The second fundamental relationship concerning exchange rate changes is the extension of equation (11.3) to an international context, sometimes referred to as the International Fisher effect. If the expression holds in each national financial market, there will be a real interest rate in each currency. If investors can freely choose in which currency to invest their money, this real interest rate must be the same everywhere, otherwise investors would arbitrage the differences away. If we consider the US dollar and sterling, for example, we can write equation (11.3) for each of them:

$$(1 + R_{£}) = (1 + r_{£})(1 + E(infl_{£})) \tag{11.3a}$$

$$(1 + R_{\$}) = (1 + r_{\$})(1 + E(infl_{\$})) \tag{11.3b}$$

If the real interest rate in dollar terms is equal to the real interest rate available in sterling, we must have

$$1 + r_{£} = 1 + r_{\$}$$

So,

$$\frac{1 + R_{£}}{1 + E(infl_{£})} = \frac{1 + R_{\$}}{1 + E(infl_{\$})} \tag{11.4}$$

Rearranging equation (11.3) and subtracting 1 from each side, we get

$$\frac{R_{\$} - R_{£}}{1 + R_{£}} = \frac{E(infl_{\$} - infl_{£})}{1 + E(infl_{£})} \tag{11.5}$$

Both equations (11.4) and (11.5) are different ways of expressing the International Fisher effect. Let us, as before, suppose that inflation is expected to be 8% in the UK and 4% in the US. If nominal interest rates in the UK are 10%, we can use equation (11.5), or (11.4), to derive the level of nominal interest rates in the US

$$\frac{R_\$ - 0.10}{1 + 0.10} = \frac{0.04 - 0.08}{1 + 0.08}$$

Rearranging,

$$R_\$ = 0.10 + \frac{(1 + 0.10)(-0.04)}{1 + 0.08}$$

$$R_\$ = 5.9\%$$

Interest rates will be lower in the US, because of the lower rate of expected inflation. In both countries, however, the *real* interest rate will be the same:

$$(1 + r_\$)(1 + 0.04) = (1 + 0.059)$$

$$r_\$ = 1.9\%$$

$$(1 + r_£)(1 + 0.08) = (1 + 0.10)$$

$$r_£ = 1.9\%$$

The assumptions underlying the existence of a single real interest rate world-wide include, as for PPPT, that of completely free international trade, this time in interest-bearing securities. However, interest rates are often manipulated by governments as part of their economic policies and, as mentioned earlier, foreign investors may not be allowed to hold fixed interest government securities, or may be taxed more highly than domestic investors. The Fisher relationship between *expected* inflation and interest rates is most likely to hold in the eurocurrency market, where interest rates are not *directly* government-influenced.

Since it is difficult to estimate the *expected* inflation rates implied in nominal interest rates, studies of whether the Fisher relationship holds have looked at returns in different currencies net of *actual* inflation. Such studies appear to suggest that netting out actual inflation does not give the same real interest rate for each currency.[17] As with PPPT, there are currently too many barriers and costs to international investment for

---

[17] See, for example, Madura (1986) ch. 7.

different currency capital markets to offer the same real interest rate on equivalent risk investments.

Exchange risk with PPPT and International Fisher

If these two fundamental relationships, PPPT and International Fisher, did hold, the international investor would not need to concern himself with exchange risk; there would be no *additional* risk to international as opposed to domestic investment.[18] Example 11.5 shows how, if these relationships did hold, Mr Cook would achieve the same sterling return, without hedging, whether he invested in a sterling eurobond with one year to redemption or an equivalent dollar eurobond with the same maturity.

Unfortunately, neither of these fundamental relationships holds in the real world exactly as in Example 11.5, although exchange rates do, to some extent and in the long run, adjust for differences in inflation and nominal interest rates. So, exchange risk remains a factor to be considered when investing in foreign currency securities. As we have seen, hedging on the forward market or borrowing in the currency of the investment or asset swaps, can provide a solution to the problem of exchange risk when investing in securities with predetermined foreign currency cash flows but these techniques only provide a partial solution to the problem of exchange risk in overseas securities with uncertain future cash flows.

Advantages of exchange risk

However, exchange risk may not be as much of a disadvantage to international investment as it appears. It may act in such a way as to dampen the market risk of buying overseas equities or bonds. For example, the risk to Mr Cook of buying a diversified portfolio of US shares is made up of the risk of the shares (measured in terms of volatility or standard deviation of returns in the local currency) plus the exchange risk of an adverse move in the dollar relative to sterling. As we saw in Chapter 8 on Portfolio Theory, combining risks is not strictly additive but depends on the correlation between the return patterns. Thus, the total risk of investing in US shares for Mr Cook would be:

---

[18] Ignoring political risk and any differentiation between foreign and domestic investors. Of course the fundamental riskiness of the investment (which may vary between countries) will still exist.

Example 11.5   International investment without exchange risk

---

Suppose PPPT and International Fisher hold

Assumptions:

Current exchange rate X_0 = $1.60
Real interest rate on eurobonds = 2%
Expected inflation, 8% in UK, 4% in US

PPPT gives

$$\frac{X_1}{1.60} = \frac{1.04}{1.08}$$

where X_1 = year-end exchange rate

X_1 = $1.54

International Fisher gives the nominal interest rates which will prevail on sterling and dollar eurobonds, $R_£$ and $R_\$$

In the US

$(1.02)\,(1.04) = (1 + R_\$)$

$R_\$ = 6.1\%$

where $R_\$$ = nominal return on dollar bond

In the UK

$(1.02)\,(1.08) = (1 + R_£)$

$R_£ = 10.2\%$

where $R_£$ = nominal return on sterling bond

Sterling eurobond
The return, $R_£$, on the sterling eurobond will be 10.2%
£100 invested at 10.2% gives **£110.20**

Dollar eurobond
The return, $R_\$$, on the dollar eurobond will be 6.1%
The current spot exchange rate is $1.60 = £1
The year-end exchange rate will be $1.54 = £1
So, £100 converted at $1.60 gives $160
$160 invested at 6.1% gives $169.80
$169.80 converted at $1.54 gives **£110.20**

$$S^2 = S_M^2 + S_{Fx}^2 + 2S_M S_{Fx} \, \text{CORR}_{M,Fx} \tag{11.6}$$

where S_M is the standard deviation of returns on US shares expressed in US dollars; S_{Fx} is the standard deviation of changes in the \$/£ exchange rate; and $\text{CORR}_{M,Fx}$ is the correlation coefficient between US equity returns and \$/£ currency movements. The corresponding risk of investing in a portfolio of US shares for a dollar-based investor. Mr Wan, would be

$$S^2 = S_M^2 \tag{11.7}$$

In practice, the correlation coefficient between equity returns and currency movements in most markets around the world is usually around zero or slightly negative. So, if we assume 17% market volatility for US equities, 10% volatility for the \$/£ exchange rate, and a correlation coefficient of -0.1, we can see from inputting these numbers into equation (11.7) that the risk for Mr Cook of investing unhedged in US shares would be

$$S^2 = (0.17)^2 + (0.1)^2 + 2 \times 0.17 \times 0.1 \times -0.1$$

$$= 0.0355$$

So,   **S = 18.8%**

The risk for Mr Wan, with no exchange risk, from equation (11.7) would be

$$S^2 = (0.17)^2$$

So,   **S = 17.0%**

In this example, exchange risk has only increased Mr Cook's risk of investing in US equities by 1.8% when compared with the risk of investing in US shares without exchange risk, as is the case for Mr Wan, although the exchange risk on its own is assumed to be 10%.

Note that the actual impact of currency risk will depend on the market considered and on the period under consideration. Standard deviation and correlation coefficient measures will vary according to the time period analysed, whether weekly, monthly or quarterly numbers are used, and according to the base currency used. However, on a global basis, exchange risk only accounts for around 15% of total equity market risk. This figure is closer to 50% for the global bond markets, since the typical correlation coefficient between bond returns in a particular country and its currency movements is more likely to be positive than is the case for equities.[19]

---

[19] See Solnik (1991) chs 1 and 2. An economic explanation for the positive correlation between bond returns and exchange rate movements is that governments or central banks tend to raise interest rates (and hence depress bond prices) when their currency is depreciating. This type of intervention is known as 'leaning into the wind'.

Thus, in conclusion to this section on exchange risk, investors such as Mr Cook are free to reduce exchange risk to a minimum by hedging the *expected* values of their equity and bond portfolios (if a forward or swap market exists for them to do so). Alternatively, they can accept the relatively small amount of exchange risk which in practice attaches to investment in overseas stock and bond markets, particularly if only a percentage of Mr Cook's portfolio is invested in non-sterling investments.

International diversification

However, despite the increased volatility created by exchange risk, there may be other advantages to international investment which outweigh the potential risks. Should the UK investor add foreign currency securities to his portfolio and, if so, which securities and markets should he consider?

Portfolio theory

We saw in Chapter 8 that the investor, when combining securities into a portfolio, is concerned not only with the expected return and standard deviation of each security but also with the correlation coefficients between returns on pairs of securities, since these inter-relationships affect the overall risk of the portfolio. This approach, which we confined to a domestic equity portfolio in Chapter 8, can equally well be applied to a global equity portfolio, where the constituent elements of the portfolio are not individual shares but individual stock markets.

In Figure 8.9 (p. 252) we saw that a *naïve* diversification policy on UK equities could reduce the risk of a portfolio to around 34% of the average risk of holding one share. This figure is somewhat lower at around 30% for US investors because of the greater diversification potential offered by a larger stock market. However, another piece of research by Solnik showed how just by holding 40 securities from both US and European stock markets, the risk for a US investor would be around half that of a US portfolio of stocks with the same number of shares. This result which emphasises the size of the risk reduction benefits which international diversification can bring is shown in Figure 11.1.

The risk reduction benefits of international diversification would therefore be even greater to UK investors and other investors from smaller markets than the US with less domestic diversification potential.

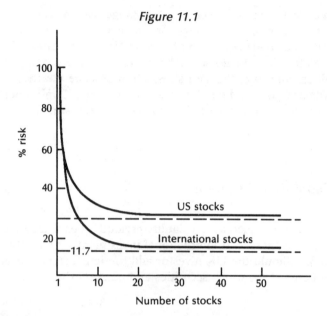

Figure 11.1

Source: Solnik (1974) p. 50.

However, again using the results from portfolio theory,[20] risk reduction can be improved by concentrating on poorly correlated stock markets. Example 11.6 gives the correlation coefficients between major stock market returns expressed in sterling terms, of 18 major stock markets for the period 1981 to 1990. It also gives the average annual returns and standard deviations of returns for all these markets. The returns, calculated quarterly, allow for changes in exchange rates and therefore include exchange risk. Notice how the correlation coefficients vary between a high of 0.77 for the Swiss and German stock markets and a low of 0.14 between Austria and Japan. These correlation coefficients between stock markets are in general lower than are correlation coefficients between shares in the same market; hence the risk reduction benefits of international diversification. By using a quadratic programming computer software package and inputting return, risk, and correlation coefficient data for all these markets, a lower risk portfolio than that achieved by naïve diversification can be derived.

Of course, there is little point in trying to reduce risk to a minimum if returns are substantially reduced as well. If, say, returns on all overseas investments were substantially less than those available to Mr Cook on the UK stock market, it might be that the benefit of reduced risk obtained from international diversification was more than offset by reduced returns.

---

[20] See Chapter 8, pp. 235–44.

Example 11.6 Returns, risk and correlation coefficients of major stock market (in sterling terms)

Equities	Return Volatility			Correlation - GBP																	
	%	%	Ratio	US	JP	UK	DM	CH	F	ND	I	SW	ES	B	DK	NW	OE	CN	AS	SING	HK
USA	16.3	21.6	0.8	•																	
Japan	21.8	22.9	1.0	0.43	•																
UK	18.8	20.4	0.9	0.61	0.42	•															
Germany	20.7	23.0	0.9	0.48	0.36	0.43	•														
Switzerland	14.9	18.5	0.8	0.64	0.45	0.55	0.77	•													
France	20.0	25.1	0.8	0.49	0.42	0.42	0.62	0.60	•												
Netherlands	22.2	20.1	1.1	0.72	0.47	0.61	0.70	0.74	0.58	•											
Italy	16.0	26.8	0.6	0.40	0.40	0.38	0.50	0.47	0.54	0.49	•										
Sweden	26.9	24.5	1.1	0.53	0.46	0.52	0.49	0.56	0.36	0.53	0.47	•									
Spain	21.5	26.1	0.8	0.47	0.46	0.43	0.41	0.48	0.49	0.45	0.43	0.46	•								
Belgium	28.4	21.3	1.3	0.56	0.46	0.47	0.62	0.62	0.63	0.63	0.47	0.42	0.47	•							
Denmark	20.8	20.4	1.0	0.49	0.35	0.28	0.48	0.51	0.40	0.50	0.33	0.33	0.29	0.44	•						
Norway	17.9	27.5	0.7	0.56	0.30	0.56	0.46	0.54	0.48	0.61	0.27	0.48	0.38	0.51	0.38	•					
Austria	21.7	23.7	0.9	0.28	0.14	0.21	0.60	0.46	0.39	0.39	0.36	0.35	0.28	0.35	0.19	0.29	•				
Canada	10.4	21.8	0.5	0.83	0.39	0.63	0.39	0.60	0.42	0.67	0.43	0.50	0.41	0.45	0.46	0.51	0.23	•			
Australia	9.4	31.5	0.3	0.53	0.29	0.57	0.32	0.46	0.34	0.44	0.26	0.43	0.44	0.37	0.29	0.51	0.15	0.64	•		
Singapore	8.6	32.6	0.3	0.67	0.37	0.52	0.40	0.50	0.50	0.54	0.25	0.50	0.40	0.47	0.42	0.57	0.29	0.59	0.59	•	
Hong Kong	11.0	39.1	0.3	0.48	0.31	0.55	0.40	0.44	0.31	0.54	0.33	0.48	0.46	0.37	0.24	0.50	0.26	0.49	0.53	0.51	•
World - GDPppp	19.3	17.4	1.1	0.48	0.31	0.55	0.40	0.44	0.31	0.54	0.33	0.48	0.46	0.37	0.24	0.50	0.26	0.49	0.53	0.51	

Source: UBS Phillips & Drew, World Markets Review, Table 3.1(c) for data from January 1981 to September 1990.

However, this is not the case, as we can see from Example 11.6, which also shows the average annual sterling returns which could have been obtained on the 18 different stock markets during the period January 1981 to September 1990. Nine of those outperformed the UK stock market over that period, with the Japanese stock market outperforming the UK market by 3% per year over 10 years. If Mr Cook had chosen the right overseas stock markets in which to invest, not only could he have reduced risk by diversification but he could have significantly increased his achieved sterling returns.

However, suppose Mr Cook were trying to decide in September 1990 in which overseas markets it was optimal to invest. He would be concerned with *expected* returns and risks of markets rather than the historical figures given in Example 11.6. If he used historical figures, he would doubtless have put a substantial amount of his overseas portfolio into Japanese shares which offered, during the 1980s, relatively high returns, risk on a level with that of the UK market, and relatively low correlation with the other stock markets. However, past performance is no guide to the future and the Japanese market in fact crashed in December 1990 and fell almost continously for the next two years.

In practice, therefore, investors using a portfolio theory model to determine their optimal international equity portfolio use their own forecasts for expected returns (bearing in mind their view of future exchange rate movements) but will generally use historical estimates of market volatilities and correlation coefficients, since it is more difficult to have an intuitive feel for these.[21] They, then, as for the domestic equivalent, are offered by their computer model a range of portfolios on the efficient frontier, each with its own risk and return levels. Investors can choose whichever portfolio most suits their risk preference.

Notice that investors from different countries looking at market returns, risks and correlation coefficients for the same historical period will be shown different numbers, reflecting the use of a different base currency. Returns for US investors will be calculated in dollars and returns for German investors in deutschemarks and will be different from those given in Example 11.6. This will naturally lead to different opportunity sets, efficient frontiers and optimal portfolios for different nationality investors. Also, investors within the same country may have different return expectations for markets or different tax positions, again leading to variations in optimal portfolios between investors.

---

[21] However, one problem with this model must be noted: a small change in expected return could radically affect the composition of the optimal portfolio. So, changing views on market returns could lead to expensive rebalancing costs on portfolios.

Capital asset pricing model

Having seen that portfolio theory can be successfully applied to the problem of international investment, this leads us naturally to look at the role of the CAPM in an international context. As we saw in Chapter 9, the CAPM was derived in a purely national framework by US researchers with the largest Stock Exchange in the world and the least to gain from international investment. Can it be extended to an international framework?

There are two main ways in which the CAPM could be viewed in an international framework. One would be to assume that all capital markets were integrated, meaning that all securities were priced relative to a world capital market. In this case, the CAPM would be a 'world' CAPM, with world betas, of the form

$$E(R_j) = \alpha_j + \beta_j\, E(R_w) \tag{11.8}$$

For this to happen, investors would have to be able to invest freely in any capital market and so would naturally compare the risk and return of any security in a world-wide context.

Alternatively, each security's return could be determined, as postulated by the original CAPM, purely in its domestic market. Each country i would have its own CAPM of the form

$$E(R_{ji}) = \alpha_{ji} + \beta_{ji}\, E(R_{mi}) \tag{11.9}$$

where each country's risk–return relationship could be different. For there to be this multiplicity of different equations (11.9), a different one for each country, one must envisage some impediment or disadvantage to international investment to explain why investors do not value securities on an international basis and why markets are thus segmented.[22] There is at present no real agreement on the form that an international CAPM would take,[23] but this view of the capital markets as integrated or segmented does give an understanding of how international diversification reduces risk. If markets were fully integrated, and investors had identical expectations and investment preferences (that is, were passive investors as opposed to the more active investors inputting expected returns into the portfolio theory model), a world CAPM would lead, as does the domestic CAPM, to the result that all investors should hold the same market portfolio, in other

---

[22] Factors leading to segmented markets could include tax, legal, or information barriers to overseas investment as well as differences in consumption preferences between investors in different countries.

[23] For example, there are problems in defining a risk-free interest rate in an international CAPM context.

words, hold a proportion of all the stock markets in the world in amounts reflecting the market's relative importance. In this case, if investors chose to restrict themselves to a purely domestic portfolio, they would be bearing diversifiable risk for which they would not be rewarded.

On the other hand, if markets were segmented, international investment would also offer a reduction in risk since risk which was systematic in a national context would become diversifiable in an international context. However, markets are segmented if there are impediments preventing investors from including non-domestic securities in their portfolios, so only those investors lucky enough to be able to circumvent the restrictions would be able to benefit from international diversification if markets were segmented.

There is some evidence that markets are partially segmented[24] although the tax, legal and informational barriers are gradually being removed. More and more investors are able, if they wish, to invest in international portfolios or index funds, designed to represent an international market portfolio. Thus, if they are passive investors as assumed by the CAPM, they can in practice apportion their assets between, say, Treasury bills in their domestic currency and a world index fund.

Example 11.7 shows the relative sizes of the major stock markets expressed as percentages of the total world stock market valued at the end of 1991. In Example 11.7, the US represents the largest single stock market, followed by Japan, the UK, France, and Germany. If these five markets are added up, they represent 85.3% of the total global stock market capitalisation. Integrated CAPM says that all investors, regardless of which country and currency they are based in, should put the majority of their money into these five stock markets. The optimal portfolio under CAPM will include countries according to the size of their stock markets. This is in contrast to an optimal portfolio under a portfolio theory model approach, which will choose countries according to their expected returns, risks, and the correlation coefficients between countries. The CAPM model assumes that the investor is passive, accepts the market consensus on stock market values and returns, and wishes to achieve an average return on a fully diversified portfolio. The portfolio theory model assumes that the investor is more active, with views different from the consensus. He will therefore expect to achieve a better return for risk ratio than the investor in a global index fund by being 'overweight' in those stock markets which he thinks will outperform and 'underweight' in those which he considers undervalued.

Although there is less theoretical support for an international CAPM than for its domestic counterpart, international index funds which offer investors the opportunity to invest in countries in proportion to their stock

---

[24] For a discussion of the research in this area, see Levi (1990) ch. 13.

Example 11.7   Relative importance of major stock markets (end 1992)

	% of total
US	42.8
Japan	25.4
UK	10.5
Germany	3.3
France	3.3
Switzerland	2.0
Canada	1.8
Other	10.9
	100.0

Source: WM Performance Measurement Services.

market and bond market[25] values have had some success. This has been helped by the practical difficulties which investors face when attempting to select likely outperforming stocks in foreign stock markets, where they have to deal through unknown intermediaries and are not as at ease with the local accounting methods and types of equity analysis employed. Such index funds are available to individual investors through the medium of unit trusts but are not as popular as the more conventional unit trusts and investment trusts which adopt a more active approach, attempting to outperform their index fund counterparts. Also, it must not be forgotten that investing in the UK stock market does expose investors such as Mr Cook to exchange risk and to some element of international diversification, due to the large element of revenues and costs incurred overseas by UK-based companies.

Finally, most UK investors consider sterling to be their base currency. Whatever the time horizon of their investment strategy, their future liabilities are likely to be expressed in sterling terms. Both the portfolio theory and CAPM approaches to international investment should lead UK-based investors to hold a majority of non-sterling-denominated bonds or equities in portfolios which are optimal in terms of expected returns per unit of risk. This type of asset structure would expose the investors to significant exchange risks although, as we saw earlier in the chapter, investors who do not wish to bear the exchange risk inherent in overseas investment can, to a large extent, hedge this away, However, it is still the case that UK and other investors tend to keep a majority of their investments in securities

---

[25] Both the portfolio theory and CAPM extensions to an international contract can be applied to bonds as well as equities.

denominated in their base currency, applying integrated CAPM only to the funds which are not dedicated to domestic investments or adjusting the portfolio theory model to include a predetermined percentage of domestic security markets.

Summary

This chapter has looked at the advantages and disadvantages to the UK investor of international investment which has become an increasingly important part of stock market investment.

The major additional factor to be considered when investing in foreign currency securities is exchange risk, the risk that the return on investment, when converted back into sterling, will be different from expected, due to changes in exchange rates. Exchange risk can be partially hedged by using the spot and forward foreign exchange markets, both of which are efficient, or by borrowing the expected proceeds in the foreign currency. Forward rates are also the best available, albeit poor, estimates of future spot exchange rates.

Although the factors determining changes in exchange rates are as yet inadequately understood, two basic relationships ought to hold in a world with no barriers or costs to international trade. These are purchasing power parity and the International Fisher effect. If these hold, even if only in the long term and approximately, exchange risk is not as great as it originally appears. Also, because exchange rate movements and stock market returns are not significantly correlated, exchange risk is not a significant risk factor for international equity investment. The correlation between currency movements and bond market returns is more positive, making currency risk a more important element in international bond portfolios.

Exchange rate movements alter returns on overseas stock markets when expressed in sterling terms and this reduces the correlation of these returns with those of the UK stock market. As a result, investment in these overseas stock markets can substantially reduce the portfolio risk of a UK-based portfolio. This international extension of portfolio theory shows that, unless expected returns are *much* lower on overseas securities (due to transaction costs, taxes, or political risk), investors should not restrict themselves to domestic investment and should always take advantage of the increased returns and reduced risk available from internationally diversified portfolios determined from the investor's best estimates of expected returns, risks, and correlation coefficients allowing for exchange rate movements. An identical approach can be adopted for bond portfolios.

The CAPM, on the other hand, when applied to an international context, suggests a global index fund approach, with all investors (whatever their base currency and stock market) investing in each stock market in the world in proportion to its size. This passive approach to international investment is based on accepting the market consensus for the returns expected on each stock market.

It has now become common, particularly for UK investors who have a long tradition of overseas investment in bonds and equities, for investors to hold a significant proportion of their investment portfolios in international investments. Many countries are still limited in the proportion of non-domestic investments which they can hold but, as deregulation gathers pace, the trend towards increased international investment will accelerate. However, given that the currency of consumption for UK investors is the pound sterling, most investors will still choose to keep the majority of their investments in sterling-denominated securities.

Appendix: the euromarkets

Eurocurrency

A eurodollar bank deposit is simply dollars placed on deposit outside the US. It is exactly the same as a normal bank deposit except that it represents money placed outside the US national banking system.

This type of bank deposit was first developed during the 1950s and 1960s when dollars became available for lending outside the US for various reasons. For example, persistent US balance of payments deficits meant that there was a surplus of dollars held by other countries. Also, the US government chose to restrict the level of interest rates payable on dollar bank deposits placed in the US. Demand for these dollars offered outside the US came from US companies unable to borrow in the US to finance overseas expansion and from a general upsurge in international trade. Since these early days, the eurodollar market has grown dramatically and now includes other currencies such as euroyen, eurodeutschemarks and eurosterling. Eurocurrency is thus a general term for a currency available for lending in a centre which is not its home centre.

Borrowing and lending in eurocurrency constitutes what is known as an offshore banking system, in the sense that it is outside any national boundaries and unregulated by any national authorities. Despite its lack of a 'lender of last resort' (such as the Bank of England in the case of the UK banking system), the eurocurrency market has experienced very few defaults. London is the main centre with most major international banks in London being actively involved. Eurobonds, which are eurodollars or other eurocurrencies issued in the form of bonds other than bank loans, are described in the last Section of Chapter 4 on Fixed Interest Securities.

Eurobonds can have a range of maturities, with terms from, say, six to over fifteen years. Eurocurrency deposits are shorter-term than eurobonds with terms of up to one year although both deposits and loans can be 'rolled-over' to extend their maturity. For example, a eurodollar loan can have an overall maturity of five years, but the interest rate will be based on the three- or six-monthly eurodollar borrowing rate. So, every three or six months, the loan will be 'rolled-over' and the interest rate will change.

This very brief introduction to the euromarkets should be supplemented with further reading. For example, see Levi (1990) ch. 11.

Problems

1. Mr Brooks is trying to calculate the expected return in £ sterling from two investments, one in Etiquette plc, a UK company, and the other in Protocol Inc., a similar US company. The current share prices are 114p for Etiquette and $26 for Protocol and the prevailing £/$ exchange rate is £1 = $2.25.

   Mr Brooks has asked his stockbroker for advice on the likely dividends and future share prices for the two companies in exactly one year's time. He has been given the following estimates:

	Share price in one year's time	Dividend to be received in one year's time
Etiquette plc	120p	9p
Protocol Inc.	$28	$3

   The broker is unwilling to commit himself on the future exchange rate; he is only prepared to give the following probability distribution:

	Exchange rate in one year's time	Probability
	$1.50	0.2
	$2.00	0.2
£1 =	$2.50	0.3
	$3.00	0.3

   (i) Calculate the expected one-year sterling return for Mr Brooks on both Etiquette plc and Protocol Inc.
   (ii) If the most pessimistic exchange rate forecast turns out to be true, how much does Mr Brooks stand to lose in £ sterling if he invests £1,000 now in Protocol?
   (iii) If the expected earnings per share for Etiquette and Protocol are 12p

and $5.14 respectively, calculate the *PE* ratio, dividend yield and dividend cover for each company. Explain the meaning and relevance of each of these terms for investment decision-making and comment on the figures you have calculated for Protocol and Etiquette.

2. Miss King wishes to buy 100,000 shares in a US company, BBB Inc., which are currently quoted at $46 per share. She expects BBB to pay a dividend of $3 per share in three months' time and she wishes to sell the shares three months later for an expected price of $55. Miss King wishes to hedge exchange risk as much as possible and her bank has provided her with the following quotations. The bank also states that it will charge ¼% commission.

	£	$
Three-month eurocurrency rates (% p.a.)	11	9
Six-month eurocurrency rates (% p.a.)	12	9.5
Spot exchange rates	$1.50/£1	

(i) Does Miss King wish to buy or sell forward dollars?
(ii) Use the interest rate parity theory to determine the equilibrium three- and six-month forward rates.
(iii) Will the commission charged increase or decrease the number of $/£ in the transaction?
(iv) What return in sterling can Miss King expect to get and to what extent can she hedge exchange risk?

3. In January 1993 (when £1 = FFr 8.50), the inflation rate for 1993 expected in the UK was 5% and in France was 3%. Suppose the required real interest rate in both countries is 4%.
(i) Use the Fisher relation to estimate the nominal interest rates which will prevail in each country.
(ii) Use the purchasing power parity theory to determine the expected spot French franc/sterling exchange rate in one year's time.
(iii) Use the interest rate parity theory to estimate the one-year forward French franc forward rate.
(iv) Compare your estimate of the current forward rate with the expected spot rate in (ii). What does this imply about the need to hedge using the forward markets?

4. Describe the different ways in which an investor can invest internationally, and the advantages of each.

5. (i) What does the interest rate parity theory state? What are the implications for transactions in the forward foreign exchange and money markets?
(ii) Suppose you are a UK investor considering purchasing one of the following securities on 1 April 1992. Each security is redeemable at par on 30 September 1992, at which date the last semi-annual coupon is also payable.

Government bond	Coupon (%)	Nominal value	Price on 1 April 1992 (ex interest)	Spot exchange rate (FX/£)	Six-month forward exchange rate (FX/£)
US$	7	$100	$101.78	1.9470–1.9480	6.50–6.46 c pm
UK£	10	£100	£99.82	–	–
German DM	8	DM 1,000	DM 992	2.7950–2.8000	⅜–¼ pf pm

(a) If you wished to make a riskless investment, which security would you choose? Do your results comply with the interest rate parity theory?

(b) If, however, the securities do not mature on 30 September 1992, but have a ten-year life from 1 April 1992, what, if any, exchange risk would you incur by purchasing the US or German security?

6. Mr Crunch wishes to buy shares in a company in the food manufacturing industry. Mr Crunch's stockbroker advises either Beastly Biscuits in the UK or Weevil Wafers in Moldovia, both of which have the same beta in their respective markets. Mr Crunch expects to spend £1,000 on whichever shares he chooses and to hold them for one or three months. Neither share is expected to pay a dividend within the next three months. Mr Crunch's broker and a study of the *Financial Times* have provided the information in the table below.

(i) Calculate which of the four possible investments (Beastly Biscuits or Weevil Wafers for one or three months) offers the highest expected return, explaining your calculations. The Moldovian currency is the Liverwort (L).

(ii) State which investment opportunity you personally would choose, bearing in mind the advantages and disadvantages of overseas investment and the problems of comparing investments for different holding periods.

Shares	Current share price	Expected share price in	
		1 month	3 months
Weevil Wafers	L30	L32	L34
Beastly Biscuits	90p	95p	101p

Exchange and interest rates		1 month	3 months
Eurocurrency interest rates	L	17¼–17½%	17¹¹⁄₁₆–17¹⁵⁄₁₆%
	£	14¼–14⅝%	14¼–14½%

	Spot	1 month	3 months
Spot and forward rates L/£	1.7945–1.7955	0.45–0.55c dis	1.50–1.60c dis
		(≡ −3.34% p.a.)	(≡ −3.45% p.a.)

Investing institutions

Introduction

This chapter stands apart from the others in this book, in the sense that it is not directly concerned with how to value particular securities or with how to value an investment portfolio. It is concerned instead with a group of principal actors on the Stock Exchange investment stage, that is, with those financial institutions which are the major investors in Stock Exchange securities. No book on investment can ignore these institutions – pension funds, insurance companies, investment trusts and unit trusts – firstly, because they are the intermediaries through which the vast majority of people knowingly or unknowingly invest in stock market securities and, secondly, because their presence is now so major that every facet of investment, from performance measurement to the role of market makers and analysts, is affected by their existence.

The role of these institutions as major investors in Stock Exchange securities is clearly highlighted by their holdings of UK listed securities, as shown in Example 12.1.

Example 12.1   Investing institutions' ownership of UK gilts and equities, 1962–89*

	At end year: % held of total market value in issue			
	1957	*1967*	*1978*	*1989*
UK equities	19	31	47	58
UK gilts	17	27	46	52

*Investing institutions are defined to include pension funds, insurance companies, unit trusts and investment trusts.
Source: Wilson (1980) and various *Bank of England Quarterly Bulletins*.

The figures in Example 12.1 show the rapid growth in the holdings of the UK investing institutions over the past few decades. They now hold around 60% of UK equities compared with 47% in 1978 and a mere 19% in 1957. Their growth in control of the UK gilt market has been as rapid, with only 17% of gilts in issue in 1957 being held by investing institutions compared with over 50% by 1989. This growth, which represents a substantial increase in the assets of these institutions, for reasons which will be described later in the chapter, has led to their being the most powerful security holders in the stock market today.

Example 12.2 breaks the UK investing institutions down into the four main types – pension funds, insurance companies, unit trusts, and investment trusts – to show their relative importance as investors in UK equities in 1989.[1]

Example 12.2   Ownership of UK equities (as at 1989)

	% held
Pension funds	30.4
Insurance companies	18.4
Unit trusts	5.9
Investment trusts	3.2
	57.9
Personal sector	21.3
Overseas holders	12.4
Other	8.4
	100.0

Source: CSO, 1989 Share Register Survey.

---

[1] No later statistics are available although total figures of nearer 70% of UK equities held by UK investing institutions are often quoted in the press.

Pension funds and insurance companies are now the two major types of investing institution, with pension funds having overtaken insurance companies during the 1980s in terms of the value of the assets under their control. Investment trusts have suffered a decline relative to unit trusts as an investment medium for the personal investor due to the greater ability of unit trusts to market themselves via investment intermediaries such as insurance brokers.

Example 12.1 and 12.2 also document the simultaneous decline in importance in the stock market of the individual investor, a decline which is most marked in the context of UK equities. This decline was not reversed or even slowed by the major privatisations of the 1980s, in which shares in companies being denationalised, such as British Telecom, British Gas, and the water and electricity shares, were actively aimed at small investors in the declared aim of widening share ownership. Although the *number* of shareholders has gone up from 3 m. at the beginning of the 1980s to 11 m. by the end of the 1980s, the *percentage* in market value terms of equities held by individuals fell from 28% to 21% during that period.[2] However, as we saw in the introduction to Chapter 5, the individual investor has not abandoned Stock Exchange investment. He has merely moved from direct to indirect investment of his savings in quoted securities, either because he has had no choice, as in the case of an employee required to contribute to a pension fund, or because of the tax and other advantages of investment in, say, a long-term insurance savings policy.

This growth in the use of intermediaries for channelling private sector savings has many implications in the investment field. For example, there may be duplication of investment analysis by stockbrokers and the investment institutions. Also, there has been increased demand for the regulation of these intermediaries, which culminated in the Financial Services Act 1986, and for increased performance measurement. A private investor who deals direct with a stockbroker, and listens to his advice without having to take it, is largely responsible for his own investment decisions. An investor in a pension fund, on the other hand, transfers the responsibility for investment decisions to a thirdy party for a long period of time. As a result, he will wish to know that the intermediary is not likely to commit fraud – hence the demand for regulation – and is competent – hence the demand for performance measurement. However, the discovery in 1991 of fraud in the pension funds of companies controlled by Robert Maxwell has shown that there are still major problems associated with the dominant role of investment institutions as intermediaries which have not been solved by the regulatory framework introduced in the 1980s.

The influence and scope of these institutions has to a certain extent taken the City and the government by surprise. For example, Harold Wilson, in the parliamentary debate following the publication of the Wilson Report

---

[2] See the Stock Exchange *Quality of Markets Review* (Summer 1991).

on Financial Institutions published in 1980, referred to 'the pension fund revolution having occurred with no formal notice, and without debate or decision in this House'. One of the points made by the Wilson Committee, of which he was the chairman, was the lack of accountability of the pension funds to their beneficiaries, despite the volume of assets under their control. In 1980, pension funds controlled assets of approximately £55b, and yet many did not provide annual reports and accounts to present or future pensioners. Despite these warning signals, by 1991 pension funds controlled £357b. of assets and were still regulated by an archaic trust deed mechanism, which failed to stop fraud on a massive scale by Robert Maxwell and fraud on a less dramatic but nonetheless tragic scale in a number of other sizeable pension funds.

The increase in importance of both pension funds and life assurance companies as investment institutions has been largely the result of active government encouragement. Life assurance companies benefitted from major tax advantages attached to life assurance policies until 1984 in the form of full tax relief at the marginal income tax rate on life assurance contributions; since that date, there are still certain advantages for particular types of life assurance savings schemes, particularly for the higher rate taxpayer. Life assurance companies also still benefit from less stringent constraints of marketing – they are allowed to employ salesmen who can 'cold call' potential policyholders at home. These advantages date from the days when pension schemes were not widespread and pension benefits, such as they were, did not provide an adequate retirement income individuals catered for their own retirement through savings schemes related to life insurance and, to encourage this, the government accorded tax relief and marketing advantages for such investments.

Despite the reduction in tax incentives for individuals to save via life assurance policies, life assurance companies have continued to grow, this time helped by the government offering financial incentives to encourage private sector pension schemes. Since 1975, when legislation was introduced in the Social Security Pensions Act, companies have been obliged to either contract into the state scheme, SERPS,[3] for their employees, or to provide their own scheme. These privately organised pension schemes are either run as pension funds separate from the company or managed by a bank or an insurance company on behalf of the company. In 1986, the Social Security Act also allowed employees (as well as the self-employed) to take out personal pension plans which are tied to the individual rather than to the company for which he works. At the same time, they offered financial incentives for employees to switch out of the state scheme, SERPS, into private sector schemes. This gave a boost to life assurance companies who are the main providers of personal pension plans.

---

[3] State Earnings Related Pension Scheme (different from the basic state pension scheme which pays a fixed pension regardless of income).

Thus, as pension schemes have spread and as benefits and hence contributions have been increased, so the assets of the pension funds (and insurance companies) have grown. Since contributions to pension schemes are tax-deductible and the returns on investments made by pension funds are not liable to tax, 'investment' in a pension fund can offer a more tax-efficient method of saving to the individual investor than does direct investment in Stock Exchange securities.

Unit trusts and investment trusts, on the other hand, did not develop as tax-efficient forms of saving for retirement. They were set up to offer small investors a way of holding a stake in a diversified portfolio of fixed interest securities and ordinary shares, an opportunity which was otherwise unavailable (without high transaction costs). Perhaps because unit and investment trusts have not had the same advantages of government support as insurance companies and pension funds, and also because investment trusts (as limited liability companies) have had to comply with company disclosure requirements, a greater tradition of disclosure of investment policy and investment performance has been established for these types of intermediary. For example, both the Unit Trust Association and the Association of Investment Trust Companies publish *Year Books* giving brief details of the past performance and the spread of investments of each unit or investment trust.

The next section of the chapter considers each of the four main types of investing institution – pension funds, insurance companies, unit trusts and investment trusts – in more detail. A brief description of each type of institution will be given, how it arose, what its investment objectives are, and how these determine its investment strategy. The final part of the chapter will be devoted to a discussion of the main areas of investment which have been affected by the growth of these investment institutions, for example the efficiency of the stock market, the role of stockbrokers and market makers, regulation, and, last but not least, the impact on the individual investor.

Pension funds

The growth of the pension funds has been the fastest of the four investing institutions, rising from £2b. of assets invested in 1957 to approximately £302b. at the end of 1990, equivalent to over 16% annual average growth in nominal terms or 8% annual average growth in *real* terms. The net new inflow of cash in 1990 to be invested was £19.2b. and is still rising. Unfortunately, one of the problems in talking about the pension funds and their investments is the lack of data concerning them. One reason for this is that, as we saw above, pension funds are not accountable to their beneficiaries in the same way as investment trusts are to their shareholders and, to date, the level of disclosure of pension funds does not reflect the volume of funds under their control.

This rapid increase in pension assets, whether controlled by insurance companies or pension funds, is due, as we have already seen, to the extension of pension fund schemes to a greater proportion of the working population as a result of legislation, to higher earnings and benefits requiring greater contributions, to fiscal incentives offered by the government, and to the rise in the value of assets already managed, particularly during the bull markets of the 1980s.

The way in which a pension fund works is as follows. The employer and, in many cases, the employees of an organisation pay contributions into a separate pension fund. This usually operates as a legal trust, with the present and future pensioners as beneficiaries. The trustees, made up of representatives from management and the current employees, invest the contributions to provide pensions as required by the terms of the trust. Pension funds are designed so that contributions from employees and the employer plus the income flow from the assets already held can meet the future pension payments. The amounts contributed by employees are usually fixed at a percentage of salary. The amounts contributed by the employer are determined by an actuary, bearing in mind the pensions promised, the characteristics of the workforce (with respect to age, sex, leaving rates, retirement ages, and so on), and the expected returns on the investment of the contributions over time.

Thus, the actuary has to be an expert in investment as well as in such matters as expected labour turnover and death rates. Actuaries will vary in their estimates of future cash flows according, for example, to the return they expect to be achieved from the pension fund investments over the next ten or twenty years. The more conservative the actuary's estimates of future returns on investment, the higher will be the employer's contributions to the pension fund. Less conservative actuaries will require lower contributions in the early years of the fund, with a higher probability that the employer will have to 'top up' the fund in later years. Although employers are not required by law to take the advice of their actuaries, it is usual for them to do so.

One of the consequences of the bull equity markets of the 1980s was the rapid rise in the value of pension fund assets (which were predominantly in equities) and the creation of a surplus of the present value of the assets in the fund over the present value of the liabilities of the fund. Indeed, in some cases, for example that of Dunlop, the pension fund became so large that it was worth more than the company itself! This led to some takeovers of companies (for example, BTR acquired Dunlop) where the acquirer was able to use the pension fund surplus to reduce future pension contributions and thus boost earnings after the acquisition. Indeed, in some cases, the acquirer was able to close the pension fund down, move the employees to their own scheme, and take the surplus out as a reduction to the cost of the acquisition. In fear of this, many UK companies then declared pension contribution holidays themselves, reducing the cash inflows to pension funds from their previously high levels.

Up to now, we have been describing what is known as a 'defined benefits' type of pension scheme. This is a fund which promises the employee a fixed percentage of final salary for every year of service. An alternative type of scheme, offered by smaller companies and used for personal plans, is the 'defined contributions' pension scheme. With this, the contributions are invested by the pension fund manager as for the defined benefits schemes, but no promise is made as to the size of the future pension; this is determined by the rate of return achieved on the contributions and so, by definition, there can be no surplus.

Before we go on to discuss the investment objectives and policies of pension funds, it is useful to note that pensions do not have to be provided for via funded pension schemes, as is the norm in the UK and the US. For example, in France and Germany, UK-style pension funds are unheard of and an Appendix to this chapter describes the mechanisms used in other countries to provide pensions. However, the trend is definitely towards the model of a separate, funded pension scheme and there is rapid growth world-wide in pension fund assets.

Investment objectives and policy

Given that pensions in the UK are usually funded through a separate pension fund, how are the contributions invested to provide in the best manner possible for future pension liabilities? What factors do pension fund managers take into consideration when making investment decisions?

One of the most contentious areas of pension fund management is how to decide on the objectives and policy of the pension fund. This is because there are a number of interested parties: shareholders, managers, trustees, employees, pensioners, actuaries, and fund managers, some of whom may be taking on more than one role.

Although they may all have the underlying objective for the fund of being able to pay pensions as and when required, they may have conflicting views on what the pension fund's investment objectives ought to be to do just that. In other words, given the future liabilities of the pension fund, how should its asset structure be determined and what level of risk should be assumed? For example, managers may wish to maximise the returns on the fund so that any surpluses made can be paid back to the company to boost earnings for shareholders. Owner-shareholders may wish to use the pension fund assets to finance the purchase of a luxurious head office.

Trustees may wish to meet the liabilities of the fund with the minimum of risk. Alternatively, fund managers may have the investment objective of outperforming other pension fund managers to improve their ratings. In practice, although trustees have the power to determine investment policy, they may have no expertise in this area and defer to the advice of consultants, actuaries, or fund managers responsible for the implementation of the investment policies and the management of the funds on a day-to-day basis.

(i) LIABILITIES

Pension funds have very long-term liabilities. For example, an employee joining a company at the age of twenty will not in general become eligible for a pension for a further forty or forty-five years. We saw in Chapter 2 that one way of reducing risk is to 'match' assets and liabilities; so, if, say, a pension liability will fall due in twenty years' time, an asset can be bought which will also mature in twenty years' time and which will exactly cover the liability. It is thus likely that pension funds, with substantial long-term liabilities, will hold long-term assets. For example, as can be seen in Example 12.3, in so far as pension funds hold gilts, these are long-term, that is, gilts with maturities of at least fifteen years or undated gilts. Note that the statistics for pension funds in Example 12.3 include figures for the three main groups of pension funds – local authorities, other public sector (mostly nationalised industries) and private sector (mostly companies).

However, this risk reduction strategy only works if the liabilities and the assets are subject to the same economic effects. If, for example, a liability is fixed in real terms and the matching asset is fixed in nominal terms, there is a risk that the asset will not be worth enough in real terms to match the liability. Corporate pensions in the UK are usually linked to final salaries, and final salaries are linked to earnings.[4]

Over the past 25 years, earnings have grown by an average of 2.5% over the rate of inflation. So, by investing in gilts, pension funds run the risk of not earning a high enough real rate of return, particularly if inflation is higher than expected over the investment period. This is why pension funds have been substantial investors in index-linked gilts since they were first issued in 1981, since they offer *guaranteed* real rates of return of 2–4%, enough to meet the liabilities of final salary-related future pensions.

Another consequence of the need to match assets with liabilities which are increasing with inflation has been a search for assets which are seen to be hedges against inflation. One such type of asset is property, and this performed well in the 1970s when gilts were earning negative real rates of

---

[4] Increases in pensions, however, once started, are *not* linked to earnings and may not even keep up with the rate of inflation.

Example 12.3 Portfolio holdings of investing institutions

(End 1991*) (£b., % in brackets)	Pension funds		Insurance companies General		Long-term		Unit trusts		Investment trusts	
Short-term assets	21.6	(7.1)	5.9	(15.7)	15.7	(6.8)	2.6	(4.8)	1.7	(6.6)
UK gilts										
M† ≤ 5	1.2	(0.4)	2.9	(7.6)	1.8	(0.8)	0.5	(0.9)	0.4	(1.6)
5 < M ≤ 15	12.7	(4.2)	2.5	(6.7)	18.5	(8.0)				
M > 15	4.3	(1.4)	0.1	(0.3)	7.1	(3.1)				
Index-linked	9.8	(3.2)	–	–	3.8	(1.6)				
	27.9	(9.2)	5.5	(14.6)	31.1	(13.5)	0.5	(0.9)	0.4	(1.6)
Ordinary shares										
UK	142.1	(46.9)	7.9	(21.1)	81.0	(35.1)	29.6	(54.9)	11.6	(44.5)
Overseas	47.5	(15.7)	2.1	(5.7)	19.2	(8.3)	18.2	(33.8)	9.8	(37.5)
	189.6	62.6	10.0	(26.8)	100.1	(43.4)	47.8	(88.7)	21.4	(82.0)
Other securities										
UK	6.3	(2.1)	2.0	(5.4)	13.3	(5.8)	1.5	(2.8)	0.9	(3.5)
Overseas	7.0	(2.3)	3.8	(10.2)	5.8	(2.5)	0.8	(1.5)	1.1	(4.1)
	13.3	(4.4)	5.8	(15.6)	19.2	(8.3)	2.3	(4.3)	2.0	(7.6)
Unit trust units‡	5.8	(1.9)	0.2	(0.6)	21.1	(9.1)	–	–	0.3	(1.1)
Loans and mortgages	0.3	(0.1)	1.9	(5.0)	7.3	(3.2)	–	–	–	–
Land, property and ground rents	26.4	(8.7)	3.8	(10.2)	35.1	(15.2)	–	–	–	–
Agents' balances	–	–	3.7	(10.0)	0.7	(0.3)	0.5	(1.0)	0.1	(0.4)
Other‡	17.8	(5.9)	0.5	(1.4)	0.5	(0.2)	0.1	(0.3)	0.2	(0.7)
TOTAL	302.7	(100.0)	37.3	100.0	230.8	100.0	53.9	100.0	26.1	100.0

* Pension funds and insurance companies at end 1990.
† Maturity in years of gilts.
‡ Of which, for pension funds, £1.656b. was in property unit trusts.
⁺ Including, for pension funds, £10.778b. investment in insurance-managed funds.
Source: CSO, Business Monitor.

return in a high inflation environment. By 1980, pension funds held 18% of their assets in property. However, property became unpopular in the 1980s when it failed to act as an inflation hedge *and* it underperformed equities as an asset class, and by 1990, it represented only 9% of pension fund assets.

As can be seen in Example 12.3 the emphasis in UK pension fund portfolios is on equities, which represented 63% of pension fund assets in 1990. The attraction of equities is that, of all the securities available for investment, only equities are likely to increase at a substantial real rate of return, approximately equal to GNP growth. So, whereas actuaries will phrase a pension fund's objectives in terms of the need to achieve a certain real rate of return, trustees may ask fund managers to try and match a stock market index, such as the FT-Actuaries All-Share Index. The implicit assumption is that share prices will match GNP growth, providing a growth pattern to match that of the liabilities, and hence that the fund will be able to meet pension payments in the future.

Of the 63% invested in equities by UK pension funds, 47% is invested in UK equities and the remaining 16% in overseas equities. One of the arguments raised against pension funds investing overseas (apart from the political question of whether pension funds ought to invest for the good of the economy[5]) is that UK pension funds are expressed in sterling terms and that assets denominated in foreign currencies cannot be matched to these liabilities because of exchange risk. However, as was discussed in Chapter 11, exchange risk is not as substantial as it first appears and the benefits of international diversification more than outweigh the added exchange risk on only part of a large portfolio.

(ii) TAX

As already mentioned, pension funds are exempt from income and corporation tax on their investments.[6] This also now includes futures and options insofar as they are used for hedging rather than trading purposes. Thus, pension funds should be indifferent, other things being equal, between high- and low-coupon gilts and between dividends and capital gains on shares. Of course, other factors will influence the decision on which securities to choose but, unlike the individual investor with a high marginal tax rate, pension funds need not, in principle, take tax into account when making investment decisions. However, in practice, gilt prices will reflect

---

[5] This issue was raised in a famous court case between trustees appointed by the National Union of Mineworkers and trustees appointed by the National Coal Board in 1984. The union-appointed trustees argued against international investment; academic expert witnesses put the case for portfolio theory in an international context. The academics won.

[6] Except that withholding taxes on income from overseas investment may not be recoverable.

Example 12.4   Effect of tax on choice of gilts

Gilt	Coupon paid annually (%)	Price £	One-year net holding period return to pension fund (%)	One-year net holding period return to 40% tax-payer (%)
A	3	94	9.6	8.3
B	12	101	10.9	6.1

the *net* yields available to investors with different tax rates and so certain gilts will be attractive to 'gross' pension funds in exactly the same way as other gilts will be attractive to taxpaying investors. For example, Example 12.4 shows two one-year gilts (for simplicity) offering different *net* returns according to the tax rate of the investor. (Remember that no capital gains tax is payable if the gilts are held for a year and a day, as we assume here.)

The taxpayer with a marginal rate of 40% would prefer the low-coupon gilt *A* whereas the pension fund would prefer the 12% gilt *B*. This is because the tax advantages of the low-coupon gilt for high-rate taxpayers have led to its offering a lower gross yield of 9.6% than the high-coupon gilt's yield of 10.9%.

As far as dividend yield and capital gains on shares are concerned, pension funds do not appear to be indifferent between them. They seem to prefer dividends, judging from their protests when major companies cut their dividends in the recessionary years of 1991 and 1992. This preference for dividends could be because dividends provide fund managers who may have limited cash inflows with cash to invest in new shares without having to incur transaction costs by selling existing share holdings. Pension funds also like dividends for tax reasons: since they are non-taxpayers, they can reclaim the tax credit paid by the company in the form of Advanced Corporation Tax (ACT) to the Inland Revenue. However, paying dividends when profits and cash flow are suffering is onerous for companies; it may take years for them to be able to reclaim the ACT against mainstream tax liabilities. Finally, one more factor which may affect pension funds' predilection for dividends: if neither an interim nor a final dividend is paid in any one financial year, the ordinary shares of that company cannot be held by pension funds governed by the Trustee Investments Act 1961.[7]

---

[7] See section (iv) below on asset mix for further requirements under this Act. However, most pension fund trusts view the requirements of the Trustee Investments Act 1961 as too onerous and are exempt.

(iii) TIMING AND SELECTION

Employee and employer contributions represent a form of contractual saving, certainly from the employee's point of view. The employee has no choice as to where his contributions are invested nor can he usually decide how much to contribute; his payments are automatically deducted from his pay. This enables the pension fund manager to be more or less certain of how much new money he will have to invest each month or quarter.[8] This regular inflow of new money has two effects on investment strategy. Firstly, it allows the investment manager to alter the balance of his portfolio with the new money, without having to sell part of his existing holdings. This should lead to lower portfolio turnover and transaction costs than, say, investment trusts, which have no regular new inflow of funds. Secondly, the pension fund manager can follow, if he so wishes, a form of investment strategy, known as 'pound averaging'. By spreading the purchases of securities over the peaks and troughs of the market, the pension fund manager can ensure that the average cost of these securities will be at their average prices, rather than at their peak prices, over a period. In practice, pension funds may not do this, preferring instead to keep the new money in cash until they judge that the moment is right for investment in shares or gilts, whatever the efficient markets hypothesis may say.

For example, with the Japanese stock market falling over 60% from its all-time high in 1990 to the end of 1992, pension fund managers were reluctant to use pound averaging as forecasters predicted yet further falls. However, there is little evidence that pension fund managers are good at picking just the right moment to get in or out of a market. For example, pension funds in general withheld from investment in ordinary shares during the fourth quarter of 1974, despite the fact that shares were at what was in retrospect a fifteen-year low. Similarly, before the Crash of 1987, they had the highest ever proportion of equities in their portfolios at over 85%, compared with an average during the five previous years of 63%.

(iv) ASSET MIX

The trust deed of a pension fund usually allows for the overall investment policy to be left to the discretion of the trustees, in consultation with the company and the investment advisers. A few trust deeds make no specific statement on investment policy and, in these cases, the trustees must conform to the investment policy laid down in the Trustee Investments Act 1961, which, amongst other things, restricts investments to at least 50% in fixed interest stock (excluding preference shares) and up to 50% in ordi-

---

[8] Unless a pension fund contribution or early retirement scheme is suddenly announced.

nary and preference shares, shares in building societies and units in authorised unit trusts. Another constraint on pension funds governed by the Trustee Investments Act is that they cannot invest directly in real property.

The investment policy will usually be concerned with the asset mix, that is, the proportions which can be invested in each type of security, and possibly a list of approved securities. Day-to-day decisions will be taken by the pension fund managers who can be employees of the company, or may be financial institutions such as merchant banks or insurance companies. The pension funds managed by insurance companies will usually not be in the form of a trust fund but in the form of a contract between the company and the insurance company. In these cases, the insurance company will normally have discretion over the investment policy.

The traditional view on asset mix in periods of low inflation, reflected in the Trustee Investments Act 1961, was that it was advisable to place the bulk of the funds in fixed interest securities such as gilts. As the rate of inflation increased in the 1960s and 1970s, asset mixes were adjusted to allow higher proportions to be invested in equities and property, which, as mentioned earlier, were viewed as better inflation hedges. By the 1980s, property had become unpopular as an inflation hedge and the cult of the equity had taken over. It became the norm for pension funds to place the bulk of their investments into both UK and overseas shares. Even the Crash of 1987 did not dent their enthusiasm; pension funds still held 68% of equities in their portfolios (of which 16% were overseas shares) at the end of 1988 and the percentage was back up to 74% (with 20% in overseas shares) by the end of 1991 – despite the Japanese market crash.

A common way of deciding on the asset mix, taking the impact of inflation into account, is to fund the liabilities which have crystallised, such as the future pensions of employees who have left (whose pensions will be based on their known leaving salaries) with assets having future values fixed in nominal terms – usually gilts – and to fund the uncertain future liabilities with assets which should maintain their value in real terms – usually equities. This method of determining the optimal asset mix appears to ignore the implications of the capital asset pricing model (CAPM), which suggest that the equity portfolio should approximate as nearly as possible to the market portfolio, and that the amount of fixed interest securities held should not be related to the ratio of known to unknown liabilities but rather to the required level of risk of the fund.

However, before the optimal level of risk in the fund and, hence, the optimal asset mix can be determined, the question must be asked as to who will benefit or suffer from the risks and returns of the pension fund portfolio. If, as is most common for company pension schemes, pension benefits are fixed in relation to final earnings, the company will benefit from good performance by being able to make reduced contributions in the future, and correspondingly suffer from poor performance by being asked to make increased contributions in the future.[9] So, in the cases where pension rights are linked to salary and not pension fund performance, the risk that the assets of the pension fund will be less than or greater than its liabilities will be felt more by the shareholders of the company than by the legal beneficiaries of the fund.

Given that, in these instances, the shareholders of the company may be more concerned with the risk and return of the pension fund than are the pensioners, the question of optimal asset mix should perhaps be considered from the shareholders' point of view. For example, it is likely that when the stock market as a whole does badly, and hence the pension fund's equity portfolio suffers, the company will be required to top up its contributions at a time when it, too, is suffering and is least able to do so. In this way, equities in a pension fund portfolio will increase the volatility of the company's earnings and hence the risk borne by the shareholders of the company. In contrast, fixed interest investments in the portfolio would reduce this risk without affecting the pensioners' *expected* benefits. So, by considering who actually benefits or suffers from pension fund performance in the long term, we may reach a different view of what constitutes the optimal asset mix from that usually held. Instead of investing in risky equities and property, perhaps pension fund managers should be concentrating on investing in lower risk fixed interest securities. However, this brings us back to the inadequacy of most fixed interest investments as matches of liabilities growing in real terms.

Where pension rights *are* linked to fund performance (that is, where pensions are increased when the fund does well and vice versa), it will be the beneficiaries of the pension fund who suffer or benefit from the risk and return of the pension fund portfolio. This is the case for personal pension plans managed by an insurance company or other fund manager; in this case, the future pensioner has to trust the fund manager to decide whether the level of risk is appropriate for him. In many cases, the individual can choose which types of investments to invest in, by selecting index-linked gilt funds, Japanese equity funds, and so on. The danger here is that the individual does not understand the level of risk which he is bearing and does not realise the benefits of having more than one portable pension scheme when he, rather than the company, is taking the risk of the final outcome not being as high as expected.

A similar dilemma arises when we consider how the risk of the pension fund portfolio should be measured. In Chapter 2, we chose to measure the riskiness of securities and portfolios by their standard deviations, whereas, in Chapter 9, we saw that, according to the CAPM, investors are only

---

[9] It is worth noting that a company is not *legally* bound to follow an actuary's recommendation to make good any deficit which may occur (based on the actuary's valuation of the assets and liabilities of the fund at a given date) although, provided the company is solvent, it is usual for the company to do so.

rewarded for the beta element of risk in their portfolios, due to the fact that the remaining risk of their portfolios can largely be diversified away. Applying this approach to the pension fund problem, if the shareholders of the company effectively bear the portfolio risk, the pension fund's beta will be the appropriate measure of risk, since it can be assumed that the shareholders hold these shares as part of a diversified portfolio. However, if the pensioners bear the risk, as they may do in the case of personal pensions, where their pensions are linked to the fund's performance, it must be remembered that the assets of the pension fund probably represent the major portion of their savings, especially if they are not home owners. In this case, the standard deviation, as a measure of *total* risk, may be a more appropriate measure of risk. As we shall see in Chapter 13, a risk measure appropriate to the persons at risk must be chosen before any comparable estimates of performance can be made.

Before any conclusions concerning optimal asset mix or suitable measures of risk can be drawn, it must be said that the whole area of what the financial objectives of the pension fund should be in practice is tied up with the present uncertainty as to who is responsible for pension fund deficits and who owns any pension fund surpluses. The Maxwell pension fund enquiry has led to acceptance of the need to revise the trust law basis of pension funds and to clarify responsibilities, articulate objectives and report pension fund performance to the present and future pensioners.

Insurance companies

We now turn to the second most important type of investing institution, insurance companies. UK insurance companies had assets of £4.9b. in 1957 (they were then twice the size of pension funds) compared with £268b. in 1990 (10% smaller than pension funds), with a substantial percentage related to pension fund business.

The benefits of reducing risk through pooling by an insurance company are clear. We saw, in Chapter 8, that if the independent risks of an event occurring are pooled, the combined risk is less than if the risks were separately borne. For example, the risk of a house being burgled is usually independent of the risk of other houses being burgled and is fairly easily quantified by looking at past experience.[10] Now, if an insurance company

---

[10] One type of insurance which does *not* fit this description is mortgage indemnity insurance, where insurance companies protect *lenders* against defaults on their mortgages. In this case, the risks of different individuals defaulting *are* linked through the impact of the recession on incomes and house prices. Also, before the early 1990s, there was no past experience of major price falls. This combination of factors led insurance companies to lose substantial amounts on this type of insurance during 1991 and 1992.

can take on several thousand house contents policies, it can be reasonably certain of the percentage of claims on those policies and the premium charged can take account of the fact that the risk borne by each individual house owner has been reduced through pooling. Of course, the insurance company will need to cover expenses and, if it is profit-making,[11] will require a return for its shareholders. So, the premium charged will not reflect the entire statistical benefit of pooling.

As well as carrying out an insurance role, some insurance companies have evolved as investment intermediaries. This is partly because of the nature of life *a*ssurance,[12] where the policyholder seeks to protect his dependents from financial loss caused by his premature death whilst also seeking to provide for his old age. Most life policies provide benefit on expiry of the term of the policy, say after 10 or 20 years, or on earlier death. This contrasts with non-life policies, where no benefit is paid if the event does not occur during the life of the policy. So, life assurance policies can vary from pure term *in*surance which only pays out if death occurs during the policy's term to long-term savings schemes with an element of insurance attached to provide the benefits earlier in the event of premature death.

The activities of insurance companies can thus be split into two – general business and long-term business.[13] To give an idea of their relative sizes, insurance companies held assets related to general insurance of £37b. in 1990 compared with £231b. for long-term business. Many insurance companies carry out both activities, indeed most large UK insurance companies are what is known as 'composites', although some choose to specialise in general or life business. However, whether specialist or composite, insurance companies are required by law to manage and report the two activities separately, to prevent cross-funding of two basically very different types of business.

General insurance

In this field, which includes household and motor insurance, policies are usually taken out for periods of one year at a time. Claims related to these policies are mostly settled fairly quickly, reducing the insurance compa-

---

[11] Mutual insurance companies aim to distribute profits by way of reduced premiums or, in the case of with profits life policies, through increased bonuses. For this type of insurance company, the policyholders can be regarded as shareholders.

[12] The term *a*ssurance is used where a benefit is *always* going to be paid (for example, if not on death then on expiry of the policy), as opposed to *in*surance where a benefit is only paid *if* an event such as a theft occurs.

[13] Long-term business includes life assurance, pensions business, insurance-related long-term savings policies, and long-term sickness insurance.

nies' ability to build up long-term reserves except out of profit.[14] Also, the funds held to meet these claims have to be in fairly liquid form. Thus, in Example 12.3, p. 359, we can see that 16% of the total assets related to general insurance business were held in cash or near-cash in 1990 compared with an equivalent figure of 7% for long-term business. Similarly, the gilts held for general business were of shorter maturity than for long-term business. Nevertheless, substantial long-term investments, in the form of equities and property holdings, are held by insurance companies to back the risks of general insurance.

Long-term funds

This is mostly life assurance and pension-related business. Since we have already looked at pension funds in the previous section, we concentrate here on life assurance savings-related business. The UK is one of the most heavily 'life-assured' markets in the world with almost 80m policies outstanding in 1992, representing three to four policies per household.[15] The reasons for the success of the life assurance industry in the UK are the aggressive sales techniques adopted and the success in linking life assurance to savings policies attached to mortgages or pensions.

Life assurance policies range from straightforward annuity business (where regular savings or a lump sum entitle the policyholder to an annuity in the future) through to 'with profits' policies where life assurance is only a small element of the policy and the bulk of the premiums are invested in stock market securities on the policyholder's behalf.

Given the long-tern nature of life assurance policies and of the pensions business carried out by insurance companies, funds need to be invested by the insurance companies for long periods of time. If we look at Example 12.3, we can see that this is reflected in the type of securities held for long-term business. For example, in 1990, 43% of total assets were invested in equities and a further 15% in property and land. Similarly, the gilts held were mostly those with a maturity of at least five years.

Investment objectives and policy

In the same way as for pension funds, we now examine in more detail the factors affecting the investment decisions of insurance companies.

---

[14] However, some claims, such as those associated with the Piper Alpha North Sea oil rig disaster of 1988, would take much longer to settle.

[15] However, this does include the new personal pension plans.

(i) LIABILITIES

Originally, insurance companies concentrated on offering fixed benefits from long-term savings plans, for example a fixed lump sum or an agreed annuity. The maturities of these policies could be matched with those of long-term, fixed-interest securities, notably gilts, enabling the insurance companies to provide benefits fixed in nominal terms (subject only to the risk of changes in interest rates at which premiums and coupons on the securities could be reinvested). One way to reduce interest rate risk to a minimum is to 'immunise' the investment portfolio. This can be done by matching the duration of the assets to the duration of the liabilities. By doing so, the insurance company is sure of being able to meet its future liabilities whether interest rates go up, stay the same, or go down.[16]

An extreme version of duration matching is cash flow matching, where every coupon and principal repayment of every bond is chosen to exactly match a particular cash flow payment on policies. A less onerous version is simply to ensure that the average durations of the assets and liabilities match, without making the cash flows exactly match. This type of risk reduction exploits the fact that duration takes into account the coupon and life of every bond to work out its likely price movement given an interest change. It does the same for a bond portfolio. Thus, provided the estimated change in present value on the bond portfolio for a given change in interest rates is matched by the estimated change in the present value of the liabilities for the same interest rate change, the insurance company will be able to meet its liabilities.

Fixed benefit savings plans became less popular during the 1960s and 1970s, as inflation began to erode the value of the fixed benefits when received. So, in the 1980s, insurance companies began to market more 'with profits' policies linked primarily to equity rather than fixed interest securities, since equities were perceived to be a better long-run hedge against inflation. It must be remembered that insurance companies act predominantly as intermediaries for the savings elements of these policies, passing on the majority of the investment risks to the policyholders. If they cannot immunise their liabilities through duration matching, insurance companies prefer not to commit themselves on the actual benefits to be paid, usually guaranteeing only a low fixed benefit plus a bonus related to 'investment performance' – a 'with profits' policy.

There are two types of 'with profits' policy: 'endowment' and 'unit-linked'. Endowment policies are sold every year and the funds invested in a large pool. Each year a certain number of the endowment policies mature and a terminal bonus is declared. The size of this bonus is a function of how well the fund has done over the past few years and of how competitive the market for life assurance is. The more competitive the market, the higher

---

[16] For a quick revision of the duration of fixed interest securities, see Chapter 4, pp. 98–103.

the terminal bonus will be in order to draw in new business. However, the major effect of the insurance company having the right to decide on the terminal bonus is to smooth the bonuses over time. If a policy matures in a bull market, the payout will not be as high as that on a unit-linked policy which is a direct function of the value of the units on maturity; if a policy matures in a bear market, the endowment policyholder should do better than the unit-linked holder whose payout will reflect depressed shares prices. In other words, unit-linked holders bear more risk than endowment policyholders who share market risk with other endowment policyholders over time.

However, although primarily invested in equities, many of the 'with profits' policies still retain some gilts for diversification and risk reduction purposes. Annuity policy premiums are entirely invested in gilts with suitable maturities. As a result, a higher proportion of the long-term business liabilities of insurance companies is invested in gilts than is the case for pension funds, less of whose liabilities are fixed in nominal terms and who have a more aggressive approach to equity investment to meet their longer-term liabilities.

(ii) TAX

Both types of insurance, general and long-term, are taxed on their profits, essentially defined to be income including investment profits less expenditure including management charges. However, the tax on long-term business is complex, varying according to whether it is pension (tax exempt), with profits, or annuity business. The standard rate of corporation tax, currently 33%, is charged on long-term business unless the profits relate to investments destined for policyholders, in which case it is reduced to the current basic rate of 25%.

This tax treatment for life assurance business has two effects. Firstly, insurance companies, because they *do* pay tax, are not generally 'gross' investors like the pension funds (except on pensions business). Secondly, the effect of investors choosing to invest via life assurance-linked savings schemes is that the tax advantage of so doing is less than investing via a 'gross' pension scheme, but superior to investing via a unit or investment trust. This is because payouts on 'qualifying'[17] insurance policies, for example, are exempt from income tax in the hands of the recipient – since the insurance company is already deemed to have paid tax, and this advantage will be particularly beneficial to a higher-rate taxpayer. In practice, the relative tax advantages of each form of indirect investment are not easy to calculate, but it has been estimated that if unit-linked life

---

[17] To qualify, the policy has to have a life of at least ten years, with at least annual premiums, and the amount insured must be equal to a certain percentage of the premiums paid.

assurance profits were taxed in the hands of the insurance companies in the same way as unit trusts are taxed on the income from their investments, the tax burden on the insurance company profits might increase by as much as 25%.[18]

(iii) LEGISLATION

The insurance industry is heavily controlled by law, as evidenced, for example, by the careful separation of general and long-term business. The aim of the legislation is to try to prevent insurance companies from being unable to meet claims and to minimise the risk of fraud, a potential problem with any form of investment intermediary, particularly one which has control of the policyholders' funds for ten years or more.

For example, UK insurance companies involved in *general* business are required to maintain certain solvency margins (expressed as a percentage of net assets to net premiums written). UK legislation does not specify exactly which type of securities insurance companies must hold, in contrast to a number of countries including the US where insurance companies are restricted predominantly to fixed interest securities. This restriction does not, however, prevent problems since US insurers were big investors in property and junk bonds during the 1980s, which caused some insurance companies to declare bankruptcy.

In the UK, during the 1970s and 1980s, insurance companies found that nominal premiums and claims were increasing by more than the rate of inflation. They therefore tried to ensure that the market value of their assets also increased, in order for solvency margins to be maintained and to allow them to expand as they wished. As a result, they switched emphasis from fixed interest securities to investments such as equities more likely to maintain their value in real terms. However, too great a dependence on risky assets increases the probability of reduced solvency margins and this caused some insurance companies to switch emphasis from equities back to bonds in 1992.

In terms of profits, general insurance companies depend to a great extent on their returns from investment to make a profit. Underwriting losses (from claims exceeding premiums paid) can be more than offset by profits generated by good management of the premiums invested. Portfolio performance can make all the difference between a profit-making and loss-making general insurance company.

Turning to long-term business, there are few restrictions on the types of investments which can be made, again in contrast to non-UK life com-

---

[18] For further details of a complex subject, see the Report on Taxation of Life Assurance produced for the Association of British Insurers in 1988 in response to a consultative document by the Inland Revenue.

panies. One form of restriction which is imposed on some non-UK life assurance companies is a *minimum* required rate of return which must be awarded to 'with profits' policyholders. In Switzerland, this is currently 4%, which encourages an all-bond portfolio able to achieve this with minimum risk. However, Switzerland has until recently had a strong currency and low inflation, so that 4% in nominal terms represents a comparable *real* rate of return when compared to UK life policy returns expressed in pound sterling terms.

Investment and unit trusts

We will treat these two types of investing institution in the same section since, although they have different histories and structures, they both have similar investment objectives and policies.

Investment trusts

We start with the older investment trusts which have been in existence for more than 100 years. Designed to offer the small investor a way of holding a diversified portfolio, the emphasis of investment trusts had switched from over 50% in fixed-interest securities in 1930 to over 80% in equities by 1990. There has always been a strong international flavour to investment trust portfolios, as can be seen in Example 12.3, where 42% of total investment trust assets were invested in overseas securities. Assets have grown from £1.1b. in 1957 to £26b. in 1991, representing an annual average growth rate of 10% p.a. This conceals a decline in real terms in the 1970s, with many investment trusts being wound up, converted to unit trusts, or taken over, followed by a minor resurgence in the 1980s.

Investment trusts (ITCs) are limited liability companies and are *not* trusts in the legal sense, as are their competitors, unit trusts. Investors in ITCs acquire the ordinary shares of the ITCs and their return is therefore in the form of dividends and capital gains or losses from their shares. ITCs use the funds raised from shareholders to invest in a diversified or specialised portfolio of securities. An example of a diversified portfolio is the Foreign and Colonial Investment Trust with 39% of its assets in UK equities, 26% in North American equities, 12% in Japanese and Far Eastern equities, 16% in European and other equities, and the remaining 7% in cash and fixed interest securities on 31 July 1992. An example of a specialised portfolio is the Baillie Gifford Japan Investment Trust, with

Example 12.5   Effects of gearing on Wary Investment Trust shareholders

	£m.
Market value of all-equity portfolio	100
less: 5% Loan Stock 2010	(25)
Net assets for ordinary shareholders	75
Suppose that market value of all-equity portfolio increases by 20% to:	120
less: 5% Loan Stock 2010	(25)
Net assets for ordinary shareholders	95
Representing an increase of	27%

94% of its assets in Japanese equities and the remaining 6% in cash.

New money for investment can only come from a rights issue or from borrowing, either from a bank or by issuing debt such as debentures or loan stock. This ability to raise fixed interest capital allows the ITCs to 'gear' themselves up and to effectively increase their beta. In the 1960s, when interest rates were low, fixed-interest rate loans were commonly raised by ITCs in order to take advantage of this gearing potential. However, in the 1970s and 1980s, interest rates were high relative to the dividend yield income of ITCs and there was a fall in the level of gearing of ITCs. Many now have negative gearing, since the amount of cash and fixed interest securities in their portfolios usually exceeds any debt they may have.

Example 12.5 illustrates the impact of positive gearing on the ordinary shareholders of Wary Investment Trust. Because of the fixed interest loan stock in issue, an increase of 20% in the market value of the all-equity portfolio managed by Wary Investment Trust would lead to a 27% increase in the net assets belonging to Wary shareholders. A decline in the value of Wary's portfolio would have a similarly magnified detrimental effect on the value of Wary's net assets.

However, a gearing innovation in the last few years for some ITCs, for example, Scottish American Investment Trust, is loan stock which is index-linked to the FT-Actuaries All-Share index. This type of loan stock pays a coupon equal to the dividend yield on the particular index and has a principal payment equal to 100 plus the percentage rise in the capital value of the index over the life of the loan stock. The implication for the ITC concerned is that the managers *must* expect to outperform the index (capital plus income) with the funds raised from the loan stock, or else the ITC shareholders will be worse off than with no debt.

Since investment in ITCs is via the purchase of Stock Exchange-listed ordinary shares, one might expect an ITC's share price to be equal to the market value per share of the underlying investment portfolio which is held on behalf of the shareholders. However, this has not been the case in practice and ITC share prices commonly stand at a discount and occasionally a premium to their underlying portfolio or net asset value. Recent discounts have been of the order of 15%–20%, on average, with a maximum of 32% reached in 1977. Many reasons have been put forward to explain this phenomenon, which implies that shares held through the medium of an investment trust are in some way less valuable than if they were held directly. Reasons put forward have included the limited marketability of some ITC shares and the fact that investment trusts do not distribute 100% of the income they receive, some being absorbed by management costs and some reinvested.[19] There is still no agreement on which of these and other factors lead to the discounts frequently observed on ITC shares.

Premiums on net asset value, which sometimes exist on ITC shares, are just as difficult to explain. In these cases, investors are paying a premium for management of the portfolio. This either implies that investment trust managers are credited with superior stock selection skills (although this is unlikely to be a permanent feature – see the discussion in Chapter 10 on efficient markets) or that they have created a portfolio which could not easily be replicated by the shareholders on an individual basis. One example of an ITC trading at a premium to net asset value is CU Environmental Trust, an ITC specialising in 'green' investments and in demand by local authority pension funds and other investors seeking a portfolio of 'ethical' investments. Another is the Aberforth Smaller Companies ITC, whose managers are doubtless credited with being able to obtain better information than individual shareholders on 'good buys' in the sector.

Whatever the reasons for premiums or discounts on the net asset value of ITC shares, their existence adds an extra dimension of risk to investment in ITC shares when compared with buying shares directly. An investor in ITC shares takes on not only the risk of the underlying investments but also the risk that the level of premium or discount will change. This will affect the holding period return in a positive or negative way depending on whether the discount, for example, has narrowed or widened.

However, if large discounts persist, there are various ways in which they can be reduced or removed. One method would be for a pension fund seeking to make equity investments to buy 100% of an ITC. Even if it offered a premium to the share price, it might still be able to acquire a large equity portfolio at a small discount to net asset value and with low transaction costs. For example, The Globe Investment Trust, at the time the largest ITC listed on the Stock Exchange, was acquired by the British Coal Pension Fund in 1990 for a price equal to net asset value.

---

[19] To qualify as an investment trust for tax purposes, ITCs must distribute at least 85% of the investment income they receive.

Aware of their vulnerability to takeover if the discounts to net asset value are large enough, ITCs have evolved a variety of methods to combat the threat. One method is to convert the ITC into a unit trust; as we shall see below, this automatically wipes out the discount since unit trust units are quoted *at* net asset value and not below it. Another is to enter the market and to buy their own shares to support the share price. A third method is to set a fixed date for the redemption of the shares, at which point the share price *must* equal the net asset value. This type of ITC is usually what is known as a split trust, with income shares paying an income based on the dividend income of the ITC and capital shares paying nothing until redemption.

Another important by-product of ITCs being organised as limited liability companies is that they are not allowed to promote the sale of their own shares. Investors buy and sell shares in ITCs exactly as they buy and sell ICI shares, through brokers or market makers on the Stock Exchange. Unit trusts, on the other hand, can and do spend substantial amounts on marketing their units and on commissions to agents. This is the main reason for their relatively greater success relative to ITCs in recent years, despite their higher running costs and worse investment performance.

Unit trusts

Unit trusts are a more recent phenomenon than ITCs, only taking off in the 1960s. However, unit trusts have experienced a much faster growth rate than ITCs. In 1980, ITCs managed assets worth £8.4b., almost double the equivalent figure for unit trusts of £4.6b. By 1991 the position was reversed, with unit trust assets of £54b. compared with ITC assets of only £26b., reflecting an average growth rate for unit trust assets of over 18% per annum. Also, other EC countries, such as France, Germany, and Italy, have very few ITC-type investment vehicles, preferring the unit trust structure.

Unit trusts, like the modern-day investment trusts, have concentrated on equity investments, with 89% of assets invested in UK and overseas shares in 1991 (see Example 12.3), 55% in the UK and 34% overseas.

An investor in unit trusts invests by buying units from the unit trust managers. Unit trusts are also known as 'open end' funds (as opposed to ITCs which are known as 'closed end') because of the fact that the size of a unit trust varies with the number of units in issue. If investors wish to invest in the trust, new units are created to meet demand and the managers invest the new money (less a 'front end fee' as management charge) in securities to increase the size of the portfolio. If investors wish to disinvest, they will sell their units back to the managers and the trust will shrink in size as money is paid out, the managers in principle[20] being forced to realise part of the portfolio in order to buy back the units from the holders. The managers of the unit trust buy and sell units at prices based on the underlying value of the portfolio, with the portfolio valued on a daily basis. However, there will be a difference between the price at which they are prepared to buy units and the price at which they are prepared to sell units, the equivalent of the market maker's bid-ask spread, and this is typically 5–8% of the net asset value per share.

From this description of unit trusts, we can see the major difference between unit trusts and investment trusts as investment intermediaries. The capital of an ITC is fixed (unless it borrows or has a rights issue), with the discount or premium of the share price to the net asset value reflecting current demand for the shares. The unit trust units, on the other hand, are bought and sold at prices equal (bar the bid–ask spread) to the underlying net asset value, so that there are no discounts or premiums. Demand for unit trusts is reflected in the number of units in issue, which defines the size of the unit trust.

Investment objectives and policy

In the case of an investment trust company, the board of directors will determine investment policy. In the case of a unit trust, although the board of trustees will check that the investment policy is being properly carried out, the actual policy itself will usually be chosen by the unit trust managers. Management of both types of trust is mostly delegated to a management company, sometimes an outside company such as an investment bank, sometimes owned by the trust. Some management companies run a whole 'stable' of trusts and this is particularly useful for unit trusts since one of the trusts is bound have done reasonably well in the past year and this is the one which will be promoted in the marketing literature. Each trust is characterised by its own investment policy, which may be geographic specialisation such as Framlington American Smaller Companies Unit Trust, or a stress on income such as Dunedin Income Growth Investment Trust, or simply offer a diversified portfolio spread across different industrial sectors and across several markets. However, most of these funds will have a majority of their portfolio in UK securities, preferring not to take on too much exchange risk to increase the volatility of their portfolios. Typically, 40% of balanced portfolios will be in overseas

---

[20] In practice, the managers will keep part of the portfolio in cash to meet such requests. They will also often be able to 'match' purchasers and sellers of units on a day-to-day basis without having to touch the cash or securities in the portfolio.

securities, with all the benefits of international diversification which this brings, and yet these unit trusts are normally judged against the FT-Actuaries All-Share Index which does not have the improved return for risk advantages open to the internationally diversified trusts.

As already mentioned, a number of ITCs have a split capital structure and a predetermined redemption date, as a means of ensuring that the shares do not trade at a large discount to net asset value. An example is Kleinwort High Income Investment Trust, which has 20m. zero dividend preference shares and 30m. ordinary shares in issue. The preference shares receive no income during the life of the ITC but are promised an average annual return of 9.9% over their eight-year life, by paying back 212.70p for every 100p invested on issue. The ordinary shares are promised the balance of the value of the portfolio (after expenses) on redemption, which is scheduled for 30 June 1998.

(i) Legislation

Unit trusts, as a special kind of intermediary not subject to company and Stock Exchange regulation (as are investment trusts) are tightly controlled by the Department of Trade and Industry, the Securities and Investment Board, and the Investment Management Regulatory Organisation. In order to be able to market units direct to the public in the UK, unit trusts have to be 'authorised' although there are a number of 'exempt' trusts subject to less onerous regulation whose units can be held by pension funds and charities. One of the more famous regulations concerning unit trusts is that, on every marketing document, the phrase 'the value of your units can go down as well as up' has to appear.

Investment trusts are regulated by Companies Acts and by all the regulations applying to companies listed on the Stock Exchange. Neither ITCs nor unit trusts are regulated on their management charges, provided these are suitably disclosed. Unit trust managers typically charge a 6% front end fee when units are purchased, and this is deducted from the amount invested, with 1.5% of the value of the fund charged every year thereafter as a management charge. It is difficult to compare overseas unit trust charges with this, since it is common in some countries to charge lower management fees but to charge a custody fee for dealing with security transfers. ITCs typically have no front end fee although the broker will charge a commission on the purchase of the ITC shares. The annual management charge is also lower at around 0.5% of the value of the assets under management.

Both types of trusts have restrictions imposed on their investment policies. For example, unit trusts may not have more than 5% in any one security and ITCs may not have more than 15% of their assets invested in any one company.[21]

These types of restriction ensure a reasonable amount of diversification, a sensible policy according to portfolio theory. Interestingly, ITCs, which have the longer history of the two, have reduced the average number of the securities they hold over time, with an ITC perhaps holding as many as 1,000 securities 50 years ago compared with around 100 now. This suggests that they realise that they can have efficient portfolios in the risk–return sense without incurring the huge transaction and monitoring costs associated with holding large numbers of securities.

(ii) TAX

A basic problem of any investment intermediary is to provide benefits, whether from economies of scale, pooling of risk, or diversification, without these benefits being eroded by tax disadvantages. For example, given the corporation tax system as applied to insurance companies, non-taxpaying investors might be at a tax disadvantage if they invested in securities via certain types of life assurance policy. Similarly, investors would be reluctant to invest via investment or unit trusts if they were taxed twice, once in the hands of the trust and once in their own hands. This potential double taxation is avoided by, for example, the tax credit attached to dividends from UK shares being able to be passed on intact, and by trusts not being liable to capital gains tax on their own disposals, any such liability being incurred only by the ultimate investor.

Of course, intermediaries will benefit from any tax advantages attached to investment through their particular medium. For example, investing via a pension fund is tax exempt. Also, personal equity plans (PEPs), created by the government in order to encourage *direct* investment in Stock Exchange listed shares in 1986, can now be used as a means of investing several thousand pounds per annum in equities *indirectly* via unit trusts or investment trusts, with no liability on the part of the investor to higher-rate tax on dividend income or to capital gains tax on disposal, provided the shares are held in the PEP for a minimum of five years.

(iii) TIMING AND SELECTION

Investment trusts have a fixed amount of money raised from shareholders to invest. If investors wish to leave the ITC, they do so by selling their

---

[21] This and other requirements are imposed by the Inland Revenue on ITCs before they can gain approved status and qualify for certain tax concessions (some of which will be discussed in the next section on tax).

shares in the secondary market. If enough investors wish to sell, the share price will fall relative to the net asset value and the discount to net asset value will increase. However, this will have no impact on the investment trust portfolio and hence need not affect the timing or selection of investments by the fund manager.

On the other hand, demand and supply for units affect the cash flow available to the unit trust manager. A popular unit trust will have a regular inflow of cash to invest from the sale of new units, although it must retain a certain proportion of its portfolio in liquid assets to be able to buy back units on demand. A unit trust which suffers a decline in popularity (and this is common in bear markets when investors panic and sell their units) may well find itself with a shrinking number of units and need to liquidate part of a carefully constructed portfolio in order to be able to buy back the units. As a result, unit trusts have an unpredictable cash flow, which complicates the implementation of investment policies. One way round this has been for unit trusts to market their units aggressively, in the hope of increasing or at least maintaining the size of the investment pool;[22] another has been for unit trust managers to link the sales of their units to life assurance policies with regular payments into the trust over a predetermined number of years. Finally, unit trust managers encourage investors to buy 'accumulation' rather than 'income' units. The latter pay dividends out to the investor; the former reinvest the dividends in the fund, giving a boost to the trust's cash flow.

Unit trusts have the highest portfolio turnover of all the four categories of investment institution, with purchases and sales of assets equal to 126% of the average value of the assets under management during 1991. Many unit trusts do not seem, therefore, unduly inhibited by any lack of new money, being prepared if necessary to sell existing securities in their search for high performance. Investment trusts have a lower portfolio turnover (77% during 1991) which is understandable given the greater pressure on unit trusts to perform in order to encourage unit purchases and discourage unit sales. However, we saw in Chapter 10 on Efficient Markets that it is unlikely that any investing institution can consistently achieve superior performance in the long run. This implies that a high level of portfolio turnover will be unproductive, merely resulting in unnecessarily high transaction costs, and this is certainly reflected in the poorer performance of unit trusts relative to ITCs in both the short and long term. Studies of UK unit trusts and ITCs have not found any evidence of long-run abnormal returns, leading one to conclude that the high levels of turnover in unit trusts and, to a lesser extent, investment trusts, may waste some of the benefits they offer the investor in the form of diversification.

---

[22] Note that management fees are a function of the value of the funds under management and so a decreasing number of units in a bear market has a doubly depressing effect on unit trust managers' fees.

(iv) ASSET MIX

As we have already seen, the objectives of both investment trusts and unit trusts are to provide the advantages of diversification. Since most trusts make clear what their investment policy is, it is relatively simple for the investor to estimate the level of risk he is going to take on by choosing a particular trust. For ITCs, the investor has the advantage of being able to look at the trust's beta. For the larger, UK-oriented ITCs, the beta is typically around 1. For example, in 1992, Electra Investments had a beta of 0.99 and the average for the industry was 0.98. ITCs with a high overseas content or a substantial proportion of the portfolio in cash or fixed interest securities should have somewhat lower betas.[23]

Investment trusts with a high level of gearing (described in Example 12.5) have relatively higher betas, because of the increased volatility of the ordinary shareholders' assets. Unit trusts, without the advantage of betas determined from share price movements relative to the movements of the UK stock market, have to make do with a rather rudimentary risk categorisation provided by the Unit Trust Association.

Impact of the investing institutions on the stock market

Having looked at each of the above types of investing institution separately, we can now consider their overall impact on Stock Exchange investment. As we have seen, the investing institutions are now the dominant investors in the stock market, both in terms of the proportion of securities held and in terms of turnover. By 1991, the investing institutions were responsible for over two-thirds of all Stock Exchange customer turnover in value terms. As they have increased their investment portfolios and as commissions on trading securities have fallen or, in the case of gilts, disappeared, so they have increased their portfolio turnover rates. This dominance of the investing institutions as the major traders in the stock market has led to larger average bargain sizes for all types of security and to the increasing dependence of market makers and brokers on the investing institutions for business.

---

[23] For example, BZW Convertible Investment Trust had a beta of 0.60 in 1992. See the *Risk Measurement Service* published by London Business School for further details of investment trust betas.

Investment analysis

Post-Big Bang, the average commission paid on large trades by investing institutions fell dramatically. Both agency brokers and market makers now depend on large turnover to survive, and the quality of their investment analysis is one of the major factors in their getting business. Most brokers and market makers employ large teams of equity analysts to follow companies and to make recommendations to the investing institutions. However, the quality of the analysis is not always high and may be flawed by a conflict of interest. Most of the market making firms, and some of the agency brokers, act as brokers or investment banks to the companies on which they are advising. There have been a number of occasions on which analysts have been known to have been guided away from a 'sell' recommendation on a company which brings in substantial corporate finance fees to the organisation. There may also be a conflict between the analyst and the salesman and market maker. The salesman and market maker may wish to dispose of a large 'line of stock' which has been acquired on the books through normal market making activities. They will not be happy if the analyst is recommending a 'sell' to investors.

Firms counter criticism by saying that reports written by analysts should not be taken too seriously; it is the telephone conversations with investors which convey the truth about the firm's views. However, there is little evidence that this was done for, say, Polly Peck before its sudden demise either in written or conversation form. Also, such emphasis on telephone conversations naturally favours the investing institutions over the smaller investor who has to rely on written material and recommendations mentioned in the press for his access to fundamental analysis.

Worries about the independence and quality of the investment analysis received from brokers and market makers have led to investing institutions employing their own equity analysts in-house. This is also a result of the fact that they often hold substantial percentages of particular companies' shares which allows them privileged contact in the form of company visits and telephone calls, not available to brokers in the City. This privileged treatment could in theory lead to the investing institutions gaining access to 'inside' information, information which may not be generally available to all investors.

So, with privileged contacts with City analysts and with their own analysts having superior direct access to the companies in which they are investing, there does appear to be a two-tier shareholder information structure, with the smaller shareholders less well-informed. However, as we saw in Chapter 10 on Efficient Markets, whether they have access to privileged information or not, the investing institutions do not appear to earn long-run excess returns with it. Similarly, their greater economies of scale in investment analysis (in the sense that only one pharmaceuticals analyst is needed whether thousands or billions of pounds are being invested) do not seem to show up in their performance.

Finally, since the investment institutions are so dominant in trading Stock Exchange securities, they are clearly buying and selling from each other. Although there is little evidence of investing institutions consistently outperforming relevant benchmarks, it may well be the case that some investing institutions do consistently badly over a number of years. Given that most investing institutions make it difficult or expensive for individuals to remove their money in the short run, and that information about performance is often slow to be disseminated or is limited in content, it may take a considerable period of time for individual investors to realise the poor performance of the investing institution which they have chosen as their intermediary.

Relationships with company managements

The importance of the investing institutions as the majority shareholders in many large UK quoted companies has caused much discussion. Over recent years, this has culminated in the 'short-termism' argument put forward by company management, angered at the ease with which their companies can be taken over by hostile bidders. They argue that investing institutions, in particular pension funds and life assurance companies, have long-term investment horizons and should be long-term holders of the shares in their portfolios. However, they appear to hold a short-term view, since they are only too willing to accept a takeover bid, even if the incumbent management is against it. This is despite the effort company managers have put in to improve relations by making company presentations direct to the major investing institution shareholders and by keeping the institutions informed of projects and profits through the medium of 'investor relations' managers.

Investing institutions argue that they are experts in investment and not in management and that it is not their job to get too closely involved with company managements else they would lose their independent stance. They point out that it is the managers of *other* companies who initiate the takeover bids, not the investing institutions. It is also a fact that, in the UK, takeovers are often the only way to achieve a change in management, which may well be needed if the company has been doing badly relative to its competitors. However, in the past few years, institutional investors, often via the Institutional Investors Committee, have intervened to force board resignations, to query large payouts to retiring managers, and to bring in new managers when needed. They have begun to recognise that, given the size of their percentage shareholdings, they have no choice but to help companies with ailing share prices to improve. If they attempted to dispose of their large shareholdings on the stock market, this would radically affect the share price, leading to an even greater loss on the investment.

Impact on share prices

The investing institutions may also affect the relative pricing of different types of security. For example, we have seen how high-coupon gilts and low-coupon gilts have different gross redemption yields, reflecting the relative demand from gross investors such as pension funds and from high tax-paying individuals. Prices of shares in the FT-SE 100 share index may also be affected by the investing institutions. Shares in all the largest 100 companies are held by the vast majority of investing institutions, either as part of index funds or simply to gain exposure to the most important elements of the stock market. If a new issue is made of a company which will immediately form part of the FT-SE 100 share index, as was the case for many of the utility privatisation issues such as British Telecom and British Gas, there is likely to be high demand from the institutions which will drive the share price up relative to other share prices.

Since the majority of investment decisions are now made by perhaps a few hundred institutional investment managers, there may also be greater homogeneity of beliefs in respect of future returns and risks on particular securities or stock markets than when large numbers of individual investors dominate the stock market. If this is so, one of the assumptions underlying the CAPM would more nearly hold, but it could also imply greater volatility of share prices and lower liquidity in the stock market if institutional investors wish to buy and sell at the same time. However, there is no academic research to support this viewpoint although the more frequent occurrence of sudden large crashes in share prices could perhaps be partly explained by the sudden desire to sell shares of a majority of fund managers controlling billions of pounds' worth of portfolios.[24]

Summary

This chapter has investigated the impact of the long-term investing institutions on stock market investment. The four main types – pension funds,

---

[24] There are many other possible explanatory factors for crashes, for example the switch to different method of trading shares and the general reduction in transaction costs. For a more detailed survey, see the 1988 Report by the Brady Committee for the US Presidential Task Force on Market Mechanisms, published after the 1987 stock market crash.

insurance companies, unit trusts and investment trusts – are major holders of UK and overseas equities, gilts and international bonds, as well as being more and more involved in futures and options. Their investments, both in terms of the size of their portfolio holdings and the turnover of securities they generate, dominate the stock market. The majority of individual investors now invest the bulk of their savings devoted to securities indirectly via these investing institutions.

The chapter has examined each of the four types of investing institution separately, concentrating on how they have evolved and discussing how their particular characteristics affect their investment objectives and policy. Factors such as tax and legislation also affect the structure and turnover of their investment portfolios.

The chapter concluded with a discussion of the main ways that investing institutions have affected the stock market, in terms of the impact on investment analysis and share prices as well as on the companies in which they invest and the other investors in the stock market.

Appendix: alternatives to funded pension schemes

Although the UK and US governments have legislated for funded pension schemes, which are legally separate from the companies concerned, other countries have chosen different systems.

For example, in Germany, pensions are provided for internally, in the sense that companies make provisions for pension payments in their balance sheets but still have the use of the money for investment purposes. With this system, in the event of a company going into liquidation, the company's assets would be used in paying all the creditors and the present and future pensioners could lose all or most of their benefits. So, pension schemes in Germany are insured against such an eventuality. The same system was commonly used in the UK in the 1930s and 1940s but not necessarily with the protection of insurance. The legal separation from the company of the funded schemes now largely in operation in the UK means that, in the event of a liquidation, the creditors of the company cannot reach the assets of the pension fund. However, the assets of a legally separate pension fund, although reserved for the pension liabilities of the company, may still not be sufficient to fund all the pension liabilities incurred before liquidation; in other words, the pension fund may have 'unfunded liabilities'.

In France, companies usually prefer the 'Pay As You Go' method of providing for pensions. Under this system, no provision is made, either in the company's balance sheet or in a separate fund. Pension payments are made as they fall due out of current income and only then appear in the accounts. This system obviates the need for intermediaries and avoids the problem of having to quantify future uncertainties in order to decide the necessary level of contributions.

However, the Pay As You Go system suffers from the same disadvantage as the German schemes. If a company goes into liquidation, there will be no assets, whether notional or real, set aside for the provision of pensions. Again, Pay As You Go works only if there are insurance schemes in existence to protect the pensioners. In France, these are provided by state guarantees and funds. Thus, non-funded schemes usually require more government intervention than funded schemes. They also allow each company to use the funds set aside as pension provisions for investment as they wish. Funded schemes, on the other hand, channel a substantial proportion of corporate sector savings via the pension funds, and it is up to the managers and trustees of the pension funds to decide how best to invest these resources.

One potential advantage of a funded pension scheme is that it should lead to the employer concerned being aware of the cost of his pension scheme. It is tempting under Pay As You Go to promise generous pension entitlements which may cause problems when there is a declining workforce. In the UK, only the government operates Pay As You Go schemes with respect to state pensions and the pensions of civil service employees. Both local authorities and nationalised industries operate funded pension schemes.

Problems

1. (i) What are the main differences between a unit trust and an investment trust? How do these differences explain the increased popularity of unit trusts relative to investment trusts in recent years?
    (ii) Suggest reasons why a large proportion of the shares in investment trusts are held by pension funds? Why would pension funds and insurance companies wish to invest via authorised or exempt unit trusts?

2. Pension funds, insurance companies, unit trusts and investment trusts are the major investors in the UK stock market. Which types of securities do each of these investing institutions prefer, and why?

3. What are the major arguments for and against institutional investors becoming involved in the management of the companies in which they hold shares? Do you think that investing institutions should be limited to a maximum percentage of any one company's share capital which they can hold?

4. You have been asked to design the Report and Accounts of a pension fund to be sent to all pensioners and contributors of the fund. Describe the main items you think should be included.

5. (i) Describe all the costs incurred by investors in unit trusts and investment trusts, in particular the management charges. How should this affect the time the investor in such trusts expects to hold his investment?
    (ii) The *Investment Trust Year Book* gives ratios of management expenses/assets managed and management expenses/total gross revenue. Are high ratios good or bad for the investor?
    (iii) Suppose a unit trust manages its portfolio as an index fund. How should management be remunerated in this case?

PART IV

CONCLUSION

CHAPTER 13

Investment objectives, investment policy and performance measurement

Introduction

In the first twelve chapters of this book we looked at different types of Stock Exchange securities, how to value them and how to compare them through the medium of expected holding period return and risk. We also considered the advantages of portfolio investment, both domestic and international, and the different requirements of the institutional (as opposed to the individual) investor. In this final chapter, we examine the investor's overall strategy, from the factors he should take into consideration when quantifying his objectives to the measurement of his actual investment performance.

Before the investor can make any investment decisions at all, he must decide on the *objectives* he is trying to achieve. Although all investors will have an implicit investment policy, this is all too often not stated explicitly. Again, the growth of investment intermediaries has emphasised the need for clearly stated objectives. The objectives of these intermediaries have to be known before their performance can be meaningfully measured and compared. There is no point in comparing the performance of an investment trust with the FT-Actuaries All-Share Index when its objective was to be 50% invested in the US and 50% in Japan.

Objectives can only be set once certain characteristics of the beneficiaries or investors are known. These characteristics will include their required risk and return, details of their existing wealth, their tax positions, liquidity requirements, future liabilities and a host of other factors. Until recently, the approach of investment advisers has been to concentrate more on the characteristics of the securities or market they are investing in rather than on the characteristics of their clients. As understanding of the efficient markets hypothesis and the capital asset pricing model (CAPM) has spread, more emphasis has been placed on the construction of 'optimal' portfolios, optimal in the sense of being the best portfolio given the investor's risk and return requirements, rather than in the sense of optimal securities (those offering the highest expected excess returns) to put into the portfolio.

Once the objectives of the investor or fund have been established, the investment policy to be pursued must be decided upon. This hinges very much on the beliefs of the investor or fund manager concerned. Two major investment strategies can be identified – passive and active. A passive investment policy corresponds to the 'fair return for risk' approach discussed in Chapter 10 and will be adopted by investors who believe that markets are efficient with respect to information; in other words, that there are no undue monetary rewards to be gained from studying market trends or trying to pick winners. Such investors believe that their selection skills are not sufficient to warrant an active search for excess returns, after transaction costs. All that they expect is, on average, a fair return for the risk they choose to bear. Active investors, on the other hand, follow a 'picking winners' approach and try, by searching for mis-priced securities or by attempting to time investments correctly, to beat the market.

Investment policy does not just involve a once and for all portfolio decision. Both active and passive strategies require that the portfolio, however constructed, be amended from time to time. The frequency and extent of the portfolio revisions are also investment policy decisions, taking into account the objectives of the portfolio and the transaction costs involved.

Finally, investors will be interested in measuring the performance of their investment portfolios, for many different reasons. For example, they will wish to check (particularly if they have used an intermediary) that the investment objectives laid down have been followed. Also, they may wish to compare the performance of alternative investment funds. Performance measurement will in addition identify particular investment skills, such as the ability to pick winners, and allows comparison between active and passive investment strategies.

Despite a clear need for performance measurement, techniques could only be developed in the wake of portfolio theory and the CAPM since these were the first models which explicitly quantified risk and return. Once risk could be measured, comparisons could be made between portfolios of different risk. Similarly, once a passive investment strategy based on the CAPM had been identified, comparisons could be made between active and passive investment policies. Performance measurement is now commonplace in the US, where portfolio theory and the CAPM were developed, and in the UK, and is becoming more usual in Continental Europe, in preference to the traditional cursory comparison with an often non-comparable share index.

This chapter begins with a discussion of possible investment objectives and considers the factors which must be taken into consideration when deciding on objectives, for example inflation and tax. The second section compares alternative investment policies, that is, active and passive approaches to investment management. The third and final section describes the alternative, risk-adjusted performance measures which can be used, together with a discussion of their relevance, in different situations.

Investment objectives

These will of course vary widely according to the type of investor. For instance, an individual investor may wish to maximise his return over a ten-year period, taking on a reasonably high level of risk since he already has a substantial earned income. A pensioner would be more likely to require a constant level of income in real terms, to be achieved with minimum risk. A pension fund manager might have the objective of meeting a specified set of future liabilities at minimum overall cost.

Rather than specifying in detail particular sets of objectives, we shall concentrate instead on those factors which must be considered before any investment objectives can be set. We group these factors under five headings – consumption preferences, required risk and return, tax, inflation and asset allocation.

Consumption preferences

Each investor will be aware of his own consumption preferences. These will include preferred currency of consumption, so that an investor who spends half the year in New York may require a portfolio denominated in both sterling and dollars. Also, part of the portfolio may need to be in liquid assets, to meet unforeseen liabilities and to allow the investor to pursue an 'active' investment policy. The preference for income or capital gain will be determined partly by the tax position of the investor but also by the need for a regular income as opposed to long-term capital growth. However, this does not always follow; for example, as we saw in Chapter 12, pension funds, despite the fact that they do not necessarily need income, still prefer regular dividends.

The time horizon of concern to the investor will vary from a few hours or days for the speculator who believes he has inside information to several decades for the pension fund manager. The time horizon will thus be a function of the future consumption needs of the investor and of the type of investment policy he prefers. The time horizon will also affect the investor's attitude to transaction costs. For example, if the investor wishes to invest in property in the near future, he will wish to minimise the risk and transaction costs associated with his short-term investments. On the other hand, a salaried investor with ten years to go before retirement may be willing to invest in a unit-linked life assurance scheme, where the long-term capital growth and tax advantages outweigh the relatively high transaction costs.

Attitude to risk and return

As we have seen throughout the book, the investor's attitude to risk and return is the most important factor needed to be able to quantify his investment objectives. Whether he wishes to pursue a 'picking winners' or a 'fair return for risk' investment policy, the investor needs to state how much risk he is willing to bear and how much return he requires on average in order to choose between alternative efficient portfolios. The investor can either concentrate on maximising return subject to a maximum risk level, for example an investor merely supplementing his earned income, or on minimising risk subject to a minimum return, such as the pensioner living off his investments. Risk can be expressed in terms of the standard deviation of returns, if the investor is considering his entire wealth and the possibility of its loss, or in terms of beta if the investment considered represents only part of his total wealth.

Since it may be difficult for investors to be able to state the maximum standard deviation of returns that they will accept or the minimum return they require, a simpler solution might be to face the investor with a set of alternative portfolios which lie on his efficient frontier,[1] each of which will have different risk–return characteristics, and to ask the investor to choose the one he prefers.

Tax

Tax is also an extremely important factor in real life, as we saw in Chapter 12, although tax was excluded from the discussion of portfolio theory and the CAPM. Tax can render certain investments unattractive to the investor, as is the case with high-coupon bonds for high tax rate investors. Similarly, tax can make certain types of investment more attractive than they would otherwise be, such as investing in equities via a pension scheme rather than directly in the stock market. Also, personal equity plans (PEPs) allow investors, provided they hold the equities for a five-year period, to avoid capital gains tax on any gains over the period.

So, tax can affect preferences for income or capital gains, high- or low-coupon stocks, direct versus indirect investment. The tax position of the investor must therefore be taken into account when determining the investment objectives of his portfolio and portfolio returns must be compared net of tax.

Inflation

Another factor to be considered is the impact of inflation on the value of investments. Investments and liabilities can no longer be viewed purely in nominal terms. For example, in Chapter 2, Mr Stone wished to buy a house in five years' time. Even if he bought gilts which had fixed redemption values and which matured exactly at the right moment, he could not be sure that house prices would remain fixed in nominal terms over the five years. Similarly, pension funds' liabilities are related to salaries which are certainly not constant in nominal terms. Because of this inflation risk, investment objectives must take account of inflation in assessing the investor's requirements, that is, whether the need is to keep up with inflation or merely to cover a nominal liability, such as the repayment of a fixed loan.

---

[1] As we saw in Chapter 8, the efficient frontier represents those portfolios which offer the best returns given their risk. The investor will choose amongst these according to his utility function.

Most investors, whether individuals or institutions, need to maintain the value of their investments in real terms. This leads us to consider the different types of investment available in the light of how good a hedge they are against inflation.

We have already noted in Chapter 11 that investment intermediaries, in particular insurance companies, pension funds and investment trusts, all experienced losses from their fixed interest investments in the 1960s and 1970s as interest rates and inflation rates rose. Since then, there has been a general movement right up to and before the 1987 Crash away from fixed interest investments towards equities which were believed to represent a better hedge against inflation. According to classical economic theory, ordinary shares were supposed to maintain their value in real terms. As interest rates and the required rate of return on equities went up, so would the income of the companies as revenues and costs went up correspondingly. The overall impact on share prices would represent no change in real terms.

Let us first consider a world with no inflation. The value of a share, P_0, can be written, according to the dividend valuation model discussed in Chapter 5, as

$$P_0 = \sum_{n=1}^{\infty} \frac{D_n}{(1+R)^n} \tag{13.1}$$

where D_n is the dividend to be paid in year n and R is the required rate of return on the share. How will inflation affect equation (13.1)? If the revenues as well as the outgoings of the firm increase in line with inflation, thus allowing dividends also to keep up with inflation, the numerator of equation (13.1) will become, simply, $D_n(1+i)^n$ where i is the annual inflation rate expected to prevail for the foreseeable future. Similarly, the required rate of return will also adjust for expected inflation, so that the denominator $(1+R)$ will become instead $(1+R)(1+i)$.

Substituting into equation (13.1) gives

$$P_0 = \sum_{n=1}^{\infty} \frac{D_n(1+i)^n}{(1+R)^n (1+i)^n} \tag{13.2}$$

The term $(1+i)^n$ cancels out and equation (13.2) reduces to

$$P_0 = \sum_{n=1}^{\infty} \frac{D_n}{(1+R)^n} \tag{13.3}$$

which is exactly the same as equation (13.1).

From equation (13.3), we can see how the classical theory works. If, in an inflationary environment, the dividends of the company are maintained

Example 13.1   Correlation between returns on equities, gilts, and cash

	Correlation coefficients		
	1923–50	*1951–70*	*1971–91*
Equities/Cash	(0.01)	(0.25)	(0.04)
Long Gilts/Cash	0.03	(0.11)	0.09
Long Gilts/Equities	0.48	0.18	0.65

Source: Frank Russell International

in real terms (as a result of revenues and costs going up exactly in line with inflation) and if the required rate of return also adjusts exactly for expected inflation, the current value of the share, P_0, will remain unchanged, thus representing a complete hedge against inflation.

In real life, there are many reasons why the classical theory may not hold. For example, the company's cash flows may not maintain their value in real terms as a result of, for example, prices not keeping up with costs; the tax system penalising nominal, as opposed to real, increases in profits; or simply lags between changes in costs and changes in revenues. Also, the required rate of return, R, only takes *expected* inflation into account. No allowance is made in equation (13.2) for unexpected inflation.

Example 13.1 shows us the correlation coefficients between UK equities and cash (represented by treasury bills) over three periods: 1923–50, 1951–70 and 1971–91, and between gilts and cash over the same periods. Returns on equities and gilts are correlated with returns on treasury bills to see how good equities and gilts are as a hedge against *expected* inflation. Investment in treasury bills, because of their short life, minimises the risk that inflation will be different from expected. Returns on treasury bills are therefore good indicators of the expected inflation rate.[2]

From Example 13.1 we see that, for each of the three periods, the correlation coefficient between returns on equities and returns on treasury bills and between returns on gilts and returns on treasury bills hovered close to zero or was small and negative. There appears to be no evidence, therefore, that equities or gilts are a good hedge against inflation.

However, in the case of gilts, as we saw in Chapter 3, the introduction of index-linked gilts in 1981 appeared to offer a true hedge against inflation. (Index-linked gilts were not considered in Example 13.1). But even with index-linked gilts, the problem of inflation is not completely solved. First of all, the current supply of index-linked gilts, of around £13b., is by no means sufficient to hedge all the pension funds' inflation risk, let alone that of other investors. Secondly, the gilts are indexed to the retail prices index

---

[2] We saw in Chapter 2 that Miss Silver might be better off investing in the most short-term government securities (e.g. treasury bills) in times of uncertainty about future inflation.

which is meant to reflect the cost of living of the 'average' consumer. It may be that the investor wishes to hedge against a particular price change, such as Mr Stone with his prospective house purchase, and this can be greater than or less than the change in the retail prices index. Thirdly, the required *real* rate of return on gilts may vary and this will affect the price of index-linked gilts. The investor cannot therefore be sure of a certain real rate of return unless he holds the index-linked gilts to maturity.

An alternative way of coping with risk, as we saw in Chapter 2, is by pooling or diversification. One method, discussed in Chapter 11, is to diversify internationally. This will reduce the dependence of the investor's portfolio on domestic inflation. Another is to diversify across types of security which may have different reactions to inflation.

Asset allocation

Portfolio theory suggests that combinations of equities which are poorly correlated will improve the risk–return characteristics of an investor's portfolio, when compared with holding just a few shares or a naïvely diversified portfolio. This argument can, as we saw in Chapter 11, be extended to the international arena since the correlation coefficients between certain stock markets will be lower than between shares in the same stock market.[3]

We can now go one step further and consider portfolios made up of combinations of different types of asset. We can see from Example 13.1 that, for example, returns on cash and long gilts are poorly correlated in the UK and even returns on gilts and equities have a correlation coefficient substantially less than one. Clearly, the time period chosen affects the correlation coefficients significantly, but this does not detract from the fact that spreading assets amongst different types of asset as well as internationally will improve the risk–return characteristics of an investor's portfolio, and this approach has been adopted (as we saw from the portfolio details given in Chapter 12) by all UK pension funds and insurance companies.[4]

When considering the asset mix and the objectives of his investment portfolio, the investor should also bear in mind the characteristics of his existing wealth. For example, if the investor works in the chemical industry, it might be sensible to include an objective to hold a smaller proportion of his portfolio than might otherwise be the case in the chemical sector.

---

[3] See Chapter 11, p. 339.

[4] See Example 12.3. Also, note that the British Rail Pension fund took diversification of the asset mix one stage further by investing in Impressionist paintings as a separate asset class.

This is because the level of the investor's future earnings will be to some extent linked to the fortunes of the chemical industry. The investor would therefore reduce his risk by having an investment portfolio whose returns were poorly correlated with the chemical industry and hence his other main source of income.

Investment policy

As mentioned in the introduction to this chapter, there are essentially two types of investment policy which can be pursued by the fund manager or by the individual investor. The first is an *active* investment strategy which attempts to capitalise on a particular investment skill, such as stock selection or market timing and the other is *passive*, attempting merely to achieve an average return on a well-diversified portfolio.

Active investment policy

There are two main ways of attempting to actively outperform a benchmark: one is to pick stocks which do better in return terms than the stocks in the benchmark portfolio – we shall call this 'stock selection'; the other is to buy and sell stocks at the right time so that they are bought at a lower than average price and sold at a higher than average price – we call this 'market timing'.

Stock selectors believe that markets are in some way inefficient and that some securities are under- or over-valued. They believe that, with the help of fundamental analysis, they can identify over-valued stocks and that portfolios including substantial or 'overweight' holdings in them will therefore outperform a more diversified index benchmark. The most common kinds of techniques used to try to identify potential outperformers include more accurate earnings forecasts than the consensus, detailed analysis of the impact of accounting techniques on the declared profits, identifying high or low *PE* stocks (according to the stage in the economic cycle) and quantitative techniques where computers are used to identify stocks with a particular range of characteristics which the analyst believes will do well over the investment time horizon – for example, by attempting to identify possible takeover candidates.

The second way to do well in investments is to attempt correct timing of purchases and sales, often through the use of technical analysis (or possibly insider information!). This can be done either at the individual security level, say with point and figure charts (Figure 10.4), or at the market level. One method, provided by the CAPM, would be to acquire high beta shares before a bull market and to switch into low beta shares before a bear market. This would allow the fund manager or investor to alter the risk of the equity element of his portfolio without altering the amount invested in equities. Another method involves switching from equities into bonds or cash if a stock market fall is forecast and moving into equities before a stock market rise. This technique is also referred to as 'tactical asset allocation' and can be undertaken by making a study of the typical historical relationship of, say, the yield gap between the return on treasury bills and the dividend yield on equities and switching between treasury bills and equities according to whether the current yield gap is high or low relative to its historical average. Tactical asset allocation involves short-term switches between asset classes and differs from *strategic* asset allocation which involves the fundamental choice of how much to put into each asset type such as bonds, domestic equities, foreign equities in the longer term and was discussed earlier in the chapter.[5]

Passive investment policy

The alternative investment policy is a passive approach, based on the results of portfolio theory and the CAPM. All that is expected by the investor is a fair return for the risk involved. Thus, once the risk level has been set and an optimal portfolio (allowing for consumption preferences, time horizon, tax and inflation) has been determined, all that the investor needs to do is to maintain the portfolio at its required diversification and risk levels. Turnover and transaction costs of the portfolio will be lower than that of an actively managed portfolio, as will be management fees, since there will be less need for the advice of either technical or fundamental analysts.

The passive approach to fund management has become increasingly popular over the past few years as evidence has accumulated that the majority of fund managers do *not* consistently outperform a general share index. Over 10% of UK institutional funds' equity portfolios are now invested via index funds whilst the US figure is estimated at over 20%. An index fund is a portfolio of equities (or bonds) which attempts to track as closely as possible a stock market index such as the FT-Actuaries All-Share Index for UK equities and the S&P 500 for US equities. The aim of the active investor is to *outperform* the relevant benchmark index; the aim of

---

[5] See p. 393.
[5] See p. 393.

the passive investor is to achieve *average* performance through returns which are equal to the returns on the market as a whole, most likely achieved through investing in an index fund. In active fund management, success is judged by the size of the return in *excess* of that on the index; in index fund management, success is judged by how *small* is the difference between the fund's return and the index's return, known as the 'tracking error'.

Whether an active or passive investment policy is pursued, it must be consistent. An active policy will involve high turnover, high transaction costs and relatively poor diversification (since specific risk must be borne for excess returns to be possible). A passive policy will involve low turnover, low transaction costs and high diversification. Both, however, will require some element of portfolio revision. Active investors will need to re-examine opportunities and estimates of future share price and market movements fairly frequently in their search for 'winners'. Passive investors will only need to revise their portfolios when the factors affecting their objectives change or when their estimates of market risk and return change.

Various compromises between the two types of investment policy are now being adopted by investors, particularly the large institutional portfolio managers. One compromise is, instead of having the entire portfolio actively managed, to split the fund into a passively managed index fund element and an actively managed element. This actively managed element might be split into three or four different funds each with specialist expertise: for example, Far Eastern, global bonds, quantitative, or futures and options. This allows the overall fund manager to keep down portfolio turnover and hence transaction costs whilst attempting to outperform with part of the portfolio. A second method is the so-called tilted fund, an index fund tilted away from the index to exploit some particular investment expertise, for example the ability to identify 'good value' stocks or sectors likely to perform better than the market average. Tilted funds have the advantage of allowing the fund managers running them to charge higher fees than for the plain vanilla index funds.

Performance measurement

The final section in this chapter is devoted to performance measurement, which has a variety of possible uses. For instance, once the investment objectives of their portfolios have been set, investors will wish to know whether these objectives have been achieved. They may also wish to compare their portfolios' performance with the performance of portfolios which had similar objectives. For example, if an investor has placed his savings in a unit trust promising high income, he may wish to compare its performance with other high-income unit trusts. When investment is via intermediaries, performance measures also serve other functions. They help to check that the fund managers are neither fraudulent nor incompetent and that they are keeping to their stated objectives.

Performance measures can also be used to evaluate investment policy. We saw above that there are two main investment strategies – an active investment strategy which we have called 'picking winners' and a passive strategy referred to as 'fair return for risk' based on the CAPM. Given this, any actively managed investment portfolio can be evaluated not only relative to portfolios with similar objectives but also relative to an equivalent passive portfolio of index.

If we consider the quantity of performance measurement carried out in industry, such as measuring achievement against profit targets or examining variances[6] between actual and budgeted performance, it is surprising to note how little has been done in the field of investment. Two factors probably influenced this lack of performance measurement. Firstly, until portfolio theory and the CAPM quantified risk, there was no way that two portfolios of different risk could be fairly compared. Secondly, the relative paucity of disclosure concerning the investment portfolios and policies of the investment intermediaries, especially when compared with the level of disclosure required of companies, has not allowed detailed assessments of performance.

However, as investment has become more and more institutionalised, so performance measurement has become more prevalent. Once confined to the US, performance measurement is common for all UK investing institutions and is now spreading to Continental Europe and Japan. Performance measures are increasingly being used by trustees of pension funds as a form of monitoring and as a means of identifying the particular investment skills (or lack of them) of the managers of pension funds. Detailed performance measurement is not yet part of the services offered to private client investors, who still tend to get statements of the value of their portfolios with no information on how their assets performed relative to a benchmark or adjusted for the risk of their portfolios but, over the next few years, competitive pressures in the fund management industry, coupled with increased computerisation, will see more sophisticated measures of performance for all types of fund management.

Now, in order to determine a measure of performance for any portfolio, two figures must be known, the *return* the portfolio achieved and the level of *risk* it assumed. There are four main aspects which must be considered when measuring performance, the first in calculating the return, the second in coping with risk and the third in breaking the measure down to analyse

---

[6] A budget variance is the difference between the amount forecast for a cost or revenue item and the amount actually incurred.

performance in greater depth. The fourth aspect relates to the general applicability of the performance measures derived.

Calculating return

Let us consider the calculation of the return of a portfolio run by an investing institution. As we saw in Chapter 12, investing intermediaries have varying patterns of cash flows, the size of which the fund managers may or may not be able to control. For example, pension funds will have cash inflows and outflows at regular intervals representing employer and employee pension contributions and pension payments, whereas unit trusts will experience irregular cash inflows and outflows reflecting demand for the units. So, when comparing the performance of two funds, the timing of their cash flows must be taken into account. If one unit trust experiences a large inflow of funds to be invested just before a bull market whereas another experiences a cash outflow at that time, the first unit trust may well appear on a superficial look to have done better although it may actually have achieved lower returns overall.

Suppose units trusts *A* and *B* have identical equity portfolios and investment policies but they experience different timing of cash flows over years 1, 2 and 3, as outlined in Example 13.2. Unit trust *B* appears to have done

Example 13.2   Impact of timing of cash flows on performance

	Now	End of Year 1	End of Year 2	End of Year 3
Unit trust A				
Value of fund (£)	100	110	131	**209**
Cash inflow (at end of year 2)			+100	
Annual rate of return (%)		+10	+19	−9.5
Average R of R[7]	6%			
Unit trust B				
Value of fund (£)	100	110	250	**226**
Cash inflow (at end of year 1)		+100		
Annual rate of return (%)		+10	+19	−9.5
Average of R of R[7]	6%			

---

[7] The average calculated is the geometric mean

$$GM = \sqrt[n]{(1 + r_1)(1 + r_2) \ldots (1 + r_n)} - 1$$

The geometric mean is used rather than the arithmetic mean when averaging percentage increases over time.

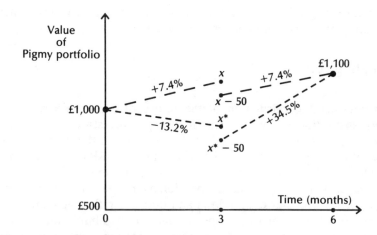

Figure 13.1   Calculating TWROR when value of portfolio unknown

x = Value of portfolio estimated using IRR method = £1,074.
x^* = Value of portfolio estimated using CAPM method = £868.

better, with a higher terminal value of £226, because, although both trusts received cash inflows of £100 during the period, unit trust *B* received its cash flow before a general market rise in year 2 and unit trust *A* only before a market fall in year 3.

In order to allow for different timing of cash flows, the time-weighted rate of return (*TWROR*) can be used to compare the performance of unit trusts *A* and *B*, instead of simply comparing the terminal values of their portfolios. To do this, we calculate the average of the rates of return achieved in each period between cash flows. From Example 13.2, we can see that, despite the difference in timing of cash flows, unit trusts *A* and *B* are in all other respects identical, including their annual rates of return, which leads to identical *TWROR* of 6%.

To determine the *TWROR*, the date on which each cash flow occurs and the value of the portfolio on each such date must be known. Whereas this may be practicable for units trusts (which have to calculate the market value of their portfolios on a daily basis[8]), it may be costly for small funds which experience frequent cash inflows and outflows. In these cases it may be necessary to *estimate* the value of the portfolio at the time the cash flow occurred.

For example, suppose that Pigmy Trust plc achieves a return on its portfolio of 10% over a period of six months, as shown in Figure 13.1, with the portfolio increasing in value from £1,000 at the beginning of the period to £1,100 at the end of the six months. Suppose also that Pigmy experienced a cash outflow of £50 half-way through the six-month period. Be-

---

[8] Because the bid and offer prices for units are based on the market value of the portfolio.

cause of this, Pigmy's *TWROR* must in fact be greater than 10% but it cannot be determined since the value of the fund at the date of the cash outflow is unknown.

However, the *TWROR* can be estimated if it is assumed that the rate of return achieved in the first three months, say R, was the same as that achieved in the second three months. We can then write, if x is the unknown value of the portfolio at the half-way point, that the returns in each three-month period must be equal. Thus,

$$R = \frac{x - 1,000}{1,000} = \frac{1,100 - (x - 50)}{x - 50} \tag{13.4}$$

Cross-multiplying to solve for x in equation (13.4) gives

$$(x - 1,000)(x - 50) = (1,100 - (x - 50))(1,000)$$

$$x(x - 50) - 1,000(x - 50) = 1,100,000 - 1,000(x - 50)$$

$$x(x - 50) = 1,100,000$$

$$x^2 - 50x + 1,100,000 = 0$$

Using the quadratic equation formula[9] to find x we get

$$x = \pounds 1,074$$

Therefore, the return in each three-month period, P, was 7.4%, compounding up to a six-month *TWROR* of 15.3%.

Although this method, known as the internal rate of return (or IRR) method, allows *TWROR* to be estimated, it makes no allowance for market movements during the period under consideration. It assumes that the overall return for the six months was mirrored in the two three-month sub-periods. It could have been the case that there was a downswing in the first three months followed by an upswing in the next three months.

An alternative to the IRR method uses the CAPM to take into account any such market movements when estimating x. Suppose that a suitable market index dropped from 196 at the beginning of the period to 172.5 three months later, a fall of 12%. If the beta of Pigmy Trust's portfolio against that market index was 1.1, the portfolio could have been expected to fall in value by $1.1 \times 12\% = 13.2\%$. Thus an estimate of x, allowing for market movements, would be £868, 13.2% below the original £1,000.

---

[9] The formula used to solve for x when $ax^2 + bx + c = 0$ is

$$x = (-b \pm \sqrt{(b^2 - 4ac)})/2a$$

(Note that this assumes Pigmy Trust's portfolio to be well diversified.) This CAPM method leads to two different sub-period returns,

$$\frac{868 - 1{,}000}{1{,}000} = -13.2\%$$

in the first three months and

$$\frac{1{,}100 - 818}{818} = 34.5\%$$

in the second three months, giving a total *TWROR* of 16.7%.[10]

Adjusting for risk

Having dealt with the measurement of return for use in performance measurement, we now turn to how to adjust for risk. As a first step, we are aware, from Chapter 12, that the investor can use either the standard deviation or the beta of the portfolio as a measure of risk, according to whether the portfolio under consideration includes all his assets or represents only part of his well-diversified portfolio.

There are two main types of performance measure which can be derived (for either measure of risk) according to whether the risk of the particular portfolio whose performance is being measured is pre-specified or not. For example, unit trusts and investment trusts choose their own levels of risk and investors in these trusts can adjust the level of risk of their investment if they so wish, by borrowing or lending. In these cases, the individual investor may wish to know which trusts offer the highest return allowing for their risk. Only by doing this will he be able to compare trusts which have different levels of risk, however that risk is measured. On the other hand, a pension fund manager may be operating under a set level of risk, which has been imposed on him by the trustees of the fund. The question to be asked in this case is, given the level of risk imposed, did the pension fund manager do well or badly?

Risk measures have been developed to cater for either of these circumstances and to deal with either measure of risk. This gives rise to a matrix of performance measures, reproduced in Figure 13.2.

The two measures in the reward per unit of risk column give a reward–risk ratio which can be used to rank funds or portfolios. Both the Sharpe

---

[10] The *TWROR* figures of 15.3% and 16.7% are for a six-month holding period.

	Reward per unit of risk	Differential return
Standard deviation	$$\frac{R_p - R_r}{S_p}$$ 'Sharpe' measure	$R_p - R_{benchmark}$ where $R_{benchmark} = R_B$ and $$R_B = R_r + \frac{(R_m - R_r)}{S_m}S_p$$
Beta	$$\frac{R_p - R_r}{\beta_p}$$ 'Treynor' measure	$R_p - R_{benchmark}$ where $R_{benchmark} = R_B$ and $R_B = R_r + (R_m - R_r)\beta_p$ 'Jensen' measure

Risk

Figure 13.2 Risk-adjusted performance measures

measure, which uses the standard deviation as a measure of risk, and the Treynor measure, which uses beta as a measure of risk, are based on the CAPM. (As has already been said, no risk-adjusted measures can be derived unless some model which quantifies risk is used.) Investors can then, using whichever of the Sharpe and Treynor measures is most appropriate to their personal circumstances, choose to invest in the highest-ranking portfolios. They can adjust to their required risk levels by borrowing or lending. For example, suppose three unit trusts have performed as in Example 13.3 in the last year.

Mr Adonis, wishing to place the majority of his funds in one of the above unit trusts, might choose *B*, which has the highest Sharpe measure.

Example 13.3 Reward per unit of risk performance ranking

		Risk			
Unit trust	Return (%)	Standard deviation (%)	Beta	Sharpe measure	Treynor measure
A	12	25	1.3	0.16	0.031
B	10	10	1.1	0.20	0.018
C	13	30	1.4	0.17	0.036
Risk-free rate	8				

Mr Zeus, however, wishes to place only a small part of his total portfolio in one of these unit trusts and so might prefer C, which has the highest Treynor measure of performance. Both Mr Adonis and Mr Zeus can then adjust for risk separately. If Mr Adonis wishes to bear a total risk of 20% (measured by standard deviation), he should invest all his funds in unit trust B and borrow a further 100% and invest that in unit trust B as well. In practice, Mr Adonis may not be able to borrow 100% of his investment at the risk-free rate. In this case, he might settle for a unit trust with a slightly lower Sharpe measure, such as trust C. He could then achieve his total required risk level by investing ⅔ of his funds in C and ⅓ risk-free.[11]

Of course, for both Mr Adonis and Mr Zeus, basing investment decisions on rankings derived from past returns and risk will not necessarily provide optimal returns in the future.

The two measures denoting differential return in Figure 13.2 can be used in cases where the risk is pre-specified, which usually occurs in cases where the portfolio is managed by a fund manager. What is required in these instances is a benchmark portfolio with the same risk as the fund in question. This benchmark portfolio should represent a realistic investment alternative which was open to the fund manager. Again, the CAPM provides a suitable benchmark portfolio. For example, if we are considering beta as a suitable measure of risk, the CAPM tells us that the optimal investment policy is to hold the market portfolio (or as near as is feasible, say an index fund) and to adjust for risk by borrowing or lending. A comparison of the actual fund's performance with such a benchmark portfolio, which has the same beta, is effectively a test for abnormal returns or alphas, and a comparison of an active investment policy with a passive one. If the Jensen measure yields a positive differential (or abnormal) return, the fund manager may be 'beating the market' because he is good at picking winners. Of course, a positive Jensen measure may also be due to luck, and the fund's performance over a number of periods would have to be examined to gauge whether the positive measure is more likely due to luck or to skill.

For instance, suppose that a company has allocated 10% of its pension fund to be managed by QED investment managers. Since QED only has 10% of the total funds of the company's pension fund, we can say that beta is the appropriate measure of risk in this case. Now, suppose that the beta

---

[11] His total risk would be

$$S^2 = x^2 S_C{}^2 + (1 - x)^2 S_{RF}{}^2 + 2x(1 - x)S_C S_{RF} CORR_{CRF}$$

where x is the proportion invested in fund C and $(1 - x)$ the proportion invested at the risk-free rate, R_F. Since $S_{RF} = 0$ (it is risk-*free*) we get

$$S = xS_C$$

The required $S = 20\%$ and $S_C = 30\%$. so $x = \dfrac{2}{3}$.

required by the trustees of the pension fund is 0.9. If the yield on gilts was 10% last year and the return on the FT-Actuaries All-Share Index was 17%, the benchmark portfolio would have yielded

$$R_B = R_F + (R_m - R_F) \beta_p$$

$$= 0.10 + (0.17 - 0.10) \, 0.9$$

$$= \mathbf{16.3\%}$$

If the fund managed by QED actually achieved a return of 18% with a beta of 0.9, the differential return was $18 - 16.3\% = 1.7\%$. It would remain to be seen whether this level of performance could be maintained in the future, but from the conclusions of Chapter 10 this would appear to be unlikely.

The other differential return measure of performance, which uses standard deviation as a measure of risk instead of beta, will be used in those cases where the portfolio under consideration represents the total wealth of the investor. Interestingly, if the portfolio is fully diversified, this measure will give the same differential return as the Jensen measure since, for a fully diversified portfolio, there is no specific risk and the total risk of the portfolio is simply its beta risk. We can see this in equation (13.5), previously given in Chapter 9 as equation (9.11) on p. 267.

For each security i, we can write

$$V_i = \beta_i^2 \, S_m^2 + S^2(e_i) \tag{9.11}$$

So, for a portfolio, we have

$$\text{Variance}_p = V_p = \beta_p^2 S_m^2 + \sum_{i=1}^{i=n} S^2(e_i) \tag{13.5}$$

$$\text{(Total risk} = \text{beta risk} + \text{specific risk)}$$

where β_p is the weighted average of the individual β_i.

Since, in a fully diversified portfolio, specific risk is zero, the standard deviation of the portfolio will simply be equal to its beta times the standard deviation of the market:

$$\text{Standard deviation } S_p = \beta_p S_m$$

or

$$\beta_p = \frac{S_p}{S_m} \tag{13.6}$$

If we look at the two differential return measures in the matrix of Figure 13.2, we can see that, if the equality in equation (13.6) holds, the two differential return measures are identical.

Analysing performance measures

Once a measure of performance has been derived, the next obvious question to ask is how was that performance achieved? The differential return measures discussed in the last section give some indication since, by comparing the performance of the portfolio with that of a passively managed portfolio, we know that the differential abnormal return achieved must be due to some form of active portfolio management.

How can we find out which type of active investment policy was pursued? Unfortunately, the state of the art of performance measurement is still not far advanced and, as we shall see in the next section on the relevance of performance measures, there are problems in placing too much emphasis on the results obtained. However, some attempt can be made to identify the success of selectivity or timing policies, the two basic ways of 'picking winners'.

(i) SELECTIVITY

We start by looking at the Jensen measure of performance. This differential return figure shows whether active portfolio management has achieved positive or negative abnormal returns. What it does not take into account, however, is that in order to achieve those abnormal returns, diversifiable or specific risk is likely to have been borne which would not have been the case if a fully diversified, CAPM portfolio strategy had been adopted.

Fama (1972) graphically analysed the Jensen measure of performance as in Figure 13.3.

In Figure 13.3, the Jensen measure will be the difference between the return on the portfolio under consideration, A, and the return on that combination of the market portfolio and risk-free borrowing or lending which has the same beta as A. In Figure 13.3, this CAPM portfolio is represented by portfolio B. So, the Jensen measure is given by $R_A - R_B$.

Since portfolio B is fully diversified, it will only have beta risk whereas A will have both beta risk and diversifiable risk. The total risk of portfolio A, measured by the standard deviation of its returns, will thus be greater than the total risk of portfolio B. Because of this, it would be fairer to compare the performance of portfolio A with that of a CAPM portfolio which had

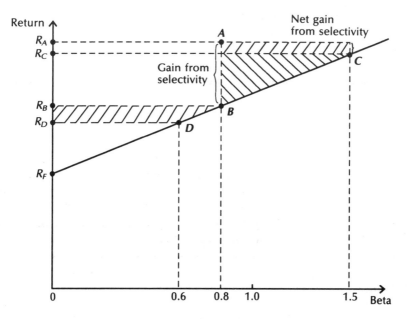

Figure 13.3 Analysis of Jensen performance measure

Source: Fama (1972). By permission of the *Journal of Finance*.

the same *total* risk, portfolio C in Figure 13.3. C can be found by equating the standard deviation of portfolio A with the market risk of a CAPM portfolio, as in equation (13.7):

$$S_A = \beta_C S_m \tag{13.7}$$

So,

$$\beta_C = \frac{S_A}{S_m}$$

Once we know the total risk of portfolio A we can use equation (13.7) to find the beta of a CAPM portfolio with the same total risk.

For example, suppose that the risk of portfolio A is made up as follows:

$$\beta_A = 0.8$$

Specific risk$_A$ = 25%

and that the market standard deviation of returns, S_m, is 20%.
Substituting these values into equation (13.5) gives:

$$S_A^2 = (0.8)^2 (0.20)^2 + (0.25)^2$$

$$S_A = 0.3$$

To find portfolio C, we simply substitute the necessary figures into equation (13.7) to get

$$0.3 = 0.2 \, \beta_C$$

Thus,

$$\beta_c = \textbf{1.5}$$

Note that portfolio C has a higher beta than portfolio A in order to achieve a higher level of risk simply from market risk.

We can now see that the *true* abnormal return earned by A, given its total risk, is not $R_A - R_B$ but the smaller $R_A - R_C$. Fama denoted the first measure the 'gain from selectivity' and the second measure the '*net* gain from selectivity'.

Figure 13.3 can also be used to monitor how closely the portfolio manager has kept to his objectives, provided that these were expressed either in terms of return or of beta. For instance, if the manager had been told to keep to a target beta of 0.6, compared to the actual beta of 0.8, he obviously added to the investors' risk, presumably in the belief that a bull market was on the way. The difference between portfolio D (which has a beta of 0.6) and portfolio B is therefore the return earned by the portfolio manager for correct timing using betas. Note, however, that this analysis will only use the beta at the beginning or end of the period or the average beta and thus will not allow for any changes in the beta of the portfolio which may have occurrred during the period under consideration.

The Fama breakdown of the Jensen performance measure gives us a way of identifying more closely the true gains or losses from a 'picking winners' strategy based on selectivity. It shows us that we must take into account the extra risk the manager takes on to try to 'beat the market'. A simple measure which assesses how much diversifiable risk has been taken on is provided in the London Business School *Risk Measurement Service* and is called R^2. This measures the extent to which the portfolio's returns are explained by market returns. In other words, it shows how much of the portfolio's total risk is explained by its beta. The higher the R^2, the more the portfolio's returns are explained by market risk and the lower the amount of diversifiable risk.

(ii) TIMING

We saw above that the Fama analysis did not really help us to examine the extent to which fund managers or investors try to earn abnormal returns through correct timing of purchases and sales of particular shares or of a more general market portfolio. This is because, as mentioned earlier, this investment strategy will involve changing the risk of the portfolio over time either through changing the shares held in the equity portfolio to alter the equity portfolio's beta or through the use of equity options and futures which can impact dramatically on the portfolio's overall beta. So, performance measures which assume constant risk over a period will be of no use in this instance.

One way of examining the impact on a portfolio of changing its beta is to compare graphically the changes in beta with the changes in the market. If the manager got it right, a change to a higher beta should be mirrored by a rise in the market and vice versa. If the manager got it wrong, there should be no clear relationship between the two, as in Figure 13.4, or even a negative relationship.

This rough-and-ready appraisal of performance achieved through correct timing is obviously unsatisfactory. The only consolation that we have is that the evidence supporting the ability of investors to time the market correctly is weak. We have only to look at how pension funds increased (whether actively or passively) the proportion of equities in their portfolios from around 70% in January 1987 to over 85% just before the Crash in October 1987, whereas they were net sellers of equities in early 1975, during the last major bear market.

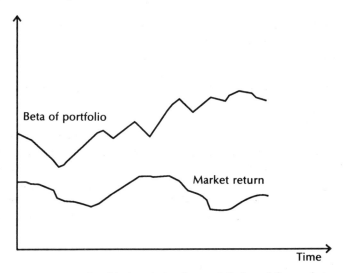

Figure 13.4 Graphical analysis of correct timing of the market

Relevance of the measure

Despite the advantages of performance measures for comparative and monitoring purposes, great care must be taken in their use. For example, we have just seen that the performance measures given in Figure 13.2 are of little use when trying to determine that element of performance which is due to attempts to time investments correctly.

Also, a factor which must be taken into account when using the differential return measures is the possibility that the benchmark portfolio made up of the market portfolio and risk-free borrowing and lending is not a realistic alternative. One reason could be because a high-risk fund could not adopt the benchmark alternative and borrow at the risk-free rate (as was a problem for Mr Adonis). Rankings using the Jensen measure would thus be biased against high-risk funds. Similarly, a particular fund might be precluded from holding certain securities which form part of the market portfolio; it should not, therefore, be compared with a benchmark portfolio which it could not, in practice, hold.

Thought must also be given to the way betas are measured for, say, the Treynor measure. Betas may be measured in different ways against different indices, all of which might be suitable surrogates for the market portfolio. So, rankings using one index could be different from those using some other index. Further, we know that although the CAPM implies that securities' returns are determined by their betas (and the market and risk-free rates of return), in practice other variables affect security returns, such as industry factors and so on.[12] This will provide another form of bias in the measures.

In addition, transaction costs affect performance. However much they would prefer not to, fund managers have to pay transaction costs on securities transactions. If the passive fund ignores transaction costs, the comparison is unfair.

The time horizon is also relevant. Whichever measure of performance is used, it can only be really valuable if a number of periods are examined, to separate out the effects of chance from the effects of skill. The need to consider more than a short-term horizon is acknowledged by investment trusts and unit trusts which publish five-year cumulative returns for investors to judge their performance. (Only the mutual funds, as yet, publish risk-adjusted returns).

Although there are problems in using performance measures, this should not preclude their use in the investment field. Performance measures in

---

[12] We saw that this was the case when we considered multi-index models at the end of Chapter 9.

industry, such as return on investment (ROI),[13] also have drawbacks and yet some measure of performance is considered better than none at all.

As yet, few European investing intermediaries are publishing performance measures such as those shown in Figure 13.2. However, acceptance of the inclusion of risk in measuring performance is growing. The most common form of risk-adjusted performance measurement is simply to plot returns of funds against the standard deviation of their returns; betas tend to be ignored. However, more emphasis is being placed on the breakdown of performance, not as in the Fama analysis shown in Figure 13.3 for domestic portfolios, rather in the currency and country selection skills shown by fund managers managing global portfolios.

Summary

The emphasis of this chapter is somewhat different from that of the rest of the book since it deals with the more subjective aspects of investment, namely objectives, policy and assessment of performance.

The chapter has discussed the setting up of explicit investment objectives, which must be done before a suitable investment policy can be decided on or a portfolio built up. The factors which have to be considered for investment objectives include consumption preferences, attitude to risk and return, tax, inflation and asset allocation.

The two basic types of investment policy which can be adopted can be categorised as active or passive. An active policy is based on the desire to beat the market and to make excess returns and involves either 'selectivity' (the search for mis-priced securities) or correct 'timing'. A passive investment policy is based on the results of the CAPM which finds that all investors will hold the 'market' portfolio and borrow or lend at the risk-free rate. The investor with a passive policy will therefore hold a well-diversified portfolio or an index fund and not indulge in a high turnover, high transaction cost, management strategy.

Using the results of the CAPM, performance measures can be derived which allow the investor to assess how well he has done, given the risk of his portfolio, both relative to other comparable portfolios (which may have different risk) and relative to the alternative portfolio he could have

---

[13] *ROI*, return on investment, is usually calculated as profit before tax divided by capital employed. Because of such factors as accounting conventions, *ROI* can be misleading as a measure of performance. For example, the older the machines, the lower their depreciated book value. A lower book value gives a lower capital employed and a higher *ROI*. There may thus be an incentive not to replace old machines which may adversely affect the future profitability of the firm.

constructed based on the CAPM with the same risk as his portfolio. However, care must be taken when using the performance measures to ensure that relevant comparisons are being made, bearing in mind the original objectives of the portfolio.

Problems

1. A unit trust manager wishes to set up a new trust for retired persons. A typical investor is seen as one who has just entered retirement at sixty. He has sold his house for, say, £160,000 and bought a small bungalow in a seaside resort for, say, £100,000. He wishes to invest the balance to provide a regular annual income to supplement his pension for himself and his wife who is ten years younger than he is.

   Advise the manager on the type of investments which the trust should hold and state why you think they will fulfill requirements.

2. You are one of the trustees of the Widget Company pension fund, which has £50m. currently invested and a net cash inflow of £5m. per annum. The fund is managed internally. Explain how you would:
   (i) establish objectives for the fund and direct investment accordingly, and
   (ii) evaluate the performance of the pension fund investment manager.

3. Mrs Brown is a widow of forty with three school-age children. She works as a schoolteacher and earns £12,000 a year but has difficulty making ends meet. Her aunt has recently died and left her a legacy of £50,000.

   Mrs Brown has been to see her friend Mrs Smith who is an accountant and who has suggested the following ways of investing the money.
   (i) Building society account. Interest of 8.5% per annum (after tax) paid six-monthly.
   (ii) Save As You Earn. Monthly investment of any amount over £10 per month for five years and a fixed sum received at the end of it equivalent to a return of 7% per annum tax-free.
   (iii) Unit trust, for example, those managed by the Schroder group. These include Schroder 'Growth', Schroder 'Fixed Interest', Schroder 'Gilt Income' and Schroder 'European Smaller Companies'.
   (iv) Shares of companies such as Royal Insurance with a dividend yield (before income tax) of 11.3% per annum, or Courtaulds with a dividend yield (before income tax) of 3.3% per annum.
   (v) Gilt-edged stock with a gross redemption yield of 8% for a 3% coupon 5-year gilt or 10% for a 10% coupon 5-year gilt or a gross redemption yield of 9.5% on a 15-year 9% coupon gilt.
   (vi) A life assurance policy.

   Advise Mrs Brown on which of the above investments she should make, and explain what factors you are taking into consideration.

4. Suppose you are an investment adviser. What questions would you ask each client before advising on a suitable portfolio?

5. Data on six investments trusts' performances last year are shown below:

Trust	Actual return (%)	Standard deviation (%)	Beta
A	19	6	1.5
B	17	4	0.5
C	21	8	1.0
D	15	6	0.5
E	25	10	2.0

(i) Calculate the reward to variability measure, $(R_p - R_F)/S_p$, known as the Sharpe index, for each trust and rank them accordingly. Suppose $R_F = 9\%$.

(ii) Rank the trusts using the Treynor index, $(R_p - R_F)/\beta_p$.

(iii) What is the essential difference between the Sharpe and Treynor indices of portfolio performance? Which do you think is preferable? Why?

(iv) Calculate the excess return of these trusts (i.e. compared with a portfolio having the same beta) assuming last year's R_m was 13%. This method of judging portfolio performance is known as Jensen's measure. In what way does it differ from the Sharpe and Treynor indices?

(v) Consider investment trust B. How would you break down an overall measure of performance, such as the Jensen measure, into different aspects of performance to get a better picture of how well managed the trust was – i.e. which aspects would you like to measure, and how would you attempt to measure them?

(vi) Suppose you are considering buying shares in one of the investment trusts listed above. What additional facts would you like concerning the trusts and how would *you* decide between them?

6. What have been the implications of the results of empirical studies on investment trust, unit trust and mutual fund* performance for the efficient markets hypothesis?

*Mutual funds = US investment trusts and unit trusts.

Appendix 1: transaction costs

Commission

Commission is charged on purchases and sales of government and corporate securities and of financial futures and options. There are no minimum commissions: rates are negotiable between the client and the broker, with the average size of the transactions and the frequency of trading being taken into consideration.

Commission are expressed as a percentage of the value of the transaction and do not currently attract Value Added Tax.

Typical commissions on ordinary share purchases and sales are 1%–1.5% for transactions of below £5,000 in value falling to 0.5% for transactions of over £10,000 and 0.2% for institutional-size trades.

Typical commissions on gilt purchases and sales are 0.5%–1% for transactions of below £5,000 falling to 0.2% for over £20,000 and no commissions are payable for transactions in excess of £1,000,000 in value. Notice that the gilts can be purchased from the National Savings Stock Register via the post office. Transaction costs here are fixed at 50p per £125 in value (with a £1 minimum) for purchases and sales.

Typical commissions on futures and options transactions might be 2.5% for purchases worth up to £5,000 with no commission being charged on sales. However, for larger value transactions, commissions would be quoted as an amount in pounds per contract, typically £10–£20 for both a purchase and sale, known as a 'round trip', depending on the particular contract.

Stamp duty

Transfer stamp duty is payable by the purchaser of UK-registered securities (whether or not listed on the Stock Exchange) which require completion of a transfer form. This Stamp duty is payable at the rate of 50p per £100 of consideration or part thereof.

Purchases of bearer securities are exempt. Also pension funds and charities are exempt from payment of transfer stamp duty.

Once the Stock Exchange has changed to a rolling[1] rather than account settlement system for listed securities, purchases of these securities will no longer attract transfer stamp duty.

Transactions in futures and options do not attract transfer stamp duty.

PTM levy

A levy (currently 10p) is charged on all purchases and sales of UK equities listed on the Stock Exchange or the Unlisted Securities Market where the consideration is in excess of £5,000. This levy is used to finance the panel on Takeovers and Mergers.

Clearing charges

Buyers and sellers of futures or options contracts are also liable to clearing charges which compensate the broker for clearing charges paid by the broker to the clearing house. The current contract clearing charge imposed on their clients by brokers is around £2 per contract.

FSA charge

Brokers have to comply with regulations laid out by the Financial Services Act 1986. For example, they have to sign a contract with each client detailing their terms and conditions of service and also have to ensure that their clients are aware of the risks of their investments. Some brokers include a charge for this on every contract note. Although the term 'FSA charge' may sound compulsory, this is not the case since it is up to the individual broker as to whether or not he chooses to pass on the costs of complying with regulation.

---

[1] A rolling settlement system is one in which settlement takes place a *fixed* number of days (usually 1 to 7) after a transaction has occurred.

Appendix 2: annuity and present value tables

Present value of 1 at compound interest: $(1 + r)^{-n}$

Years (n)	Interest rates (r)														
	1	2	3	4	5	6	7	8	9	10	11	12	13	14	15
1	0.9901	0.9804	0.9709	0.9615	0.9524	0.9434	0.9346	0.9259	0.9174	0.9091	0.9009	0.8929	0.8850	0.8772	0.8696
2	0.9803	0.9612	0.9426	0.9246	0.9070	0.8900	0.8734	0.8573	0.8417	0.8264	0.8116	0.7972	0.7831	0.7695	0.7561
3	0.9706	0.9423	0.9151	0.8890	0.8638	0.8396	0.8163	0.7938	0.7722	0.7513	0.7312	0.7118	0.6931	0.6750	0.6575
4	0.9610	0.9238	0.8885	0.8548	0.8227	0.7921	0.7629	0.7350	0.7084	0.6830	0.6587	0.6355	0.6133	0.5921	0.5718
5	0.9515	0.9057	0.8626	0.8219	0.7835	0.7473	0.7130	0.6806	0.6499	0.6209	0.5935	0.5674	0.5428	0.5194	0.4972
6	0.9420	0.8880	0.8375	0.7903	0.7462	0.7050	0.6663	0.6302	0.5963	0.5645	0.5346	0.5066	0.4803	0.4556	0.4323
7	0.9327	0.8706	0.8131	0.7599	0.7107	0.6651	0.6227	0.5835	0.5470	0.5132	0.4817	0.4523	0.4251	0.3996	0.3759
8	0.9235	0.8535	0.7894	0.7307	0.6768	0.6274	0.5820	0.5403	0.5019	0.4665	0.4339	0.4039	0.3762	0.3506	0.3269
9	0.9143	0.8368	0.7664	0.7026	0.6446	0.5919	0.5439	0.5002	0.4604	0.4241	0.3909	0.3606	0.3329	0.3075	0.2843
10	0.9053	0.8203	0.7441	0.6756	0.6139	0.5584	0.5083	0.4632	0.4224	0.3855	0.3522	0.3220	0.2946	0.2697	0.2472
11	0.8963	0.8043	0.7224	0.6496	0.5847	0.5268	0.4751	0.4289	0.3875	0.3505	0.3173	0.2875	0.2607	0.2366	0.2149
12	0.8874	0.7885	0.7014	0.6246	0.5568	0.4970	0.4440	0.3971	0.3555	0.3186	0.2858	0.2567	0.2307	0.2076	0.1869
13	0.8787	0.7730	0.6810	0.6006	0.5303	0.4688	0.4150	0.3677	0.3262	0.2897	0.2575	0.2292	0.2042	0.1821	0.1625
14	0.8700	0.7579	0.6611	0.5775	0.5051	0.4423	0.3878	0.3405	0.2992	0.2633	0.2320	0.2046	0.1807	0.1597	0.1413
15	0.8613	0.7430	0.6419	0.5553	0.4810	0.4173	0.3624	0.3152	0.2745	0.2394	0.2090	0.1827	0.1599	0.1401	0.1229
16	0.8528	0.7284	0.6232	0.5339	0.4581	0.3936	0.3387	0.2919	0.2519	0.2176	0.1883	0.1631	0.1415	0.1229	0.1069
17	0.8444	0.7142	0.6050	0.5134	0.4363	0.3714	0.3166	0.2703	0.2311	0.1978	0.1696	0.1456	0.1252	0.1078	0.0929
18	0.8360	0.7002	0.5874	0.4936	0.4155	0.3503	0.2959	0.2502	0.2120	0.1799	0.1528	0.1300	0.1108	0.0946	0.0808
19	0.8277	0.6864	0.5703	0.4746	0.3957	0.3305	0.2765	0.2317	0.1945	0.1635	0.1377	0.1161	0.0981	0.0829	0.0703
20	0.8195	0.6730	0.5537	0.4564	0.3769	0.3118	0.2584	0.2145	0.1784	0.1486	0.1240	0.1037	0.0868	0.0728	0.0611
25	0.7795	0.6095	0.4776	0.3751	0.2953	0.2330	0.1842	0.1460	0.1160	0.0923	0.0736	0.0588	0.0471	0.0378	0.0304
30	0.7419	0.5521	0.4120	0.3083	0.2314	0.1741	0.1314	0.0994	0.0754	0.0573	0.0437	0.0334	0.0256	0.0196	0.0151
35	0.7059	0.5000	0.3554	0.2534	0.1813	0.1301	0.0937	0.0676	0.0490	0.0356	0.0259	0.0189	0.0139	0.0102	0.0075
40	0.6717	0.4529	0.3066	0.2083	0.1420	0.0972	0.0668	0.0460	0.0318	0.0221	0.0154	0.0107	0.0075	0.0053	0.0037
45	0.6391	0.4102	0.2644	0.1712	0.1113	0.0727	0.0476	0.0313	0.0207	0.0137	0.0091	0.0061	0.0041	0.0027	0.0019
50	0.6080	0.3715	0.2281	0.1407	0.0872	0.0543	0.0339	0.0213	0.0134	0.0085	0.0054	0.0035	0.0022	0.0014	0.0009

n	16	17	18	19	20	21	22	23	24	25	26	27	28	29	30	n
1	0.8621	0.8547	0.8475	0.8403	0.8333	0.8264	0.8197	0.8130	0.8065	0.8000	0.7937	0.7874	0.7812	0.7752	0.7692	1
2	0.7432	0.7305	0.7182	0.7062	0.6944	0.6830	0.6719	0.6610	0.6504	0.6400	0.6299	0.6200	0.6104	0.6009	0.5917	2
3	0.6407	0.6244	0.6086	0.5934	0.5787	0.5645	0.5507	0.5374	0.5245	0.5120	0.4999	0.4882	0.4768	0.4658	0.4552	3
4	0.5523	0.5337	0.5158	0.4987	0.4823	0.4665	0.4514	0.4369	0.4230	0.4096	0.3968	0.3844	0.3725	0.3611	0.3501	4
5	0.4761	0.4561	0.4371	0.4190	0.4019	0.3855	0.3700	0.3552	0.3411	0.3277	0.3149	0.3027	0.2910	0.2799	0.2693	5
6	0.4104	0.3898	0.3704	0.3521	0.3349	0.3186	0.3033	0.2888	0.2751	0.2621	0.2499	0.2383	0.2274	0.2170	0.2072	6
7	0.3538	0.3332	0.3139	0.2959	0.2791	0.2633	0.2486	0.2348	0.2218	0.2097	0.1983	0.1877	0.1776	0.1682	0.1594	7
8	0.3050	0.2848	0.2660	0.2487	0.2326	0.2176	0.2038	0.1909	0.1789	0.1678	0.1574	0.1478	0.1388	0.1304	0.1226	8
9	0.2630	0.2434	0.2255	0.2090	0.1938	0.1799	0.1670	0.1552	0.1443	0.1342	0.1249	0.1164	0.1084	0.1011	0.0943	9
10	0.2267	0.2080	0.1911	0.1756	0.1615	0.1486	0.1369	0.1262	0.1164	0.1074	0.0992	0.0916	0.0847	0.0784	0.0725	10
11	0.1954	0.1778	0.1619	0.1476	0.1346	0.1228	0.1122	0.1026	0.0938	0.0859	0.0787	0.0721	0.0662	0.0607	0.0558	11
12	0.1685	0.1520	0.1372	0.1240	0.1122	0.1015	0.0920	0.0834	0.0757	0.0687	0.0625	0.0568	0.0517	0.0471	0.0429	12
13	0.1452	0.1299	0.1163	0.1042	0.0935	0.0839	0.0754	0.0678	0.0610	0.0550	0.0496	0.0447	0.0404	0.0365	0.0330	13
14	0.1252	0.1110	0.0985	0.0876	0.0779	0.0693	0.0618	0.0551	0.0492	0.0440	0.0393	0.0352	0.0316	0.0283	0.0254	14
15	0.1079	0.0949	0.0835	0.0736	0.0649	0.0573	0.0507	0.0448	0.0397	0.0352	0.0312	0.0277	0.0247	0.0219	0.0195	15
16	0.0930	0.0811	0.0708	0.0618	0.0541	0.0474	0.0415	0.0364	0.0320	0.0281	0.0248	0.0218	0.0193	0.0170	0.0150	16
17	0.0802	0.0693	0.0600	0.0520	0.0451	0.0391	0.0340	0.0296	0.0258	0.0225	0.0197	0.0172	0.0150	0.0132	0.0116	17
18	0.0691	0.0592	0.0508	0.0437	0.0376	0.0323	0.0279	0.0241	0.0208	0.0180	0.0156	0.0135	0.0118	0.0102	0.0089	18
19	0.0596	0.0506	0.0431	0.0367	0.0313	0.0267	0.0229	0.0196	0.0168	0.0144	0.0124	0.0107	0.0092	0.0079	0.0068	19
20	0.0514	0.0433	0.0365	0.0308	0.0261	0.0221	0.0187	0.0159	0.0135	0.0115	0.0098	0.0084	0.0072	0.0061	0.0053	20
25	0.0245	0.0197	0.0160	0.0129	0.0105	0.0085	0.0069	0.0057	0.0046	0.0038	0.0031	0.0025	0.0021	0.0017	0.0014	25
30	0.0116	0.0090	0.0070	0.0054	0.0042	0.0033	0.0026	0.0020	0.0016	0.0012	0.0010	0.0008	0.0006	0.0005	0.0004	30
35	0.0055	0.0041	0.0030	0.0023	0.0017	0.0013	0.0009	0.0007	0.0005	0.0004	0.0003	0.0002	0.0002	0.0001	0.0001	35
40	0.0026	0.0019	0.0013	0.0010	0.0007	0.0005	0.0004	0.0003	0.0002	0.0001	0.0001	0.0001	0.0001	0.0000	0.0000	40
45	0.0013	0.0009	0.0006	0.0004	0.0003	0.0002	0.0001	0.0001	0.0001	0.0000	0.0000	0.0000	0.0000	0.0000	0.0000	45
50	0.0006	0.0004	0.0003	0.0002	0.0001	0.0001	0.0000	0.0000	0.0000	0.0000	0.0000	0.0000	0.0000	0.0000	0.0000	50

Source: Samuels and Wilkes, *Management of Company Finance*, 3rd edn, Van Nostrand Reinhold (1980). By permission of the publishers.

420

Present value of an annuity of 1: $\dfrac{1 - (1 + r)^{-n}}{r}$

Years (n)	Interest rates (r)															(n)
	1	2	3	4	5	6	7	8	9	10	11	12	13	14	15	
1	0.9901	0.9804	0.9709	0.9615	0.9524	0.9434	0.9346	0.9259	0.9174	0.9091	0.9009	0.8929	0.8850	0.8772	0.8696	1
2	1.9704	1.9416	1.9135	1.8861	1.8594	1.8334	1.8080	1.7833	1.7591	1.7355	1.7125	1.6901	1.6681	1.6467	1.6257	2
3	2.9410	2.8839	2.8286	2.7751	2.7232	2.6730	2.6243	2.5771	2.5313	2.4869	2.4437	2.4018	2.3612	2.3216	2.2832	3
4	3.9020	3.8077	3.7171	3.6299	3.5460	3.4651	3.3872	3.3121	3.2397	3.1699	3.1024	3.0373	2.9745	2.9137	2.8550	4
5	4.8534	4.7136	4.5797	4.4518	4.3295	4.2124	4.1002	3.9927	3.8897	3.7908	3.6959	3.6048	3.5172	3.4331	3.3522	5
6	5.7955	5.6014	5.4172	5.2421	5.0757	4.9173	4.7665	4.6229	4.4859	4.3553	4.2305	4.1114	3.9975	3.8887	3.7845	6
7	6.7282	6.4720	6.2303	6.0021	5.7864	5.5824	5.3893	5.2064	5.0330	4.8684	4.7122	4.5638	4.4226	4.2883	4.1604	7
8	7.6517	7.3255	7.0197	6.7327	6.4632	6.2098	5.9713	5.7466	5.5348	5.3349	5.1461	4.9676	4.7988	4.6389	4.4873	8
9	8.5660	8.1622	7.7861	7.4353	7.1078	6.8017	6.5152	6.2469	5.9952	5.7590	5.5370	5.3282	5.1317	4.9464	4.7716	9
10	9.4713	8.9826	8.5302	8.1109	7.7217	7.3601	7.0236	6.7101	6.4177	6.1446	5.8892	5.6502	5.4262	5.2161	5.0188	10
11	10.3676	9.7868	9.2526	8.7605	8.3064	7.8869	7.4987	7.1390	6.8052	6.4951	6.2065	5.9377	5.6869	5.4527	5.2337	11
12	11.2551	10.5753	9.9540	9.3851	8.8633	8.3838	7.9427	7.5361	7.1607	6.8137	6.4924	6.1944	5.9176	5.6603	5.4206	12
13	12.1337	11.3484	10.6350	9.9856	9.3936	8.8527	8.3577	7.9038	7.4869	7.1034	6.7499	6.4235	6.1218	5.8424	5.5831	13
14	13.0037	12.1062	11.2961	10.5631	9.8986	9.2950	8.7455	8.2442	7.7862	7.3667	6.9819	6.6282	6.3025	6.0021	5.7245	14
15	13.8651	12.8493	11.9379	11.1184	10.3797	9.7122	9.1079	8.5595	8.0607	7.6061	7.1909	6.8109	6.4624	6.1422	5.8474	15
16	14.7179	13.5777	12.5611	11.6523	10.8378	10.1059	9.4466	8.8514	8.3126	7.8237	7.3792	6.9740	6.6039	6.2651	5.9542	16
17	15.5623	14.2919	13.1661	12.1657	11.2741	10.4773	9.7632	9.1216	8.5436	8.0216	7.5488	7.1196	6.7291	6.3729	6.0472	17
18	16.3983	14.9920	13.7535	12.6593	11.6896	10.8276	10.0591	9.3719	8.7556	8.2014	7.7016	7.2497	6.8399	6.4674	6.1280	18
19	17.2260	15.6785	14.3238	13.1339	12.0853	11.1581	10.3356	9.6036	8.9501	8.3649	7.8393	7.3658	6.9380	6.5504	6.1982	19
20	18.0456	16.3514	14.8775	13.5903	12.4622	11.4699	10.5940	9.8181	9.1285	8.5136	7.9633	7.4694	7.0248	6.6231	6.2593	20
25	22.0232	19.5235	17.4131	15.6221	14.0939	12.7834	11.6536	10.6748	9.8226	9.0770	8.4217	7.8431	7.3300	6.8729	6.4641	25
30	25.8077	22.3965	19.6004	17.2920	15.3725	13.7648	12.4090	11.2578	10.2737	9.4269	8.6938	8.0552	7.4957	7.0027	6.5660	30
35	29.4086	24.9986	21.4872	18.6646	16.3742	14.4982	12.9477	11.6546	10.5668	9.6442	8.8552	8.1755	7.5856	7.0700	6.6166	35
40	32.8347	27.3555	23.1148	19.7928	17.1591	15.0463	13.3317	11.9246	10.7574	9.7791	8.9511	8.2438	7.6344	7.1050	6.6418	40
45	36.0945	29.4902	24.5187	20.7200	17.7741	15.4558	13.6055	12.1084	10.8812	9.8628	9.0079	8.2825	7.6609	7.1232	6.6543	45
50	39.1961	31.4236	25.7298	21.4822	18.2559	15.7619	13.8007	12.2335	10.9617	9.9148	9.0417	8.3045	7.6752	7.1327	6.6605	50

	16	17	18	19	20	21	22	23	24	25	26	27	28	29	30	
1	0.8621	0.8547	0.8475	0.8403	0.8333	0.8264	0.8197	0.8130	0.8065	0.8000	0.7937	0.7874	0.7812	0.7752	0.7692	1
2	1.6052	1.5852	1.5656	1.5465	1.5278	1.5095	1.4915	1.4740	1.4568	1.4400	1.4235	1.4074	1.3916	1.3761	1.3609	2
3	2.2459	2.2096	2.1743	2.1399	2.1065	2.0739	2.0422	2.0114	1.9813	1.9520	1.9234	1.8956	1.8684	1.8420	1.8161	3
4	2.7982	2.7432	2.6901	2.6386	2.5887	2.5404	2.4936	2.4483	2.4043	2.3616	2.3202	2.2800	2.2410	2.2031	2.1662	4
5	3.2743	3.1993	3.1272	3.0576	2.9906	2.9260	2.8636	2.8035	2.7454	2.6893	2.6351	2.5827	2.5320	2.4830	2.4356	5
6	3.6847	3.5892	3.4976	3.4098	3.3255	3.2446	3.1669	3.0923	3.0205	2.9514	2.8850	2.8210	2.7594	2.7000	2.6427	6
7	4.0386	3.9224	3.8115	3.7057	3.6046	3.5079	3.4155	3.3270	3.2423	3.1611	3.0833	3.0087	2.9370	2.8682	2.8021	7
8	4.3436	4.2072	4.0776	3.9544	3.8372	3.7256	3.6193	3.5179	3.4212	3.3289	3.2407	3.1564	3.0758	2.9986	2.9247	8
9	4.6065	4.4506	4.3030	4.1633	4.0310	3.9054	3.7863	3.6731	3.5655	3.4631	3.3657	3.2728	3.1842	3.0997	3.0190	9
10	4.8332	4.6586	4.4941	4.3389	4.1925	4.0541	3.9232	3.7993	3.6819	3.5705	3.4648	3.3644	3.2689	3.1781	3.0915	10
11	5.0286	4.8364	4.6560	4.4865	4.3271	4.1769	4.0354	3.9018	3.7757	3.6564	3.5435	3.4365	3.3351	3.2388	3.1473	11
12	5.1971	4.9884	4.7932	4.6105	4.4392	4.2784	4.1274	3.9852	3.8514	3.7251	3.6059	3.4933	3.3868	3.2859	3.1903	12
13	5.3423	5.1183	4.9095	4.7147	4.5327	4.3624	4.2028	4.0530	3.9124	3.7801	3.6555	3.5381	3.4272	3.3224	3.2233	13
14	5.4675	5.2293	5.0081	4.8023	4.6106	4.4317	4.2646	4.1082	3.9616	3.8241	3.6949	3.5733	3.4587	3.3507	3.2487	14
15	5.5755	5.3242	5.0916	4.8759	4.6755	4.4890	4.3152	4.1530	4.0013	3.8593	3.7261	3.6010	3.4834	3.3726	3.2682	15
16	5.6685	5.4053	5.1624	4.9377	4.7296	4.5364	4.3567	4.1894	4.0333	3.8874	3.7509	3.6228	3.5026	3.3896	3.2832	16
17	5.7487	5.4746	5.2223	4.9897	4.7746	4.5755	4.3908	4.2190	4.0591	3.9099	3.7705	3.6400	3.5177	3.4028	3.2948	17
18	5.8178	5.5339	5.2732	5.0333	4.8122	4.6079	4.4187	4.2431	4.0799	3.9279	3.7861	3.6536	3.5294	3.4130	3.3037	18
19	5.8775	5.5845	5.3162	5.0700	4.8435	4.6346	4.4415	4.2627	4.0967	3.9424	3.7985	3.6642	3.5386	3.4210	3.3105	19
20	5.9288	5.6278	5.3527	5.1009	4.8696	4.6567	4.4603	4.2786	4.1103	3.9539	3.8083	3.6726	3.5458	3.4271	3.3158	20
25	6.0971	5.7662	5.4669	5.1951	4.9476	4.7213	4.5139	4.3232	4.1474	3.9849	3.8342	3.6943	3.5640	3.4423	3.3286	25
30	6.1772	5.8294	5.5168	5.2347	4.9789	4.7463	4.5338	4.3391	4.1601	3.9950	3.8424	3.7009	3.5693	3.4466	3.3321	30
35	6.2153	5.8582	5.5386	5.2512	4.9915	4.7559	4.5411	4.3447	4.1644	3.9984	3.8450	3.7028	3.5708	3.4478	3.3330	35
40	6.2335	5.8713	5.5482	5.2582	4.9966	4.7596	4.5439	4.3467	4.1659	3.9995	3.8458	3.7034	3.5712	3.4481	3.3332	40
45	6.2421	5.8773	5.5523	5.2611	4.9986	4.7610	4.5449	4.3474	4.1664	3.9998	3.8460	3.7036	3.5714	3.4482	3.3333	45
50	6.2463	5.8801	5.5541	5.2623	4.9995	4.7616	4.5452	4.3477	4.1666	3.9999	3.8461	3.7037	3.5714	3.4483	3.3333	50

Source: Samuels and Wilkes, *Management of Company Finance*, 3rd edn, Van Nostrand Reinhold (1980). By permission of the publishers.

Appendix 3: sources of information

The following list details the main sources of information on UK companies and. UK quoted securities. It is by no means comprehensive.

Company report and accounts

Available free of charge from the company secretary.

Extel cards

Summaries of published information, one card for each company.

McCarthys

Press comment on companies.

Stockbrokers' reports

These can be on specific companies, industries or countries.

Financial Times (and other main daily and Sunday newspapers)

The results of UK companies are published in the *Financial Times* and there will usually also be comment for the major companies.

Industry surveys

Many market research companies produce industry reports. These will not usually be available to the general public free of charge.

Topic

Real-time stock exchange prices available on television on payment of a monthly subscription. Teletext has share prices which are changed several times a day for no charge.

Bloomberg

Real-time analytic service on bonds and equities, and their derivatives, available for institutional investors.

Datastream

Provides analyses of all UK and many foreign securities interactively on computer terminals. All the major city institutions are subscribers.

Weekly financial press

Note:
The main library in London at which most of the above information is available is the City Business Library. This library is open to the general public and is situated at 106 Fenchurch Street, London EC3.

Appendix 4: summary of formulae used

Chapter 2

Holding period return

$$HPR = \frac{D_1 + (P_1 - P_0)}{P_0}$$

Fisher's relation

$$(1 + R) = (1 + r)(1 + E(\mathit{infl}))$$

where R is the nominal interest rate and r the real interest rate

Expected return

$$E(R) = \sum_{i=1}^{i=n} p_i R_i$$

Variance

$$V = \sum_{i=1}^{i=n} p_i (R_i - E(R))^2$$

Standard deviation

$$S = \sqrt{V}$$

Expected utility of wealth

$$E(U(W)) = \sum_{i=1}^{i=n} p_i U(W_i)$$

Interest yield

On a fixed interest security

$$\text{Interest yield} = \frac{D}{P_0} (\times 100)$$

Multiplying by 100 simply expresses the result in percentage rather than decimal form.

Dividend valuation model

$$P_0 = \frac{D_1}{(1 + R)} + \frac{D_2}{(1 + R)^2} + \ldots + \frac{D_n + P_n}{(1 + R)^n}$$

Chapter 3

Redemption yield

The redemption yield is the R in the equation

$$P_0 = \frac{D}{(1 + R)} + \frac{D}{(1 + R)^2} + \ldots + \frac{D}{(1 + R)^n} + \frac{100}{(1 + R)^n}$$

Linear interpolation formula

$$r = r_1 + (r_2 + r_1)\, \frac{PV_1}{(PV_1 + PV_2)}$$

Duration

$$D = \frac{1.\, PV_1}{P_0} + \frac{2.\, PV_2}{P_0} + \ldots + \frac{N.PV_N}{P_0}$$

Chapter 4

Spot rates

These are interest rates r_i in the expression

$$P_0 = \frac{D}{(1 + r_1)} + \frac{D}{(1 + r_2)^2} + \ldots + \frac{D}{(1 + r_n)^n} + \frac{100}{(1 + r_n)^n}$$

Forward rates

These are implicit in the spot rates. For example,

$$(1 + r_1)\,(1 + {}_1f_2) = (1 + r_2)^2$$

Chapter 5

Gross dividend yield

$$GDY = \frac{D_0}{P_0} \times \frac{100}{(100 - A)}$$

where D_0 is the net dividend paid and A the ACT rate in %.

Net dividend yield

$$NDY = \frac{D_0}{P_0}$$

Dividend cover

$$\text{Dividend cover} = \frac{eps_0}{dps_0}$$

PE ratio

$$PE = \frac{P_0}{eps_0}$$

Gordon's growth model

$$P_0 = \frac{D_1}{R - g} \qquad R = \frac{D_1}{P_0} + g$$

Payout ratio

$$K_i = \frac{dps_i}{eps_i}$$

Chapter 6

Fair futures price

$$F = C + i \times \frac{N}{365} - \text{div yield over period}$$

Number of gilt contracts for hedge

$$G = \frac{\text{Nominal value CTD gilt} \times \text{Conversion factor}}{\pounds 50,000}$$

Chapter 7

Minimum value of call option

$$C \geqslant S - PV(X)$$

Relationship between put and call option on expiry

$$S + P = C + X$$

Black–Scholes formula

$$C = S\,N(d_1) - Xe^{-R_F t}\,N(d_2)$$

(See Appendix to Chapter 7.)

Value of CULS

$CULS$ = value of equivalent ULS + value of option to convert into ordinary shares

Chapter 8

Expected return and risk of portfolio of two securities

$$E(R_p) = W_1 \, E \, (R_A) + W_2 \, E \, (R_B)$$

$$V_p = W_1^2 \, S_A^2 + W_2^2 \, S_B^2 + 2 \, W_1 W_2 S_A S_B CORR_{AB}$$

Expected return and risk of portfolio of n securities

$$E(R_p) = \sum_{i=1}^{i=n} W_i E(R_i)$$

where W_i is the proportion held of security i

$$V_p = \sum_{i=1}^{i=n} W_i^2 S_i^2 + \sum_{i=1}^{i=n} \sum_{\substack{i=1 \\ i \neq j}}^{j=n} W_i W_j COV_{ij}$$

Covariance

$$COV_{AB} = \sum_{i=1}^{i=n} (R_{A_i} - E(R_A)) \, (R_{B_i} - E(R_B)) \, p(R_i)$$

Correlation coefficient

$$CORR_{AB} = \frac{COV_{AB}}{S_A S_B}$$

Chapter 9

Sharpe's market model

$$R_i = a_i + b_i R_m + e_i$$

Capital market line

$$E(R_p) = R_F + (E(R_m) - R_F)\ \frac{S_p}{S_m}$$

Securities market line

$$E(R_i) = R_F + (E(R_m) - R_F)\ \frac{COV_{im}}{S_m^2}$$

or

$$E(R_i) = R_F + \beta_i(E(R_m) - R_F)$$

Security risk

$$V_i = \beta_i^2 S_m^2 + S^2(e_i)$$

(Total risk = market risk + specific risk)

Arbitrage pricing model

$$E(R_i) = a_i + b_{i_1}\beta_1 + b_{i_2}\beta_2 + \ldots$$

Chapter 10

Excess return

$$\epsilon_{j,t+1} = (R_{j,t+1}) - (E(R_{j,t+1})/\phi_t))$$

Fair game

$$\sum_{i=1}^{i=n} \epsilon_{j,t+1} = 0$$

Chapter 11

Forward exchange rate

$$X_f = X_0 \quad \begin{array}{l} + \textit{discount} \text{ quoted in } \textit{Financial Times} \\ - \textit{premium} \text{ quoted in } \textit{Financial Times} \end{array}$$

Interest rate parity

$$\frac{X_f}{X_0} = \frac{1 + R_\$}{1 + R_\pounds}$$

where $R_\pounds$ and $R_\$$ represent the interest rates available in each currency.

Purchasing power parity

$$\frac{X_1}{X_0} = \frac{P_{f_1}/P_{f_0}}{P_{d_1}/P_{d_0}} = \frac{1 + E(\textit{infl}_f)}{1 + E(\textit{infl}_d)}$$

International Fisher

$$\frac{1 + R_{£}}{1 + E(infl_{£})} = \frac{1 + R_{s}}{1 + E(infl_{s})}$$

Chapter 13

Measures of portfolio performance

Sharpe measure $= \dfrac{R_p - R_F}{S_p}$

Treynor measure $= \dfrac{R_p - R_F}{\beta_p}$

Jensen measure $= R_p - R_B$ where $R_B = R_F + \beta_p (R_m - R_F)$

Geometric mean

$$GM = r = (^n\sqrt{(1 + r_1)(1 + r_2) \ldots (1 + r_n)}) - 1$$

Solution to quadratic equation

If $ax^2 + bx + c = 0$,

$$x = \frac{(-b \pm \sqrt{b^2 - 4ac})}{2a}$$

Bibliography

G. J. Alexander (1986) *Portfolio Analysis*, 3rd edn, Prentice-Hall.

L. Bachelier (1900) *Théorie de la Speculation*, Gauthier-Villars.

R. Ball (1990) 'What do we know about market efficiency?', unpublished manuscript, William E. Simon Graduate School of Business Administration, University of Rochester.

Bank of England Quarterly Bulletin (1989) 'Chart analysis and the foreign exchange market' (November) pp. 548–51.

W. H. Beaver (1981) *Financial Reporting: An Accounting Revolution*, Prentice-Hall.

F. Black (1972) 'Capital market equilibrium with restricted borrowing', *Journal of Business* (July) pp. 445–55.

M. Blume (1975) 'Betas and their regression tendencies', *Journal of Finance*, vol. 10, no. 3 (June) pp. 785–95.

R. A. Brealey (1983) *An Introduction to Risk and Return*, 2nd edn, Basil Blackwell.

S. J. Brown and J. B. Warner (1985) 'Using daily stock returns: the case of event studies', *Journal of Financial Economics*, vol. 14, pp. 3–32.

T. E. Copeland and J. F. Watson (1988) *Financial Theory and Corporate Policy*, 3rd edn, Addison-Wesley.

E. Dimson and P. Marsh (1984) 'An analysis of brokers' and analysts' unpublished forecasts of UK stock returns', *Journal of Finance*, vol. 39, no. 5, pp. 1257–92.

E. J. Elton and M. J. Gruber (1991) *Modern Portfolio Theory and Investment Analysis*, 4th edn, Wiley.

E. F. Fama (1970) 'Efficient capital markets: a review of theory and empirical work', *Journal of Finance*, vol. 25, no. 2 (May) pp. 383–417.

——— (1972) 'Components of investment performance', *Journal of Finance*, vol. 27, no. 3 (June) pp. 551–67.

——— (1984) 'The information in the term structure', *Journal of Financial Economics*, vol. 13, pp. 509–28.

——— (1991) 'Efficient capital markets: II', *Journal of Finance*, vol. 46, no. 5 (December) pp. 1575–1617.

E. F. Fama, L. Fisher, M. C. Jensen and R. Roll (1969) 'The adjustment of stock prices to new information', *International Economic Review*, vol. 10, no. 2 (February) pp. 1–21.

I. Fisher (1930) *The Theory of Interest*, Macmillan.

M. D. Fitzgerald (1978) 'Media and investment advisory service recommendations and market efficiency', Salomon Brothers Center for the Study of Financial Institutions, *Working Paper*, no. 159, New York University.

R. L. Hagin (1979) *The Dow-Jones Irwin Guide to Modern Portfolio Theory*, Dow-Jones Irwin.

P. Hastings (1977) 'The case of the Royal Mail', in *W. T. Baxter and S. Davidson* (eds), *Studies of Accounting Theory*, 3rd edn, Institute of Chartered Accountants in England and Wales, pp. 339–46.

R. T. Henriksson (1985) 'Market timing and mutual fund performance: an empirical investigation', *Journal of Business*, vol. 57, pp. 73–96.

J. Hull (1991) *Introduction to Futures and Option Markets*, Prentice-Hall.

R. A. Ippolito (1989) 'Efficiency with costly information: a study of mutual fund performance, 1965–1985', *Quarterly Journal of Economics*, vol. 104, pp. 1–23.

R. A. Jarrow and A. Rudd (1983) *Option Pricing*, Irwin.

R. W. Kolb (1992) *Investments*, 3rd edn, Kolb.

M. D. Levi (1990) *International Finance: The Markets and Financial Management of Multinational Business*, 2nd edn, McGraw-Hill.

London Business School, *Risk Measurement Service*, quarterly.

J. H. Lorie and M. T. Hamilton (1973) *The Stock Market: Theories and Evidence*, Irwin.

J. Madura (1986) *International Financial Management*, West.

H. M. Markowitz (1991) *Portfolio Selection: Efficient Diversification of Investment*, 2nd edn, Basil Blackwell.

Midland Bank Series New Issue Statistics, February issues, *Midland Bank Review*.

A. B. Moore (1962) 'A statistical analysis of common stock prices', unpublished Ph. D. dissertation, University of Chicago.

V. Niederhoffer and P. Regan (1972) 'Earnings changes, analysts' forecasts, and stock prices', *Financial Analysts' Journal*, vol. 28, no. 3 (May–June) pp. 65–71.

J. M. Patell and M. A. Wolfson (1984) 'The intraday speed of adjustment of stock prices to earnings and dividend announcements', *Journal of Financial Economics*, vol. 13, pp. 223–52.

H. V. Roberts (1959) 'Stock market "patterns" and financial analysts', *Journal of Finance*, vol. 14, no. 1 (March) pp. 1–10.

S. A. Ross (1976) 'The arbitrage theory of capital asset pricing', *Journal of Economic Theory*, vol. 13 (December) pp. 341-60.

W. F. Sharpe (1963) 'A simplified model for portfolio analysis', *Management Science* (January) pp. 277–93.

B. H. Solnik (1974) 'Why not diversify internationally rather than domestically?', *Financial Analysts' Journal*, vol. 30, no. 4 (July–August) pp. 48–54.

———— (1991) *International Investments*, 2nd edn, Addison-Wesley.

Wilson Report (1980) *Report of the Committee to Review the Functioning of Financial Institutions*, Cmnd 7937 (June) HMSO.

Index